*Peasant Cooperatives and Political Change in Peru*

*Cynthia McClintock*

# PEASANT COOPERATIVES AND POLITICAL CHANGE IN PERU

PRINCETON UNIVERSITY PRESS
PRINCETON, NEW JERSEY

*For my Mother*

# Contents

## PART ONE
### Self-Management, Reform Government, and Changing Political Culture

# Illustrations

# Tables

# Acknowledgments

THE strengths of this study reflect generous contributions of time, knowledge, and moral support by many people. My friends and advisers will disagree with some of my interpretations, but they will see their contributions on many pages of this study.

I did not plan to do research in Peru originally. When I arrived in Peru, my orientation was facilitated by the advice and friendship of John Pate and Gael and Gavin Alderson-Smith. As I formulated my research plans, the key importance of the data collected by the Instituto de Estudios Peruanos and Cornell University became apparent, and Giorgio Alberti and William Whyte of these institutions offered not only to share the data with me but also to help me replicate their study. In making my own additions to the survey instrument and planning my research strategy, I received excellent advice from Wayne Cornelius, John Gitlitz, and Christopher Arterton.

Of course, this study could not have been done without the support and goodwill of the people in my research sites in Peru's countryside. I am especially grateful to the residents of my key research enterprises, Estrella, Marla, and Monte. Many times over a period of seven years they have welcomed me into their homes, and shared their thoughts with me. They let me come to know and be a part of their world; they trusted me to tell their story. Particularly meaningful for me has been the friendship of Efraím Amesquita, Leoncio Ramón Veliz, Walter Carranza, Pedro Lazo, Lorenzo Leon, the Otiniano family, my compadres Mario and Justina Ramos Valverde, and my compañero Lorenzo Villareal.

Over the years of my research in Peru, I have gained many insights into the nation and its agrarian reform from conversations with scholarly analysts living in Peru. I am especially grateful to Miguel Candiotti, of Huancayo; to José Elías Minaya and Pat and Clara Brennan, of Trujillo; to Roberto Abusada, Giorgio Alberti, José María Caballero, Oscar Espinoza, Douglas Horton, Helán Jaworski, and Peter Knight, all of whom were living in Lima during key periods of my research.

When I returned to M.I.T. to analyze my data and write my dissertation, various individuals were extremely helpful. Christopher Arterton and Douglas Hibbs provided excellent advice on my data analysis. Wayne Cornelius, Suzanne Berger, and Lucian Pye, the members of my dissertation committee at M.I.T., all asked the probing questions that led me to new insights. As I became more interested in the scholarly debates about corporatism, my thoughts were stimulated by discussions with Professors Cornelius and Berger as well as with Kevin Middlebrook and Scott Palmer. I am also grateful for the insightful comments on drafts of the work or related papers made by José María Caballero, Richard L. Cole, Henry A. Dietz, Jorge I. Domínguez, David Garson, Merilee Grindle, Abraham F. Lowenthal, Eric Peterson, Martin Scurrah, Nelle Temple, and Fred Temple.

I have been fortunate to have the research assistance of Rodolfo Osores Ocampo and Eduardo Friedman. For several years, Rodolfo has skillfully assisted me with interviewing in Peru, and Eduardo with coding, tabulating and proofreading in the United States. I am also indebted to Juan Chiroque, Nancy Cosavalente, Flora Ruíz, Sonia Yupanqui, and Rolando Yupanqui for their help as interviewers; to Jane Baird and Karen Nurick for their work coding data; to Alan Melchior, Steven Forman, and Lydia van Hine for their proofreading and editorial aid; and to Annette Holman, Muriel Goodridge, and Gladys Becker for their typing assistance. For much of this aid, I am grateful to my brother-in-law, Charles Atkinson, who provided me access to all his office resources at various critical periods.

Financial support for the research and writing of the dissertation was generously provided by the Foreign Area Fellowship program of the Social Science Research Council. I am particularly thankful for the Council's renewal of my grant for follow-up research in 1975. The M.I.T. Political Science Department gave the funds for extensive data processing.

The dissertation might never have become a book but for the assistance of Sanford Thatcher at Princeton University Press. He read my massive thesis carefully and in its entirety, and provided extremely helpful suggestions for revisions. His interest and encouragement kept me at the revision process. I am also grateful to Gail Filion of Princeton University Press, who skillfully edited the manuscript.

I also owe some very special thanks to certain individuals. From Huancayo to Washington, Richard Webb, Luis Deustua, and Pedro Ortiz have been the best of friends. Richard Webb was a guide through many mazes at various times, especially during my first difficult days in Huancayo. Luis Deustua and Pedro Ortiz gave me an enormous wealth of insight and information into Peru's agrarian reform. Luis allowed me to accompany him on visits to cooperatives in different regions, providing me with a much broader perspective on the reform than would otherwise have been possible. They have shown a faith in my abilities and a cariño that carried me through difficult moments.

I have dedicated this book to my mother, Beatrice Kellogg McClintock. She has always asked important questions about society and politics, and encouraged me to do the same. She passed on to me an appreciation of the value of accomplishment, and an understanding of the importance of endurance.

# Glossary of Acronyms and Spanish Terms

| | |
|---|---|
| anexo | distant hamlet of a peasant community |
| APRA | foremost Peruvian political party, the American Popular Revolutionary Alliance |
| Aprista | an affiliate of APRA |
| CAP | agrarian production cooperative, typically established on one geographical site, comprising only ex-hacienda workers; the predominant type of cooperative in Peru |
| capacitación | training and adult education, usually to some extent of a political nature; literally, consciousness-raising |
| caporal | work supervisor, below the status of mayordomo |
| CCP | anti-government, pro-Marxist Peruvian Peasant Confederation |
| CENCIRA | center for capacitación and research on the agrarian reform |
| CI | the Industrial Community, a self-management program for the industrial sector |
| CNA | National Agrarian Confederation, established in 1974 under government auspices |
| COAMA | Council of Advisers to the Minister of Agriculture |
| comerciantes | commercial middlemen, usually at the socioeconomic apex of the community |
| compadre or comadre | ritual co-parent; godfather or godmother |
| comunero | member of peasant community |
| CONACI | National Confederation of Industrial Communities |
| DESCO | Center for Studies and Advancement of Development, an independent Lima-based institution, involved in social and political research |
| ejido | Mexican agrarian cooperative |
| El Chalán | ex-hacienda in Virú valley studied by Greaves (1968) and contiguous to Estrella and Marla |
| eventuales | temporary workers, usually landless |
| faena | collaborative work project that does not entail financial transactions. A peasant community tradition, generally discouraged in haciendas. |

| | |
|---|---|
| FENCAP | peasant organization of the political party APRA |
| feudatario | literally, a sharecropper, but in the Virú valley, the term applied to prosperous men who cultivated their land individually, gaining it under the Belaúnde agrarian reform. Thus, a kulak, Peru-style. |
| gerente | technical administrator of cooperative |
| hectare | measure of land; one hectare equals about 2.47 acres |
| huacchas | privately owned sheep in the highlands |
| IPC | International Petroleum Company (subsidiary of Standard Oil) |
| jornal | daily wage |
| ladrilleros | brick makers |
| Loroya | ex-hacienda contiguous to Monte |
| mayordomo | head work supervisor, second only to the administrator and sub-administrator (if any) |
| minifundistas | individual cultivators of small parcels |
| panllevar | basic foods, in contrast to food for export; i.e., potatoes rather than sugar |
| peasant community | a traditional agrarian group in Peru, typically including about 100 peasant families who own and work the land individually, but are bound together by kinship. Some peasant community members work in an enterprise temporarily for extra cash. |
| SAIS | an Agrarian Social Interest Society that combines peasant communities and ex-haciendas in one cooperative |
| sectorista | lowest level bureaucrat in the Ministry of Agriculture |
| SINAMOS | National System for the Support of Social Mobilization |
| SNA | National Agrarian Society, the traditional organization of landholding elites |
| soles | Peruvian currency, exchanged at $1 for 38.7 soles in 1969-75 |
| sub-gerente | assistant to the gerente |
| tarea | daily work quota |
| trabajador | worker; in this study, generally the worker on an agrarian ex-hacienda |

Part One · *SELF-MANAGEMENT,*
*REFORM GOVERNMENT,*
*AND CHANGING*
*POLITICAL CULTURE*

# I · *Introduction*

> We must forge a new political consciousness in Peru. A new con-
> sciousness built in struggle against all that before meant citizenship
> in our country... This establishes ambitious objectives, [but]...aspir-
> ing to recreate the world of our people... and to forge a new society
> for a new man, we have no other recourse but to confront bravely the
> formidable challenge.
>
> Juan Velasco Alvarado[1]

A CRITICAL and dramatic goal of many radical governments has
been to change traditional political values and forge a "new man."[2]
The most prominent leftist leaders of recent years—Cuba's Fidel
Castro, Tanzania's Julius Nyerere, China's Mao Tse-tung, Chile's
Salvador Allende—all hoped to develop a new political consciousness in their countries. Whereas in the past citizens had been
divided from one another and cowed in front of superiors, they
were to begin to collaborate with their fellows as equals, trust them,
and share authority with them. Together, citizens would work hard
to advance their own living standards and those of the nation as a
whole. There would also be a new awareness and openness to the
world beyond one's own community, resulting in a sense of identification with the nation and a willingness to recognize the achievements of the national government.

In Peru, the challenge of developing such new political values was
taken up by a military chief, General Juan Velasco Alvarado. Leading Peru between 1968 and 1975, Velasco claimed that his military
government was radically transforming the entire economic and
political structure of Peru and building a "fully participatory social
democracy." The proclaimed revolution was to be a "humanistic"
one because it wished "the full actualization of man, within a community where there is solidarity and where the essential and insepa-
rable values are justice and liberty." Posters stated the goals of the
military government in simpler terms: "In unity lies strength." "No
more peasant tears. The agrarian reform is changing the very back-

---

[1] Speech given at the Center of High Military Studies (CAEM), December 27,
1972, cited in Delgado (1973: 221).

[2] The terms "radical," "reform," and "leftist" will be used interchangeably in this
study to imply some movement toward equality.

bone of Peru." "Peasants! Herdsmen! United to produce more!" This study examines the economic and political structures developed in Peru under the Velasco government—in particular, the self-management structures—and assesses their impact on the values and the behavior of Peru's peasants. Was the Velasco government doing what it claimed, and was a new political consciousness forged in Peru?

## CAN PEASANT ATTITUDES CHANGE?

To bring about rapid change in key human values is an arduous and complex task. Some argue that such values originate in a major historical crisis and are transmitted through the family to the individual as a young child, in a process that continues for generations.[3] Other analysts agree that these values are very difficult to change, but suggest that their source is economic, and that dramatic improvements in economic well-being are necessary to modify them.[4] These scholars consider the possibility that new political structures could change traditional attitudes and behavior of this type to be remote because they believe that these values and practices define and penetrate the political system itself; individual attitudes and behavior are inextricably intertwined with the political system in an

---

[3] Examples abound from many nations. Burmese images of authority as arbitrary and unstable derive from Burmese colonial experiences and from Burmese family patterns (Pye, 1962). In Mexico, the traditional relationship between hacienda patron and hacienda peon colors many Mexicans' attitudes toward hierarchy today (Fromm and Maccoby, 1970). In one Italian community, mistrust was pervasive, and was believed to result from children's fears of orphanhood (Banfield, 1958). The development of achievement motivation has been thought to depend not only on the content of children's school readers but also on the role of the mother (McClelland, 1967). The political loyalty of French peasants was found to be captured by syndicalist anti-Paris organizations in the early days of the Third Republic, and to be difficult to redirect thereafter (Berger, 1972). Many other studies can also be cited. On attitudes toward authority, see Hagen (1962: 168-175); on social trust, see Paz (1961) and Carstairs (1967); on achievement, again see Hagen (1962); on commitment to the nation, see LaPalombara (1965) and Scott (1965).

[4] See for example Acheson (1972); Maccoby (1967: 341); and Lopreato (1967: 425). Although dramatic changes in economic well-being would certainly be conducive to change in values and practices, mere "modernization"—increasing education and mass media exposure—has been shown to have scant impact. Modernization may increase political information but rarely participation, egalitarianism, or trust. Consider for example Lerner (1963), Rogers (1969), and Inkeles and Smith (1974). Despite some implications to the contrary, these studies primarily reveal correlations between modernization and information (McClintock, 1976: 26-28).

enduring political culture.[5] In part for this reason, although local grassroots organizations may encourage participatory, egalitarian, and trusting attitudes and behavior among members for a time,[6] they gradually dissolve as the outcome of specific pleas becomes evident and the countervailing weight of the overall political culture thus seems greater (Mangin, 1965; Goldrich, Pratt, and Schuller, 1970: 185). (As the nature of attitude change is a complex issue, so is the definition of various terms used in its study. The next section of this chapter clarifies my use of the concepts "attitude," "behavior," "structure," "incentives," "political participation," and "peasants.")

Although from the perspective of radical leaders it is important to try to change the values of the peasantry, these values are also considered particularly resistant to change. Peasant attitudes and behavior are targeted for modification because peasants are usually the largest and most downtrodden group in Third World nations, and their orientations the most antithetical to those of the "new man." Both political leaders and social scientists see peasants as politically cowed rather than participatory; socially atomized rather than collaborative; skeptical of the value of hard work; and at best fearful and at worst disinterested in the larger world around them. Of course scholars generally make these characterizations with a certain amount of caution about the errors of stereotypes and over-generalization, especially in light of the current recognition of the important role of the peasant in revolutionary movements in China and Cuba, but they have yet effectively presented a rather negative image of the peasant.[7]

[5] For definitions of political culture, see Pye and Verba (1965). This volume and many of the books cited in footnote 3 hold this vision of the tenacity of political culture.

[6] Cornelius (1973, 1975) suggests a particularly strong impact for issue-specific urban organizations, especially for individual political participation. Pratt (1968) also finds a significant impact, although his study is marred by a very small sample. Goldrich, Pratt, and Schuller (1970) perceive a more limited impact. With respect to issue-specific rural organizations, a dramatic effect was found for Venezuelan peasant unions, primarily on political efficacy, by Mathiason and Powell (1972).

[7] As Shanin (1966: 5) notes, "The image of the peasant has swung from that of an angelic rustic humanist to a greedy, pig-headed brute." One of the earliest analysts to take a dim view of the peasantry was Karl Marx, whose references to the class as "sacks of potatoes" and to peasant life as "rural idiocy" are well-known. Heath (1969: 179) has listed all the epithets applied to the Bolivian Aymara peasants by various observers and anthropologists; the peasants were described as "anxious, apprehensive, brutal, careless, closed, cruel, depressed, dirty, dishonest, distrustful, doubtful,

The tendency of the peasant to adopt a subordinate role before authority figures from within and beyond the community has been widely noted (Banfield, 1958: 85-95; Maccoby, 1967: 341-346; Lopreato, 1967: 425-426; Arora, 1967; Huizer, 1972: 9-10). Peasants do not seem to be able to participate politically because they fear alienating individuals in authority and assume that a humble, know-nothing posture is their best defense. Paz describes the Mexican peasant thus: "He is afraid of others' looks and therefore he withdraws, contracts, becomes a shadow, a phantasm, an echo. Instead of walking, he glides; instead of stating, he hints; instead of replying, he mumbles." (1961: 42-43).

In social and economic matters, the peasant is perceived to be particularly competitive (Lewis, 1963: 287-305; Banfield, 1958; Fromm and Maccoby, 1970; Foster, 1967; Lopreato, 1967). Peasant jealousy and distrust are the correlates of an "image of limited good"—the idea that all good things, material and spiritual, exist in finite quantity and that one person can progress only at the expense of another (Foster, 1965). The peasant rarely collaborates with neighbors at work or even on special community projects. Fearing betrayal or deception, peasants usually shrink from close friendships.

At work, peasants are considered to believe that effort and initiative are futile against the impossible odds of life (Banfield, 1958: 114; Foster, 1965; Lopreato, 1967: 421-427). They are faced by many unknowns beyond their control: earthquakes, the weather, the timely arrival of credit, the continued operation of worn machinery, the honesty of intermediaries and the stability of product prices. The economic success of peasants is attributed to good luck or to good contacts among middlemen and bureaucrats, but not to hard work in the fields.

Peasants are also perceived to be apprehensive about outsiders (Wolf, 1969: 294; Maccoby, 1967; Lopreato, 1967; Alderson-Smith, 1973: 17-18). The essence of the peasant position is often emphasized as powerlessness before outsiders (Powell, 1973: 87;

---

drunken, dull, fearful, filthy, gloomy, hostile, ignorant, insecure, irresponsible, jealous, malevolent, malicious, melancholic, morose, negative, pessimistic, pugnacious, quarrelsome, rancorous, reticent, sad, silent, sinister, slovenly, stolid, sullen, suspicious, tense, thieving, treacherous, truculent, uncommunicative, unimaginative, unsmiling, untrustworthy, violent, and vindictive." Only a few scholars have refined theories of the peasantry to consider the impact of distinct agricultural modes or macropolitical context on peasant attitudes. For such perspectives, see Migdal (1974); Powell (1974); Paige (1975); Scott (1975); and Handelman (1975a).

Redfield, 1953: 31; Wolf, 1966: 11). Peasants rarely interact with peasants from communities other than their own; when they do interact, it is often to struggle over rights to land or water with contiguous communities.[8] Most outsiders approaching the community are put into the class of "authority figures" by the peasant. Although the outsider may be a scholar or a government official sincerely interested in the development of the community, he is suspected of being a tax collector, a labor recruiter, and/or a political spy. The peasant almost automatically assumes ill will on the part of the government and its representatives. The fears and cynicism of the peasant toward outsiders are illustrated in a vignette from an Italian peasant village:

> Dr. Gino [a community resident] tells a story about a peasant father who throws his hat upon the ground. "What did I do?" he asks one of his sons. "You threw your hat upon the ground," the son answers, whereupon the father strikes him. He picks up his hat and asks another son, "What did I do?" "You picked up your hat," the son replies and gets a blow in his turn. "What did I do?" the father asks the third son. "I don't know," the smart one replies. "Remember, sons," the father concludes, "if someone asks you how many goats your father has, the answer is you don't know."[9]

Most of these profiles of the peasantry were done by anthropologists concerned with describing the peasant's world view rather than the possibility of changing this view. However, the very fact that the possibility of change is not discussed, despite the bleak image presented, implies considerable immutability to these characteristics. Political scientists who have analyzed peasant communities with a view toward the possibilities for change have been pessimistic. Various founders of the "political culture" approach to politics examined the peasantry as a key case study. Emphasizing that important political attitudes are communicated through the family and only over generations, these political scientists were profoundly negative about the potential for change (Banfield, 1958; Hagen, 1962; Pye, 1962 and 1968). As mentioned above, a

---

[8] Because peasants' interaction with neighboring villagers is rare, it is not widely discussed in the major studies of peasant political culture. On the paucity of interaction and the proclivity to intercommunity strife over land and water rights, see Stein (1961: 163) and Paige (1975: 188).

[9] Story is told by Banfield (1958: 120), and recounted by Paige (1975: 31).

major theme of the political culture approach is that individual attitudes and behavior are so intertwined with political structures that it becomes impossible to isolate the structures from the orientations and then modify the structures to modify the orientations.

The argument of the political culture school was given considerable support by the results of the most well-known efforts to forge a "new man," the attempts in China, Cuba, and Tanzania. Although the character of these results is disputed, in part because difficulties of access by North Americans have impeded scholarly research, it is clear that the "new man" in these nations did not emerge without birth pangs.[10] In all three countries, change in attitudes and behavior has been most dramatic in the realm of identification with the nation, including both concern for peasant outsiders and loyalty to the government.[11] In Cuba change also apparently occurred with respect to political participation and stance vis-à-vis authority figures. In contrast, in China and Tanzania, peasants seem to have remained politically cowed before authority figures.

Changes in commitment to the nation and support for the national government seem to have been sparked by the effective and engaging leadership of Mao, Nyerere, and Fidel, all of whom achieved leadership through long political struggles, which involved violent revolution in China and Cuba and the achievement of national independence in Tanzania and China. All three leaders are considered charismatic. Under their leadership, each government was able to develop an evocative national ideology as well as

[10] Access has been best in Tanzania, although even there it was limited during some periods. There are various studies of villages based on actual residence and observation in the sites. See for example Ingle (1972); Hyden (1975); Samoff (1974); Finucane (1974); and Van Velzen (1973). The few works on China based on actual recent observation are rarely scholarly in nature; see for example Printz and Steinle (1973). However, there are various studies that have effectively used sensitive, in-depth interviews with refugees in Hong Kong, such as Solomon (1971), Whyte (1974), and Unger (1978). Other scholars have used documents and primary research by non-American analysts to present rather intimate portraits of Chinese attitudes and behavior, including Meisner (1978). Opportunities for independent observation and intensive interviews seem to have been most limited for Cuba. Although recent work is generally based on at least some time in Cuba, it lacks descriptions of events and references to personal interviews. See for example Fagen (1969), Perez-Stable (1975), and LeoGrande (1978). The major recent study of changes in Cuban political culture by Domínguez (1976a) is based primarily on documentary research.

[11] Chapter X discusses the concept of "identification with the nation" and my use of support for the government as an important indicator of this attitude.

to provide considerable material gains to the peasantry.[12] Although survey data on attitudes toward the nation and the government before and after the emergence of the new leaderships are not available, the survival of these governments in the politically unstable Third World, combined with visitors' analysis of current attitudes, strongly points to such a change.

Prior to 1949, governments of China were not able to maintain central control over the country; the creation and maintenance of the Chinese nation were achievements of the Mao government. Internal support for the Chinese Communist political system seems to be widespread (Solomon, 1971: 248-526; Bryan, 1975; Cell, 1977: 183-195; Townsend, 1974: 350-351; Mehnert, 1975; Printz and Steinle, 1973). Although the period after the death of Mao has been a difficult one for the Communist government, it apparently has fared better than earlier governments, which were traditionally very short-lived after the death of the original leaders. In Tanzania, Nyerere is often hailed as "The Teacher." He regularly receives over 90 percent of the vote in national elections. Important national policies such as "villagization" and the holding of elections within the single party have been implemented with an eye to the development of a sense of national identification, and have apparently been successful in this respect (Samoff, 1974; Ingle, 1972; Pratt, 1976: 259-263; Blue and Weaver, 1977; and Rigby, 1977). In Cuba, too, the traditional peasant cynicism toward the national government has apparently been transformed, and strong loyalty to Fidel Castro's government has been reported by most scholars and visitors to the island (Fagen, 1972a: 218; Domínguez, 1976a: 5; Mankiewicz and Jones, 1975: 17-36).

In other spheres, however, the success of the Chinese, Tanzanian, and Cuban efforts is more uncertain. In China and Tanzania, the government relied heavily on the official political party and on government bureaucrats to promote changes in citizens' attitudes and behavior. This strategy may have been more effective in communicating the needs of the nation and the importance of national loyalty than in developing popular participation or social trust. Whereas party cadres are critical integrative links between government and citizen, they are also symbols of political hierarchy. If cadres are too forceful in their exhortations or too quick to support

[12] These points are not the subject of controversy. Particularly informative analyses of the role of ideology are provided by Unger (1978) for China; Pratt (1976) for Tanzania; and Fagen (1972a) for Cuba.

their arguments on the grounds of government doctrine, they can only discourage a peasant's political interest and confidence. Although the central government may try to check authoritarian behavior by officials, it can probably never completely succeed in this effort, especially in remote agricultural areas. Moreover, peasants would still be looking upward for "correct" political stances, useful social "contacts," and perhaps even economic success; looking upward rather than at peers, peasants would not be fully collaborating politically, socially, or economically with fellow community members.

In both China and Tanzania, officials and cadres have been frequently commandeering and at times corrupt.[13] In both nations, the final decision on such important factors as the size and structure of agricultural cooperatives and production policies usually rested with government officials. Officials often seemed to feel they could afford to be arrogant, as is evidenced by the words of this Tanzanian official at a community gathering:

> I am new to this area, so it will be useful if I tell you something of my character. I am not a kind and polite man: I am cruel! If I see that government orders are not obeyed, I will know where to find you and how to punish you. I do not care if you hate me, for me it is only important that the orders of the government are fulfilled. I know you are truly blind; otherwise you would have appreciated more the progress that staff have brought to Bulambia. Now we are going to make you rise from a long sleep. I have a strong medicine for this job, we will give it to all lazy people (Van Velzen, 1973: 157).

According to an account reported by Meisner (1978: 52), a Chinese official who, during the Cultural Revolution, sought to force peasants to criticize their local leaders at a meeting in the community took a similar tone: "Livid with rage, Hsing [head of the work team in the area] pounded the table and bellowed, 'What makes you all side with your cadres? If you don't have big complaints, you must have small ones. Or some suspicions at least.'" When a peasant did stand up with a "suspicion," Hsing responded, "Out with it, quick. We'll help you analyze it." When the peasant

---

[13] On China, see Vogel (1969: 189); Whyte (1974: 154); Schurmann (1968: 490); Gayn (1974); on Tanzania, see Samoff (1974: 118-121); Van Velzen (1973); Finucane (1974); and Rigby (1977). On the extent of officials' authority, Unger (1978) is especially informative with respect to Tanzania.

replied that he suspected Hsing himself, the cadre "flew into a fury. 'What grounds have you for saying this?' he yelled."

Although in the Chinese case cited above the peasant responded assertively to the official's abuse, many reports suggest that Tanzanian and Chinese peasants remain fearful of authority figures and are reluctant to be active politically. In Tanzania,[14] as it became apparent that local development meetings were a vehicle for officials' exhortation rather than peasants' input into policies, peasants declined to attend; the rate of participation in such meetings was reported to be under 50 percent on the average. In many regions, development committees gradually stopped meeting altogether. Another reason for the low level of local collective political activity was that the wealthiest peasants continued to be chosen as local leaders—for example, as cell leaders in the official political party—and they often discouraged meetings. Frequently rather large landowners, they feared peasant political activity.

In China, the option of nonparticipation has not been as feasible as in Tanzania, although a few scholars have suggested that interest and participation in community meetings and in leadership positions is rather limited.[15] The more common assessment of scholars somewhat critical of the Chinese experience is that meetings are manipulated by cadres, and that peasants accept this because they appreciate what the Revolution has brought them on the whole, because they have no theoretical and practical grounds on which to resist, and because of a mixture of opportunism and fear.[16] One scholar comments:

> before open meetings are held to discuss whether grain should be dedicated to the country, or whether "political struggle" against bad-class village residents should be intensified,... special smaller meetings of militia squad leaders and other activists are organized to discuss a game-plan for generating enthusiasm amongst the audience for the forthcoming proposals. At the sub-

[14] On Tanzania, Finucane (1974) provides the most detailed study of peasant participation, including data on meetings in four communities. Feldman (1975) offers a stimulating analysis emphasizing the implications of the high socioeconomic status of local party leaders. See also Van Velzen (1973), Lewin (1973) and Barker (1974).

[15] See especially Whyte (1974: 162-165) on participation in *hsiao-tsu* groups, and Townsend (1974: 225).

[16] Not surprisingly, the more critical studies are usually based on interviews with emigrated Chinese in Hong Kong. See Whyte (1974); Bernstein (1977); Meisner (1978); and Unger (1978).

sequent larger meetings young militiamen and League members help lead the outbursts of applause and jump to their feet at appropriate moments to give short speeches or to shout slogans approving the new measures. It is manipulative, but usually sincerely so. Everyone knows the nature of the game, and . . . most of the villagers usually consider it a fair game to participate in (Unger, 1978: 598).

To support this argument, Unger cites the response of peasants at a village meeting to a request from cadres that they dedicate some of their production team's rice to the commune as a whole; the response was recollected by an emigrated peasant:

We'd had a good harvest that year. The peasants naturally wanted more from the team's surpluses. But the teams had someone stand up as a representative of the peasants and say "Let us dedicate some of this rice to the revolution and the world." Team members felt, "Here we have a good harvest, but of what good is that to us?" But they dared not say this. One big problem was that the cadres wanted to show how activist they were, and to show what revolutionary spirit existed in the village and also to demonstrate their ability to persuade the villagers (Unger, 1978: 594).

Analysis of changes in the political attitudes and behavior of the peasantry in Cuba is difficult for North American social scientists because of the particularly serious lack of opportunity for prolonged observation or interviews there. It appears, however, that most citizens, including the peasantry, are politically rather active and confident in Cuba. Local authority seems considerable, much greater than in Tanzania or China, especially with respect to the selection of leaders.[17] There are very few reports of abuses by officials in Cuba, perhaps in part because until recently the Communist party did not have much authority; a great deal of authority tended to rest with Fidel Castro himself.[18] In any case, an easy camaraderie apparently prevails among officials and citizens in

[17] Contrast LeoGrande (1978) with Printz and Steinle (1973: 53) and Stavis (1974a: 114-124), discussing the selection of local Chinese authorities, and with Finucane (1974: 158-162), Van Velzen (1973: 163) and Rigby (1977: 97-103), discussing the selection of local Tanzanian authorities.

[18] Discussions of Cuban political institutions include Fagen (1969 and 1972a); Domínguez and Mitchell (1971); Domínguez (1976b); and LeoGrande (1978). Fagen (1972a), Gonzales (1974), and Mankiewicz and Jones (1975) emphasize the role of Fidel Castro himself.

most Cuban communities and enterprises (Zimbalist, 1975a; Yglesias, 1968; Fagen, 1969: 179). This camaraderie may not, however, be a *new* value among Cubans, but rather a component of the traditional political culture (Domínguez, 1976a: 3).

Forging a "new man" thus proved difficult in China and Tanzania. Although the process was apparently less difficult in Cuba, a definitive assessment must await further research. Relying heavily on the government-guided political party as an agent of change, the Chinese and Tanzanian regimes were unable to resolve a critical contradiction: the exhortative, aggressive political official may be able to explain the achievements of the national government and to encourage a sense of national identification and loyalty to the regime, but this official may simultaneously become a symbol of political hierarchy.

If leaders such as Mao, Nyerere, and Fidel encountered difficulties in changing basic political values, what chance did a relatively obscure Peruvian military man have to do so? Velasco came to power in 1968 in a sudden coup, staged without revolutionary combat and without the kind of intense popular affiliation such an experience stimulates. Although nationalism was an important issue in the coup—the International Petroleum Company, a subsidiary of Standard Oil, had long been a symbol of Peruvian economic dependence and actual expropriation was virtually the first act of the new military junta, and a very popular one—formal national independence was not at stake. Velasco himself was not a charismatic leader; further, after his leg was amputated in 1973, he was unable to travel beyond Lima to any extent. He was the son of a "medical helper" (a kind of pharmacist without a pharmacy), who grew up not in Lima but in a lesser coastal city, and had to struggle just to stay in grade school; he was not a rigorously trained intellectual who developed an innovative body of political thought. He had been in the army since high school, and was seen as a military man with a military personality—in a country where the military had an inglorious history and was not popular.

Even more important, it was not entirely clear what the Velasco government wanted to do. The government claimed to be dramatically changing Peru's economic and political structures, building a "fully participatory social democracy," and nurturing the "new man." But the government chose a distinctive—and, to some, suspect—strategy for the achievement of these goals. In contrast to most revolutionary governments, the Velasco regime opposed the establishment of a pro-government political party, on the grounds that authority remained based on traditional superior/subordinate relationships in parties and that political games and manipulation among party leaders were virtually inevitable (Delgado, 1973: 49-52, 221-267). Rather, influenced in part by the Yugoslav model and perhaps also by the cooperative modes established in other Latin American nations, the Peruvian government emphasized self-management as a strategy for change.[19] Referring to the participation of enterprise workers in the decisions of the enterprise and often in the ownership of the enterprise, self-management is also termed "workers' participation," "workers' control," "industrial democracy," and "economic democracy." Velasco frequently said that self-management principles or programs were "the basis of the revolutionary plan of the government" or "perhaps the most important step of the Revolution."[20] However, as Chapter II will elaborate, many analysts of the Velasco regime have criticized self-management. They have argued that self-management was not really a leftist reform aimed at workers' participation or control, but rather a rightist tactic for co-optation, manipulation, and the conciliation of classes.

Moreover, not only self-management but also the other goals and programs of the Velasco government were often ambiguous, as Abraham F. Lowenthal first pointed out and as Chapter II will describe in detail. Ideological conflict and confusion were marked, and government policies were different in different spheres and at different times. Various questions were asked and never satisfactorily answered by the military government, in the opinion of most Peruvians: Is not a military regime inherently biased toward hierarchy and order and thus inherently opposed to a real revolution? If the government truly sought popular participation, and really advanced self-management to this end, why did it not hold elections

[19] The Velasco government rarely compared its goals or strategies to those of other countries. However, Yugoslav influence was clear. The Czech-American economist Jaroslav Vanek and the Yugoslav economist Branko Horvat, both of whom have written major works on self-management with reference to Yugoslavia, visited Peru several times and consulted with high Peruvian officials on the Social Property program (Knight, 1975: 375-379). Influence from the self-management experience in other Latin American nations is evident from the similarity of Peruvian agrarian cooperative laws to their Chilean and Mexican counterparts. For example, the provision for two councils in the cooperatives, one a "vigilance" body to check any irregularities by the major executive body, seems to be a Latin American tradition. See Chapter XI for further discussion.

[20] First citation is from Velasco (1972a: 24-25) and the second is from Velasco (1974).

for top offices and bring civilians into these offices, or at least institutionalize strategies for popular input into national-level decision making? Moreover, if SINAMOS (National System for the Support of Social Mobilization), the agency charged with promoting popular participation, was actually designed for this purpose, why was there not greater citizen involvement in its personnel recruitment decisions and its basic policies? Why, if self-management were to be the bedrock of the new order, was the role of the state in the economy accelerating so rapidly? Why, if the government were to establish its political and economic autonomy from the United States or the international capitalist system in general, was the country seeking capital-intensive technology and foreign loans more vigorously than ever before?

The Velasco government's descriptions of its own aims and policies were often vague, indicating what they were not rather than what they were. Thus, for example, the regime emphasized that it was "neither capitalist nor communist." The ambiguities of the Velasco government, coupled with perceptions that a major clique within it was abusive and corrupt, but increasingly powerful, were important factors behind the 1975 palace coup in which another general, Morales Bermúdez, ousted Velasco.

The character of the Velasco government and its primary strategy for changing attitudes and behavior were thus very different from the governments and strategies in Mao's China, Nyerere's Tanzania, and Fidel Castro's Cuba. Given that the most salient and most widely documented changes in attitudes and behavior in these nations were in the sphere of commitment to the nation and were related to persuasive and exhortative leadership, the institutionalization of political parties, and considerable material benefits for most peasants, and given the emphasis of most social scientists on the difficulties of changing peasant attitudes and behavior, I wondered whether the Velasco government with its self-management strategy had been able to encourage new peasant orientations within the few years it held power. Was the general pattern of change observed in China and Tanzania, and to a lesser extent in Cuba, the only possible pattern of change? Or would the different mode of government and different strategy for change in Peru stimulate new orientations?

Finally, in general, how quickly and how rationally would peasants, given the general characteristics attributed to them, perceive and react to the specific features of Peru's new political structures and new incentives of these structures? Examination of the Peruvian experience seems important because if Velasco's government, with so much less going for it than Mao's, Nyerere's, or Fidel Castro's, could stimulate change in political culture, then presumably other governments could do so as well. In the terms of political science, Peru was perhaps not a "least likely case," but it was certainly a relatively unlikely one.

If the self-management strategy of the Peruvian government did encourage new values appropriate to the new structures, a second question then emerged: what kind of new values would appear? Considerable controversy existed concerning the "real" nature of self-management, a controversy raging not only in Peru but also in many nations throughout the world. One of the reasons for the controversy was that self-management had been considered primarily from a theoretical perspective and had rarely been rigorously assessed in practice. Although programs that resembled the Peruvian were implemented in Yugoslavia under Tito, Chile under Allende, and Mexico under Cárdenas, rigorous study of the impact of these programs had been impeded by difficulties of access, the absence of pre-reform baseline data on attitudes and behavior, and, in the Mexican case, the demise of key aspects of self-management prior to the emergence of scholarly interest. (Sufficient research on self-management programs in these nations has occurred, however, to provide the opportunity for some comparison with the Peruvian effort, as will be done in Chapter XI.) In contrast, the research opportunity in Peru promised to be excellent: live-in access to the self-managed agrarian cooperatives for both observation and interviews was possible without any government supervision and for long periods of time, and pre-reform baseline data on the enterprises in the study were available.

In Peru, I selected three cooperatives for intensive study: Estrella and Marla, two small crop enterprises on the north coast near Trujillo, and Monte, a livestock enterprise that is one site among many in the very large cooperative Huanca, located in the central highlands near Huancayo. My selection was based on the fact that all three enterprises had been included in the sample survey study of attitudes in rural Peru by Cornell University and the Instituto de Estudios Peruanos (IEP) during 1969, immediately prior to the agrarian reform. Fortunately, the Cornell-IEP scholars had been concerned with the representativeness of their rural sites, and the three enterprises were about as representative of the universe of rural cooperatives in 1973 as any three could have been. I also selected a village that had not become a cooperative in each site as a "control": the peasant community Agustín in the Huancayo area and the village Virú in the Trujillo area. Both these villages had also been included in the Cornell-IEP study. As the three enterprises were the only ones available to me for study included in the Cornell-IEP research, I was very fortunate that the leaders in all three decided to approve my applications for research. I worked in Huanca and Agustín for about four months in mid-1973, and in Estrella, Marla, and Virú for another four months, from October 1973 to February 1974, and returned various times thereafter. My research included not only a replication of many items in the 1969 Cornell-IEP sample survey but also participant observation, analysis of documents, and informal interviews. In this work, statements by peasants made in formal interviews are cited by questionnaire number (e.g. Q345) and other designations to indicate year and site (e.g. Q1977 E8). This citation procedure, the research sites, and my research methodology are fully described in Chapter IV. Names of sites and individuals are pseudonyms, except the site Virú.

I believe that, with these research advantages, this study sheds considerable light on the analytical issues posed above. Self-management was a very "real" reform. In the self-management structures of the Peruvian agrarian cooperatives, political activity and social collaboration within the enterprise dramatically increased and, in some cases, collective work achievement increased too. Fully developed only at the local level, however, self-management could not establish incentives for new loyalties or commitments beyond the enterprise. Nor were any other structures with such incentives established by the Velasco government. Nor did peasants become more sympathetic to outsiders—be they other disadvantaged peasants or government officials. The new pattern of orientations was often labeled "group egoism" by Peruvian analysts. It was a dramatic change in peasants' attitudes and behavior, and also a very rational and appropriate one, but it proved distressing to the Velasco government. Some scenes from my visits in the cooperatives illustrate the pattern of change.

*June 1973:* It was a very cold night in the new agrarian cooperative Monte, high and remote in the Peruvian Andes. It was the night set for the celebration of the birthday of Monte's "administrator," Julio Melchor, the only technician remaining in the cooperative. The party was to be a gala one; many sweets had been baked and records sorted for dancing. But many of the peasants who came to the large Monte dining hall that evening did not seem enthusiastic.

As usual, older people entered slightly hunched, and exchanged only brief formal salutations. Quickly the men and women took their places around the tables, and food and drink were served. Silence hung over the tables for a while. Then, the administrator, seated at the head of the table, began to talk. As he drank more, he talked more, totally dominating the conversation. He embarked on a long, drunken toast to the "prominent" guest—namely myself. The peasants looked tired and bored. Why had they come, I wondered: to curry the administrator's favor? And how many similar parties had taken place throughout the decades in Peru and other Latin American countries?

*May 1975:* I was back in Monte after some time. It was the lunch hour, and I approached the dining hall expecting the customary situation—school-children would eat quietly, adult peasants would be absent, and I would be placed alongside the schoolteachers and the social worker at the most comfortable table (the warmest one, close to the kitchen). The administrator would be eating in his house in solitary splendor. But all had changed. The administrator and the social worker had been transferred. The "elite" table was gone. I joined a new young schoolteacher and social worker at a regular table with some six peasants. The men eagerly discussed the Monte union and its politics. Their tone was assertive as they debated strategies. The former leader of the union had left Monte for various reasons, and I asked a peasant if his departure had hurt the union. Although in the past Monte peasants had been extremely preoccupied by the possibility of betrayal of the union by its leaders, as well as of its repression by technicians, there seemed to be no fear in the peasant's answer. "If one man deserts the cause, two will take his place; and if two leave, four will take their places, that's how it will be," said the peasant. Yet, I noted that the peasants' attention was riveted upon their own union: they were proud of the demands they had won together through the union and wanted to advance more demands. They did not seem to worry whether or not satisfaction of their needs would hurt other peasants in the area, or whether or not their action would damage the cooperative movement as a whole and thus potentially the Velasco government as well—a real possibility in this case because Monte was part of one of the best-known cooperatives in Peru.

*January 1974:* Many peasants in the cooperative Estrella, on Peru's north coast, were eagerly anticipating a general assembly of the cooperative's members, where new enterprise leaders were to be selected. I was also eagerly awaiting it. The current leaders were blatantly corrupt, having won power through bribes and other devious strategies. Individually, many members had expressed to me their outrage at how these leaders were robbing the cooperative. But nothing had been done about it to date. The assembly was scheduled for 10 a.m. on a Sunday morning. A few hours before the scheduled time, I began visiting members and talking with them about the upcoming meeting. 9:30 a.m. came around and I wondered why the bell had not rung to call peasants to the meeting hall. By 10:00 a.m. the bell still had not rung, and few peasants had gathered. At 10:30, there was still no action. At 11:00, I went to ask one of the leaders what had happened. "Well, few people are coming to the meeting, so we'll just have to cancel it," he said. What kind of conspiracy was afoot, I wondered.

*May 1977:* About three days after my return to Estrella, my comadre held a party for me and some of her friends in Estrella. It had been two years, since May 1975, that Estrella's corrupt leaders had finally been thrown out. The ouster had come about largely through the vigorous effort of the union, which had taken the issue to political agencies in a nearby city and won a change in the very structure of the cooperative. The two subsequent presidents of the enterprise had been honestly elected and had led the cooperative to remarkable achievements. At the party, one member after another mentioned a new achievement in Estrella: the new school, the new medical post, the new library, the new consumers' cooperative, the new sports stadium, the new investments in pigs and cows. Then, the current Estrella president stood up to make a toast. He recounted the list of Estrella's accomplishments, and exclaimed "All by our own efforts!" to the happy group.

Clearly, Estrella's members had done a great deal to "raise themselves up by their bootstraps." Yet, it was also true that much of Estrella's success was due to government loans and was predicated upon the agrarian reform. And it was true that by 1977 Peru was in the midst of an economic crisis that would presumably soon impinge upon the cooperative. Estrella peasants seemed oblivious to these facts. Their concern was with Estrella, not Peru. Indeed, Estrella peasants were not even sympathetic to the problems of troubled nearby enterprises. Their stance was competitive, even on minor points. When I showed Estrella peasants this manuscript, for example, they eyed the photographs jealously. Why had I included a picture of the sports stadium in a nearby town rather than of the one in Estrella?

The extent to which new values emerged among Peruvian cooperative members offers considerable hope to those who favor the development of more collaborative and egalitarian societies but, aware of the implications of Freudian psychology and the political culture literature, fear that traditional, "engrained" personal values raise an insurmountable obstacle to the establishment of such societies. This study suggests that the greatest problem confronting a reform government with aspirations to encourage the "new man" is not that citizens' attitudes and behavior change too slowly in response to new political structures and new patterns of incentives. Rather, the greatest problem confronting such a government is to design structures and incentives appropriate to the kind of new attitudes and behavior that the regime is trying to encourage. The reform government must attend carefully to the examples it sets and the incentives it offers, and must also analyze in detail the nature of new organizational structures that it established. On the basis of the national experiences analyzed in this study, it appears that, alone, neither self-management structures confined to the local level—as in Peru—nor persuasive leadership offering an engaging ideology and material gains and new government-guided political parties—the change agents established in China and Tanzania—are sufficient to the task of developing a "new man" who is both committed to the nation and politically assertive. To this end, new structural amalgams and incentives must be sought.

## CLARIFICATION OF CONCEPTS IN THE STUDY

The terms "attitude," "behavior," "structure," "incentives," "political participation" and "peasants" are prevalent in social science research, but are often used vaguely. The fuzziness reflects the fact that the social phenomena that the terms try to define are themselves elusive, and indeed often—though not always—interrelated in the real world.

The concept of attitudes is surrounded by considerable controversy. The question of the degree of stability and coherence necessary for classification as an attitude and the issue of the relationship between attitudes and behavior have been especially disputed (Kiesler, Collins, and Miller, 1969; Zimbardo and Ebbesen, 1970). Some social scientists even contend that truly basic attitudes may be unconscious, and thus cannot be captured without a psychoanalytic interview. However, common social science practice, as indicated by such major studies as Almond and Verba (1965), Cornelius (1975), Nie, Verba and Petrocik (1975), Dietz (1980), and Mathiason and

Powell (1972), is to construe survey responses and verbal comments as attitudes. This practice is followed in this study. Similarly, as in most social science, behavior here refers to the actions of people, observed by the researchers and not merely reported by the individual.

In short, this study attempts to make the terms "attitudes" and "behavior" as concrete as possible by defining them primarily in terms of their modes of operationalization. When a word that refers loosely to both attitudes and behavior is necessary, the term "orientations" is employed. "Values" is used as a synonym for "attitudes."

"Structure" can be used informally as a synonym for "pattern" or "composition." Here, I employ the term more rigorously. "Structure" is applied primarily to the agrarian cooperatives, and emphasizes the legal basis of organization, production, and ownership. The legal connotation of structure is important to separate the meaning of structure from behavior. We can demonstrate the importance of this connotation by considering the phenomenon of political meetings: are they a component of the new cooperative structure or an example of politically collaborative behavior? Consideration of the law about political meetings in the cooperatives facilitates an answer; the number of political meetings that are held to satisfy a legal requirement for assemblies may be considered a component of the new political structure; any meetings held beyond that number may be considered an example of politically collaborative behavior.

Particular attention must be given to the term "incentives" because it is rather new in social science research. Indeed, one contention of this study is that, too often, political scientists focus only on the nature of political structure as a change agent and neglect the impact of other government policies and other reasons for change generally. The term "incentives" was originally developed by social psychologists (especially Skinner, 1953), to explain the adoption of new attitudes and behavior. Incentives are benefits or rewards.[21] They may be material gains—money, or a new house, school, or tractor—or they may be social rewards—more opportunities for a good time, a greater sense of pride or status. A government policy entails incentives of one kind or another as it affects citizens in these ways. Incentives are usually classified as collective or individual;

[21] The classic analysis of incentives from a political perspective is Olson (1965). Other important studies addressing the nature of the concept include Blau (1964), Wilson (1973), and Migdal (1974).

collective incentives are enjoyed by the group and cannot be denied to any member of the group, whether or not the member participates in the effort to win the benefits, whereas individual incentives are enjoyed by one member alone. Although government policies may offer either individual or collective incentives, or both, it is important to note that key collective incentives are usually related to government policy. It should be pointed out too that "incentives" may overlap not only with "policy" but also with "structure." For example, Velasco's agrarian reform was a policy that established new legal structures in the countryside; the policy entailed various kinds of incentives, some of which were related to the new structures and some of which were not.

The concept of incentives and the potential role of incentives in changing attitudes and behavior have been neglected by political scientists, at least until recently, for various reasons. One important reason has been that, from the perspective of the political culture school of theorists, incentives would not exist apart from the context of citizens' values. In other words, it would be considered difficult if not impossible to extricate "incentives" for change from individuals' attitudes and behavior. Indeed, at times in this study "incentives" were not sufficiently clear or sufficiently great to stand apart from traditional orientations. For example, profits from the cooperative enterprise never attained a level sufficient to promote a dramatic increase in collective work achievement, and a vicious circle of skepticism of collective work → limited collective work achievement → marginal profits → skepticism of collective work continued.

The political culture school might also point to analytical difficulties in the concept of incentives. At times, the term seems a reification; the stipulation of what is or what is not an incentive may depend upon its effect, and thus an incentive may be distinguished from a disincentive only *after* the evaluation of changes in attitudes and behavior. Thus, description of incentives as great or as small may seem analytically questionable because estimation of the size of incentives seems possible only through observation of their impact on attitudes and behavior. However, despite these analytical difficulties, the concept of incentives is useful because it compels the consideration of reasons for changes in attitudes and behavior.

Moreover, the role of collective incentives, and thus government policy as well, as change agents was neglected in large part because Olson (1965) argued strongly that "collective incentives" are inherently weak. Olson contends that because policy benefits or, in his term "public goods," are received by the entire organization, without differentiation according to each individual's efforts, the rational person contributes to the group endeavor as little as possible. Olson terms this conundrum the "public goods dilemma." The individual is stimulated to participate only if the benefit from the public goods allocation is "so great" that the individual would gain from its implementation even if he had to try to provide the good all by himself, thereby incurring significant costs. Thus, Olson concludes that individual financial and social inducements are most important in stimulating political participation.

Olson's argument was, however, based on a consideration of public goods—or government policies—that were of marginal importance, such as street repair and pollution control. In Third World nations, particularly leftist ones, public goods may be of critical significance to citizens. To a prosperous peasant with twenty hectares of land, the possibility that the government might reduce the legal landholding maximum to ten hectares is obviously of overwhelming importance. Thus in many Third World nations where government policy decisions critically affect individuals, the public goods dilemma is rarely operative.

In part for this reason, the role of collective incentives, and specifically government policy, in changing attitudes and behavior has recently been reconsidered by some scholars. The image of the organization member as a rational analyst of the costs and benefits of participation and cooperation has gradually been developed (O'Brien, 1975; Schonfeld, 1975; Langton, 1975). In the United States, the failure of grassroots, anti-poverty organizations to achieve major policy benefits was seen to discourage participation and political efficacy among the poor (Marshall, 1971). In Mexico, Cornelius (1975) found that the long-term prospects for government assistance or secure land tenure was an important collective incentive to political involvement. Support for the government was based not on distant memories of the spirit of the Mexican Revolution but on positive evaluations of actual contact with officials. Examining the reasons for greater radicalism in urban squatter settlements in Chile than in other countries, Handelman (1975b) emphasizes that Chilean migrants, unlike their counterparts in most Latin American countries, perceived real opportunities to contribute to a reformist movement. Recently too, this image of the rational participant, calculating the costs and benefits of political participation as well as different life styles, has even been applied to the peasant by some scholars (Mathiason and Powell, 1972; Migdal, 1974; Popkin, 1976; Bates, 1976).

Although the definition of political participation has not been debated as intensely as the concepts of attitudes and incentives, the term has been used in various ways by scholars. Recent major works examining individual and community action in the politics of non-democratic Third World nations, especially Cornelius (1975: 74-75) and Dietz (1980: Chapter 1), point out that conventional definitions of political participation often over-emphasize activities aimed at the selection of government leaders, activities that may not be relevant in many Third World political systems. Following both Cornelius and Dietz, I adopt a broader definition of political participation that recognizes internally oriented political activity, or in the phrase of Cornelius and Dietz "community problem solving," as an important kind of political participation, as well as the more traditional, externally oriented activities. Again after Cornelius and Dietz, I propose the following definition of political participation by Leeds (1972): "Any action, interest, expression, or attempt to maneuver public or private bodies which is aimed at extracting rewards from a given system."

The definition of "peasant" has also been controversial. Following Powell (1972: 97), Redfield (1953: 5), and Wolf (1966: 11), I use a broad definition of peasants, encompassing all rural residents who are largely involved in agricultural production and whose lives are shaped to a significant extent by powerful outsiders. Some peasants, however, must also be considered "workers" because they are employed for a daily wage by an enterprise. The cooperative members of this study can thus be referred to as peasants and as workers.

## II · Self-Management and the Velasco Government as Agents of Change: Theory and Practice

> Every revolution is an unconcluded task, a great effort of approxima-tion toward ends that are always elusive and, in their entirety, unattainable.
>
> (Delgado, 1973:9)

GENERAL VELASCO said that in the "new Peru" there would gradually emerge from the vulnerable and socially isolated peasant a confident individual, expressing his concerns proudly, collaborat-ing with others to resolve those concerns, and working hard to improve Peru's living standard. Velasco presumably hoped that the "new peasant" would also be concerned with the development of Peru as a nation and appreciative of government efforts on behalf of the peasantry. As Chapter I observed, Velasco's government emphasized self-management at the level of the single enterprise as the critical agent of transformation. This chapter reviews key theo-retical issues relevant to self-management and describes Peru's self-management structures.

Despite the focus by the Peruvian leadership, and by many self-management theorists as well, upon self-management at the level of the single enterprise, self-management is of course embedded in a national political and economic system. The impact of self-management at the enterprise level filters through the national-level political and economic structures.[1] Political participation within the enterprise is futile if all demands made by enterprise members are disregarded by government officials; social assertive-ness is discouraged if enterprise members are treated disdainfully by officials; hard work seems futile if the government squanders resources and lazy officials earn large salaries; loyalty to the govern-ment is illogical if the government is not benefiting citizens. Hence, this chapter also considers the controversy about the nature of the

[1] Self-evident as these points may appear, they have often been ignored. See Stephens (1977) for a cogent cross-national analysis of self-management and the importance of considering national-level structures. Espinosa and Zimbalist (1978: 24-28) also make this point.

Peruvian military government and its policies and then describes that government itself.

## SELF-MANAGEMENT AS AN AGENT OF CHANGE: THEORETICAL PERSPECTIVES

What is self-management? The term refers to the participation of enterprise workers in the key decisions of the enterprise and often in the ownership of the enterprise.[2] Self-management theorists have often stressed the distinction between "political democracy" and "economic democracy," arguing that there is only political democracy and not economic democracy in most so-called democratic nations. In other words, in these countries the decisions of government are subject in various ways to citizen influence, but the decisions of enterprises are rarely subject to organized employee influence.

Self-management is most often defined as the *exclusive* control and management of productive organizations by their *full,* active membership on the basis of voting equality (Vanek, 1975: 14). In practice, however, the term has been applied to various degrees and types of workers' control.[3] The gamut begins with such limited forms as opportunities for profit sharing and information and consultation, implemented in various Western European countries. The gamut then moves toward forms in which workers gain minority, parity, majority, and finally entire representation on the decision-making bodies of the enterprise. The range also encompasses situations in which some workers have representation rights (usually the workers employed full-time at the moment of the transformation of the firm from a traditional one into a self-managed one), but other workers do not (for example, part-time, seasonal, or new workers). An important distinction among self-managed firms is whether, if workers share power over enterprise decisions with another group, they share it with the traditional owners and managers or with the state. In Western European nations, the power is typically shared with the traditional owners and managers. In Yugoslavia, in Chile under Allende, and in some sectors of the Peruvian economy, power was shared in various ways with the state.

[2] This usage is evident in most studies of specific cases, such as Adizes (1971); Bernstein (1974); Garson (1974 and 1977); Hunnius, Garson, and Case (1973); Espinosa and Zimbalist (1978); and primarily theoretical works, such as Blumberg (1969); Garson and Smith (1976); Gramsci (1977); and Pateman (1970).

[3] Excellent reviews of the range of self-management experiences include Espinosa and Zimbalist (1978: 1-8); Garson (1977: 1-25); and Stephens (1977).

Although self-management theorists have traditionally empha-sized the micro enterprise level, some recent consideration has been given to macro self-management at the national level. What national-level self-management would mean is still disputed and unclear, however. Vanek (1970) defines self-management at the national level to apply only to the economy, implying decentralized decision making within all firms, a free market in goods, labor, and investment funds, and rental of capital assets from an agency ex-ternal to the firm. Borgese (1975), on the other hand, envisions the application of self-management to the political system, implying that the representatives of economic enterprises have seats in gov-ernment alongside the traditional political representatives. Horvat (1975) suggests a complex set of political linkages for the coordina-tion of the self-managed economy, including a regulative and ad-ministrative federation. Gramsci (1977: 92) also recommends that the workers' councils be "linked and coordinated systematically in such a way that they culminate in a general congress at their apex expressing their national unity." However, in contrast to the three previous analysts, Gramsci perceives the purpose of such a congress as being to help build a revolutionary movement that will ultimately overthrow the government. Gramsci also believes that workers' councils and workers' congresses should work with the Communist party, although his view of the specific role for the party is not clear; primarily, his emphasis is that the party should persuade and edu-cate workers (Clark, 1977: 62-73).

One of the most controversial issues with respect to self-management is the ideal role of the state in the self-managed system.[4] Many of the original proponents of self-management pri-marily sought libertarian goals and tended to regard any state role in the decisions of the enterprise as a violation of the principles of self-management. Increasingly, however, self-management theo-rists have become concerned that if self-managed enterprises operate entirely within a free market economy, the tendencies for capital to be allocated to already richer enterprises will prevail, and inequality will be exacerbated.[5] They suggest that the state might orient taxation, investment, and other policies to encourage eco-

[4] Interesting discussions of this issue are highlighted by Malenkovitch (1971). See also the debates in 1974 and 1975 issues of the newsletter of *People for Self-Management*, based at Cornell University.

[5] See for example the critiques of Yugoslav self-management during the 1960s, many of which are incorporated in Malenkovitch (1971). Similar beliefs are held by Knight (1975), Espinosa and Zimbalist (1978: 6-7), and Huberman and Sweezy (1964).

nomic equality among enterprises, although a considerable range of decision-making power would yet remain with workers.

What is the impact of self-management on the attitudes and behavior of enterprise members? The debate on this question, although intense, has been largely theoretical because until recently the only self-management program approximating the ideal had been implemented in Yugoslavia. In the controversy, the key questions are: Is the workplace a significant political arena? Is self-management an impetus to the solidarity and political strength of enterprise workers, or a strategy for the conciliation of different classes in the enterprise? What is the relationship between self-managed enterprise and unions? Does self-management enhance collective work achievement? Well-known radical theorists who advocated self-management are Antonio Gramsci, Henri de Man, and André Gorz. Recently, a number of social scientists have promoted self-management, including Blumberg (1969), Pateman (1970 and 1976), Hunnius, Garson, and Case (1973), Adizes and Borgese (1975), Horvat, Marković, and Supek (1975), Vanek (1975), and Espinosa and Zimbalist (1978). The most prominent criticism of self-management was by Clegg (1960); other scholars have criticized self-management primarily from the perspective of a specific national experience.

Advocates of self-management share a vision of the workplace as a critical political arena. Workers spend a large amount of their time on the job, and decisions made there have an immediate effect. For these reasons, the worker feels his subordination to the enterprise boss with special intensity. The hierarchical structure of traditional enterprise teaches workers to act as inferiors in all political arenas. In his studies of the psychology and politics of the workplace, de Man emphasizes the extent of workers' subordination in the enterprise and workers' frustration at their lot; modern capitalist enterprise represents "a mortifying hierarchy of social power" (1929: 203) and has entailed "boredom with work, the loss of all opportunity for the worker to exercise his skill, his initiative, to utilize in his work the highest powers of his mental faculties" (1979: 121). De Man stresses, too, the importance of democracy in workplace organization, and the meaninglessness of socialism without such a change:

> You go to elections only once every four years; you go to the shop, the factory, the workyard every day. You spend there the best part of your life; you expend there the power of your muscles and of your nerves. Democracy will be realized nowhere

unless it is realized there. . . . There are comrades who like very much to speak of the revolution and who always have in their mouths certain banal formulas by which they conceive of it, such as "the dictatorship of the proletariat." . . . [But] To change laws is not very difficult! To bring about a political overthrow, . . . sometimes only machine guns are necessary. . . . Before such an enterprise can succeed it is indispensable to change the general outlook, to transform institutions, customs, ideas, not only in political life, but in work life, everyday life (de Man, 1979: 132-133).

Proponents of self-management also contend that enterprise democracy builds solidarity among the workers in the firm. If self-management has been fully implemented and thus the boss or government cadre does not dominate the enterprise, the traditional hierarchical authority structure of the enterprise is smashed. No longer competing for the favors of the boss or the official, workers are able to talk with each other and trust each other. As they meet and forge their own decisions about enterprise policy on the one member/one vote principle, they develop a sense of their own political equality with other members. As their decisions are implemented, political competence also emerges among members. On this score, self-management is contrasted to government-guided organizations, where capitalists may only be replaced by bureaucrats in the enterprise, leaving the worker still subordinate.

Even if self-management is only partially implemented, many proponents of enterprise democracy argue that the reform builds workers' social solidarity and political will. Workers gain access to important information; they perceive that enterprise owners profit not necessarily because of their work, but often because of their machinations. Management's veils are penetrated. Moreover, even in partial forms of self-management, workers' political skills and confidence are strengthened by allowing them to take part in making the policies they best understand. The potential for building workers' political strength through self-management is emphasized by Gramsci:

Such a system of workers' democracy [ward committees] . . . would provide a permanent form and discipline to the masses. It would be a magnificent school for political and administrative experience and would include all of the masses down to the last man; within it the masses would learn tenacity and perseverance and would become accustomed to regarding themselves as an army in the field that requires a strong cohesiveness. . . . Meetings held in the shops and ceaseless propaganda and persuasion by the most conscious workers should bring about a radical transformation of the workers' psychology, improve the preparedness of the masses to exercise power and their ability to do so, and inculcate an awareness of the rights and duties of both comrade and worker, an awareness that is both concrete and effective because it is derived from living historical experience (Gramsci, 1975: 223-224).

Self-management advocates suggest that enterprise democracy plays a role in developing workers' solidarity and participation that the union cannot. Self-management is generally considered to complement the union rather than to displace it. In the union, workers act within the bounds of the legal industrial system; they accept the definition of their role as a "commodity" in a market (Gramsci, 1975: 224). Unions merely voice realistic and "negotiable" demands for wage increases or fringe benefits. In contrast, in self-managed organizations, workers make enterprise decisions and feel their capacity to act more positively as "producers" and "makers of history" (Gramsci, 1975: 227; Clark, 1977: 67-73).

Advocates of enterprise democracy contend further that self-management promises a positive impact on collective work achievement (Adizes and Borgese, 1975: 116-118; Vanek, 1971; Tornquist, 1973: 384-385). As members receive enterprise profits and learn the mechanisms of profit generation, they would understand the need for economic sacrifice and investment. Self-management would also encourage members to study and learn how to operate the enterprise, and thus develop important new technical skills. Self-management would promote responsibility, initiative, and discipline. These virtues were considered important by both de Man (1979: 100-130) and Gramsci. Gramsci believed that they were critical not only to maintaining production after the revolution but also to achieving the revolution because workers otherwise were too often inclined to "useless insurrectionism" and "mindless rioting and striking" (Clark, 1977: 69-70). To support their contention about the positive impact of self-management upon work achievement, advocates frequently point out that Yugoslavia's average annual GNP growth rate was the third highest in the world between the mid-1950s and mid-1960s (Blumberg, 1969: 22; Ulmer, 1973: 15). They also contend that the limited schemes of workers' participation in many West European countries increased workers' productivity (Blumberg, 1969: 123-129; Greenberg, 1975: 206-207).

The claims made for self-management have been disputed by various scholars. However, with the exception of Clegg (1960) and Kramer (1972), these analysts have focused on only one self-management experience. Yet, some of these analyses of a single national experience, such as the study of Yugoslav self-management by Zukin (1975) and the studies of Peruvian self-management by Cotler (1972 and 1975) and Quijano (1975), imply inherent disadvantages to the program, wherever it would be implemented.

From these analyses, self-management emerges as co-optive and manipulative. In self-management organizations, politics is obfuscated by technocratic issues such as investment policy and downgraded to minor problems of everyday life, such as the location of the enterprise sports facility. Moreover, critics argue that class consciousness is destroyed and the maintenance of traditional hierarchies is facilitated by self-management. Classes in the self-managed enterprise are "conciliated" or "integrated," but still essentially unequal. Self-management thus integrates classes under false pretenses. Either the traditional owners remain in the enterprise, and thus capitalist owners and workers are "integrated," or, in non-capitalist systems, government officials dominate the enterprise and thus government officials and workers are "integrated." Working closely with managers or bureaucrats, labor leaders increasingly identify with their superiors, and co-optation of the leaders is facilitated. Self-management organizations are contrasted with unions, which are perceived to engage workers around the more critical issues of higher wages and class struggle. To the extent that capitalists or bureaucrats are able to stimulate work achievement through self-management, they are only creating larger profits from which they themselves will be the primary beneficiaries. Self-management is thus primarily an effort to destroy class consciousness and enlist workers' support for a team effort.

Discussion of the implications of self-management for national-level politics and, in particular, attitudes toward the government is scant. Proponents generally suggest that participation in the enterprise will develop political knowledge, skills, and confidence relevant to participation in the national system (Blumberg, 1969: 223; Pateman, 1970: 110). Gramsci (1977), de Man (1979), and Gorz (1973) perceive the development of these political skills as the prelude to revolution, as well as the assurance that the eventual revolution will not degenerate into state-run authoritarianism. In contrast, critics of self-management suggest that members of these enterprises are easily cowed and controlled by the state, generally via technicians. Technicians are considered representatives of the state who, through their expertise and power, persuade workers to act as the state desires (Zukin, 1975: 257-258; Cotler, 1975: 77). Self-management is often perceived as a component of a corporatist political system, a type of political system to be discussed below.

Neither advocates nor critics of self-management thus consider the implications of self-management for a reform government that would, in the opinion of many observers, be worthy of support—especially if the likely successor to that government would be a rightist one. In other words, if self-management does prove to enhance political skills and confidence and thus encourage demands on the government, but also if the government is weak and beleaguered, as most reformist Third World governments have been, how might the regime be able to deal with the new political configuration?

Another issue that has not been analyzed in depth by proponents or critics of self-management is the relationship among enterprises, or more generally among the various popular strata. The controversy about self-management has been so focused on the question of the relationship between the owners and/or technicians and the workers and/or peasants that the issue of the relationship among the popular strata—i.e., among groups of workers and peasants—has been slighted. As proponents for some role for the state in a national self-management system have noted, however, if self-management is implemented within an entirely free market economy, members remain in competition with other enterprises and cannot be expected to show solidarity toward them. Further, profit motivations continue, and the desire for profits may conflict with the social responsibility of the enterprise. As some enterprises accumulate profits and others do not, socioeconomic inequality among enterprises increases.

To date, in sum, little attention has been given by self-management theorists to the impact of workers' control beyond the individual enterprise. This study suggests that such issues as the relationship among distinct self-managed enterprises, as well as among enterprise members and citizens outside the enterprise, and the implications of self-management for a reformist Third World government deserve much more thorough consideration.

## SELF-MANAGEMENT IN PERU

What kind of self-management program was established in Peru? How much power over decisions devolved to enterprise members, and when members shared power with others, did they do so with the former owners or with the state? This section outlines Peru's self-management structures. These structures were a dramatic change from those of pre-reform Peru, as the description of the pre-reform structures in Chapter III indicates. Parts Two and Three of this study will analyze the impact of the new self-management structures and the implications of the Peruvian experience for the theoretical debate on self-management.

Self-management was more radical in the agricultural sector, giving more power to enterprise members, than in any other sphere, although the state did retain various prerogatives. Almost all the haciendas (estates, usually longstanding) of any size or significance in Peru were expropriated and transformed into cooperatives. The two major types were the Agrarian Production Cooperative (CAP) and Agrarian Social Interest Society (SAIS). Land was collectively adjudicated and worked in the ex-haciendas of both types. Both were subject to the same law on agrarian cooperatives, Supreme Decree 240-69-AP of November 1969, as well as other corollary decrees. The next few paragraphs describe the main features of this law.

All the permanent workers of the hacienda became "members" (*socios*) of the new cooperative enterprise: they were to be simultaneously the workers, managers, and shareholders in the enterprise. The workers did not share these rights with the former hacienda owners. Ex-owners were granted neither political nor economic rights in the new enterprise, and in the great majority of cases they left the area. (In contrast, in Chile and other nations, owners were allowed to retain a portion of their acreage, up to the legal limit; this land usually included major enterprise facilities.) However, the workers did not "own" the enterprise in the traditional sense because their right to transfer the property was restricted. Only field workers were legally eligible to be members, although in practice many white-collar employees were included. Frequently, however, the cooperative had a wage ceiling for its members; some prosperous white-collar employees and skilled workers rejected membership in order to maintain their higher salaries.[6] Unless women were permanent employees of the enterprise, they were not members. One important component of the ideal self-management mode was missing: temporary workers had neither membership rights nor any other rights in the enterprise.

[6] This was the case in both CAPs of this research. No formal law was issued to my knowledge, however.

Every member was entitled to one vote in the General Assembly, by law the ultimate authority in the cooperative. The assembly approved major decisions of the enterprise, such as production, investment, and the budget. The assembly also elected delegates to the executive organs of the cooperative, the Vigilance Council and the Administrative Council. Including a minimum of three full members and two alternates, the Vigilance Council was to check that the Administrative Council fulfilled its duties. Including a minimum of five full members and two alternates, the Administrative Council was charged with the major responsibility for policy development in the enterprise. The council was to formulate policy with the technical advice of the enterprise director or administrator (*gerente*).

The director was the professional technician in the enterprise; he usually had a degree in agronomy, veterinary medicine, or the like. The Administrative Council selected three candidates for the position of director; the Ministry of Agriculture selected one from the three. The council could fire the administrator. At first, many enterprises evaded the requirement for a director, but gradually the ministry enforced the stipulation in more enterprises. From December 1973 to May 1975, the percentage of enterprises with directors rose from 30 to 60, roughly; the figure stayed at about 60 percent through 1977.[7] Some large enterprises also hired other technicians; the hiring and firing responsibilities for these technicians sometimes lay with the director and sometimes with the Administrative Council. Frequently, the responsibility was given at first to the director but then taken away from him by the council.

Although not envisioned in the legal cooperative structure and initially opposed by the government, unions continued to operate in most sites. In 1975, the government formally approved union activity (Torres y Torres Lara, 1975: 61-63). The functions of the union were typically similar to those of the cooperative organs, although more emphasis was placed on wage questions. Leadership was often interchangeable, and technicians attended union meetings as they did General Assemblies.

Although considerable power was thus wielded by enterprise members, the government did restrict this power in various important ways. The structure of the cooperative as outlined above—the

[7] Interviews with Dr. Rodolfo Masuda Matsuura, Dirección de Apoyo Técnico Contable a las Empresas Campesinas, Ministry of Agriculture, June 4, 1975, and July 25, 1977. 1973 data were provided from the Dirección de Producción, Ministry of Agriculture, Lima, December 1973.

role of the General Assembly, councils, and director—had been decreed by the government and for the most part could not be changed by members. Supreme Decree 240-69-AP also required that the cooperative allocate some of its economic resources in specific ways. Certain percentages of enterprise profits had to be allocated to reserve funds, investment, and the like. Also, in the corollary Supreme Decree 265-70-AG (articles 173 through 181), it was required that the enterprise pay the "agrarian debt"—a sum theoretically paid by cooperative members to the former hacienda owners through the state in compensation for the hacienda.

Perhaps most important, however, were restrictions on the cooperative members' power that were not explicitly stated in the main law. In the adjudication contracts of most cooperatives, the Ministry of Agriculture was given the right to authorize salary increases. Exact ministry power was unclear, however; after widespread evasion of the ministry's "authorization" rights, the ministry's responsibility for all salary increases was formalized and clarified by Decree Law 21583 in August 1976, following the demise of Velasco. At about the same time, the government began to establish regional minimum wages; ironically, whereas the ministry's concern prior to 1976 had been to limit salary increases, the regional "minimum" wages were often higher than the cooperatives could pay.

The government also put some restrictions on the cooperative's decisions in production and marketing. Decree Law 20610, the "Law of Panllevar," requested that "food crops" such as potatoes be cultivated on at least 40 percent of certain lands—or, conversely, that "export products" such as cotton and sugar be cultivated on a maximum of 60 percent. This law was enforced only in certain regions on a rather haphazard basis and was widely evaded, however. The government also played an increasingly assertive role in pricing and marketing for the agricultural sector, but policy in this area was particularly confused. Another government power was potentially important: the government was the only major external source of credit and investment funds. Finally too, during 1976, after Velasco's fall, the government asserted a new power, the power to "intervene" in the cooperative under certain circumstances. The nature and criteria for "intervention" were vague, and varied across time and place.

Although these basic structural features were characteristic of both the CAP and the SAIS, the two enterprise modes differed in some important ways. Usually, the CAP was established from only one ex-hacienda and was a geographically integral unit. In contrast, the SAIS was typically geographically disjointed; appropriate primarily to the context of the Peruvian highlands rather than the coast, the SAIS was to comprise not only at least one ex-hacienda but also nearby peasant communities. (The term "peasant community" has a very specific and important meaning, provided in the glossary at the beginning of this study.) Further, whereas individual workers were the members of the CAP, entire sites were the "members" of the SAIS. Specifically, each peasant community was one member, as was a Service Cooperative (CS) that included all the ex-haciendas.

The restriction of all ex-haciendas to one membership unit even if there were twenty or thirty peasant community members meant that, given the allocation of one voting share and one profit share per member, the ex-haciendas were at a disadvantage to the peasant communities in the SAIS. In many SAIS, the ex-haciendas argued that this situation was unfair because they were the only "enterprises" in the SAIS and its only income producers; the peasant communities continued to produce and consume by themselves, as their residents saw fit. The peasant communities countered that the SAIS should benefit them even more, because they deserved full revenge against the haciendas and their workers. The haciendas had in the past seized much peasant community land (Martínez Alier, 1973; Paige, 1975: 160), and peasant communities wanted this land back. Tensions were exacerbated by the fact that the peasant community member saw the hacienda worker as a man who had sold out to the patron (Stein, 1961: 220), trading his independence for a substantial and secure income; the hacienda worker, who typically had tried but failed to subsist on a tiny plot in his native community, felt that he had no other choice (Montoya, 1975: 99; Dew, 1969: 72-78). Thus, the SAIS incorporated two distinct groups with a history of conflict under terms disliked by both groups; yet, it is unclear what kind of cooperative would have been fairer and more effective in this complex context.

The CAP was a more prevalent cooperative mode than the SAIS. As of September 1976, the CAPs included roughly 35 percent of reform beneficiaries and the SAIS about 21 percent (Ministry of Agriculture, 1976). Peasant communities and "peasant groups" incorporated the remainder of the beneficiaries.

Peasant communities benefited from the agrarian reform because contiguous ex-hacienda land was adjudicated to them. Peasant communities were also affected by a new "peasant community statute" (Supreme Decree 37-70-A). This statute required a General Assembly of all members and popular elections for Administrative and Vigilance Councils, as in the CAPs and SAIS. Perhaps the most important clause in the law was the so-called "disqualification" provision (article 23). Peasants whose primary residence was not in the community and whose income was not largely derived from livestock or agriculture were disqualified from membership in the community. The announced aim of the clause was to reduce the political influence of wealthy middlemen, a traditional elite in most communities.

In contrast to the peasant community but like the SAIS and the CAP, the "peasant group" was a new land ownership mode, first set down in Supreme Decree 240-69-AP. Ex-hacienda land was adjudicated to peasants as a group, but worked individually. Specific arrangements varied considerably. The peasant group mode was applied primarily in later years of the reform program in disadvantaged, remote areas—a time and place of greater doubts about the viability of the collective enterprise and greater difficulties in imposing any kind of state regulations on the peasants.

From the perspective of some government officials, the National Agrarian Confederation (CNA) was an effort to establish self-management on the national level for the agricultural sector. However, the amount of decision-making power to be transferred to peasants through the CNA was more uncertain than that transferred through the individual cooperative. Whereas members of the enterprises could make their own decisions about enterprise policy, constituents of the CNA could only make recommendations to the state. On the other hand, the CNA could potentially play a role in decision making at the national level, which of course the individual enterprise rarely could.

The CNA grew out of the ashes of the hacendados' association, the National Agrarian Society (SNA). The SNA was abolished by the Velasco government and the CNA established in its stead through Decree Law 19400. The CNA was a structural pyramid with four tiers. At the base of the organizational pyramid were single agrarian associations—peasant communities, CAPs, SAIS, and groups of individual cultivators and of landless peasants. In most cases, each base association chose two delegates to the next step in the pyramid—the Agrarian League. In turn, each league elected five delegates to the department-level Agrarian Federation. The General Assembly of Delegates from the Agrarian Federations was formally the maximum authority in the pyramid. It elected for two-year terms the eleven directors of the CNA's Leadership Board. The legal seat of the CNA was a luxurious Lima building that was formerly the seat of the SNA.

The CNA proved an active and ambitious organization. Its goals were the integration of the Peruvian peasantry, the support of rural development efforts, and expressing interests and guarding rights common to its members "in harmony with the national interest."[8] However, the powers of the CNA were circumscribed by the state. The CNA was explicitly asked to work within state-established parameters and to cooperate with government organizations.[9] Government officials were active in the establishment of the CNA, and the CNA was dependent on the government for funds.[10]

The control over economic and political resources given to peasants through the self-managed agrarian cooperatives was considerably greater than that given workers in Peruvian and foreign industrial enterprises through the Industrial Community program. In the Industrial Community (CI), workers were to gain gradually ownership shares in a firm until they owned 50 percent of the company; workers were represented on the firm's board of directors in proportion to the amount of shares held by the Industrial Community. Many enterprise owners obstructed the participation scheme, however. In May 1974, the CI averaged only about 9 percent of a company's shares (Knight, 1975: 370-371). Further, the law applied only to larger industrial concerns, so merely 200,000 workers, approximately 38 percent of the industrial labor force, belonged to a CI by the end of 1974 (Fitzgerald, 1976: 34). Moreover, a federation of Industrial Community members called CONACI was quickly at odds with the state, and never gained a significance commensurate to that of the CNA.

In the early 1970s, leftists in the Velasco government became dissatisfied with the "group egoism" and elitism of many agrarian

[8] See Articles 5 and 6 of the CNA statute.

[9] See Decree Law 19400, Article 4. The point was modified in the CNA's own statute, from "to cooperate with state organizations" to "to establish and maintain relations with organizations whose goals are similar to those of the CNA." See article 5 of the CNA statute.

[10] Originally, the CNA was to gain funds from membership dues. However, these were not forthcoming. Ministry of Agriculture officials favored a law that would allocate 0.5 percent of the proceeds from the sale of agricultural products to the state for the CNA. However, the Ministry of Food refused to implement this law. Thus, in late 1975, the government authorized an annual grant of 35 million soles (about $60,000) to the CNA. This discussion of CNA funds is based on interviews with Ing. Luis Deustua of COAMA in August 1976.

cooperative members and disgruntled also with the workers' limited participation in the Industrial Communities. To correct these deficiencies, a major new self-management mode was developed, called "social property." The social property mode was to apply primarily to industrial and agrarian enterprises that opted for this mode. Firms were to be attracted into the sector by the assurance of government advice, finance, and a protected market. Influenced by recent self-management thinking in Yugoslavia and at Cornell University in the United States, social property was an effort to combine the national interest, as perceived largely by the state, with workers' participation (Knight, 1976; Fitzgerald, 1976: 35; Béjar, 1976: 124-131). To check group egoism and inequality among enterprises, the state was to have a strong say in the wage and employment policies of the firm, and a considerable share of enterprise profits was to be returned to the government for allocation to new projects or disadvantaged enterprises. In contrast to the Industrial Communities, there would be no "owners" of the firm whose capital assured them power over resources in it. Workers held almost as large powers vis-à-vis the hiring and firing of technicians as in the agrarian cooperatives. Ultimately, although private, state, and cooperative enterprises were to continue in the new Peru, social property was to be the "preferred" variety and was to emerge as "predominant." However, social property was neglected after Velasco's fall; as of mid-1976, only three firms were classified as full social property enterprises.[11]

## THE VELASCO GOVERNMENT: THEORETICAL MODELS

Self-management may be a significant new structure and new policy, but it remains only one component of the overall national design of a government, a design that necessarily colors the character of the self-management program. Thus, the nature of the Velasco government as a whole becomes a key question. Was it, overall, an agent of change, or at least a potential agent of change? What were its main features? Before offering my own answers to these questions, this section describes the two most salient views of the government to date, presenting in some detail the key points made by each approach. The two models are virtually polar images of each other. The first is the Velasco government's own vision of itself as the "Revolutionary Government of the Armed Forces" and

---

[11]*Business Latin America*, May 26, 1976, p. 163.

1.   Juan Velasco Alvarado, President of Peru, 1968-1975

of the new political system as a "fully participatory social democracy." Second is the perspective held by many scholars that the government was certainly one of the "armed forces" but by no means "revolutionary," at least in the usual sense of the term, and that it was seeking a corporatist political system.

Velasco claimed that his government was leading a "Revolution," changing the basic economic and political structure of Peru, and constructing a "fully participatory social democracy,"[12] which he described thus:

> we must build in our nation a fully participatory social democracy, that is to say, a system based in a moral order of solidarity, not of individualism; in an economy fundamentally self-managed, in which the means of production are predominantly social property, under the direct control of those whose work generates the wealth; and in a political order where the power of decisions, rather than being the monopoly of political and economic oligarchies, is widespread and rooted in social, economic and political institutions directed, with little or no mediation, by the men and women who form them (Velasco, 1972b: 271).

[12] Most of my statements about the "fully participatory social democracy" are loose translations of Velasco's declarations. See Velasco (1972a; 1972b; and 1974). The discussion also draws heavily from Delgado (1973).

To develop the "fully participatory social democracy," various structural changes were advanced by the government. The state was to play an exclusive or major role in economic spheres that had traditionally been dominated by foreign enterprise, including petroleum, mining, fishing, transportation, communication, and export. The power of domestic elites was to be curbed not only through self-management programs in agriculture and industry but also through state action in banking, marketing, and newspaper publication. The government promised reforms in the areas of health, social security, and education.

Through these efforts, all citizens would gain the resources that would enable their effective participation, according to the government. Participation was to be the "cornerstone" of the revolution, the component that distinguished it from all other revolutions. "In the concept of participation," said Velasco, "there converge the essential parts of the humanist, libertarian, socialist, and Christian traditions to which our Revolution is historically tied." Participation meant the exercise of decision making, and had to be based on real power, including economic power (Velasco, 1974: 9). Participation was to be "authentic," "autonomous," and "equal." Decisions were "to rise more and more from the popular base of our nation, that is to say, from the autonomous organizations of the majoritarian social groups in Peru."[13] The new self-managed enterprises and workplace-based federations were to be critical to this development. Of the CNA, for example, a Peruvian official said:

[This organization] must express the profound voice of the people who were always exploited, always marginalized. Your voice is the voice of the real Peru, the real people, who were previously silenced, but today raised with pride . . . it is necessary that this voice be listened to, that it transmit what you think, that we all know your problems and your proposals. . . . You are now able to present your problems and suggestions in an autonomous way (Confederación Nacional Agraria, 1974: n.p.).

The government was not to control or intervene in these new

[13] The concluding quotation is from General Leonidas Rodríguez Figueroa, cited in "63 Preguntas y Respuestas," SINAMOS, n.d., p 3. The phrases "authentic," "autonomous," and "equal" were frequently applied to popular participation. See especially Velasco (1972b: 105-144) and Delgado (1973: 221-267). Further elaboration can be found in many pamphlets, especially those put out by SINAMOS, which are usually not dated. See particularly its "63 Preguntas y Respuestas"; "Movilización Social: De Quién y Para Qué?"; and "8 Preguntas a la Revolución Peruana."

organizations; rather, it would "support" them (Delgado, 1973: 247-251). A primary support strategy was to be the provision of policy benefits—changes in policies or resolutions of problems—to politically active and united groups.[14] Explained Velasco's main speechwriter, Carlos Delgado: "Now, the incomparable weight of popular influence in critical moments of the development of a revolution is a key factor that supports the collective action of the masses" (Delgado, 1973: 79).

In my view, the "fully participatory social democracy" was really a vague sketch of some leftist officials' utopia. Little attention was given to the resolution of possible tensions between military rule and popular participation, or between liberty and equality. For example, Velasco stated that full participation was to be welcomed almost in the same breath that he said the military was to "conduct the revolutionary process until it was no longer reversible" (Velasco, 1974: 24). Why, if SINAMOS was to stand for a new political way of life "without masters," were the officials of SINAMOS chosen by the government, rather than by citizens, and accountable to the government, rather than to citizens?[15] The viability of the plans for a "pluralist" economy, including state, self-managed, and private firms, was not examined in detail. The "fully participatory social democracy" seemed an "ideological collage" (Ortiz, 1978: 124).

The military leadership's promises of a revolution culminating in a "fully participatory social democracy" were rejected as propaganda by many analysts. The majority of critics emphasized that Velasco was aiming to establish a corporatist political system (Cotler, 1972 and 1975; Quijano, 1975; Malloy, 1974; Middlebrook and Palmer, 1975; Agut, 1975).

"Corporatism" as a concept has engaged a great deal of scholarly attention in the last decade. Corporatism is not invariably seen in a negative light; it is, after all, a term with many meanings. Wiarda (1973) emphasizes corporatism as an Iberian tradition of hierarchy that pervades social and political structures. Schmitter, in contrast, perceives corporatism as a set of structural arrangements in which

---

[14] This statement is one example: "Considering that the satisfaction of material needs provides a great part of human motivation, the united effort of the group must be a consequence of that fact. The satisfaction of common needs, the understanding of the different problems of each and all the workers, must be the motive that stimulates united effort in the countryside" (Ministry of Agriculture, 1974a: 55).

[15] See Dietz and Palmer (1978) for a fine discussion of the embodiment by SINAMOS of the tension between citizen participation and government control.

groups are organized not according to "horizontal class categories" but according to "functional categories" (i.e., place of work), and in which group activity is controlled and monitored by the state. Schmitter defines corporatism as:

> a system of interest representation in which the constituent units are organized into a limited number of singular, compulsory, non-competitive, hierarchically ordered and functionally differentiated categories, recognized or licensed (if not created) by the state and granted a deliberate representational monopoly within their respective categories in exchange for observing certain controls on their selection of leaders and articulation of demands and supports (Schmitter, 1974: 93-93).

Stepan (1978) incorporates both Schmitter's structural view of corporatism and Wiarda's cultural view. He suggests that corporatist political culture is a specific response to crisis in Latin America rather than a constant Iberian tradition. Stepan analyzes the ideal role of the corporatist state in greater detail than other theorists; the state is to serve as an overseer or referee of groups and classes in the nation, working for the common good and the "harmonious organic social whole." Stepan also stresses, as do Collier and Collier (1977), that corporatism is not a single phenomenon but a series of characteristics, and that the scholar must analyze which, if any, of these traits is present in each specific national context.

Whatever "corporatism" means, the term was used rather loosely in the early 1970s by those writing on Peru, often primarily as a derogatory label. Historically, corporatism has been closely associated with fascism, and the association was brought up at times by proponents of the corporatist label for Velasco's Peru. The label has also been applied to Salazar's Portugal, post-1964 Brazil, and Franco's Spain, and comparisons to these regimes were made at times by proponents of the classification for Peru.

Although corporatism does not theoretically entail either leftist or rightist orientations of government policy, most proponents of a corporatist classification for Peru have emphasized the limits of the transfer of wealth and power to disadvantaged groups under Velasco. These analysts have been skeptical about the military government's reforms: The reforms were sops to the masses, carried out for pre-emptive and defensive reasons only. The demands of the disadvantaged masses had frightened political leaders and spurred them to believe that reform was the only alternative to revolution (Malloy, 1974: 65-66; Astiz and García, 1972: 680-681).

The reforms were directed not at a major redistribution of wealth and power in Peru but at the industrialization of the country along capitalist lines (Cotler, 1975; Quijano, 1971). The military first hoped that its reforms would encourage the development of an industrial bourgeoisie in Peru, and when this hope proved illusionary, decided to assume the mantle of the bourgeoisie itself, setting Peru on the road to state capitalism (Cotler, 1975; Quijano, 1971). The state's role in the economy would dramatically increase, but the primary purpose would be the military's self-aggrandizement, or support for foreign and domestic capitalists fallen on hard times.

These analysts believed that the military's major political aim was to develop state control over citizens (Cotler, 1972 and 1975; Middlebrook and Palmer, 1975; Malloy, 1974; Agut, 1975). Although new organizations would be formally encouraged, they would mobilize citizens on a promise of political influence that would not be fulfilled; all major decisions would still be made by the military. The organizations would be a kind of confidence trick, as they had been thought to be in Portugal; they would be "founded 'in order to exist,' then exist 'in order not to function'" (Manuel Lucena, quoted in Schmitter, 1975: 57). Politically correct activity would be assured in all associations by rigging the membership laws or the electoral system, by state monitoring via a watchdog agency of political spies, and by bribing or repressing dissident leaders. The military would be the "new patron" in a system of "institutionalized clientelism," in which superiors co-opt and control inferiors. Self-management was considered an organizational component of the corporatist political system, conciliating classes and undermining effective political participation in unions (Cotler, 1975).

In my view, neither the "fully participatory social democracy" model nor the corporatist model adequately describes the Velasco government. Any model is by definition a simplification, but in the case of the Velasco government, where unknowns and uncertainties were so much a part of the political scene, such simplification is inappropriate. Much as we might yearn for a label for the Velasco government, none can be applied. I indicate various analytical shortcomings of both models below and provide my own description of the government in the next section.

A central feature in the two paradigms is the ultimate aim of the military leaders. In the "fully participatory social democracy" model, the government is said to desire revolution out of idealism and sincere sympathy for the disadvantaged. In contrast, proponents of corporatist models suggest that the government had its back to the wall and, frightened by the possibility of a real revolution, initiated reforms to check it. However, neither model offers a method to assess intent. Both schools tend to dismiss government officials' words as propaganda when this suits their purposes and to take them at face value when that is most convenient. Alternative sources of information about the leaders' aims are not suggested.

Lacking direct analytical strategies, proponents of a corporatist model for the Peruvian reforms often assess policymakers' intent as defensive because mass demands or unrest preceded reform. This interpretation is not necessarily valid, however. First, such an analysis does not explain why the government did not merely repress those making demands. Repression had been effective in quieting demands in Peru in the early 1960s, as it had been in various other Latin American countries. Brazil's experience shows that repression was not antithetical to industrialization in a country whose socioeconomic level was similar to Peru's. Second, popular demands may not be independent of government action. Citizens often make demands in accordance with their perceptions of the possibility of a positive government response. At times, officials may even stimulate citizen demand making; for example, leftist groups in the government may encourage agitation in the hope that the demands will stir government action.

The "fully participatory social democracy" model and the corporatist model also differ in their evaluation of the significance of the Velasco government's reforms. The questions for us become: When are policies "bandaids"? When are they "reforms"? and When are they "revolution"? Answers to these questions would require a thorough examination of the change strategies available to the government and of the structure of classes and strata in the nation. Neither model provided such an examination. Consider, for example, the agrarian reform program. To proponents of the regime, the reform accomplished a key goal: it removed the economic and political base of the traditional oligarchy, and benefited ex-hacienda workers—individuals who worked hard under difficult conditions and earned less than their counterparts in most Latin American countries. In contrast, some critics of the government's program argued that the reform was hardly significant because it had not benefited the most disadvantaged peasants, the ones in highlands areas without permanent jobs in enterprises. The reform had merely made cooperative members a newly privileged elite. Both visions of the reform hold truth. So, how should it be evaluated? Could the Velasco government simultaneously have removed the richest landowners (the great majority of whom resided on the Peruvian coast) and helped the poorest peasants (the great majority of whom lived in the remote highlands)? Were the new cooperative members "workers" or a "privileged elite"? Careful answers to such questions were not forthcoming.

Questions must also be raised on the issue of government control over citizen participation. Although the two schools disagree on the extent of government control sought by the Peruvian military, they agree that government control of citizen participation should be avoided. In both models, the more negative term "control" is generally used, rather than more positive words such as "influence," "guide," or "direct." Yet, if vast socioeconomic inequalities exist in a nation, state action may be necessary to curb elites and transfer political and economic resources to disadvantaged groups. The possibility of a justifiable purpose for government control was not examined in either model.

Another question about government control is not answered in either model: What are the criteria by which a citizens' organization may be considered "controlled" or "autonomous"? If an organization embraces virtually all official policies or rejects virtually all, the case for control or autonomy is presumably made; but frequently an organization may take some stands for the government and others against. Calculation of pro versus con stands may be meaningless given the variety of issues and the differences in the importance of the issues. Further, even if an organization consistently favors government policy, it may still not be controlled by the government. For example, on many issues, the CNA and leftist government officials were in agreement. However, the CNA was not controlled by SINAMOS; the CNA and SINAMOS were two sympathetic groups trying to push government policies further to the left (see Chapter IX).

Third, and perhaps most important, both models assume that the government was sufficiently united and strong to carry out its will. The two models imply that the government was developing coherent policies of either the "fully participatory social democracy" or corporatist variety and that the government was capable of implementing these policies. In fact, decrees made in a Lima government office often were never seen nor heard elsewhere. Laws were regularly subverted by citizens. Riddled by power struggles among distinct bureaucratic and socioeconomic groups, the Velasco government was not as strong as its adherents or its critics suggested.

One government policy illustrates especially well the inapplicability of both the "fully participatory social democracy" and corporatist models: the agrarian debt program, a feature of the agrarian reform. The debt was the payment by cooperative members to the ex-hacendados via the state in compensation for the hacienda. At first the debt, calculated by an official assessment of the hacienda and to be paid in bonds over twenty or thirty years at 4- to 6-percent interest, seemed very large, much larger than would be required in a "fully participatory social democracy." Moreover, corporatist model proponents pointed out, ex-hacendados were to enjoy payment in cash for their bonds at 100 percent of face value if an equal cash sum were invested in a new industrial plant. Corporatist model proponents emphasized this provision as the linchpin in the government's scheme to promote industrialization along capitalist lines (Quijano, 1971: 16-17; Cotler, 1975: 52).

But, after several years, the debt provisions were not affecting Peru's hacendados or peasants as corporatist model proponents had suggested. Perhaps wary of further expropriations, ex-hacendados did not invest in industry and thus did not take advantage of the favorable provisions in the debt program for industrial investment.[16] Very possibly, as the inefficacy of these provisions became clear in 1972 and 1973, officers who had advocated them lost influence to more left-wing leaders (see below). Moreover, the amount of the debt proved to be much less significant than originally anticipated, but not because of any new steps taken by leaders of a "fully participatory social democracy" school. In the mid-1970s, inflation skyrocketed; there was no provision for inflation in the debt law, and thus the agrarian debt became a nominal sum for most enterprises by the end of the decade. Why had there been no provision for inflation? Apparently, its absence was a legal oversight.[17] In contrast to the implications of both models, it seems that this key feature of perhaps the most significant military reform had not had the close attention of military officers.

---

[16] "Información sobre Bonos Deuda Agraria," data provided by Wilmer Castro, Agrarian Bank, July 25, 1977. He estimated that less than 5 percent of the bonds or less than 100 thousand soles was re-invested.

[17] That the absence of an inflation clause was a legal oversight was indicated by Graciela Lituma Torres and Wilmer Castro, of the Agrarian Bank, in Lima, July 25, 1977; and with Ing. Luis Deustua, of COAMA, on several occasions.

## THE VELASCO GOVERNMENT AND ITS AGRARIAN REFORM: THE REALITIES[18]

In my view, both the "fully participatory social democracy" and corporatist models greatly exaggerate the clarity of the government's aims and the unity of its leaders. Officers agreed that change was necessary, that Peru had been "behind" other Latin American nations socially and politically for too long, and that it was past time to eclipse the power of the oligarchy in Peru. They agreed, too, that the Belaúnde government had been the "last chance" for civilian governments to make these changes. Belaúnde had failed to fulfill his reformist pledges, and now the responsibility lay with the military. For these reasons, the government may be described as "left-wing military," as the term "left-wing" is fortunately vague.

But, with the role of the oligarchy eclipsed, what kind of new society would the military seek? Whatever the rhetoric of the "fully participatory social democracy," and whatever the fears of corporatist model proponents, I believe that in fact in 1969 the military did not know what kind of society it would seek, and then gradually during their years in power different officers developed quite different visions. Some visions resembled the "fully participatory social democracy" and other visions, the corporatist system. Because of the disparity of officers' beliefs, and the consequent disparity of their policies, the changes in Peru during this period are often described as the "confounding revolution," the "peculiar revolution," and the "ambiguous revolution."

In 1969, sweeping into power with limited prior political experience, the top military officers were unclear about their goals. As one officer put it, "we had a series of concerns but they were not very precise."[19] Primary concerns were to begin agrarian reform, to expropriate the International Petroleum Company (IPC), and to assure that communism did not become an important force in Peru.

The desire for agrarian reform was motivated in part by the analytical perception that some "forty families" owned an astound-

[18] Analysis of the military government has been difficult. Virtually no scholars were able to interview top officers systematically during their rule, to observe policy making "from the inside," or to review high-level correspondence or minutes from meetings. My assessment draws upon informal interviews in July 1979 with some twenty military and civilian policy makers about the Velasco years, my study of the development of agrarian policy, and on secondary sources, including in particular Henry Pease García (1977a and b); Alfred Stepan (1978); Lowenthal (1975); Cleaves and Scurrah (1978); and Philip (1978).

[19] Confidential interview with military officer, July 27, 1979, in Lima.

ingly large percentage of Peru's productive land and that such a skewed land tenure pattern had been widely criticized as a key reason for Peru's socioeconomic backwardness. It was also motivated by indignation that, in the past, these "forty families" had manipulated the military for their own purposes. Moreover, in the aftermath of guerrilla insurgencies during the 1960s, many officers apparently pinned their hopes on agrarian reform as a check against communism: to own land would be to have a real stake in Peru as a nation, to "have something to defend."

The desire to expropriate IPC was widespread and intense among all Peruvians; regulating IPC effectively had been one key promise made by Belaúnde in his victorious 1963 campaign, and the popular perception that he did not fulfill this promise had been a major reason for his downfall. Officers saw the privileges of IPC as an affront to Peru's national sovereignty. Years before, General Velasco had apparently confronted IPC over a question of transportation for a military unit in the La Brea and Pariñas area held by IPC, and the confrontation may have left Velasco especially sensitive to the unusual prerogatives of the company in Peru (Pinelo, 1973: 146-147).

Anti-communism had been an important component of the instruction in military schools in most Latin American nations during the post-war period, and Peru's military schools were no exception (Villanueva, 1973; Stepan, 1978: 117-157). An intense, visceral anti-communism was a part of the emotional make-up even of many officers who were later to be classified as "progressive."

These concerns did not constitute a plan (despite Velasco's claims to the contrary in 1974).[20] Various critical policy areas, especially political participation issues, had been given virtually no consideration by the top officers (Stepan, 1978: 136-144). Moreover, the middle-level strategies for the achievement of policy goals had not been worked out. Although Velasco restricted his inner circle and cabinet offices to military officers, he had to seek civilian advice on many policies. In my 1979 interviews with policy makers of this era, the limited critical capacities of the top officers were often emphasized. Said one analyst: "often the military leaders would reject a civilian proposal out of hand on the grounds that it was communist;

---

[20] On July 28, 1974, Velasco released the "Plan Inca"—a plan that he claimed had been drawn up shortly before the 1978 coup by its principal plotters. The plan specified a large number of actions that the government would take. Very few analysts of Peruvian politics believe the authenticity of the "Plan Inca."

but, if exactly the same project were presented a second time to the officers and its 'non-communist' principles emphasized, the project would be accepted."[21] Commented a civilian expert who worked on the industrial reform: "There was almost no understanding of the meaning of the Industrial Community in the government. . . . They liked the idea of profit sharing, but the concept of 'conciliation of classes' was way beyond their grasp."[22] Continued this expert: "The officers had the conceptual ability to win single battles, but not a war."

Moreover, as top officers sat down to spell out policies, they found that policy preferences differed widely—even with respect to agrarian reform, an area where most officers thought that at least "something" should be done. Disagreement arose over the swath to be cut by the agrarian reform and by the industrial reform; over the extent of regulation of foreign investment; over the advantages of state enterprise versus worker-controlled enterprise; and over the character of citizen participation in government.

In his analysis of military leadership and policies during the Velasco era, *El Ocaso del Poder Oligárquico*, Henry Pease García identifies three general tendencies within top military circles: the "bourgeois liberals," "the progressives," and "the Mission." Pease García emphasizes that these tendencies were no more than that—not ideologies, and not clearly defined factions. Adherents changed upon changes in international context and internal political dynamics.

Yet, the tendencies and their major adherents must be identified if policy changes are to be understood. The "bourgeois liberal" tendency was perhaps dominant in the government in 1968, with Admiral Luis Vargas Caballero as its principal figure (who was not removed from government until May 1974) and a considerable number of other ministers (most of whom were removed by 1971). The "bourgeois liberal" orientation was positive toward private enterprise and favored reform only as a means to promote efficiency and support private industrialists. The widespread doubts during 1968-1969 that the agrarian reform would do much more than discourage absentee landlordism reflected the many affirmations by the minister of agriculture, General José Benavides, of the "ra-

---

[21] Confidential interview with a civilian scholar of Peru's military, July 22, 1979.

[22] Confidential interview with expert on the industrial sector, July 23, 1979. The comment is particularly interesting because the expert would have preferred a more radical law, but did not blame military "ideology" for the rejection of such a law.

tional" and "modern" features of the upcoming law. A "bourgeois liberal," Benavides had to be replaced before the actual 1969 law could be declared (McClintock, 1980).

In contrast, the "progressive" orientation was sympathetic to socialist alternatives, and was committed to the achievement of both equality and liberty. "Progressive" views underlay much of the "fully participatory social democracy" perspective. The years 1972 and 1973 mark the apex of the power of the "progressives" in general and Velasco in particular. By this time, Velasco had consolidated the political position of the officers in his basic support group. The generals whose stars seemed to be shining brightest were particularly "progressive": Leonidas Rodríguez Figueroa and Jorge Fernández Maldonado. However, the number of "progressive" officers was never great (North, 1979).

By 1974, Peru was confronting serious economic problems, in part a result of a gamble that Peru's jungle would soon yield vast oil resources, a gamble the government lost. Further, after the fall of Allende and of left-wing officers in Bolivia and Ecuador, Peru seemed isolated geopolitically to many officers. The influence of "the progressives" waned; that of "the Mission," led by Javier Tantaleán, rose.

Although rightist in a certain sense, the proclivities of "the Mission" and its head, Tantaleán, were very different from those of the "bourgeois liberals." "The Mission" was intensely anti-communist, but in contrast to the "bourgeois liberals," its strategies for countering "communist subversion" were the development of political organizations to be controlled by the state and the enhancement of the government's role in the economy. "The Mission" was widely accused of gangsterish, McCarthy-type tactics. Overall, corporatist characteristics were strong in the make-up of "the Mission."

One further reason for the rise of "the Mission" in 1974 and 1975 was that they seemed to have Velasco's support. Although Velasco had greatly helped the "progressives" to victory over the "bourgeois liberals" in 1971 and 1972, he now seemed closer to Tantaleán than any other general. Velasco was also very sick, suffering from a cardiovascular disease that had already cost him a lower leg and that was incapacitating both physically and mentally. "Progressives" were worried by Velasco's illness, his political shift, and his inability to gather popular support behind the government's programs, most dramatically evident in the riots that broke out in Lima in February 1975. These concerns spurred the "progressives" to side with Morales Bermúdez in the coup against Velasco in August

1975. Over the next months economic problems mounted, the "liberal bourgeois" tendency regained predominance within the government, and the International Monetary Fund (IMF) pressured Peru to adopt austerity measures. In mid-1976, the Fund's views prevailed, the government devalued Peru's currency and most progressive figures left the government. Some resigned; others were exiled.

Velasco was, of course, a key figure shaping the changes of the 1968-1975 period and rallying diverse officer groups behind the reforms. But, just as the motivations and goals of the officers around Velasco were not entirely clear, nor were those of the leader himself. Velasco emerges as an outstanding strategist, a remarkable leader who could persuade, cajole, and badger at least a facade of unity among officers (McClintock, 1980). He was not an intellectual, and apparently not particularly reflective.

Information on Velasco's background and perspectives is scant. His origins might be classified as "petty bourgeois" by some, but as more humble by others. As noted in the first chapter, he was the son of a "medical helper," who by some accounts might also have worked as a schoolteacher. The family lived not in Lima but on the outskirts of Piura, a small city in the far north. One of eleven children, Velasco struggled just to finish secondary school. He joined the army as a private, in part to gain access to further education, and graduated from the Chorrillos Military School in Lima with honors. Of what we know about his adulthood prior to his rise to the presidency, nothing suggests a radical political perspective. Velasco married into an upper-middle-class family; maintained personal ties to some members of the elite Prado family; and "rose steadily but unspectacularly" within military ranks prior to 1968 (Philip, 1978: 76). Velasco was not considered "white," rather a *cholo* (an individual of Indian origin adopting Spanish ways), and was nicknamed *El Chino*.

In my 1979 interviews with Velasco's colleagues and opponents, Velasco was described as "daring" and "impetuous," with a strong moral fiber and "good intentions." One officer commented that Velasco was "tough on the surface but tender at heart." Apparently, Velasco owed his professional achievement not to his intellect but to good, solid military behavior, and a fine feel for people's strengths, weaknesses, and sensitivities. In February 1977, Velasco gave an interview to the Peruvian newsweekly *Caretas;* although he was ill, his words suggest the characteristics attributed to him in my interviews—a spunky and spirited individual not given to cautious reflection.[23]

Caretas: Now, how would you identify the objective [of your government]?

Velasco: To make Peru an independent nation and to change structures so that Peru might develop as independent, as sovereign. Not a soldout nation on its knees. What was it like here? Here the American ambassador governed! When I was President, the ambassador had to ask for a meeting and I kept him six feet away. I hassled them. I kicked out the American military mission. Here there were 50 or 60 American "big cheese" and the Peruvian government had to pay their salaries, their travel, even for the cat the family would bring. And they were part of the CIA's information network. . . .

Caretas: Many people consider you to be full of rancor. What do you think about this?

Velasco: Rancor? Against whom? Against nobody! I didn't hit anyone, I haven't struck any blows. I led a revolution. It was a well-planned revolution. Because we began to act straight-away, to operate at high speed. We have done so many things at a frightening speed. I knew that at any moment they might kick me out. Because here in Peru, tragically, the oligarchy never dies. . . .

Caretas: Do you believe that?

Velasco: . . . Many have said that one of the things the Revolution did was to eliminate the oligarchy. Well, I think we haven't seen the end of the oligarchy. Remnants are still here, and those remnants are growing once again. . . .

Caretas: And why do you believe you were ousted?

Velasco: Political ambition, the desire for power. . . .

Caretas: Some groups always reproach you as a friend of the communists, as one who was soft on them. . . .

Velasco: Not only that. They have said I made communism official. This is a stupidity. . . . How am I going to emerge a communist? I have been a military officer all my life.

[23]*Caretas*, February 3, 1977 (No. 512), 30-33. The first four questions and answers were the first four reported in the *Caretas* interview, except for a very brief opening question and answer; the last two questions and answers were given separately, a bit later in the interview.

> There were some people half reds in the govern-
> ment. . . . There was infiltration . . .
>
> *Caretas:* Did you feel any proximity to any political party?
> Velasco: I had some sympathy for the Christian Democrats, at
> the beginning. The only party that had precise and con-
> crete viewpoints was the Christian Democracy. The rest
> were pure blah-blah-blah.

The shortcomings in the military's political analysis, as well as the
tensions among key groups in the governments, were most evident
in SINAMOS, the agency responsible for the support of social
mobilization during the Velasco government and the major political organization established in the period. Announced in mid-1971
but not officially established until April 1972, SINAMOS was for
several years a "progressive" stronghold: its military head was the
staunch "progressive" Rodríguez Figueroa and its civilian head was
Carlos Delgado, a Cornell-trained sociologist and former member
of the party APRA (American Popular Revolutionary Alliance). In
the claims and in the actions of SINAMOS during 1972-1973, the
"progressives" took the government's reform program to its limit.

Yet this limit was very real and could not be transgressed: the
military was to retain final say over the participatory process. This
parameter was reflected in the very decision to establish an agency
for social mobilization, rather than to build a political party or
encourage spontaneous popular mobilization. In the so-called "no-
party thesis," the government repudiated political parties, including a Velasquista party, on the grounds that parties had served
citizens poorly in the past. However, a Velasquista political party
would have devastated the traditional criteria for advancement and
promotion in the military institution, and such politicization of the
institution apparently was not acceptable to officers. Apparently
also, given the anti-communist ideological strain in the Peruvian
military, many officers feared that spontaneous, grassroots organizing by peasants and workers would be easily susceptible to
communist influence. When Committees for the Defense of the
Revolution (CDRs) did emerge in various regions in 1970, the government viewed them suspiciously; they had "erupted like mea-
sles," said Velasco (Palmer, 1973: 88). The "progressives" and their
civilian allies either did not accept or did not admit these parameters to participation.

SINAMOS attracted many respected intellectuals and activists on
the left, including Jaime Llosa, a key actor in the development of

social poverty, and Hector Béjar, a leader in the guerrilla activity in the highlands in 1965 who was taken prisoner and jailed until Velasco's general pardon in 1970. Such SINAMOS officials often perceived themselves as bureaucratic guerrillas who could push the military to the left and, perhaps more important, use the agency as a base for advancing their own radical ideas among citizens.[24] Especially in 1971 and 1972, the bureaucratic guerrillas had some reason to believe their strategy might work. Rodríguez Figueroa was not only a firm "progressive" but also a close friend of Velasco; he had been catapulted to power as the head of the agency, and his political star was apparently still rising. There was official discussion of making SINAMOS a "super-ministry" that would coordinate the activities of all other ministries and monitor policies with a participation component in all ministries (Agut, 1975: 453-460).

"Progressives" made various arguments for the soundness of the SINAMOS idea.[25] Political parties in Peru had performed poorly, becoming the personal vehicles of their leaders and accomplishing little; a government agency would have a better chance to fulfill the social mobilization task. The agency would not be deflected from its broader goals by partisan politics and the rhetorical games of electoral competition. Theoretically without an ideology of its own, SINAMOS would not be absorbed in endless and divisive ideological debate. As a government institution, with a budget over $90 million in its first year, SINAMOS would enjoy an access to state agencies and a level of funding beyond what most political parties could anticipate. When analysts brought up the contradictions of a government agency supporting popular mobilization, "progressives" would respond that SINAMOS was to be a transitional organization that would wither away after popular mobilization was achieved, and that strategies for citizens' selection and recall of SINAMOS officials could be devised as well (Woy-Hazleton, 1979: 17).

Whereas Peru's political parties had tended to concentrate their efforts in major coastal cities, SINAMOS was organized on a territorial hierarchy that required attention to all parts of the nation: 384 local planning offices were established in 91 zones under 11 regional offices (Woy-Hazleton, 1978b: Ch. III). Although the national office retained major prerogatives, regional autonomy was

---

[24] A full discussion of this conception is given in Santistevan (1977a: 133).
[25] A thoughtful, sympathetic discussion of major principles of SINAMOS is provided by Woy-Hazleton (1979).

considerable; for example, the activities of the Huancayo SINAMOS were different from those of the Trujillo SINAMOS, and the background and skills of field agents (*promotores*) also varied greatly (Woy-Hazleton, 1978b: Ch. III).

By "progressive" criteria, some SINAMOS activities were successful. Perhaps its most important success was its work with the CNA. The CNA was the first organization in Peru to bring thousands of peasants into national politics. SINAMOS worked with the CNA, but did not co-opt it (see Chapter IX). SINAMOS worked with the CNA—and even at time with the CCP, the Peruvian Peasant Confederation, an anti-Velasco, pro-Marxist group[26]—to press for land expropriations. The pressure from these groups was important to the advance of the agrarian reform into the more remote and disadvantaged areas of the countryside after 1973. It is interesting to note that, although the corporatist model would have required that expropriations proceed most rapidly in these traditionally impoverished and politically agitated areas, in order to reveal the military's desire for pre-emption, in fact these regions were affected more slowly than other areas.[27] Many of SINAMOS's "progressive" initiatives in the agrarian sector were at odds with positions held by the Ministry of Agriculture, and the conflict between the two agencies heightened confusion in the countryside (see Chapter X). For the most part, SINAMOS promotores were idealistic, left-wing young people without specific skills; Ministry of Agriculture officials were experienced technicians who had usually worked previously on haciendas.

Yet, the "progressive" vision of SINAMOS was flawed. The

[26] On alliances among SINAMOS, the CNA, and the CCP, see Agut (1975: 522-524); Valderrama (1976: 119); and *Latin America, 11* (March 11, 1977), 75; *8* (April 26, 1974), 127; and 7 (July 13, 1973), 222-223.

[27] The most disadvantaged departments of Peru are Apurímac, Ayacucho, Cajamarca, Cuzco, Huancavelica, and Puno. The relative intensity of political unrest in these areas is emphasized by Handelman (1975a; 155-187 and 246-248), Philip (1976: 37), and Chaplin (1968). During 1974-1975, the number of families gaining land in these six departments more than doubled the number during 1970-1973, whereas it increased by only 60 percent in the country as a whole. Over the mere 18 months between January 1975 and June 1976, 47 percent of all reform enterprises in these six departments were adjudicated, versus 22 percent in five wealthier departments (Ica, Junín, La Libertad, Lambayeque, and Lima). In the most politically mobilized department, Cuzco, only 98 reform enterprises had been adjudicated by January 1974, but by June 1976 the number had jumped to 252. (All figures are taken or calculated from "Reforma Agraria en Cifras," a serial publication of the Ministry of Agriculture.)

hopes of the "progressives" were dashed against the wall of the military's refusal to surrender power, a refusal that undercut SINAMOS from the heady days of its inauguration to its retreat in 1975 and 1976. The very decision to establish a government agency for the social mobilization task reflected the government's fears of political activity beyond its own purview.

SINAMOS preached a doctrine of participation that it did not practice. Neither its personnel nor its policies were chosen with civilian involvement. The agency remained closely tied to the military hierarchy. High-ranking military officers became directors of eight of the ten regional offices in 1972 and heads of seven of the sixteen top positions in the agency's national office (Palmer, 1973: 94-96). The commander of the military region was also head of the Tenth Region of SINAMOS, the one responsible for Lima's migrant settlements (Collier, 1976: 108). In January 1974, Rodríguez Figueroa was replaced as head of the agency by General Rudecino Zavaleta, who was aligned with "the Mission." The change triggered a dramatic shift in SINAMOS's policies and signaled the decline of the "progressive" tendency in the government—but it was a decision made exclusively by the inner officers' circle. Whatever the expectations of the "progressives," local promotores were recruited by and responsible to their superiors in the zonal and regional offices. Despite a measure of regional autonomy and efforts to select promotores from the area, who would be familiar with its indigenous population and would speak the language of the area, most SINAMOS employees had relatively middle class origins: as of 1974, about 70 percent of all promotores had studied beyond the secondary level (Woy-Hazleton, 1978a: 184).

The non-partisan and non-ideological claims of SINAMOS were also flawed. The agency's criticisms of Peru's political parties as organizations run by their leaders for personal goals had some validity. However, such charges only exacerbated the traditional rivalry between civilian political leaders and the military. In practice SINAMOS had many features of a political party, or at least a military version of a party, and did in fact compete with political parties. In its denial of these aims and its claims to a higher legitimacy than parties, the military enraged many party leaders.

Moreover, although ideology may be divisive, without a clear-cut ideology SINAMOS confronted other problems just as serious. As ideology was not a valid criterion in recruitment, citizens of all political perspectives, and often unknown political perspectives, were hired. Probably a majority were not "committed to the Revolution," in the phrase commonly used in Peru. At the regional level, many top officials thought the government's reforms were going too far, whereas most promotores, often young people with social science backgrounds and loosely Marxist sympathies, thought the reforms were not going far enough.[28] The result was conflict and confusion.

Further, theoretically non-ideological, SINAMOS did not give sufficient attention to its own principles. For example, the government said that SINAMOS should promote both authentic participation, i.e., that it should respect the authentic political voice of a community, and equal participation, i.e., that it should encourage equal access to participatory organizations and equality in general.[29] But in many situations both principles could not be upheld simultaneously. In their assemblies, cooperative members would authentically vote to restrict the membership opportunities of temporary workers, thereby violating the tenet of equal participation. What should the SINAMOS official do in such instances? No guidelines were ever established, and often officials did try to overrule community decisions to advance equal access.

Overall, rather than resolving the contradictions in the military government's ideas and the conflicts between different tendencies among military leaders, SINAMOS embodied them. The goals and structure of the agency were confused, and citizens saw the confusion and feared what might emerge from it. To citizens' queries about what SINAMOS was, the agency usually could explain only what it was *not:* It was *not* a Peruvian FBI, it was *not* a corporatist trick. Other explanations were rather poetic, but remarkably uninformative:

> SINAMOS is you. We are all SINAMOS, the men and women of the coast, the highlands and the jungle, . . . those who want to construct a revolutionary nation. SINAMOS is you, me and all our brothers, who in the cooperatives, the SAIS, the labor communities, the universities, the neighborhood assemblies, the public administration . . . are working and learning, constructing a new society of participation in the revolutionary Peru. So don't ask what SINAMOS is. SINAMOS is you.[30]

[28] This assessment is based on my own observation of the Trujillo and Huancayo SINAMOS, and on Woy-Hazleton (1978a).

[29] See Decree Law 18896 on SINAMOS and the pamphlets on SINAMOS published by the agency itself in 1972-1973.

[30] "Movilización Social y SINAMOS," SINAMOS, Lima (n.d., back cover). See also the various other SINAMOS pamphlets, "8 Preguntas a la Revolución Peruana," "63

After the days and years of political struggle and political learning among military officers and civilian leaders, what had been done and what not done? Unfortunately, a neat assessment of Velasco's achievements and failures is difficult. It is hard to separate what was from what might have been. In the early 1970s, there was a strong feeling of uncharted new possibilities in Peru, and the mere fact that Peru did "experiment"—whatever the results—was a dramatic alteration of the traditional rules of the game. Changes in attitude through these years may have been the most important and most enduring achievement; traditional elites were confronted with their vulnerabilities, and many disadvantaged citizens became aware of their capabilities. But it is also hard to separate what was from what was reversed several years later under Morales Bermúdez. By 1978, after several rightward turns, the agrarian reform was the only Velasco program still by-and-large intact. Gradually, SINAMOS was decimated, social property, forgotten, the Industrial Community weakened, major enterprises offered back to private buyers, and repression sharply intensified. What may be said, however, is that the major original goal of the Velasco government was achieved: the power of the oligarchy was challenged.

The government took various steps to advance Peru's political and economic autonomy. At international gatherings, Peru spoke prominently for Third World concerns. Ties with the Soviet Union, China, Cuba, Yugoslavia, and Japan were strengthened. The government expropriated many large foreign enterprises: the International Petroleum Company, the telephone and cable networks of International Telephone and Telegraph, banking institutions, fishmeal firms, and various mining concerns. These firms were transformed into state-owned enterprises. Although the government sought new U.S. investment for technically complex or expensive projects such as petroleum exploration and copper mining, the military tried to negotiate more favorable terms for Peru. The state did not carry its ambitions for independence into the arena of financing: Peru's foreign debt rose sharply between 1968 and 1975, reaching four billion dollars in 1976.[31]

The role of the state in the Peruvian economy was greatly enlarged. The government took control not only of many foreign enterprises but also of various domestic ones including cement,

Preguntas y Respuestas," "De Quién y Para Qué?" all published in Lima without dates (probably in 1973).

[31]*Business Latin America*, January 19, 1977, p. 18.

paper, and fertilizers. State monopolies were developed in steel, airlines, several export marketing lines, and other areas. By 1974, the state accounted for one-third of output and one-fifth of the labor force in the modern productive sector, excluding government itself (Fitzgerald, 1976: 33). The government played an increasing role in investment; its share of national investment jumped from 13 percent in 1965 to almost 50 percent in 1974 (Lowenthal, 1975: 8). Although the mounting foreign debt was later to bring into question the government's economic strategy, in the early 1970s the economic record seemed good, suggesting that the government's property reforms had been handled effectively. The gross domestic product grew by over 5 percent annually during the five years between 1970 and 1974; it was over 6 percent in 1973 and 1974, dipping to 4 percent in 1975.[32]

Announced in 1969, the agrarian reform gradually became the most important challenge to Peru's elites.[33] The massive agroindustrial sugar haciendas of the north coast were expropriated virtually overnight. The limits of size established for agrarian holdings were rather stringent.[34] For several years there were many doubts that the agrarian reform law would be implemented, in large part because liberal bourgeois elements in the government were still seeking to weaken the law (Harding, 1975; McClintock, 1980). However, by 1972, these elements were defeated, and the swath of the law grew greater.[35] By 1977, there were virtually no more haciendas in Peru.[36]

Table II.1 shows that reform in Peru did more to challenge the hacendados than reforms in Chile, Mexico, Bolivia, or Venezuela.

[32] Figures from *Latin America Economic Report*, *3* (April 11, 1975), 54, and *Información Política Mensual*, No. 40 (January 1976), 23. Similar figures are reported in most studies, including Cabieses and Otero (1977: 209-210).

[33] The entire law is known as Decree Law 17716. However, this Decree Law actually includes many supreme decrees, a good number of which were issued before or after 1969. See Horton (1974) for excellent background material on the law.

[34] Supreme Decree 265-70-AG set 150 hectares as the maximum holding for coastal irrigated farmland, 300 for coastal non-irrigated land, 15 to 55 (depending on the province) for highland and high-jungle irrigated land, and that number of hectares sufficient to sustain 5,000 sheep (or the equivalent of 5,000 sheep in other species) for highland and high-jungle non-irrigated land.

[35] The annual rate of expropriations is provided by Padron Castillo and Pease García (1974:273). The number of hectares adjudicated in 1972 was roughly double the number adjudicated in 1971, and the 1972 record was surpassed in 1973.

[36] There is little disagreement on this point. See for example *The Andean Report*, (March 1977), 47.

Impact of Various Latin American Agrarian Reforms

| | Were large, lucrative tracts still owned by well-capitalized individuals? | Number of hectares expropriated | Percentage of agricultural land in reformed sector | Number of families benefited | Percentage of rural families benefited | Number of landless temporary workers | Terms of Compensation |
|---|---|---|---|---|---|---|---|
| Peru, through 1977 | No | 8,383,677[a] | 35 | 356,276 | 24 | 250,000 | Bonds payable in 20-30 years with 4-6% interest but no inflation adjustment, based on official fiscal evaluation of hacienda, 0-5 years of grace with prolongations pending. |
| Chile, through May, 1973 | Yes | 9,780,300 | 36 | 56,159 | 9 | 160,000 | Bonds payable in 25-30 years with 3% interest and adjustment for inflation, based on declared tax value of hacienda, 3 years of grace. |
| Mexico, 1960 | Yes | 44,500,000 | 36 | 1,500,000 | 25 | 3,500,000 | Compensation was legally required, but most landowners were not paid. |
| Cuba, 1966 | No | 5,513,700 | 60 | 470,120 | 90 | Few or none | 75% of lands confiscated; 25% of lands paid for in 20 years with 4% interest. |
| Bolivia, 1969 | Yes | 9,740,681[a] | 30 | 208,181 | 39 | N.A. | In law but not in fact. |
| Venezuela, 1969 | Yes | 4,605,594[a] | 18 | 117,286 | 16 | 220,965 | Compensation to landowners was good. About 50% of total obligations paid in cash. |

SOURCES: See Appendix 3. Figures must be considered *rough estimates*.
[a] Figures for Peru exclude colonization, but include individual adjudications. Figures for Bolivia and Venezuela include colonization.

About 35 percent of all Peru's agricultural land was expropriated, and over half of the irrigated agricultural land (Caballero, 1976: 7). Whereas the land not expropriated in Mexico, Bolivia, and Venezuela was often fertile land still owned by hacendados, in Peru unexpropriated land was usually the less fertile land of peasant communities and small owners. In Mexico and Bolivia, the government encouraged the settlement of promising agricultural areas by prosperous individuals, and provided these regions with credit and irrigation facilities, thus contributing to the gradual re-emergence of the large, individual estate (Stavenhagen, 1975; Burke and Malloy, 1974: 57-60). In Venezuela, the reform never pretended to be an attack on efficient haciendas; the peasants were benefited primarily by colonization efforts (Kirby, 1973). As a result, in these countries most properties in the reformed sector are the poorest in the country (Stavenhagen, 1975: 146; Burke and Malloy, 1974: 57-60; Kirby, 1973). In Chile, the most prosperous estates were expropriated, as in Peru; but yet the Peruvian reform was more radical than the Chilean for various reasons, especially the right of landowners to retain "reserves" and their right to subdivide their haciendas among family members during the Frei government.[37] As suggested previously, one feature of the Peruvian law that is difficult to evaluate is the compensation scheme.[38]

Although the Peruvian reform thus hurt hacendados severely, it helped only some 10 or 15 percent of the nation's peasantry,

[37] Chilean landowners were allowed to keep up to the land ownership maximum of 80 "basic irrigated hectares" in "reserves." (A "basic irrigated hectare" referred to top-quality irrigated land in the fertile central valley, and translated into some 500 hectares in other regions.) Landowners were permitted to choose the most desirable land. About 35 percent of the Chilean landowners exercised their reserve option (Steenland, 1974: 135). Perhaps most important, subdivision occurred: Between 1965 and 1972, the number of farms between 40 and 80 "basic irrigated hectares" increased from 13 percent of the total agricultural land area to 27 percent (Steenland, 1974: 135). Thus, many Chilean hacendados did not leave the countryside, but rather retreated into smaller farms along with their livestock, machinery, and vehicles and were still in a position to influence contiguous new cooperatives (Steenland, 1974: 134-136; Chinchilla and Sternberg, 1974: 122).

[38] At the proclamation of the reform, hacendados claimed they were being robbed (Goodsell, 1974: 135; and my own interviews). Meanwhile, peasant leaders maintained they should not have to pay anything, on the grounds of social justice and retribution. In the early 1970s, the agrarian debt did weigh heavily on the new cooperative members (see Chapter VIII). However, inflation skyrocketed after 1974, and as a result the value of agrarian bonds decreased sharply (see Chapter VIII). Finally, in 1979 the outstanding debt was written off, as had occurred previously in Mexico and Bolivia (*Latin America Weekly Report*, 79-04 (November 23, 1979), 37.)

namely those on the large coastal and highland haciendas that became CAPs and SAIS (see Table IV.4 and Caballero, 1976). About 40 percent of the peasants classified as "benefited" by the reform actually only gained additional hectares from expropriated haciendas to the lands of their peasant communities, and sometimes, as with respect to the adjudications to "peasant groups" as well, these hectares were not of sufficient quantity or quality to make a large difference to the peasant communities.

The reform did virtually nothing for the poorest peasants, landless temporary workers. However, other Latin American reform programs also scored poorly in this respect. Table II.1 shows 1) the ratio of hectares expropriated to families benefited and 2) the ratio of families benefited to landless workers in Chile, Mexico, Bolivia, and Venezuela. With the exception of Bolivia, for which no data are available, Peru did better than these other nations in equalizing benefits. The Chilean reform emerges as particularly deficient, granting each family beneficiary some 175 hectares while leaving almost three times more landless temporary workers than beneficiaries. The Peruvian reform granted each family beneficiary merely about 23 hectares, with considerably more beneficiaries than landless peasants.

Subsequent chapters will examine to what extent the new self-managed enterprises established by the Velasco government stimulated change in the orientations of Peruvian peasants. The concept of incentives is used to analyze the impact not only of new political structures but also of government policy and political outputs generally. To understand the character of change under the Velasco government, however, it is necessary to look first at the traditional agrarian structure and traditional peasant values of Peru.

# III · "Before": Peruvian Agrarian Structure and Peasant Political Culture Until 1969

> ...the world is a jungle; hence it is appropriate to claw and scratch in a struggle for survival. It is a world where power is the main good and where dominance and submission are the main human postures.
>
> (Lane, 1974:432)

BEFORE 1969, the Peruvian political system was considered an oligarchy.[1] "Forty families" were widely believed to dominate Peru's polity and economy. Often, elite families did not formally lead the Peruvian government but backed military officers and politicians who sought the presidency. Although the families extended their influence throughout the Peruvian economy by extensive ties in banks, commerce, and industry, a significant share of their wealth was derived from their haciendas even in the 1960s (Bourricaud, 1970: 39-40; Astiz, 1969: 49-65). The families controlled the major Peruvian agricultural exports, including sugar, cotton, and wool. The dominance of Peruvian agriculture by a small elite is indicated by the fact that Peru's Gini index of land distribution in 1961 was the most unequal reported for 54 nations (Taylor and Hudson, 1972: 267). The Peruvian pattern of income distribution was one of the most skewed in the continent.[2] The Peruvian elite blocked economic and political reforms during the 1960s more effectively than their counterparts in other Latin American countries.

Peruvian hacendados owned a scarce and important resource, and they were able to monitor their peasant employees closely and inhibit their contacts beyond the hacienda.[3] The landowners were

---

[1] On the pre-1969 political system, especially its oligarchical nature, see Astiz (1969); Bourricaud (1970); Larson and Bergman (1969); Malpica (1968); Chaplin (1968); and Matos Mar (1969). An illuminating portrait of several key families is provided by Gilbert (1977).

[2] In 1961, the top 5 percent of Peruvian income recipients received 48 percent of the income, a considerably larger percentage than in Brazil, Bolivia, Colombia, Chile, Mexico, or Ecuador, countries somewhat close to Peru in per capita GNP ($237 in Peru in 1961). See the Overseas Development Council (1975: 214-215).

[3] These criteria for the structural bases of the patron's power are drawn from Scott (1972: 197-201). The final criterion with respect to proximity is my own, drawn from

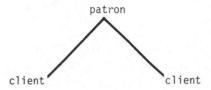

patron

client         client

2. The Baseless Triangle

thus able to encourage clientelism on their haciendas. Clientelism may be defined as a private, hierarchical relationship between people of unequal status, based on expectations of mutual exchange.[4] The patron and client engage in frequent face-to-face contact and exchange a variety of goods or services, in accordance with the needs of the moment. The exchange is an informal one, without conditions or rules of conduct. In such a relationship, the client must adopt attitudes and behavior that are deferential and individualistic, accepting the inequality and atomization that the relationship assumes. Clientelism is contradictory to solidarity, equality, and national identification.

The degree of clients' submissiveness and atomization may vary.[5] Typically without alternative opportunities for employment, without job security, and without employment, peasants on a hacienda are extremely subordinate and isolated. Hacienda clientelism may be identified as the archetypal mode and depicted as a "baseless triangle" (Fig. 2) in which the patron is at the apex, indicating his high status, and the clients are at the base.[6] The clients are linked only to the patron and not to each other. The patron channels all information and communication through himself. The clients perceive each other as competitors for the favors of the patron. Each believes that the pie of benefits from the patron is limited and that one client's gain is another's loss.

the definition of clientelism given by Powell (1970). They are discussed in greater detail in the second section of the chapter.

   [4] For definitions of clientelism, see Powell (1970); Scott (1972); Lemarchand and Legg (1972); Kaufman (1974); Sandbrook (1972); and Grindle (1975: 66-74).

   [5] For discussion of various types of clientelism and stipulation of criteria for the types, see especially Scott (1972) and Powell (1971).

   [6] The geometric figure of the "baseless triangle" was first used to describe Peruvian peasant society by Cotler (1969) and has been applied subsequently by Tullis (1970: 40-50), Singelmann (1975), and Scott (1972: 96), and Whyte and Alberti (1976) among other scholars.

"Archetypal" clientelism on the hacienda may be contrasted with a modern variant that is often found among landed peasants, urban migrants, and even elites (Powell, 1971; Lemarchand and Legg, 1972; Grindle, 1977; Scott, 1972: 105-113). In this variant, clients have greater resources vis-à-vis their patron. The context for this variant is more likely to be migrant settlements in cities or private landholdings than the traditional hacienda. In these settings, clients often have somewhat more secure economic positions through their possession of more specialized work skills or land ownership. They are more likely to be able to go to school, read the newspaper, listen to the radio, travel to different parts of the country, and in general gain access to alternative sources of information and ways of life than in the hacienda. Possession of the vote may thus become a more important resource too. Such clients will increasingly want to form bonds with other clients—in other words, to "close the base" of the triangle. Moreover, as economic growth occurs and political awareness rises, new "brokers" emerge, replacing the patron. An individual who can deal both with traditional elites and clients, the broker may be a union leader, a middleman buying and selling between a provincial city and small private farms, the leader of a migrant settlement with close ties to a major political party, or the like. A client, or a broker, may have ties to more than one broker, and a broker may be a client in a relationship to another, higher-up broker. Such a configuration may be depicted as a complex of closed triangles, as in Figure 3.[7]

Hacienda clientelism thus signifies a much greater degree of clients' atomization and inferiority before their patron than

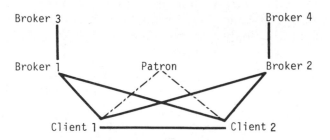

3. A Complex of Closed Triangles

[7] The figure is modified from Singelmann (1975: 392). A similar model has been suggested by Tullis (1970: 43-47) and Cotler (1969).

modern clientelism. The second section of this chapter discusses in greater detail why hacienda clientelism was so entrenched, describing the traditional agrarian structure. The final section elaborates the nature of clientelist attitudes and behavior among hacienda peasants. I will suggest how deeply clientelism pervaded the haciendas and thus how difficult it might be to change—but also why a reformist government would very much want to change it.

## THE PRE-1969 NATIONAL POLITICAL SYSTEM

The "forty families" held an enormous share of power and wealth in Peru as late as the 1960s. The identity of these families changed somewhat; as an export commodity's value would boom and bust, a family would often rise and fall. However, by the 1920s and 1930s, most prominent elite families held large tracts of rich coastal land that produced primarily sugar or cotton and provided the families a critical resource base. Such plutocrats as the Aspillagas, the Gildemeisters, the de la Piedras, the Prados, the Beltráns all had a resource base in coastal export agriculture. Although under great political pressures in the 1960s, these landowners succeeded in withstanding agrarian reform movements. The Peruvian highlands are less lucrative agriculturally than the coast; highlands hacendados were generally neither as rich nor as powerful as their coastal counterparts, and were somewhat less successful in blocking reform movements during the 1960s. However, even highlands hacendados could count on the timely support of the police and the military during a crisis, and for the most part better-off highlands hacendados also maintained their landowning privileges through the 1960s.

Various members of the traditional oligarchy served in prominent positions in the national government. The most important was Manuel Prado, who was elected president in 1939 and in 1956. Hacendados also often served as cabinet officers and representatives to Congress. On the whole, however, the oligarchy did not successfully develop a coherent political movement with a legitimating ideology. Conservative political parties were political machines that developed policy positions to suit the needs of the moment.

Prominent families often called upon military leaders to topple presidents who had jeopardized the oligarchy's interests. In return for conservative policies, the elite promised its military favorite financial gains and entrance into upper-class society, plus permission to raise the military budget (Payne, 1968; Astiz, 1969:

133-135). For example, after a 1912 electoral victory by the relatively reformist Billinghurst, Colonel Oscar Benavides was "es-
corted" to the presidency by two young men from the elite Prado
family (Urdanivía Gines, 1954: 17). In 1948, when the upper class
became dissatisfied with President Bustamante, General Odría was
apparently also financed and helped into office by key business
circles (Bourricaud, 1970: 305; Jaquette, 1971: 78). In part because
of this political manipulation by the elite, the military frequently
held Peru's political reins. Indeed, the military has been in power
nearly half the time since Peru's independence, for all but six years
between 1821 and 1895, as well as for 22 years between 1895
and 1969.

Peru's reformist political parties were less successful than their
counterparts in many other Latin American countries. Various
reasons for their failure are evident. First, electoral support for the
reformist parties was limited by a literacy requirement for voting
and by manipulation of the system for allocating congressional
representatives to favor large landowners and rural commercial
elites (Whyte and Alberti, 1976: 16). Further, the close ties between
the "forty families" and military leaders enabled the elite to hold the
threat of a coup constantly over the heads of reformist leaders. In
part because of the oligarchy's powerful clubs and in part because
of the personal background of the reformist leaders themselves, the
spokesmen for change also often seemed clientelist in their attitudes and behavior, forsaking their promises of reform for the
benefits of office in private deals with members of the elite.

Founded by Haya de la Torre in 1924, APRA was not only the
first but also the most important reformist political party in Peru.[8]
The party originally espoused dramatic reforms. Haya de la Torre
strongly opposed foreign imperialism, proposing the international-
ization of the Panama Canal and the nationalization of many
foreign-owned enterprises. The APRA leader also advanced the
"redemption" of the Indian through various programs that included massive land expropriations as well as new educational and
commercial opportunities. By the mid-1940s, however, APRA
gradually became more interested in gaining office than in fulfill-
ing its reform program. To win power, APRA entered a variety of
compromise arrangements with other political parties. These alliance decisions seemed opportunistic; they were made by Haya

---

[8] For discussions of APRA, see Klarén (1973); Hilliker (1971); and Bourricaud
(1970: 142-157).

alone, and reflected the top priority he gave to his personal ambitions (Klarén, 1973: 109; Payne, 1968: 28).

First, in 1945 APRA supported the candidacy of a liberal independent leader, Bustamante; the support enabled the party to occupy some cabinet posts as well as more than 40 percent of Senate and House seats (Bourricaud, 1970: 263). But even this coalition frightened the upper classes, who encouraged a coup by General Odría. APRA was again made illegal. By 1956, the party was even readier to trade in its political support for the benefits of office. Haya de la Torre allied with the conservative candidate Manuel Prado. Haya agreed to modify many traditional leftist APRA positions in its 1956 platform, including the agrarian reform. In exchange, Manuel Prado gave APRA legal recognition and access to patronage. The agreement was called the *convivencia* (living together).

In 1962, Haya again chose a strong political bedfellow. He allied not with the reformist Fernando Belaúnde Terry, but with his previous arch-enemy, General Odría, and Odría's party, the National Odriísta Union (UNO). From 1963 to 1968, the APRA-UNO coalition was the majority opposition in Congress to Belaúnde's Acción Popular, and the coalition worked to defeat many of the reformist programs that Haya had long espoused.[9] APRA pushed for the exemption of the large coastal haciendas from Belaúnde's agrarian reform bill, largely because it feared encroachment by Acción Popular on APRA's traditional political base. APRA neglected the plight of seasonal workers recruited by the agro-industrial haciendas for the harvest. The party did not encourage cooperatives or technical assistance to disadvantaged highlands peasant communities. Nor did it try to give disadvantaged peasants political weight by moving to delete the literacy requirement for the franchise or by waging literacy campaigns. Perhaps APRA's greatest betrayal of its original reformist spirit, however, was its opposition to the peasant uprisings around Cuzco in the 1960s. In part due to its jealously of the rival political federations there, APRA supported the military's brutal repression of peasant movements.

APRA's betrayal of its original reformist spirit was evident not only at the national level but also at the local level. APRA's concern with winning national office spurred its alliances with local elites

[9] Documentation of the points in this paragraph can be found in Cotler and Portocarrero (1969); Bourque (1971: 165-170); Jaquette (1971: 135-136); Hilliker (1971: 111-154); and Chaplin (1968: 420).

who, even if conservative, were eligible to vote. Further, to appeal to the electorate, which was more advantaged and conservative than the population as a whole, APRA tended to select candidates for national office who were relatively conservative. These conservative national APRA leaders often undermined radical regional leaders (Bourque, 1971: 168; Tullis, 1970: 65-66).

APRA's major peasant organization FENCAP (National Federation of the Peasants of Peru) also failed to fulfill its promises for radical improvement of the peasants' lot. Like APRA's leaders themselves, FENCAP leaders seemed clientelistic in their attitudes and behavior, encouraging particularistic, dyadic exchanges with peasants. FENCAP officials frequently offered solution of land disputes in exchange for peasants' support of APRA.[10] With respect to hacienda peasants, FENCAP often discouraged the radicalization of peasant union demands, trying to limit them to higher salaries and better working conditions (Cotler and Portocarrero, 1969: 307).

APRA's betrayal of its reformist promise became increasingly evident to Peruvians. Peasants gradually withdrew support from APRA. In 1963, literate peasants in many regions of Peru voted for Belaúnde, the leader of the new reformist party, Acción Popular. During the next year, in municipal elections, APRA's support declined even in its traditional regional bastion, the "solid north" (Astiz, 1969: 110-112; Jaquette, 1971: 133). Gradually, however, Belaúnde also abandoned many of his reformist programs.[11]

A young architect, Belaúnde was feverently committed to the potential of technology and planning for Peru. His great dream for the development of the country was the "Marginal Forest High-

---

[10] Bourque (1971: 138-140) vividly describes these clientelistic attitudes and behavior: "On a typical busy morning there are 25 to 30 campesinos crowded into the main room . . . [they] mill about . . . Avalos [the Secretary General of FENCAP] is in sharp contrast to them. . . . He dresses carefully and stylishly. There is nothing in his appearance that would suggest a campesino background. . . . Most [peasants] seek the personal intervention of Avalos . . . to solve their particular problem. Frequently, the problem is land. It is clearly a personalistic system: the campesinos identify themselves as Apristas and . . . their affiliation, they assume, is important to him. . . . [Many peasants also want to see Benitez, a second-level official] on various aspects of the agrarian reform. Usually these are land disputes or petitions for expropriation. Benitez . . . is gruff, somewhat abusive. . . . The campesinos are reticent, . . . and apologetic under his verbal barrage."

[11] On Belaúnde's programs and his difficulties in implementing them, see especially Astiz (1969: 115-118); Bourricaud (1970: 325-333); and Jaquette (1971: 132-176). Kuczynski (1977) provides an interesting insider's view into the administration.

way." To win the presidency, Belaúnde embraced a vigorous reform program. He advanced a land reform whose essential features would be "the transfer of land ownership, the resettlement of the peasantry, and the introduction of legal regulations governing the use of water and irrigation" (Bourricaud, 1970: 330). Although the proposal was qualified by an emphasis on technical and regional criteria, in his extensive travels to disadvantaged rural areas Belaúnde implied a significant redistributive effort. Belaúnde also promised that he would favorably resolve the dispute between Peru and the International Petroleum Company over the ownership rights to the oil fields in northern Peru. The Acción Popular candidate advanced tax reform, credit reform, and similar measures.

After his election in 1963, however, Belaúnde failed to keep his promises, most blatantly his promise of agrarian reform. Two-thirds of Belaúnde's cabinet officers were from landed families (Lowenthal, 1975: 26). Belaúnde acquiesced to the passage of a weak agrarian reform law favored by the APRA-UNO coalition. Under the law, any hacienda expropriation was subject to review by a committee that included representatives of landowners and of APRA, and water rights were not questioned (Jaquette, 1971: 137). By 1968, less than 2 percent of Peruvian farm families had received land (Palmer, 1973: 191). Meanwhile, anticipating a reformist government, peasants had invaded lands in various highlands regions. Pressured by the "forty families" and other landowners, Belaúnde authorized the repression of invaders. By some estimates 8,000 peasants were killed (Villaneuva, 1969: 47; Jaquette, 1971: 146-147).

Belaúnde also failed to develop the efficient, modern administrative organization he had espoused. Corruption riddled the bureaucracy as always. Car smuggling, for example, was so extensive that lost tariffs were estimated at the value of half the budget deficit for one year (Jaquette, 1969: 166). Nor was the tax system reformed; in 1965 only 17,000 Peruvians paid any sort of income tax (Astiz, 1969: 118). The loss of government revenues, exacerbated by a reduction in U.S. aid, resulted in balance-of-payments difficulties for the first time in many years. Under considerable pressure from the cotton and sugar hacendados as well as the mining and fishmeal interests, Belaúnde devalued the currency.

The supreme example of Belaúnde's failure to fulfill his campaign pledges was his handling of the IPC dispute. Since the early 1800s, IPC had operated oil fields in northern Peru as its own private domain, without paying taxes. From 1963 through 1968,

IPC and the Peruvian government fought over the terms of a new agreement, spurring the United States to withhold aid from Peru. An agreement was finally reached in 1968. However, the head of the Peruvian petroleum company alleged that the contract short-changed Peru—that the original contract included a "page 11" in which a price for IPC's crude oil was stipulated in dollars, a better deal for Peru. Belaúnde was widely believed to have sold Peru out.

Peasants were especially frustrated. Despite their initially favorable response to Belaúnde, by 1969 they had grown disillusioned, even hostile. Peasants did not believe that they could influence the government. In three highlands regions in 1969, less than 12 percent of community leaders thought that their villages could influence government policies more than slightly without outside help (Handelman, 1975a: 220-221). Asked about exerting pressure on the government, many community leaders were fearful of repression. Said one village president in the Huancayo area: "Oh, no, we could get thrown in jail if we tried that" (Handelman, 1975a: 221).

Handelman's interviews (1975a: 232) with groups of community leaders in 1969 are especially revealing of peasants' hostility. Of 27 such groups in the Huancayo and Cuzco areas, none felt that Belaúnde had shown concern for the peasantry. Further, a minority of the 13 groups in the Pasco region felt that Belaúnde was concerned. Almost a majority of the groups thought that no Peruvian administration had ever shown sympathy for the peasantry. Among a sample of migrants to two Lima settlements in the mid-1960s, an average of only 20 percent of respondents (versus an avearge of 61 percent in three Chilean settlements) strongly agreed that "In general our system of government and politics is good for the country" (Goldrich, Pratt, and Schuller, 1970: 205).

## TRADITIONAL AGRARIAN STRUCTURE

Peruvian haciendas were marked by the great wealth and power of the landowner relative to the peasants. On the basis of various criteria developed by Scott (1972) and Powell (1970) to indicate the power of a patron, the Peruvian hacendados emerge as extremely powerful. The Peruvian hacendados directly and securely owned a rare and significant "resource base" (land); they could easily replace the services of their peasant clients; they effectively controlled all the links to outside structures; and they (or their administrators) were in close proximity to the peasants, facilitating supervision. The hegemony of the hacendados was gradually weakening in the

1960s, but it was still great in comparison to that of hacendados in many other Latin American countries as well as to that of the more "modern" patrons in independent peasant communities or migrant settlements (Whyte and Alberti, 1976; Bourque, 1971; Dew, 1969; Greaves, 1968; Tullis, 1970).

Land was owned extremely unequally in Peru, as Peru's score on the Gini index of land distribution indicated. Although exact calculation of land tenure structure is impossible, rough estimates can be made (see Table IV.4 and Appendix 2). In the mid-1960s, approximately 700 hacendados owned perhaps one-third of the productive land; they owned much more than half of the best land, the irrigated coastal land. These hacendados employed the members of some 250,000 families (around 20 percent of all rural farm families). Somewhat over one-third of the productive land was owned by roughly 275,000 small farmers (perhaps 22 percent of all rural farm families). These farmers were either enterprising individuals who developed small farms on the coast, often in villages, or former sharecroppers who gradually won ownership rights to their land. The range of income among these small farmers was great. Another important mode of land tenure was the "peasant community," the traditional highlands village. The members of a peasant community, called *comuneros*, were bound by a common heritage and kinship and typically shared many community activities, although most residents worked their land individually. For the most part, the peasant community was socially and politically independent of the hacienda, although during the early 1900s the Peruvian haciendas grew primarily by encroachment on peasant community land (Martínez Alier, 1973; Hurtado, 1974). By the 1960s, although peasant communities constituted less than 25 percent of the productive land, they included about 40 percent of the rural population. The problem of unequal land ownership was exacerbated by the scarcity of land. In the 1960s, the land/man ratio in Peru was estimated at .21 hectares of land for cultivation or pasture per peasant—one of the lowest ratios in the world, approximately half that in Bolivia, Chile, or Ecuador (Valdez Angulo, 1974: 2).

Peru's scarce land was a significant resource whose ownership provided hacendados with major economic benefits. In 1960, agriculture provided 23 percent of Peru's GNP and employed 58 percent of its economically active population (Astiz, 1969: 56-63). A large share of agricultural income went to hacendados. Although data are limited, many hacendados apparently earned as much as 100 times the income of their employees (Barraclough, 1973: 280;

McClintock, 1975b: 259-260). In some haciendas where peasants were poorly nourished and illiterate, the patrons enjoyed vacations in Europe and private cars (Tullis, 1970: 97; Greaves, 1968: 360). The pattern of income distribution on Peruvian haciendas was apparently more sharply skewed than in other Latin American countries, where the hacendado's income was typically only somewhat more than fifty times larger than the peasant's (Pearse, 1970: 22).

Poor as hacienda peasants were, they were generally better off economically than peasant-community residents. The permanent worker on the typical coastal enterprise had "made it" by the criteria of Peruvian peasants. The average employee on the coastal enterprise earned at least double the income of an average peasant-community resident.[12] The typical peasant-community member worked .9 hectares of cropland (Webb, 1975: 87). Almost half of all peasant-community residents had to find some temporary employment outside the community to subsist (Paige, 1975: 193). These peasant-community residents traveled to the coastal enterprises as temporary workers (eventuales). (Work in most highlands enterprises is not as seasonal as that on the coast, and the enterprises are not as lucrative, so they rarely employ outside temporary labor.) Some temporary workers owned no land whatsoever, merely traveling from seasonal job to seasonal job. Perhaps 250,000 Peruvian peasants were primarily eventuales, constituting roughly 20 percent of economically active rural families, about the same percentage as in Chile and Mexico (Barraclough, 1973: 202 and 232).

The hacendado not only owned a scarce and important resource, but he owned it securely. Invasions of hacienda land by peasant-community members did happen, but in the great majority of cases the peasants were repelled by the landowners who could rely on the support of the police and the military. The best-known example is the repression of land invasions around Cuzco in the early 1960s. The Cuzco peasants were the best organized and most ideologically radical in Peru. Their escalating land invasions frightened Peru's agrarian elite. The hacendados begged the government to stop the invaders, and Belaúnde finally agreed.

Hacendados were able to enlist the support of the military and the police to thwart unionization efforts as well. Union leaders were imprisoned and often brutalized in many regions of the country (Handelman, 1975a: 152; Huizer, 1972: 10; Tullis, 1970: 3-4,

[12] Exact calculation is difficult, but this ratio is suggested by OIT (1975) and Webb (1974a: 2-34). The question is discussed further in Chapter IV. See also Appendix 7.

114-116, 142; Gitlitz, 1975). In some cases, the police shot peasants for very modest reform efforts:

> Serfs on a hacienda adjoining Vicos who had been impressed by the reforms introduced by the Cornell administration began constructing a new school building and petitioned the ecclesiastical authorities who held title to the land to allow them to work hacienda waste land communally. The patron of the estate, a hereditary renter, responded to these modest initiatives by summoning a fifteen-man detachment of the national police.... The police attempted to arrest the peasants, then opened fire, killing three and seriously wounding five others... (Paige, 1975: 169).

Some hacienda peasants were successful in unionizing or even in gaining hacienda land during the 1960s, but they were a minority, and typically owed their success largely to reduced commitment of the landowner to the hacienda, often because of the increased attractiveness of urban life or death in the family (Tullis, 1970; Cotler, 1969b; Delgado, 1972; Whyte and Alberti, 1976).

Because land was scarce, hacendados could easily replace the service of their employees. As the population of peasant communities grew, more peasants' sons were landless and were forced to seek employment in the hacienda as the only means to survival. As temporary workers, they jealously eyed the relatively secure and lucrative positions of the permanent workers. Most hacienda jobs were unskilled, requiring very little training. Thus, a recalcitrant peasant could be replaced virtually overnight, and the patron's capacity to fire the peasant became perhaps the most important weapon in his power arsenal. Asked why they had not unionized in the hacienda, cooperative members usually said: "Because the patron would carry me and my family off to the highway and dump us there."

Hacendados controlled peasants' access to outside structures rather effectively, at least until the 1960s. The patron ran the hacienda as his own state, acting as judge, governor, and priest himself and prohibiting the exercise of authority by outsiders.[13]

---

[13] Note these words from a highlands patron to a visiting district official: "Who do you think you are, to have yourself appointed lieutenant-governor.... I do not know you.... You should know that in this hacienda there can be no lieutenant-governor or any other authority for that matter, so go and paper the walls of your house with your appointment. In the hacienda the only authorities are those appointed by me" (Cevallos, 1965: 17-19).

Landowners were especially careful to prevent the admission of "political agitators" into the haciendas.[14] Perhaps most important, the majority of hacienda peasants were not able to affect outside structures through voting, because they were illiterate and thus ineligible. Even in areas where more peasants were literate, the patron was often able to manipulate their votes (see Chapter V).

Patrons also tried to reduce the impact of outside cultural and political influences on the hacienda. They refused to construct schools (Tullis, 1970: 2, 94, 115; Paige, 1975: 167), and discouraged trips to the provincial cities and access to newspapers and radios. The effectiveness of their efforts is indicated by the disparity in the levels of education and culture contact between haciendas and communities. In a small town near Cuzco in 1964, 39 percent of respondents were literate, 49 percent listened to the radio daily, 62 percent knew Spanish, and 75 percent traveled to the provincial capital at least once a week (Cotler, 1970a: 553). In contrast, in a nearby hacienda, only 6 percent of respondents were literate, merely 11 percent listened to the radio daily, only 16 percent knew Spanish, and merely 6 percent traveled to the provincial capital at least once a week (Cotler, 1970a: 553). Similarly, in the Huancayo region in 1969, whereas 57 percent of peasant-community residents had at least two years of education, only 44 percent of hacienda peasants did (Ministry of Agriculture, 1970a).

Traditionally, the patron was able to monitor peasants' performance and inhibit their ties to outside structures because he was in close proximity to the peasants. In many haciendas, especially in the more lucrative ones, the landowner or his administrator strictly supervised peasant activities even in the 1950s and 1960s. In all three haciendas of this study, the patron retained a forceful presence. However, as city life became more attractive, hacendados in remote highland areas were often absent a considerable part of the year by the 1950s and 1960s (Whyte and Alberti, 1976: 20).

Through their secure ownership of a scarce and important resource and their close supervision of peons, the Peruvian hacendados enjoyed great power. The patron was addressed as "Doctor," or "Engineer" or merely as "patron," and always by the respectful form for "you," *usted*. The peasants were addressed as irresponsible inferiors, through the terms *hijo* (son) and *tú* (the form of "you" reserved for intimates, children and inferiors). Most hacendados

[14] In an interview in Lima on August 22, 1973, Huanca's ex-patron bragged that he had always managed to keep reformist politicians off his hacienda.

considered the peasants animals. Said one fictional patron: "Yes, I've thrashed the Indians, and they must curse me in their hearts. But I treat them like dogs, neither better nor worse."[15] Frequently, hacendados flogged peons, violated their wives, and required that they kneel and kiss their hands (Tullis, 1970: 97-99; Paige, 1975: 167-169; Whyte and Alberti, 1976: 43-44). The cruelest landowners were believed to commit flagrant atrocities:

The *gamonal* [exploitive landlord] Alfredo Romainville strung up a naked peasant to a mango tree and, among other things, flogged him all day in the presence of his own daughters and other peasants. Another peasant could not find the horse his master told him to find. Romainville forced him down on all fours, ordered him to put on the horse's harness, and compelled him to haul six *arrobas* (150 pounds) of coffee; he made him travel in this fashion, on hands and knees, around the patio, where the coffee was dried, lashing him with a whip. He forced the women to shell peanuts without pay until their hands bled, and then with their mouths until those were bloody too. He had his own daughter, born of a peasant woman he had raped, jailed as a "communist." His brother was not satisfied with raping the peasant women himself—he forced a peasant at gunpoint to rape his own aunt.

The landlord Márquez took the children borne by the women he had raped and drowned them in the river. With a hot cattle branding iron, the landlord Barolome Paz seared into the buttocks of a peasant the emblem of his hacienda (Blanco, 1972: 94-95).

By the 1960s, this kind of physical abuse by the hacendado was rare, but the hacendado was still often verbally abusive, and still firmly in control of hacienda politics (see Chapter V).

## THE CLIENTELIST POLITICAL CULTURE ON PERUVIAN HACIENDAS

The landowner's wealth and power on the hacienda facilitated clientelist attitudes and behavior among the peasants. Peasants believed that the total pie of benefits could not grow, and hence that

---

[15] Words of Don Julian in the novel *Yawar Fiesta* by José Mariá Arguedas, translated by and cited in Bourricaud (1970. 35). Hacendados' perception of the Indians as animals is also mentioned by Tullis (1970: 116); Doughty (1971: 93); Paige (1975: 177).

each of them was competing against the others for the favors of the patron. All incentives were thus individual ones. The patron was feared, for he could use his power abusively; but he also had to be cultivated, for only he could bestow significant favors on the peasant. Relationships were tenuous, competitive calculations of advantage. No matter how generous a patron, no matter how "good," he might in the future renege on his promises; the peasant knew he had no way to hold the patron accountable. Thus he was vulnerable and withdrawn, afraid to show his real self, as was the Mexican peasant described in Chapter I. The ex-patron of enterprise Huanca was widely regarded as a "good patron," but when he returned to one ex-hacienda in 1973, his exchange with peasants was minimal.

Yet, both peasants and patrons said that the peasants interacted more with the patron than with each other. Competing for the favors of the patron, peasants eyed each other with mistrust and jealousy. Social events tended to be limited to drunken fiestas, perhaps a catharsis for peasant aggression (see Chapter VII). The 1969 Cornell-IEP attitudinal survey indicated high levels of social mistrust in all eighteen sites. For example, on the three haciendas of this study, 83 percent of the respondents thought that "If you don't watch yourself, people will take advantage of you"; 81 percent felt that "nobody is going to care if you fail"; 85 percent that "Most people here can't be trusted"; and 90 percent that "Most people are more inclined to look out for themselves than help others."[16]

Political ties among clients were also scant, as Chapter V elaborates. The Cornell-IEP survey indicated low levels of collective political activity in all my research sites in 1969. In no site did more than 10 percent of respondents declare themselves members of a political party (only 2 percent in the highlands hacienda), and only in Estrella did more than 10 percent declare themselves members of a union. In none of the three haciendas did more than 21 percent of respondents say they "had worried about a community problem so as to be willing to do something to solve it." Only 44 percent of respondents in the three haciendas felt they "could do something against a political injustice," and only 50 percent that the "community should work together to solve its problems."

Peasant organization also remained limited in the 1960s. Unions were concentrated in the largest and richest haciendas, where edu-

---

[16] Figures are *averages* from the three sites, using a sample that was not matched to my 1974 sample.

cated members could provide APRA with more votes. In contrast to the 12,528 haciendas expropriated by September 1976, only 255 rural unions had been recognized in 1966; all but five of these unions were on the coast and most were on prosperous cotton and sugar haciendas (Cotler and Portocarrero, 1969: 301). The majority of these unions did not strike between 1961 and 1965, and those that did were in larger and more prosperous haciendas, averaging roughly twice the land size of haciendas where unions did not strike (Cotler and Portocarrero, 1969: 303). During the 1960s, non-recognized unions also arose, whose numbers are difficult to estimate. However, even including these non-recognized unions, Oscar Delgado (1972: 86) estimates that only 120,000 peasants were unionized in 1969, in contrast to the 285,000 benefiting from the agrarian reform by November 1976. Delgado (1972: 86) calculates that 10 percent of Peru's agrarian families were unionized in 1969, versus 35 percent or more in Colombia, Venezuela, Bolivia, and Chile. Of my three research haciendas, only the most prosperous coastal site, Estrella, operated a union on a regular basis. Peasant federations were also weak (see Chapter IX).

The unions succeeded in improving agrarian workers' economic position, but they were less effective in developing social and political solidarity. Peasants' salaries in many coastal areas tripled from 1956 to 1969 (Bourque, 1971: 185; Rodríguez Pastor, 1969: 232). In the coastal region of my research, wages rose approximately 20 percent a year in the mid-1960s (Greaves, 1968: 299-300), and 10 percent a year from 1967 to 1969.[17] Although wage increases were roughly parallel for organized and unorganized workers (Bourque, 1971: 185), organized workers won the implementation of more social legislation, such as holiday bonuses and medical insurance (Greaves, 1968: 169). However, as Chapter V details, the impact of the union on social and political solidarity within the hacienda was only moderate. For example, although attitudes toward political unity were more positive in the research hacienda with a union—Estrella—than in the haciendas without unions, political solidarity was still significantly lower in Estrella than in the contiguous independent community, Virú.[18]

[17] Interviews with Estrella's ex-patron, Ing. Pinillos Ganoza, in Trujillo, February 4, 1974, and with Estrella peasants.
[18] In the unmatched 1969 sample, 55 percent of Estrella respondents felt that "people should get together" to improve things in the village, and 52 percent felt they "could do something against a local political injustice." In Virú, the figures were 73 percent and 60 percent respectively.

Why did Peruvian haciendas remain so socially and politically atomized, even in the 1960s? Although historical crises and the poverty of the Peruvian highlands were certainly important in establishing clientelist attitudes and behavior,[19] the hacendados themselves were crucial to their maintenance (Feder, 1971; Cotler, 1970b; Huizer, 1972: 58-62). Hacendados were aware of the inequities in their haciendas and of their vulnerability should peasants unite against them. The hacendado's major strategy to maintain his position was to divide and conquer—to prevent the closing of the baseless triangle. It was important to enforce the peasant's "image of limited good"—to assure that the peasant thought benefits could come only from the patron, and at other peasants' expense. Thus the patron blocked unionization and required that any requests be advanced by peasants individually, never in a group. Said Monte's schoolteacher and ex-patron, respectively:

Before that [the reform], you had to make your demands personally. That was the only way it could be done. (Q342)

Maray [a young man who was to emerge later as a political leader] was always eager to see me; he'd ask for things for the community, but he came alone. You had to make your requests alone.[20]

The role of the patron in inhibiting peasant unity was also stressed by the peasants in my research ex-haciendas. In the two coastal ex-haciendas, I asked some respondents if they had changed their minds on the question of the desirability of political union, and, if so, why.[21] Of the 20 respondents who indicated that they favored political union in the community now but did not in 1969, 16 gave the reason that "the patron did not permit us to unite before." Explained one peasant: "Before, nobody could trust anybody; you couldn't even talk with anyone, because the patron would

[19] To conquer the Incan leaders, the Spaniards betrayed the Indians; thereafter, Indians may have doubted their ability to negotiate effectively with white men. The conquerors of Peru were perhaps the most ruthless Spaniards in Latin America at the time of the conquest (Lockhart, 1968). Further, as the Indian looked at the vast Peruvian deserts and windswept mountains, he may in fact have decided that "goods" were "limited," and that private deals with the educated white men were the best way to enhance his life.

[20] Huanca's ex-patron was interviewed in Lima on August 22, 1973.

[21] Exact wording of the item is: "Four years ago, you say you thought that each person should solve his own problems and now you think that all should unite. Why did you change your mind?" The question was asked only in the last six weeks of the survey.

threaten to fire you" (Q429). Further, some respondents were asked if they had changed their minds on the statement, "A few are born to command, and others to obey."[22] Of the respondents, 25 (39 percent) said that whereas in 1969 they had agreed that "A few are born to command," now they disagreed. Of these 25 respondents, 22 (87 percent) gave the absence of the patron as the reason for their change of opinion: "Before, the patron was the only person who ordered, now others can." Elaborated one peasant: "Before, the patron was the only person who ordered, and if you disobeyed him, he'd kick you right out of work" (Q518).

The significance of the patron is evident when one contrasts the atomization of hacienda peasants to the solidarity found in many peasant communities. As data in subsequent chapters show, peasant community members tended to be more positive toward participation and collaboration than hacienda residents. Although Incan practices of communal property had by and large died by the 1900s, many traditional collaborative activities continued. For example, the *faena* (communal work effort) was common. It was for these reasons that, as Chapter II pointed out, the hacienda peasant was often said to have traded the collaborative and independent spirit of the peasant community for the economic security of the hacienda.

Beneath the peasant's deference toward the patron and his competitiveness toward other peasants, what did he think of the clientelist system and his own behavior in it? Despite his outward acquiescence, at one level the peasant was resentful and ashamed. The peasant wanted the material benefits provided by the patron, but he also knew that his acceptance of the system hurt other peasants, primarily the peasant-community members. Caught in a bind between material need and betrayal of friends and relatives in the peasant community, the peasant embraced a dog-eat-dog ideology. Yet, shame and resentment smoldered, and the potential for a fiery outburst against the patron was always there. The peasant's conflicting emotions were not resolved, and his attitudes thus at times seemed mercurial and incoherent (Ashford, 1969; Williams, 1969).

Asked about their attitudes toward the patron, peasants recognized that he provided them with material benefits beyond what they could find elsewhere. In two of my three research ex-haciendas, the patron was remembered as a generous man; in 1969,

---

[22] This item is discussed in greater detail in Chapter VI.

10 percent of these respondents said that the patron "helped a lot," and about 65 percent that he "helped somewhat."[23] In only one hacienda did a majority of respondents report that the patron did not help at all. If respondents did think that the patron had helped, I asked them why; the great majority (almost 70 percent) said that the patron "gave" them things—meat, milk, fodder, clothes, and the like.[24] Other respondents (11 percent) cited the patron's services, especially personal transportation to the city.

But the peasants' appreciation of the "help" of the patron did not usually imply affection for him.[25] Only some 10 percent of the individuals in my 1974 survey who thought that the patron "helped" also characterized him as a "good man." In my first site an item was applied to elicit subtle feelings about the patron—"How do you remember the patron?" It was thought that the item might tap the image of the patron as father. The question found no resonance among the peasants, and I eliminated it in other sites.

The peasant was rarely confident of the patron's help. He could not be sure that the patron would take him to the hospital if he suddenly fell sick, for example—he could only hope so. The peasant had no sanctions over the patron. To appease the peasant, the patron often made promises that he would not fulfill. The patron could stall for time, hoping that the peasant would forget the request, but more often the peasant felt betrayed. The patron's evasion of his commitments sometimes spurred peasants' desires to institutionalize and formalize the patron's promises; these efforts usually failed, however.[26]

---

[23] The item reads "Do you think that, before, the patron helped a lot to improve the life of the people of this place, helped somewhat, or not at all?"

[24] Item was a follow-up to that specified in footnote 23. Respondents who said the patron helped "a lot" or "somewhat" (N = 5) were asked "Why? What was the patron like?" Other answers to the question included references to order and stability (11 percent) and vaguer statements that the patron was good and helped the respondent (10 percent).

[25] On May 9, 1975, in Lima, I spoke on this issue with Michael Gonzales, a Ph.D. candidate in history at the University of California at Berkeley, who was studying Peru's sugar haciendas. He reported that even in those haciendas where material benefits to peasants had been great, peasants rarely indicated positive affect for their patrons.

[26] Greaves (1968: 162) emphasizes El Chalán peasants' desire to institutionalize the patron's commitments: "Rural proletarians regard contact with [the administrators] a trying experience fraught with the danger of being upbraided and humiliated or of inordinate delays in getting the simple services they request. Many of the clauses in bargaining contracts reflect the rural proletarians' desire to buttress their side of these confrontations with a written rule." Greaves (1968: 74-75) also reports that the

In many peasants' eyes, the hacendado reneged on his commitments. Peasants often said that but for fear of revenge they would kill hacendados (Larson and Bergman, 1969: 71). Usually the resentment burned quietly inside. But there were times when the anger burst out. For example, after El Chalán's patron chastised peasants one night, they exploded:

> The workers withdrew in disarray and repaired to the union hall.... Tempers began to rise. Diatribes against the hacienda ... competed for the audience's approval and great applause rewarded the most impassioned denunciations (Greaves, 1968: 160).

## SUMMARY

Peasants were cowed and atomized in the traditional Peruvian hacienda. Hacienda peasants were pitted not only against each other but also against peasant-community residents outside the haciendas, who were often jealous of the material advantages of many hacienda employees. Hacienda peasants behaved according to the ideology of dog-eat-dog materialism advanced by the patron within the structure of individual incentives, of "limited good." Yet at the same time peasants were cynical toward the patron and resentful of the clientelist system itself. Their suspicion of authority may have been intensified during the 1960s, when both major reformist political parties, APRA and Acción Popular, failed to fulfill their promises to the peasant. Yet, the peasants' frustration and resentment were not successfully channeled nor sustained in purposeful institutions,[27] in large part because the hacendados still dominated not only the local agrarian structure but also the national political system. Peasant anger dissipated amid renewed competition for material benefits, a practice encouraged by the hacendados, or amid repression, a strategy to which hacendados could always resort.

---

peasants usually failed, as, for example, in an effort to fix the amount of holiday wage bonuses.

[27] For a definition of "institutions," see Huntington (1968). Various Peruvian peasant groups held up as "revolutionary" gradually dissipated. The demise of the peasant unions in the La Convención valley around Cuzco is especially instructive. See Craig (1969).

# IV · "After": Changes in Peasant Political Culture, 1969-1977

TRADITIONALLY, hacienda peasants in Peru competed with their peers to please a single man, the patron, who controlled resources and benefits important to the peasants. The world beyond the hacienda was distant to the peasant. Yet, with the transformation of the hacienda into a self-managed cooperative in the early 1970s, the clientelist orientations of peasants gave way to a new set of orientations most simply described as "group egoism." Collaborative and participatory attitudes emerged among peasants toward their fellows in the cooperatives; but, for various reasons, a sense of solidarity did not extend to peasants beyond the cooperative, or to the Peruvian nation and its government.

This chapter will examine these changes in peasant attitudes and behavior from a somewhat different perspective than subsequent chapters. Later chapters will focus on changes in specific realms—political leadership, social trust, sympathy for disadvantaged peasant outsiders, etc., and explore in detail the reasons for these changes, analyzing various kinds of incentives and disincentives for change. In contrast, this chapter aims to document the emergence of "group egoism" as an overall pattern, rather than to examine the specific components of that pattern. It also aims to show the importance of the cooperative structure to the emergence of this new pattern, indicating that membership and participation in these structures are related more to attitudinal and behavioral change than education or culture contact, for example.

To document the rise of this new pattern of orientation, and its structural correlate, the chapter draws on two quite different kinds of evidence. First, survey data are analyzed. Second, the experiences of five individuals whom I knew well are described, permitting a more intimate view of the process of change, as well as a continuous time perspective from 1973 through 1977. Before these sets of evidence can be examined, however, the research methodology and sites must be described.

## RESEARCH METHODOLOGY

Changes in political culture are notoriously difficult to measure. Analyzing the impact of new structures requires research in a country where such structures have recently been established, but most of these nations—Cuba under Castro, China under Mao, Tanzania under Nyerere, Chile under Allende—have restricted the access of researchers. Interviews and participant observation in these nations have at times been impossible for North Americans, and at times possible only in the presence of a government official. Further, an adequate research design requires data on both the "before" condition ("baseline data") and the "after." To determine the agent of change, both experimental sites where the agent is present and control sites where it is absent are necessary.

In rural Peru during 1973-1975, the research opportunity was almost uniquely propitious. Despite the sweeping reforms in the countryside, the government did not restrict the research access of North Americans. In all sites, the decision about my research access was made by the community leadership. Access was refused at times to both Peruvians and North Americans, but I encountered no serious problems. My research assistants and I lived for several months in each major site, attending political meetings, joining in sports activities and parties, watching work activities, and contributing to community life by taking photographs, providing transportation, offering instruction in the English language, and the like. I was able to interview cooperative leaders extensively, usually in the privacy of their homes or in my car. Key documents, including financial statements, were obtained for every major site.

Further, pre-reform baseline data on attitudes and behavior were available for both experimental sites and control sites. The availability of baseline data primarily determined the selection of research sites (see Appendix 1). Baseline attitudinal data were provided by the sample survey conducted by the Instituto de Estudios Peruanos and Cornell University in the fall of 1969, just after the announcement of the agrarian reform but prior to its implementation. The Cornell-IEP survey data have been used by other scholars, and their validity was also cross-checked in my research by the application of other interview strategies.[1] Baseline data on enter-

---

[1] For others' work with the 1969 data, see Matos Mar (1969); Cotler (1970a); Bourque (1971); Buchler (1975); and Whyte and Alberti (1976). I also checked the validity of the extent of attitudinal change found between 1969 and 1974 by asking respondents at times for personal retrospection. I asked whether the individual

prise structure and peasant behavior were less abundant. My major sources were interviews with the social scientists who had been employed as research assistants by IEP in 1969,[2] with the ex-hacendados,[3] and with the peasants themselves. Baseline data on my major experimental highlands site were available in the hacienda archive in Lima.[4] My two major experimental coastal sites are contiguous with the enterprise El Chalán. All three enterprises have resembled each other in many ways, and thus the extensive data on El Chalán for the mid-1960s provided by Greaves (1968) were very useful as a proximate baseline.

To measure attitudinal change in the sites, I replicated, when appropriate, the 1969 survey research. A major effort was made to replicate 1969 field strategies, sampling techniques, and sample parameters (see Appendix 1). However, a margin of measurement error must be accepted, especially because of the change in principal investigators. My sample survey was carried out between June 1973 and February 1974; its date is referred to as 1974 for the sake of simplicity.

Table IV.1 indicates the extent of similarity of sample respondents with regard to sex, education, occupation, and age. In all sites but the peasant communities, both men and women were interviewed; temporary workers were not included in the sample at either date. A few discrepancies in sample composition were eliminated by weighting some respondents in the 1969 Estrella and Marla samples (see Appendix 1). As necessary, the 1969 Monte and Marla samples were also weighted to make their importance in the over-all 1969 sample equivalent to that in the 1974 study. Some sample discrepancies could not be eliminated, however. Most im-

---

thought his attitude on social trust or the like had changed since 1969. This method indicated patterns of attitude change similar to the comparison with the 1969 data (see Chapter III). However, I feared that too many retrospective questions would reveal the purpose of the study to respondents, creating response biases.

[2] Interviews with Dr. Elías Minaya and Manuel Ortiz were especially helpful. Dr. Elías Minaya was working in the Trujillo Ministry of Agriculture in 1973-77. He wrote his B.A. thesis on the Trujillo sites, as well as various reports on them for IEP. Manuel Ortiz worked briefly for me in 1973 and then went to teach in a Lima university.

[3] The ex-hacendados of both Monte and Estrella were interviewed, but Marla's had died.

[4] This archive is a major new resource for social scientists. It is independent of the Peruvian government, funded by the Ford Foundation. It is expected that documents from a great many haciendas will eventually be included, but by 1975 only those from large haciendas had been collected.

TABLE IV.1
Survey Samples, 1969 and 1974 (%)

| | N | Male | With complete primary education or more | Business or white collar jobs[b] | 35 years or under |
|---|---|---|---|---|---|
| ›operatives, 1974 | 229 | 63 | 23 | 6 | 53 |
| ₁ciendas, 1969 | 177[a] | 63 | 19 | 5 | 61 |
| ₁Monte, 1974 | 79 | 66 | 19 | 5 | 57 |
| ₁Monte, 1969 | 58 | 71 | 12 | 5 | 60 |
| ₁Estrella, 1974 | 89 | 62 | 32 | 11 | 46 |
| ₁Estrella, 1969 | 79[a] | 61 | 25 | 7 | 54 |
| ₁Marla, 1974 | 61 | 61 | 13 | 2 | 60 |
| ₁Marla, 1969 | 40[a] | 54 | 17 | 0 | 72 |
| ₁asi-control & control, 1974 | 184 | 50 | 44 | 25 | 51 |
| ₁asi-control & control, 1969 | 253 | 45 | 42 | 23 | 55 |
| ₁gustín, 1974 | 94 | 52 | 38 | 27 | 47 |
| ₁gustín, 1969 | 153 | 47 | 36 | 24 | 56 |
| ₁irú, 1974 | 90 | 48 | 48 | 23 | 53 |
| ₁irú, 1969 | 100 | 46 | 52 | 23 | 52 |
| IS peasant communities, 1974 | 93 | 100 | 45 | 11 | 70 |

Weighted sample. Original N is 73 in Estrella and 36 in Marla.
This category includes primarily shopkeepers and commercial middlemen. Women who tended ₁res were numerous in Agustín and Virú and were often coded in this category rather than as ₁usewives.

portant, the 1974 sample is slightly older than the 1969 one. (If the age of the samples is equalized through weighting, then the 1974 sample becomes better educated than the 1969 sample.)

One important distinction between the major site samples and the SAIS peasant-community samples is the exclusion of women from the latter. Since I wanted to replicate the 1969 effort, and because the 1969 sample included many women, I had no choice but to interview women or drastically reduce the "N" for the 1969 samples in most sites. However, no 1969 data were available for the peasant communities, so the inclusion of women was not vital. Further, the great majority of women in these communities spoke only the Indian language Quechua, in which I had no facility. The exclusion of women from the peasant-community samples is the primary reason for the more collaborative and participatory attitudes in these sites relative to the other cooperatives.

Generally, respondents seemed open and frank in the interviews (see Appendix 1). I am confident that members were not merely mouthing opinions that they thought they should hold; otherwise, they would not have expressed such strong criticism of the government (see Chapter X). Nor were they voicing opinions that they thought I or my research assistants wanted to hear; as indicated in Chapter I, I did not anticipate the amount of attitudinal change that occurred. Further, most of my research assistants were more interested in current patterns of orientations than in the character of change, and did not know what kind of survey results were necessary for one or another theoretical outcome; in any case, most were opposed to the cooperatives and the government and, on the grounds of political ideology, would probably have preferred a "no change" outcome.

Although the basic sample survey was administered only once in each site after the reform, return visits during 1974, May 1975, and July 1977 were made to monitor change. In May 1975, in-depth interviews were conducted in the two coastal cooperatives, Estrella and Marla. Estrella and Marla were selected for the intensive interviews because of the greater verbal facility of their residents. Subsequently, similar interviews were conducted in the peasant community Rachuis. Although structured, these 1975 interviews were informal and not based on strict samples. Almost all respondents were cooperative members. Eighty-eight individuals were interviewed: 38 in Estrella, 22 in Marla, and 28 in Rachuis. Quotations from the 1974 work are indicated by "Q" followed by the questionnaire number, whereas those from 1975 are indicated by "Q" followed by 1975 and the questionnaire number (i.e., Q1975, 20).

In 1977, brief follow-up interviews were conducted in all the experimental sites except the major highlands ex-hacienda. Again, interviews were informal, not based on strict samples, and were almost entirely with members. Seventeen individuals were interviewed in Estrella, 16 in Marla, and 45 in the peasant communities Patca, Varya, and Rachuis (15 in each community), for a total of 78 respondents. Quotations from the 1977 interviews are noted by "Q" followed by 1977, the initial of the site name, and the questionnaire number (i.e., Q1977 E6).

The study focuses primarily on three cooperatives. Two, Estrella and Marla, are Agrarian Production Cooperatives (CAPs) located in one coastal valley; the third, Monte, is an ex-hacienda within an Agrarian Social Interest Society (SAIS), called SAIS Huanca, located in the central highlands. Two sites where production cooperatives had not been established were selected as controls: the village of independent cultivators, Virú, and the peasant community Agustín; upon investigation, it became apparent that Agustín had been affected enough by the agrarian reform to constitute only a "quasi-control" rather than a full control site. Research was also conducted in three minor sites, Varya, Patca, and Rachuis, all poor peasant communities in SAIS Huanca. Although pre-reform data were not available for the three minor sites, the sites were included to enhance my knowledge of the SAIS and to suggest the nature of change in more disadvantaged communities.

Although no three cooperatives can be declared exactly equivalent to the "new Peruvian agrarian cooperative structure," I am confident that my research cooperatives are almost as representative as any three sites could have been in 1973. The pre-1969 experience, the structure, and the performance of my research cooperatives are representative. Post-1969 political mobilization was not merely a reflection or continuation of the pre-1969 experience; Table IV.2 indicates that, as in other haciendas of their size, mobilization was low in the research haciendas before 1969. Further, Table IV.3 shows that characteristics on which variation exists in the cooperative universe generally average out across the three sites. In terms of size and wealth, SAIS Huanca is large and prosperous, CAP Marla small and poor, and CAP Estrella average. Approximately 40 percent of the cooperatives employed enterprise directors in 1973; one of the three research enterprises did. Roughly 40 percent of coastal cooperatives included *feudatarios* (ex-sharecroppers); one of my two coastal sites did. One caveat must be made about the socioeconomic representativeness of the cooperative sites. The government expropriated the most prosperous and accessible haciendas first; thus, in later years, my research cooperatives became slightly more prosperous than average. In terms of their performance, again my sites seem quite typical; my research cooperatives were not stellar, "model" sites, and possibly performed slightly below average.[5]

[5] The study of 27 enterprises in six agrarian zones by Douglas Horton during 1973 is the most comprehensive to date. On the average, his sites seemed to perform better than mine, probably because his site selection was influenced by Ministry of Agriculture advice and because he visited primarily rather accessible cooperatives (Horton, 1974: 102-119). For example, on both economic and political criteria, SAIS Huanca was the most successful of my three sites in 1973; its performance was only average, however, on Horton's performance chart, which also evaluates both economic and political achievement. SAIS Huanca received a score of 6 on Horton's scale. His average for 23 enterprises was 4.4, but his average for livestock enterprises like SAIS Huanca was considerably higher, 7.9 (Horton, 1974: 116).

Several sites that I visited briefly with Ing. Luis Deustua also seemed to be func-

TABLE IV.2

Political Mobilization History of Research Sites in Context of Rural Peru, 1965

| | Number by 1975 | Number with recognized unions, 1964 | Union status, 1961–1968 | Strike or land invasion, 1961–1965? |
|---|---|---|---|---|
| Larger coastal enter- prises[a] | 362 | 250 | — | 27% with 1 o more strikes |
|   Estrella | — | yes | successful | 1 |
|   Marla | — | yes | repressed | 0 |
| Larger highlands enterprises[a] | 50 | 5 | — | some |
|   Huanca | — | no | — | 0 |
| Highland communities | 2,500 | 0 | 30% in Huancayo area with some union affiliation | 200 |
| Peasant communities of SAIS Huanca | 29 | 0 | 0 | 0[b] |
|   Agustín | — | 0 | 0 | 0 |

SOURCES: Data for enterprises, coast and highlands, from Cotler (1969: 301-303). Fact that son highlands enterprises had strikes indicated by Tullis (1970: 85-144); certainly many of these ha unions, although apparently not recognized. Information on SAIS Huanca, especially the peasar communities, from interviews with Dr. Gavin Alderson-Smith, community leaders, and fro Martínez Alier (1973: 25-37, 68-83). Figures for highlands communities in general are very rou estimates due to biased reports; see Tullis (1970: 199), Handelman (1975: 141 and 274), Cotl (1969: 311) and Bourque (1971: 144-145).

[a] "Larger" means that these enterprises had become cooperatives by 1975.

[b] There were, however, some land invasions in the late 1940's, although not in Patca or Vary There were also series of law suits.

---

tioning better than my research sites. I spent two days in CAP Posoconi in Puno; its economic and sociopolitical performance outshone my three sites. It was also visited by Horton, who rated it well, but still gave six of the twenty-three rated enterprises equal or better scores (Horton, 1974: 116). In 1975, I visited three cooperatives in Cañete, a sector of Ica; Ica is said to be the region where the agrarian reform has been most successful, and indeed these three cooperatives all seemed to be function- ing effectively.

On the other hand, interviews with government officials and a series of SINAMOS pamphlets published by the Centro de Estudios de Participación Popular indicate that many smaller, isolated cooperatives in backward regions were functioning marginally. There are also some advantaged cooperatives that have suffered prob- lems for one reason or another. According to Douglas Horton, CAP Túpac Amaru II near Cuzco, for example, should never have been adjudicated as a CAP, but as a SAIS; it included too many isolated, disparate peasant communities and has undergone an endless series of economic and political difficulties. Evaluations of this CAP by Gaitzsch (1974) and by Guillet (1979) are rather negative.

TABLE IV.3

Research Cooperatives in the Universe of Peruvian Cooperatives, 1974

| | N | Number of hectares | Number of families | Hectares per family | Adjudication debt in soles (without interest) | With enterprise director, 1973? | Includes ex-share-croppers? |
|---|---|---|---|---|---|---|---|
| Average CAP | 362 | 4,972 | 242 | 20.0 | 21,356,636 | 36% of CAP with director | 70% with ex-sharecroppers |
| Average Coastal CAP | 250 | 2,364 | 251 | 9.4 | N.A. | N.A. | 40% with ex-sharecroppers |
| CAP Estrella | — | 1,901 | 181 | 10.5 | 9,110,283 | Without director | With ex-sharecroppers |
| CAP Marla | — | 608 | 112 | 5.4 | 3,957,055 | Without director | Without ex-sharecroppers |
| Average SAIS | 50 | 44,931 | 1,100 | 40.8 | 27,480,272 | 58% of SAIS with director | N.A. |
| SAIS Huanca | — | 268,182 | 3,784 | 70.8 | 145,975,233 | With director | Without ex-sharecroppers |

SOURCES: Figures for average CAP, average coastal CAP, and average SAIS from "Reforma Agraria en Cifras," through 30/4/75, Office of Statistics, Ministry of Agriculture, Lima; for my sites, from "Reforma Agraria en Cifras," through 30/12/74, op. cit.; for adjudication debt, from "Reforma Agraria en Cifras," through 30/11/74, op. cit. Figures refer to date of adjudication of cooperative, and thus may not jibe with mine for 1973-75. Data on enterprise directors from "Empresas Sin Administradores Nombrados en el sistema de Ley," Dirección de Producción, Ministry of Agriculture, Lima, December, 1973. Ex-sharecropper statistics from interviews with José Elías Minaya and Luis Deustua.

My confidence in the representativeness of the research coopera-tives developed through my own acquaintance with other sites and through information from secondary sources. I visited eight ex-haciendas in various parts of the country at various times: three in a remote highlands area near Puno in April 1973, three in the coastal area of Cañete in May 1975, and two in the coastal area of Chancay in July 1977. My belief in the representativeness of my sites has also been bolstered by the results of other studies, espe-cially the 1973 research by Douglas Horton (1974, 1975a, b, c) examining 27 enterprises in six agrarian zones. The earlier re-search by Buchler (1975), exploring 75 agrarian cooperatives in many regions of Peru during 1971, was particularly useful in sug-gesting changes in members' attitudes similar to those found in this study; the Cornell-IEP survey was also used as a baseline in this research. The nature of the problems that befell Huanca in its later years is suggested by the work of Guillet (1979) on cooperative Túpac Amaru II in the southern highlands, an enterprise even more massive, diverse, and unwieldy than Huanca. The study by Bell (1977) of cooperatives in the northern coastal area of Piura was also especially helpful, reporting similar political dynamics in these sites as in mine. The 19 *Informes* by a government research group, the Centro de Estudios de Participación Popular (Center for Stud-ies of Popular Participation) provided information on relatively remote cooperatives.[6] Discussion with these and other researchers further developed my knowledge of cooperatives in various regions of Peru.[7]

Although the research cooperatives are representative of Peru-vian agrarian cooperatives, they are by no means representative of all rural Peru. Table IV.4 places the research families in the context of rural Peru, estimating the number of peasants in each type of agricultural work. The wealthiest peasants are predominantly the

[6] The Centro de Estudios de Participación Popular, a department of SINAMOS, published a series of "Informes," each on one cooperative. The number is reaching towards thirty or forty studies, of which I have notes on nineteen. The information presented in each study varies by topic; thus, in future citations of these studies, the "N" may vary. The studies were generally critical, not at all mere government propaganda.

[7] Interviewed analysts include Pedro Ortiz and William Bell, who studied in Piura; Christopher Scott and Olivia Mitchell, in several coastal rice cooperatives; Kevin Middlebrook and Ute Schirmer, in the agroindustrial sugar cooperatives; Andrea Gaitzsch, in a major Cuzco site; Douglas Horton, in 27 enterprises throughout Peru; José Maria Caballero, in Cajamarca and other regions; and Susan Bourque and Kay Warren, in a remote region bordering the department of Cerro de Pasco.

TABLE IV.4

Estimated Distribution of Peruvian Peasants by Type of Agricultural Work, 1977

|  | N | Thousands of hectares | Total farm families | Families benefiting from reform | Percentage of total rural farm families |
|---|---|---|---|---|---|
| ..PS | 578 | 2,225 | 107,137 | 107,137 | 7 |
| ..asant Groups | 798 | 1,586 | 43,945 | 43,945 | 3 |
| ..IS | 60 | 2,802 | 60,930 | 60,930 | 4 |
| ..asant Communities | 4,000 | 8,191 | 500,000 | 110,971 | 31 |
| ..vate Farms | N.A. | 8,000 | 600,000[a] | 31,918 | 37 |
| ..entuales | — | — | 250,000 | — | 16 |
| ..tal | — | 23,500 | 1,600,000 | 356,276[b] | |

ᴖOURCES: See Appendix 3. Except for the data on the CAPs, Peasant Groups, and SAIS, the figures
derived from census information that may not be reliable.

Approximately 20 percent of these farms are over 20 hectares, but under 100 hectares, and 75
..cent under 20 hectares.

Figures include 1,375 peasants in Social Property enterprises.


10 percent of private agriculturalists with farms over 20 hectares.
Some private farmers with smaller parcels are also prosperous—for
example, peasants with irrigated coastal land, such as the residents
of the research site Virú. Slightly over 10 percent of peasant families belong to a reform enterprise, either CAP, Peasant Group, or
SAIS. Most CAP and SAIS members fall in the upper-middle
ranges of the income distribution in agrarian Peru.[8] Most are considerably more prosperous than the peasant-community residents
(comuneros) and temporary workers (eventuales), who eke out sub-
sistence lives in the harsh Peruvian highlands and often migrate to
the coast or high jungle for seasonal work, as described previously.
Peasant-community residents and temporary workers are about
half of all rural residents and generally fall into the bottom half of
the rural income distribution. In all probability, an "average" CAP
or SAIS member's family earns at least twice that of an "average"
comunero/eventual.[9] (There is, however, tremendous variation in
the incomes of different members of these rural groups. The incomes of most agro-industrial sugar cooperative members surpass

[8] Exact figures are not available. Table IV.5 provides some rough estimates with
ɪespect to my research sites in 1975; Appendix 7 offers some estimates, largely by
region, for 1972. Appendix 2 also indicates the difficulties of this type of calculation.

[9] Exact figures are not available. See Table IV.5 and Appendix 7 for some relevant
data. Other information appears in Chapters VIII and IX.

even those of private agriculturalists with medium-size farms, whereas the incomes of members of isolated highlands cooperatives fall below those of comuneros in fertile, accessible regions.)

## THE RESEARCH SITES

Information on the number of members, amount of land, average income, major products, and the like in each research site is provided in Table IV.5. This section emphasizes the nature of socioeconomic conflicts within each site, because these conflicts are basic to the political and social issues in the sites discussed in subsequent chapters. Table IV.6 profiles the distinct socioeconomic groups. Figure 4 indicates the location of the sites. Three sites—Estrella, Marla, and Virú—are located on the north coast near Trujillo, and the other sites—Monte, Agustín, Patca, Varya, and Rachuis—are located in the central highlands near the prosperous town of Huancayo. All sites except the three peasant communities—Patca, Varya, and Rachuis—are slightly under an hour's car trip from their respective provincial cities. Patca, Varya, and Rachuis are much more isolated.

### Major Cooperative Sites

Estrella, Marla, and Monte are all former haciendas. After the reform, Estrella and Marla became CAPs, whereas Monte became one of seven ex-haciendas in a Service Cooperative (CS) that combines with 29 nearby peasant communities to form SAIS Huanca. As Chapter II noted, the major difference between the CAP and the SAIS is that the SAIS includes not only ex-haciendas but also peasant communities. Thus, whereas Estrella and Marla as CAPs are independent cooperatives, Monte is only one part of a more complex organization. For example, Monte does not elect its own Administrative Council; it only chooses delegates to the CS that in turn participates in elections for the SAIS Council. A union is the major base-level organization in Monte.

As the cooperative to which several of the research sites in this study belong, SAIS Huanca is an important entity. The SAIS is physically represented only by its Huancayo office. It is run largely by the leaders elected from the communities and ex-haciendas. SAIS leaders were quite autonomous from their base sites. They received stipends from the SAIS, spent much of their time in Huancayo, and often aspired to professional careers.

Huanca is by far the largest and most lucrative enterprise in this

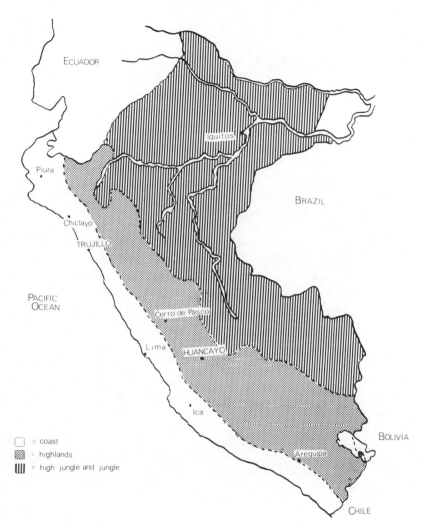

4. Location of Research Sites

study, and is probably the second largest and most lucrative in the entire highlands. Until 1969, it was a complex of five haciendas; with the reform, two ex-haciendas were added plus the peasant communities. Huanca's vast, mountainous grazing lands span both banks of a large river; travel between a community on one bank to a second on the other bank may require over a day. On the grazing

TABLE IV-5
The Research Sites[a]

| | Type of cooperative | Date(s) surveyed | Location | Number of families[b] | Number of hectares[c] | Date of cooperative adjudication | Major products | Average daily family income in soles, May 1975 |
|---|---|---|---|---|---|---|---|---|
| Cooperatives | | | | | | | | |
| Estrella | CAP | 1969, 1974, 1975, 1977 | Coast | 181 | 1,901 | 11/11/72 | Corn, tobacco, sorghum, sugar cane | 300 |
| Marla | CAP | 1969, 1974, 1975, 1977 | Coast | 112 | 608 | 10/30/71 | Asparagus, sorghum, corn | 180 |
| Huanca | SAIS | — | Highlands | 30 | 268,182 | 4/24/71 | Meat, wool, milk | — |
| Monte | Ex-hacienda in SAIS | 1969, 1973, 1977 | Highlands | 94 | 40,064 | 4/24/71 | Meat, wool, milk | 170 |
| Varya | Peasant community in SAIS | 1973, 1977 | Highlands | 186 | 588 | 4/24/71 | Potatoes, meat | 100 |
| Patca | Peasant community in SAIS | 1973, 1977 | Highlands | 231 | 464 | 4/24/71 | Potatoes, meat | 50 |

| | | | | | | | | |
|---|---|---|---|---|---|---|---|---|
| Rachus | Peasant community in SAIS | 1975, 1977 | Highlands | 84 | 121 | 4/24/71 | Potatoes, meat | 60 |
| Quasi-control Agustín | Peasant community, not in SAIS | 1969, 1973 | Highlands | 221 | 157 | — | Corn, potatoes, meat, bricks | 250 |
| Control Virú | None (individually farmed village) | 1969, 1974 | Coast | 845 | 925 | — | Corn, meat, poultry, fruit | 325 |

[a] Some figures, especially those for Patca and Varya, are estimates. The list of members in the non-cooperative sites was incomplete. Average income must be estimated even in the cooperatives because families often derive more income from privately owned animals than from their daily wage. Figures on the number of members and of hectares often vary over time as a site expands or contracts. Demographic information on SAIS sites and Agustín is from the Ministry of Agriculture (1970a). All calculations for Estrella include the *feudatarios*.

[b] Figures for members rather than families are given for Estrella, Marla, SAIS Huanca, and Monte, because they are most reliable. With regard to SAIS Huanca, members are communities such as Patca and Varya, plus the service cooperative that includes Monte. Figures refer to SAIS Huanca, members are communities such as Patca and Varya, plus the service cooperative that includes Monte. Figures refer to year of cooperative adjudication.

[c] Refers to cultivated land except in Monte and SAIS Huanca, where pasture land is included, resulting in the much larger figures. Varya, Patca and Rachuis but not Estrella or Marla also have some pasture land.

TABLE IV.6

Major Socioeconomic Groups in Research Sites

(mean scores of group on key indices)[a]

| | Number in sample | Education | Wealth | Participa- tion | Culture contact |
|---|---|---|---|---|---|
| Monte | | | | | |
| Shepherds | 16 | .3 | .4 | 1.0 | .4 |
| Operarios | 29 | 1.0 | 1.1 | 1.5 | 1.1 |
| Estrella | | | | | |
| Workers | 34 | .7 | 1.5 | 2.1 | 1.7 |
| Feudatarios | 14 | 1.6 | 2.9 | 1.8 | 2.5 |
| Marla | | | | | |
| Workers | 38 | .5 | .9 | 2.1 | 1.3 |
| Agustín | | | | | |
| Comuneros | 18 | 1.0 | 1.8 | 2.2 | 1.6 |
| Brick makers, com- erciantes[b] | 20 | 1.5 | 2.1 | 1.3 | 2.5 |
| Virú | | | | | |
| Unskilled workers[c] | 11 | .6 | 1.1 | .4 | 1.1 |
| Independent cul- tivators, comer- ciantes | 25 | 1.6 | 2.5 | 1.3 | 1.7 |
| Patca | | | | | |
| Comuneros[d] | 42 | 1.2 | .2 | 2.6 | .8 |
| Varya | | | | | |
| Comuneros[d] | 33 | 1.4 | .4 | 2.2 | 1.3 |

[a] Points on indices range from 0 to 4. The higher the score, the more education, wealth, etc. of the socioeconomic group. For construction of indices and meaning of index points, see Appendix 5.

[b] Comerciantes and ladrilleros were not distinguished in coding. Many of the comerciantes are women with shops. They tend to bring down the scores of the ladrilleros on the indices.

[c] Most unskilled workers are employed by independent cultivators.

[d] Other respondents in sample besides comuneros are students, unskilled workers, comerciantes and white-collar employees (i.e., postoffice operator in Varya).

land, sheep and cows are raised with a high degree of technological expertise. Because of its size and significance, Huanca received large amounts of government attention. For example, SAIS Huanca was never allowed to evade the requirement for a manager.

Within the SAIS, peasant-community members and the ex-hacienda workers were two distinct groups. The two groups had a history of conflict throughout Peru's highlands, and after 1969 in many cases neither group felt that the SAIS cooperative mode was sufficiently advantageous to it. This was particularly so in Huanca, where tension between the two groups had been severe, income differences were vast,[10] and the peasant-community members were heavily favored in the distribution of power and profits (29 voting and profit shares for the peasant-community members versus one for all the ex-hacienda workers).

Monte is one of seven ex-haciendas in the Service Cooperative of SAIS Huanca.[11] Although the Huanca ex-haciendas are more lucrative than most highland enterprises, they are less prosperous per capita than many coastal ones, such as Estrella. Many Monte residents are shepherds, whose socioeconomic position is the lowest of any group in the research sites. Monte is also the most "Indian" of the three major cooperative sites; for women, but not men, Indian dress is still the rule and Quechua still the common tongue. Diseases of various kinds are more prevalent than on the coast.

Of Monte's 94-odd families, about half are operarios (semi-skilled workers such as carpenters, blacksmiths, and cooks) and about half are shepherds. Although wages of the two groups were equalized under the SAIS, the socioeconomic division remains large. The shepherds live almost as wanderers in the high mountains, tending their grazing flocks. Their houses are makeshift huts in different grazing spots. They have little opportunity to communicate with one another, visiting the center of Monte only once a week to collect wages and attend union meetings. Most shepherds are older men, illiterates. In contrast, semi-skilled workers are

[10] Reliable data on the income of comuneros versus trabajadores in contiguous highlands sites are scarce. However, it can be safely assumed that workers' income was at least twice that of comuneros', at least in prosperous areas such as around Huancayo. For the 55 peasant communities and 7 haciendas around Huancayo, the Ministry of Agriculture (1970a) found family income in the haciendas more than double that in the communities. Hacienda technicians were, however, included in the sample. A study of food consumption found that Monte families averaged the equivalent of 32 soles per day for food, versus 26 soles in an economically average community in the area, Rachuis (National Institute of Health, 1971). See also the estimates of Montoya (1974: 99) and my estimates for Huanca sites in Tables IV.5 and IV.6.

[11] Information on Monte is based on observation, internal SAIS documents, the survey, and interviews. Information on Monte as a hacienda was considerable; correspondence from Monte and Huanca is available in the hacienda archive in Lima. In particular, the correspondence documents the hacienda managers' strategies for repressing and evading unionization. See also the Ministry of Agriculture (1970a) and Montoya (1974).

younger and literate. Living in small but sturdy houses in Monte's center, they can enjoy social and sports activities daily. Further, despite the salary equalizations, many still gain considerable extra income from livestock or, in a few cases, land parcels in other communities or small-scale trading.

Before 1969, Monte was the favorite hacienda of Huanca's patron. He visited it frequently and was relatively generous to it. Monte families recall the patron positively, saying that he gave presents of clothes, meat, milk, and the like. But in exchange for these benefits, Monte residents were expected to forego group activities among themselves. On the few occasions that interest in a union arose, the leaders were abruptly fired or bribed by the patron. No union ever functioned in Monte, except during one year in the late 1940s. The IEP-Cornell 1969 survey found less sociopolitical solidarity in Monte than in any other site in this study.

Estrella is a CAP in the Virú valley.[12] Estrella's families are the most prosperous of the three research cooperatives. With over eleven irrigated hectares per member upon adjudication, Estrella has a particularly favorable land/man ratio. Estrella is contiguous to Marla, but Estrella enjoys the more propitious location, only a fifteen-minute walk to the highway.

Until 1975, about half of Estrella's 150-plus members were feudatarios, and roughly half its land was operated by them. Although the name feudatarios implies tenancy, actually these individuals had won private ownership rights to their parcels through a law instituted by Belaúnde and still operative in the Velasco years. There was considerable conflict between the feudatarios and the workers for various reasons. First was the economic distance between the two groups. Estrella's feudatarios were the wealthiest group in the entire sample; some earned over $5,000 annually. Second, slightly outnumbering the workers, the feudatarios were able to dominate Estrella politically. This dominance was increasingly resented by the workers, especially because the feudatarios had no real stake in the cooperative; they worked their own land, not the cooperatives, and had no desire to change this. Most feudatarios had entered the cooperative only to assure legal security for their own plots.

Estrella has been one of the most lucrative enterprises in Virú for over a decade. Its patron could thus afford some concessions to

[12] Information on Estrella is from internal documents, observation, and interviews. See also Elías Minaya (1969b) for a description of Estrella as a hacienda.

workers. After 1963 he allowed a union and granted almost annual wage increases between 1963 and 1969.

Like Estrella, Marla is a CAP in the Virú valley.[13] However, Marla is less prosperous than Estrella. Marla's 100-odd members have only about 608 hectares, signifying a man/land ratio considerably inferior to Estrella's. Whereas Estrella is near the highway, Marla is almost an hour's trek away. For these and other reasons, a Marla worker is not as well-off as an Estrella worker, nor even as well-off as a Monte semi-skilled worker.

Group cleavages do not follow socioeconomic lines in Marla. In contrast to Estrella, Marla does not include feudatarios. (Although they were present in the ex-hacienda, after the agrarian reform they were organized into a looser service cooperative rather than the CAP.) The major cleavage is geographic. Marla is divided by a river, and each side wants either to be the cooperative center or to constitute its own new cooperative.

The relationship between the patron and the workers had been more antagonistic in Marla than in Estrella or Monte. For various reasons, the patron had fallen deeply into debt and could not pay his workers. Angry workers tried to organize, but the patron retaliated by firing a large number of them. Because of the patron's violation of the labor code, Marla was expropriated early, in late 1969.

### The Quasi-Control and Control Sites

Neither Agustín nor Virú, the quasi-control and control sites, respectively, was a hacienda before 1969, and neither became a cooperative after 1969. Both were bustling rural marketing centers, and have remained so. In both sites, all production decisions are made by the individual peasant. Nor are other key decisions—such as the contracting of technicians—made by the peasants in a collective fashion. Both Agustín and Virú are district capitals, but the district authorities are appointed by the region rather than elected by the communities.

Agustín is a peasant community in the fertile Mantaro valley, only fifteen minutes by car from Huancayo.[14] It is one of the most

---

[13] Information on Marla is from internal documents, observation and interviews. Information on Marla as a hacienda is provided in Chávez and Paredes (1970) and Elías Minaya (1969b).

[14] Information on Agustín is from observation, interviews, and the Ministry of Agriculture (1970a). The historical development of Agustín is analyzed by Alberti (1974: 91-109, 122-130).

prosperous peasant communities in the Peruvian highlands; wealth is derived not only from agriculture but also from brick making and commerce. Including both men and women, Agustín agriculturalists (comuneros) number approximately 300, compared to 75 or 100 brick makers and another 50 to 75 small businessmen and intermediaries. Although comuneros prosper on the fertile Agustín land, many brick makers are wealthier. Some employ as many as five temporary workers to mold and fire the clay in their small factories.

Virú is even more prosperous than Agustín.[15] Of its 850-odd families, about 60 percent primarily work the land, generally making a good living from their relatively lush and well-irrigated parcels, where they tend chickens and cows and cultivate corn, fruits, and vegetables. Another 40 percent of Virú's adults run the little stores and restaurants that make Virú the commercial capital of the valley. Virú boasts a secondary school, a movie theater, and a hospital. Income differences are wide in the village (about 40 percent of the farmers own less than one hectare, another 45 percent between one and five hectares, and 15 percent over five hectares), but they form a continuum, and no sharp group cleavages emerged. Socially and politically, Virú is a heterogeneous and individualistic village.

Although both villages were designated as controls at the start of the study, it became apparent that Agustín is more correctly classified as a quasi-control because it was affected by the agrarian reform in various ways. Agustín is a highlands peasant community, and thus falls under the peasant community statute described in Chapter II. Political structures similar to those in the cooperatives—the General Assembly and Councils—were thus established, and the community elite, the brick makers, became subject to the disqualification clause. In contrast, Virú rejected classification as a peasant community, and was not subject to political reforms. The only major effect of the agrarian reform in Virú was to equalize irrigation allocations and to intensify government support for land tenants, enabling many to win ownership rights.

[15] Information on Virú derives from observation and interviews. Interviews with the "Vice Mayor" during 1973-74, the secretary in the municipal office, and a "permanent" Peace Corps volunteer, James Warden, were especially helpful. The demographic figures derive from Rodríguez Suy-Suy (1965), and Elías Minaya (1966 and 1969a).

*The Three SAIS Huanca Peasant Communities*[16]

The minor sites in the research design are Varya, Patca, and Rachuis. Patca and Varya were studied at length; the long survey instrument was applied in them in 1973-1974. Rachuis was not visited until 1975, and only the shorter questionnaires were ever applied. As a result, more information is available on Patca and Varya than on Rachuis, and these two communities are discussed in greater detail in subsequent chapters. The communities are poorer than other sites in the sample; even so, they are located around Huancayo, the most prosperous and most Spanish-speaking area in the Peruvian highlands, and they are more developed socioeconomically than many peasant communities, as Table IV.7 suggests.[17]

As both peasant communities and members of the SAIS, the political structure of these sites is dual. As peasant communities, they are subject to the peasant-community statute. Further, as SAIS members, they choose delegates to the General Assembly of the SAIS. Almost all Huanca communities have had at least one delegate elected to the Administrative Council of the SAIS. In some cases, the president of the Administrative Council doubles as the delegate to the SAIS, but more often the two roles are filled by different men. On the other hand, neither membership in the SAIS nor peasant-community status mandates changes in patterns of economic production, and production continues to be primarily individual. Thus, as in Agustín, the new political organs do not consider as many or as important issues as the Councils of the CAPs or the SAIS.

Without baseline data, previous sociopolitical patterns could not be definitively ascertained, but interviews with peasants and SAIS

[16] Demographic data on the peasant communities derive primarily from the Ministry of Agriculture (1970a). The figures are somewhat unreliable and were modified in line with observation as necessary. See also Montoya (1974). Other information is primarily from interviews, including many with SAIS technicians and Huancayo university students.

[17] Although estimates of the number of communities in the more prosperous regions versus those in poorer ones ("Mancha India") vary, the most judicious calculations (Webb, 1974a; Handleman, 1975a: 32) place about half in the advantaged departments and half in "Mancha India." The destitute departments of "Mancha India" (Cajamarca, Huancavelica, Ayacucho, Apurímac, Puno, and Cuzco) had an average of only 10 percent of the population with complete primary education in the early 1900s (Larson and Bergman, 1969: Table V-4) and an average annual family income under $300 in 1972 (see Appendix 7).

TABLE IV.7

Socioeconomic Development of Peruvian Peasant Communities, 1964-1973
(percentages)

| | Rural Peru 1972 | Cuzco communities (N = 8) | Junín communities (N = 13) | Huayo-pampa[c] 1964 | Agustín 1973 | Patca 1973 | Varya 1973 |
|---|---|---|---|---|---|---|---|
| Percentage speaking Spanish | N.A. | 15[b] | 90[b] | N.A. | over 98% | 95% | 90% |
| Listen to radio daily | N.A. | 8 | 45 | 75 | 65 | 35 | 65 |
| Literate (or 2 years primary school)[a] | 66 | 47 | 69 | 98 | 82 | 73 | 87 |
| Travel to city at least once a week | N.A. | 13 | 21 | N.A. | 85 | 5 | 10 |
| With electricity | N.A. | 0 | 45 | N.A. | very limited | 0 | 0 |

SOURCES: Figures are crude estimates based on family heads. Figures for communities in Cuzco and Junín are from Handelman (1975: 164). Figures for Huayopampa and Agustín from 1964 or 1969 Cornell-IEP surveys. Patca and Varya data from McClintock survey.
[a] Figures are for men only. Rural Peru, Cuzco, and Junín figures from 1972 census. It may underestimate literacy because it includes children and men over 60.
[b] Figures from Handelman (1975: 163). Numbers refer not to percentages speaking Spanish but to percentages of communities in Handelman's sample where more than 50 percent of comuneros speak Spanish.
[c] Huayopampa is located in the northern region of Chancay.

technicians were suggestive. All sites had been dominated by a socioeconomic elite: Patca and Rachuis by a merchant family, and Varya by a clique of lawyers. The same individuals allocated political positions to themselves year after year; elections did not take place. Political meetings were extremely rare. Few national issues reached the communities, especially because most residents were illiterate and thus could not vote in national elections. However, the three communities were socially more united than the haciendas. In general, socially and politically these communities seem similar to other Peruvian peasant communities described by scholars.

The communities were relatively alike in socioeconomic terms. All of Patca, most of Rachuis, and some sectors of Varya were located in high, cold, desolate mountains. Social services were limited in all cases: there was no electricity, water purification facility, medical post, or (except in Varya) secondary school. In Patca and Rachuis, poverty was so severe that most members had to migrate to the borders of the jungle for seasonal work in order to subsist. Although Varya was the most isolated site (six hours from Huancayo—four by train and two by foot), it was slightly better off, probably because it was at lower altitudes.

Politically, Patca was one of the least active communities prior to the 1970s, but advanced sharply with the SAIS; in contrast, Varya was relatively well organized in the 1960s—it had struggled for funds for its secondary school—but it did not mobilize much further under the SAIS. The degree of political organization in Rachuis was approximately average, both before and after 1969.

## AGGREGATE PERSPECTIVES ON ATTITUDINAL CHANGE

By developing various indices, this section provides a more sophisticated, aggregate analysis of attitudinal change than elsewhere in this study. One index was developed for participatory and collaborative attitudes toward fellow site residents (see Appendix 4). This index includes the five appropriate items about these attitudes asked in both 1969 and 1974. These five items concern sociopolitical organization, political efficacy, trust, help in an emergency, and working with others. A second semblance of an index, using only two items, was developed with respect to attitudes toward outsiders (see Appendix 4). To analyze the impact of various change agents on these attitudes, indices of political participation, socioeconomic status, and culture contact were also developed (see Appendix 5).

Table IV.8 reveals that the increase in the number of respondents holding participatory and collaborative attitudes was much larger in the cooperatives than in the controls. In the experimental sites in 1969, under 10 percent of respondents were positive toward participation and collaboration on more than three items, versus over 50 percent in 1974. In contrast, in the quasi-control and control sites, roughly the same percentage of respondents (8 percent) was positive on more than three items in 1969, but the percentage grew only slightly by 1974, remaining under 20 percent. The increase was significant in the cooperative sites but not in the controls. Similar results were obtained in a T-test.[18]

The importance of the cooperative structure as a change agent is particularly evident from the data in Table IV.9. The table shows the moderately strong relationship in the experimental sites between cooperative membership and actual participation, on the one hand, and collaborative and participatory attitudes, on the other.[19] Although participation was also correlated with these attitudes in 1969, at that date socioeconomic status was correlated with these attitudes too: in most sites in 1969 the correlation coefficient between socioeconomic status and the attitudinal index was about .300, versus .130 in the cooperatives in 1974. Thus, the impact of socioeconomic status on these attitudes was apparently reduced in the cooperatives. Men were more likely than women to hold participatory and collaborative attitudes at both years in all sites. Trends with respect to the influence of culture contact were unclear.

Unfortunately, aggregate analysis of attitudes toward outsiders is difficult because there are only two relevant items in the 1969 questionnaire, one on attitudes toward the government and one on attitudes toward help from outsiders in an emergency. Compounding the problem of scarcity of relevant items in the 1969 questionnaire was the fact that the item on attitudes toward the government

---

[18] By the T-test, the index mean for the collaboration index in the experimental sites in 1974 is 3.26, versus 1.76 in 1969; the two-tailed probability of this difference by chance is below .001. By contrast, the index mean for the control sites in 1974 is 2.18, versus 1.88 in 1969; the two-tailed probability of this difference is .004.

[19] Membership in the cooperative is almost a condition of participation, and the two variables are strongly related to each other. The correlation coefficient is .527 in the three major experimental sites in 1974, the highest among these indices except for the .683 coefficient between cooperative membership and the male sex.

TABLE IV.8

Changes in Participatory and Collaborative Attitudes toward Site Residents, 1969-1975[a]

(percentages scoring low or high on index of attitudes)[b]

| | N | Scores on Index of Attitudes | | | | | |
| | | 0 (most negative) | 1 | 2 | 3 | 4 | 5 (most positive) |
|---|---|---|---|---|---|---|---|
| Cooperatives, 1974 | 229 | 6 | 10 | 14 | 20 | 25 | 26 |
| Haciendas, 1969 | 177 | 14 | 30 | 33 | 14 | 7 | 2 |
| Monte, 1974 | 79 | 9 | 13 | 13 | 20 | 21 | 24 |
| Monte, 1969 | 58 | 19 | 22 | 40 | 15 | 2 | 2 |
| Estrela, 1974 | 88 | 2 | 6 | 17 | 23 | 24 | 29 |
| Estrela, 1969 | 79 | 14 | 31 | 29 | 15 | 8 | 3 |
| Marla, 1974 | 62 | 8 | 11 | 11 | 14 | 29 | 26 |
| Marla, 1969 | 40 | 6 | 39 | 33 | 8 | 14 | 0 |
| Quasi-control & control, 1974 | 184 | 9 | 25 | 30 | 18 | 13 | 6 |
| Quasi-control & control, 1969 | 253 | 11 | 25 | 37 | 19 | 8 | 0 |
| Agusín, 1974 | 94 | 10 | 23 | 27 | 17 | 14 | 10 |
| Agusín, 1969 | 153 | 14 | 29 | 38 | 15 | 4 | 0 |
| Virú, 1974 | 90 | 9 | 26 | 33 | 19 | 11 | 2 |
| Virú, 1969 | 100 | 7 | 18 | 35 | 26 | 13 | 1 |
| SAIS Communities, 1974 | | | | | | | |
| Patca | 48 | 0 | 4 | 17 | 25 | 42 | 12 |
| Varya | 43 | 2 | 0 | 12 | 35 | 46 | 5 |

[a] In cooperatives, differences between 1969 and 1974 are statistically significant at .001 level (Chi Square); Gamma = .633, Kendall's Tau B .424 and Kendall's Tau C .540. But in quasi-control and control, differences are not statistically significant at .001 level (Chi Square). Gamma = .138, Kendall's Tau B .085 and Kendall's Tau C .104.

[b] For construction of index, see Appendix 4.

## TABLE IV.9

The Impact of Various Change Agents on Participatory and Collaborative Attitudes toward Site Residents[a]

(zero-order correlation coefficients)

| | N | Cooperative membership | Political participation | Male sex | Socioeconomic status | Culture contact |
|---|---|---|---|---|---|---|
| Cooperatives, 1974 | 230 | .328 | .362 | .337 | .130 | .280 |
| Haciendas, 1969 | 177 | — | .376 | .348 | .299 | .262 |
| Monte, 1974 | 79 | .329 | .261 | .320 | .314 | .154 |
| Monte, 1969 | 58 | — | .234 | .541 | .215 | .390 |
| Estrella, 1974 | 89 | .139[b] | .346 | .144[b] | .048 | .327 |
| Estrella, 1969 | 79 | — | .336 | .363 | .397 | .296 |
| Marla, 1974 | 62 | .631 | .482 | .609 | −.065 | .303 |
| Marla, 1969 | 40 | — | .504 | .175 | .249 | .049 |
| Quasi-control & control, 1974 | 182 | — | .194 | .327 | .356 | .304 |
| Quasi-control & control, 1969 | 253 | — | .360 | .349 | .342 | .241 |
| Agustín, 1974 | 92 | — | .216 | .365 | .540 | .276 |
| Agustín, 1969 | 153 | — | .289 | .344 | .322 | .260 |
| Virú, 1974 | 90 | — | .171 | .280 | .329 | .312 |
| Virú, 1969 | 100 | — | .401 | .380 | .306 | .194 |

[a] See Appendices 4 and 5 for construction of indices. All figures are zero-order correlation coefficients between the change agent and the index of collaborative attitudes towards site residents.

[b] Estrella pattern reflects inclusion of feudatarios as members, who are anti-collaboration on the whole.

was not asked in highlands sites in 1974, because it seemed too sensitive. Given the limitations on any "index" of attitudes toward outsiders, no data are presented here to show the stability of these attitudes between 1969 and 1974. The data for single items in Chapters IX and X better document this stability.

However, in order to provide at least some kind of aggregate-level test of the relationship between various change agents and attitudes toward outsiders, a semblance of an index of collaborative attitudes toward outsiders was constructed, despite its serious short-comings (see Appendix 4). The cooperative structure appeared to have minimal impact on members' attitudes toward outsiders.[20] The zero-order correlation coefficient between political participation in the cooperative and positive attitudes toward outsiders was .112 in Estrella and Marla in 1974, an insignificant increase from the .097 coefficient of 1969. In Monte, the coefficient was .311 in 1974, a significant increase from the .203 of 1969, but the relationship between socioeconomic status and these attitudes was also strong (.400), and stronger than in 1969, raising doubts that political participation is the true independent variable. Correlations between all change agents and attitudes were rather low for the control sites Agustín and Virú.

## INDIVIDUAL PERSPECTIVES ON ATTITUDINAL AND BEHAVIORAL CHANGE

The experiences of the five individuals whom I knew best in the Peruvian cooperatives complement the survey data analyzed above. As different types of evidence that yet point to similar patterns of change and give a similar importance to membership in the cooperative as a change agent, each kind of data heightens confidence in the other. Further, the account of the five personal experiences allows a more sensitive analysis of an individual both caught up in the process of change and contributing to the character of that change. Moreover, because these individuals were interviewed and observed intensely many times from 1973 to 1977, not just at the moments of the survey interview, it is possible to gain a fuller understanding of the trajectory of attitudinal and behavioral change and of the relationship between attitudinal change, on the one hand, and behavioral change, on the other.

Various stages of change were evident. The first step in the

---

[20] Details of this analysis are provided in McClintock (1976: 232-234).

process was the perception of change in the character of government and of the enterprise. Peasants became aware that participatory and collaborative behavior might bring rewards. Anticipating benefits, the peasant thus espoused political activity and social solidarity as ideals. However, in this initial stage the peasants often doubted that their neighbors would also embrace these new attitudes. Members ranked their own willingness to collaborate and participate higher than they did their neighbors'.[21] Peasants realized that their efforts at solidarity would go for naught if their fellow members did not change too. Thus, at first many peasants' statements about unity resembled idealistic exhortations to their neighbors, and peasants hestitated to follow up their new ideals with appropriate behavior, fearing a waste of their time and energy. Despite enthusiastic espousals of political unity in the formal survey interview, for example, most peasants attended political meetings only sporadically in 1973.

The second stage of the process was initiated when a member actually attended a meeting. Often he was even drawn into a leadership position merely by having been present at a meeting or two. At these meetings or in leadership roles, the member saw that his fellows were also embracing the new orientations. Reassured that his effort would not be wasted, the peasant went more often to assemblies. As assembly attendance improved, more policy benefits were forthcoming, in terms of the resolution of problems within the cooperative and the granting of demands by the cooperative upon the government (see Chapters V-VIII). These benefits convinced more members to put into practice participatory and collaborative ideals, and they began to attend meetings. Thus, the change dynamic was renewed.

Although this discussion applies primarily to political attitudes and action, the process was similar in other spheres. Peasants

---

[21] An index of the respondents' attitudes toward collaboration showed much larger changes between 1969 and 1974 than an index of the respondents' perceptions of other residents' attitudes. The index of the respondents' own attitudes includes four items about sociopolitical organization, trust, working with others, and political efficacy, plus a question on traditionalism. The index of the respondents' evaluation of others' attitudes comprises three items, about help in the community, collaboration in the community, and envy of hard work. See Appendix 4 for details of index construction. In the cooperatives, the scores on the index of the respondents' own attitudes showed radical changes toward collaboration and participation from 1969 to 1974 (Gamma = .686; Kendall's Tau C = .587), whereas scores on the index of the respondents' evaluation of others' attitudes showed only moderate changes (Gamma = .387; Kendall's Tau C = .301).

espoused ideals of trust and friendship rapidly, but translated them into practice only occasionally, until they became more certain that other peasants would reciprocate.

It must also be emphasized that, although peasants preferred, in the ideal, participatory and collaborative orientations, they did not forswear clientelistic practices if appropriate occasions arose. Given the chance of material benefits from clientelistic behavior, peasants often wanted to pursue this possibility. For example, they looked to university students, including myself, as potential patrons.

The process of change was thus distinctly pragmatic; assurance that real benefits would result from new behavior patterns was critical to the implementation of new ideals about collaboration and participation. However, it is not always clear which came first, the attitudinal change or the behavioral change. New ideals were most evident at first. However, the peasants' ideals became much more assured as they were implemented and proven viable. Thus, the adoption of new attitudes and their practice were mutually reinforcing.[22]

These patterns and trajectories of change are illustrated through the experiences of the five individuals discussed below. They are identified by pseudonyms, as are all individual peasants in the study. If no reference is given for an individual's statement, then the statement was made in an informal context at the time and place indicated by the text.

The change in the orientations of many Monte members—a change particularly dramatic because, prior to 1969, members of Monte had been the most isolated from each other, the most engaged in clientelist styles of all the sites—is revealed by Ingenio Cruz, a watchman. At 45 and with only two years of primary school, he was older and less well educated than most semi-skilled workers. During the era of the hacienda, Ingenio had been especially indebted to the patron; without any special skills, Ingenio had been selected by the patron, Chaparro, to guard the hacienda house. In the hacienda, his behavior had been traditional. In 1968, for example, he gave a fiesta that left him in considerable debt. When we arrived in Monte, Ingenio was one of the first individuals we met, because he was still taking care of the hacienda house where, as students, we would live. He treated us as he must have treated the patron: with a respect and humility that verged on obsequiousness.

[22] Fagen (1969) found a different sequence of attitudinal and behavioral change in Cuba. He argues that value change occurred after political restructuring encouraged changes in behavior.

In our first weeks at Monte, Ingenio seemed extremely confused by the radical changes in Monte. One night he came to visit us in our room to ask what we thought of the reforms. We demurred, indicating that we were just beginning our research: what did he think of them? Ingenio seemed put on the spot. He did not really trust us yet; he worried that we might be affiliated with the ex-patron or with the current government. First he emphasized how he liked the patron:

> He was a very good person. Everything I asked of him, he did. He always made good his promises. He would call me to keep him and his wife company and give me presents.

But then he added, more hesitantly, that the patron must be forgotten and that he was thinking about the future:

> Many people here are always thinking in the past. They think about Chaparro. Not me though. One must think of the future. But at times it is difficult.

During the conversation, Ingenio remained circumspect, discussing the reforms only ambiguously. In the end, however, he seemed pleased that we had sincerely wanted to know his opinions and convinced that we did not represent either the ex-patron or the government. A few days later at a union meeting, he stood up to advocate our stay in Monte as researchers, turning the tide in our favor.

Several weeks later we interviewed Ingenio. Although his responses favored collaboration and participation, they were expressed almost entirely as ideals (Q332). About political organization, he said, "We all *ought* to get together. We all must attend the weekly sessions; every one *ought* to participate and find out what's going on here." He added that a few people were still trying to exploit the inside information learned at the meetings, betraying the union. He claimed that he tried to trust his fellows in Monte, but his wistful tone suggested that he was thinking, "It would be good if it would happen."

During our second month in Monte, a Schoolparents' Association was established. Ingenio was elected president because he had many young children and was considered honest and sensible. In this new position, Ingenio was called upon to preside over meetings. Just after his election, a Monte boy raped a young school girl, and the case was brought before the Schoolparents' Association and then before the union meeting. The rape case was legally complex, and at the union meeting, the union's president and vice-president argued legal points for some time. Illiterate, Ingenio appeared lost and intimidated by the discussion. He bemoaned the complexity of the new laws, and ultimately questioned his own authority:

> I wish I knew the laws. But the laws are all so complex, always some new statute in some other book. Sometimes I think the laws are made to confound us. . . . At the meeting, I was really on the spot, with Miguel and Basilio (two Monte leaders) taking different positions. I didn't know what to do. I was honored to be chosen president of the Schoolparents' Association, but I wonder if maybe Basilio wouldn't have done a better job. He knows a lot.

Thereafter, we left Monte. Two months later I met Ingenio at the SAIS offices in Huancayo. Assertively instead of obsequiously, he asked me to give him a ride on an errand for the SAIS. I suggested that he bring me up to date on happenings in Monte, and he was full of news, obviously participating regularly in the Friday union meetings. He said that he planned to play an important role in the upcoming drive for a large salary raise. He felt the effort would be successful, but he feared that the SAIS was trying to co-opt Miguel Maray and Basilio Ortiz, the two union leaders, by offering them better jobs elsewhere. But, he said, even if the SAIS did co-opt these two leaders, the movement would continue because new leaders from lower socioeconomic strata would replace them. His words, cited at the beginning of Chapter VI, implied that he himself had gained a new sense of his capacities as a leader.

In subsequent visits to Monte, I found Ingenio still active politically although he had been sick. In 1975, his term as president of the Schoolparents' Association was over, but he spoke enthusiastically of his former role. He was also positive about the strength of the union, taking an active interest in the new confederation with workers from other ex-haciendas of the central highlands SAIS. I asked him if he would like to play a leadership role in this organization, and he said yes, he would: "It would be interesting. I would learn a lot and see a lot. I think I could do a good job."

Ingenio was not as interested in economic collaboration as were some other Monte members. In contrast to most semi-skilled workers, he performed his job as guard solely by himself. During 1973, Ingenio purchased a small land parcel on the road between Monte and Huancayo. He spent considerable time establishing boundary specifications on the plot and planning the construction of a house.

Ingenio's experience over these years reflects key aspects of change in Monte. Intensely politicized because of the conflict with the SAIS, the Monte union grew spectacularly. Like several other Monte men, through quasi-leadership positions Ingenio gradually identified with this political struggle. Illiteracy was an obstacle, but the actual experience of leadership seemed to build both desire and ability for political authority.

One of my closest friends in Estrella was Lorenzo Lazo, a 50-year-old worker. I presented myself to Lorenzo as a friend of Dr. Thomas Greaves, who during his field research had known Lorenzo well, and the bond was struck.

Lorenzo had worked hard to reach a position of substantial economic security and respect in the community. He was one of the most upwardly mobile men in Estrella and the upward path had created some difficulties for him. Born in an isolated northern province, he lacked a primary school education. As an illiterate, he was not accepted by educated workers in Estrella, but his achievements placed him above some Estrella blue-collar workers in their eyes and in his. Lorenzo had taken several courses in veterinary medicine and practiced out of his house. Diplomas from the courses were prominently displayed. Lorenzo also owned a large number of animals that probably tripled his income from his Estrella job. Lorenzo sent his only child, an adopted daughter, to secondary school in Trujillo. Lorenzo's most intense desire was to continue his family's upward mobility. Asked what he liked about the Velasco government, he expressed this feeling: "There are more opportunities than before. Now my daughter will become a nurse. You can study and become a doctor, a professor, or another type of professional."

Immersed in the struggle for economic improvement, Lorenzo was not involved in politics during the hacienda years; he never held an important position in the Estrella union. He did not seem to have a coherent attitude toward the ex-patron; he recounted the abuses of his father's patron angrily, and he said that the Estrella patron, Pinillos Ganoza, had been stern but also "fair." At least during the late 1960s, Lorenzo had apparently received ample amounts of livestock feed and other benefits from the patron.

Probably because of his reputation for honesty, Lorenzo was one of the few workers to be elected to the Administrative Council in 1972, although only as an alternate. In the formal interview (Q404), Lorenzo favored political union; this attitude may have contributed to his election or resulted from it, or both. During the fall of 1973, however, Lorenzo was not especially engaged in politics. He did not participate regularly in council meetings, in part because he was not asked to do so. In our conversations, he gave me fatherly advice and sometimes discussed theological issues, but did not talk much about politics.

By January 1974, however, the stench of corruption in Estrella's offices was pervasive, and Lorenzo became angry. The white-collar office employees were stealing the cooperative blind, Lorenzo said, and they must be recalled. Elections were due again; a meeting was scheduled for mid-January. Lorenzo promoted meeting attendance; he spent several days traveling about Estrella to alert members to the meeting and discuss the need to depose key council members. However, on the day of the meeting, as described in Chapter I, people gathered slowly and, primarily out of self-interest, the top leaders called the meeting off.

Frustrated, Lorenzo seemed uncertain how to proceed politically. He adopted a variety of strategies simultaneously. Apparently, during an Administrative Council meeting in which several cases of beer were consumed, he first denounced the council's corruption and then demanded a piece of the action. (Lorenzo never said this to me, but two other council members claimed he had done so.) Yet he also continued the collaborative strategy; at one General Assembly, he spoke out forcefully for the rapid disclosure of the cooperative's financial record. But he did not seem sure how the corruption problem could be solved. I asked him if he supported the nomination for the Administrative Council presidency of Pedro Vásquez, a prosperous ex-sharecropper whom Lorenzo had previously criticized as a *vivo* (an excessively cunning person). Lorenzo said he did support Vásquez. When I reminded him that he doubted Pedro's honesty, he responded: "Well, who knows. We can watch Pedro, make him stay in line. You know, as soon as anybody gets into these positions, they sell out anyway. What can we do? We just have to keep an eye on them. We're learning how to do that."

The effort to gain more workers' representatives on the council was finally successful in 1975. Lorenzo became vice-president of the Vigilance Council. During the struggle, Lorenzo's sense of solidarity with workers crystallized. In 1975, answering my question, "Are you a member of a social class?" he emphasized that he was a "member worker" (*socio trabajador*), who worked hard, unlike the "men with ties" in the office. Asked about the ideal relation between political authorities and the base, he continued to emphasize the need for workers' representatives and for accountability:

The authorities and the base must be united. The leaders must tell us what they do and forge agreement with us. Everything should be done out in the open, not in secret. There should not be one little clique of men with ties and another group of workers. We want, and now we finally have, a president who is one of us (Q1975, 1).

Politically, Lorenzo thus showed considerable solidarity with other Estrella workers. In other spheres, however, he was less interested in collaboration. Because of his ambiguous socioeconomic position and his age, he rarely participated in cooperative social and sports events. At the party celebrating the baptism of my god-child, for example, he attended largely as my friend, and was not fully accepted by the feudatarios there. Riding in my packed car to Trujillo one day, he was subdued in the presence of his social "superiors." Further, Lorenzo was one of the most fervent seekers of a private plot in Estrella. When he finally won a plot in early 1975, he lavished intensive care on it, working very long hours on both it and the cooperative's land.

In April 1975, Lucho Saavedra was elected president of the Estrella Administrative Council. The election was a tremendous victory for Estrella workers, ending the dominance of a corrupt ex-sharecropper clique. I did not know Lucho well during the initial 1973-1974 research, but the formal interview provides some information on his attitudes in that period, and in 1975 I came to know him much better.

Lucho was a respected Estrella worker: about 40 years old, he had a complete primary education, and he worked as a warehouse supervisor, a position of considerable responsibility. Lucho was favored by the ex-patron, who had given him a small plot; in the 1973 interview (Q421), Lucho ranked the ex-patron as "very helpful" for Estrella.

Over time, Lucho's attitudes changed less than those of Ingenio or Lorenzo. Lucho had been a union leader prior to 1969. He had been chosen as Estrella's delgate to APRA's union federation in Trujillo, and took the position seriously. He complained that meetings had often been postponed, but said that he had made the trips to Trujillo regularly anyway. His past experience was the key to his election as Estrella's representative to the Virú Agrarian League in 1973. In the 1973 interview, Lucho embraced politically collaborative attitudes.

Although Lucho had previously held participatory and collaborative ideals, by 1975 and his rise to the presidency of the council, there was an assertiveness and confidence in his declarations that seemed new. Lucho himself emphasized the greater assurance of Estrella members like himself. Said Lucho in a statement repeated at the very beginning of Chapter V: "Now we participate and make the decisions; before, the patron did." He pointed to the many new facilities initiated by the cooperative and spoke of his own plans for Estrella's development. Asked if he preferred a less well-trained but committed person to a better-trained but less committed man as the community leader, Lucho was forthright and adamant: "We all know how to think. The feudatarios did not realize that we too know how to think. We all are waking up. While you discharge a responsibility, you acquire experience. I had the opportunity to get more training, in Lima and many other places" (Q1975, 37).

Lucho was delighted by his skyrocketing prestige within Estrella. As the president of the Administrative Council, he was the first to break traditional barriers between white-collar employees and blue-collar workers at the Estrella restaurant. In 1975, he took coffee or ate lunch frequently with the director or key white-collar men. In 1975, he sought me out, inviting me to meals with his family several times, pleased that he was of such interest to a *gringa* researcher.

However, Lucho was not a true political radical. He felt that he had worked hard and that he deserved now, at last, some real rewards from his labor. Like many Estrella members, Lucho earned more than twice his salary from private agricultural activities, and he did not want to forego these efforts. Lucho also saw that the cooperative enterprise was lucrative, and he feared encroachments on it by disadvantaged peasants or the government. Lucho's concern for the rights of the enterprise was one reason for his election as president.

With respect to encroachments on the cooperative by disadvantaged peasants, Lucho was especially firm. He did not favor helping temporary workers. "The enterprise does not yield enough to have so many members," he said (Q1975, 37). Nor did he want Estrella to sacrifice for poorer communities: "The richest places have struggled hard for their improvement. In other places, especially in the highlands, leaders have put the money in their pockets. They don't deserve help."

Further, Lucho was not especially favorable to the government. Not only did he fear more intensive cooperativization programs but he criticized the low salaries and the high cost of living, especially the high price of fertilizer and insecticides. He blamed the government for the misguided incorporation of feudatarios and trabajadores in the same cooperative. He was critical of the government's initial hostility toward the Estrella union. Despite his position as delegate to the Agrarian League, he was also critical of it: "The Agrarian League is a political organization, nothing more. It does nothing, because it has no money. When there's no money, there's no interest. The whole thing is just a struggle between the political parties. At the meetings, we can never reach an agreement" (Q1975, 37).

The selection of Lucho as the Administrative Council president indicates much about Estrella. Lucho was a blue-collar worker who had "made it," but he was still a blue-collar worker. He had recognized the rewards of political collaboration early, and his good judgment was respected in Estrella. Yet, he was certain to promote the interest of Estrella, rather than make risky sacrifices for outsiders or dubious external political alliances. Further, unlike most middle-aged Estrella workers, Lucho could read and write. He promised to be a capable and honest administrator.

Carlos Otiniano of Marla was the white-collar employee whom I knew best. As a white-collar employee, Carlos's attitudes toward the cooperative were more ambivalent than those of Ingenio, Lorenzo, or Lucho. Like the other men, Carlos favored social and political solidarity, but these orientations were mixed with more pure ambition and opportunism than in their cases.

The son of a wealthy feudatario and a payroll supervisor, Carlos was Marla's only white-collar employee who actually lived in the site. His house was the most luxurious house in Marla and was centrally located. His wife taught school in the community, and Carlos continued to cultivate some land near his father's. Prosperous and friendly, Carlos often assumed *de facto* leadership in Marla. When we first arrived, he showed us all around, jumping into the driver's seat of my Volkswagen and masterfully taking it over the dunes on the way to the beach. He said with assurance that our research proposal would be accepted by the Administrative Council.

Only 28 years old, Carlos had been the vice-president of the Vigilance Council in 1972 and delegate to the Agrarian League in 1973-1974, and he wanted to be Administrative Council president. He carefully planned political meetings, making sure that they were held regularly. He spent a lot of time every day with workers—talking, joking, and organizing sports and parties. Asked what he liked about the cooperative, Carlos stressed the security of employment, the development of new facilities, and the social and political opportunities opened by the departure of the patron. By 1975, however, Carlos's imminent succession to the presidency was dubious; Marla members were electing men of average socioeconomic status to cooperative leadership. Carlos was frustrated, and he began to scheme to enhance his behind-the-scenes political role.

Carlos also wanted more economically. He was very concerned with the cultivation of his family's land; for example, he spent several days in vigorous pursuit of onion seed when the price of onions rose in 1974. Borrowing my car, he raced from Marla to Trujillo to the town of Virú. The effort was futile. Carlos was not making as much money as he had expected in the cooperative. In 1975, Carlos was thinking of moving to Trujillo. His older brothers were in the car business there, he said, making five or ten times as much as he did in Marla. But it is also likely that Carlos was thinking of strategies to make money out of the cooperative. In 1977, Carlos was still in Marla, looking well and prosperous, and he was widely suspected of having bilked the enterprise. Obviously, such an individual would not be inclined to sacrifice for disadvantaged peasants, and indeed Carlos was steadfastly opposed to the admission of temporary workers as full members into the cooperative.

Whereas Lucho Saavedra was ambivalent toward the government, Carlos neither criticized nor praised it, but wondered how much he and Marla could gain from it. I asked Carlos why members went to the regional political meetings, and he replied that they hoped to win a lucrative job in the provincial capital or Lima. He reeled off the salary levels of several delegates from nearby areas who had won jobs. Asked what he liked about the government, Carlos emphasized the large loans that Marla had won. Yet he showed little interest in Marla's production problems. Carlos seemed proud of what he considered his ability to out-maneuver government officials. He was confident that Marla would raise its salaries and keep out eventuales, actions disapproved of by the government, but still win government benefits. He reported that, when one SINAMOS official had become adamant about Marla's incorporation of more eventuales, through his own position in the Agrarian League he arranged the transfer of the official to a distant highlands cooperative. He concluded: "SINAMOS can't push me around. They need me, for otherwise how will they know what's going on around here? They know I know. So they're friendly with me, and they treat me well."

Whereas all four cooperative members described above became more interested in community collaboration after 1969, Pedro Paredes, a 25-year-old Estrella eventual, did not. Pedro's father, a feudatario owning a mere two hectares, was qualified as a member, leaving Pedro with temporary worker status. In part because he was not a cooperative member, Pedro's demands were not accepted by the cooperative. After the failure of collaborative demand making, he turned to clientelist efforts with mixed success. Pedro's reversion illustrates the importance of the cooperative's incentives for new attitudes and behavior.

Pedro should have been a cooperative leader: he was young, bright, active. In 1973, he was dedicated to the idea of political solidarity (Q409). He was also angry at injustices against the eventuales by the cooperative leaders. He had evidence of unwarranted, sporadic wage cuts and named many temporary workers who, like him, had worked for years in Estrella and yet had not been admitted as full members. He organized weekly meetings of the temporary workers. The meetings were not successful, however; the temporary workers feared being fired.

The less successful these meetings, the more Pedro tried to rally authoritative outsiders behind his effort, in clientelist style. Pedro worked first with a young radical university student who was in Estrella to fulfill her "practical experience" requirement. The student tried to help Pedro mobilize the other temporary workers but failed. A month later, Pedro wrote a formal denunciation of the corruption and injustice in Estrella and told us that he was seeking all the temporary workers' signatures. In a few weeks, however, when he still had no signatures, he asked me to deliver the document personally to my Lima "contacts," hoping that my personal delivery would compensate for the lack of popular support. Almost simultaneously, cooperative leaders fired one-third of all the temporary workers. Pedro's document had no apparent impact on officials. Pedro's efforts were frustrated.

At the same time, Pedro was galvanizing a specific family demand. The cooperative wanted the fertile, centrally located Paredes parcel, but it was too small to be legally expropriated. Various deals were proposed, with some measure of compulsion, to the Paredes family. But neither Pedro nor his father wanted to give up the land. The Paredes's position was not supported by other cooperative members. Workers wanted the Paredes land, and ex-sharecroppers feared Pedro as a radical. Pedro sought recourse through the Ministry of Agriculture agent in Estrella, but that agent did nothing. Believing that I had "superior contacts," Pedro turned to me. I said I would try to help, but that my contacts were not so good. Ultimately, word of the case reached the Trujillo Ministry of Agriculture and Pedro's family received secure land title.

Pedro's experiences with political collaboration and with the co-operative were frustrating. As a temporary worker, his only redress was through clientelist strategies. The relative success of the clien-telist effort persuaded him to concentrate on cultivating his garden and to forget his youthful dreams of solidarity. When I returned to Estrella in 1975, he had been offered cooperative membership but had rejected it. He had married, and he wanted to help his father on the parcel. His attitudes toward any kind of collaboration had become negative (Q1975, 5), and remained so through 1977. He perceived corruption everywhere. He no longer identified with any group in the cooperative or any political struggle: "I don't see myself as a member of a social class. You know, I tried to struggle for the temporary workers, but everything entered one ear and left the other. The cooperative frightened them. I'm tired of the whole thing. I want to concern myself with my bit of land" (Q1975, 5).

The experiences of these five men suggest the nature and process of attitude and behavior change in the cooperatives. The coopera-tives encouraged the gradual adoption of more collaborative and assertive attitudes and behavior. The contrast between the experi-ences of the cooperative members and of the temporary worker Pedro Paredes illustrates strikingly the importance of cooperative membership and participation in promoting change. The tendency for new attitudes to be adopted before new behavior is suggested by the cases of Ingenio Cruz and Lorenzo Lazo: both gave interview responses that were very positive toward solidarity before their actions reflected such commitment. All five individuals demon-strated greater interest in political and social collaboration than in work cooperation. Further, none of the five showed sympathy for disadvantaged outsiders or any significant degree of support for the government. Even Lucho Saavedra, who had won a great deal from the reforms and was Estrella's delegate to the Agrarian League, was skeptical of the government on various scores.

5. Delegates at Inaugural CNA
Congress

6. Near the Center of Monte

7. Monte Workers

8. Two Monte Women

9. Estrella Tobacco Workers

10. Near the Center of Marla

11. Marla Workers and Tractor in the Field  12. Marla Worker

13. Faena in Agustín  14. Brick Making in Agustín

15. Sports Stadium in Virú  16. Relaxing in Virú

17. Varya Houses

18. Carlos Otiniano with Other Prominent Marla Residents

19. Pedro Paredes with His Family on Their Plot

20. Miguel Maray with Author's Research Assistant and Monte Worker

21. Aurelio Osores with Military Officer

22. Pedro Vásquez and Author at Baptism in Estrella

Part Two · *THE IMPACT OF PERU'S SELF-MANAGEMENT: ATTITUDES AND ACTION WITHIN THE ENTERPRISE*

# V · *Political Participation*

Now we make the decisions. Before, the patron did.
                                  (Lucho Saavedra, in Estrella, May 1975)

ON THE HACIENDA, peasant political participation was severely restricted by the patron. Virtually monopolizing the scarce
Peruvian land resources, the hacendado held tremendous economic and political power in comparison to the peasants and was
able to control their political activity. Almost all key enterprise
decisions were made by the hacendado and/or his technicians. Peasant political participation was largely limited to the kind of behavior
appropriate in a clientelist relationship: the placement of a request
upon the patron by one peasant, always individually, as an inferior
to a superior, and without assurance of any real attention to the
request by the hacendado.

In a corporatist political system, local peasant participation would
be somewhat similar to that on the hacienda. Although peasants
would be allowed to organize, the organization would be a sham,
controlled by the government. Decisions in the cooperatives would
not be made by their members, but would be manipulated by
owners, technicians, or officials. Aggressive peasant demands
would be discouraged.

In contrast, in the "fully participatory social democracy" model of
participation in the new cooperatives, peasants were to control enterprise decisions themselves. Decisions would be made according
to the majority votes in meetings. Peasants would also be able to
bring their concerns before government officials, who would try to
respond positively to them. As the peasants themselves would control enterprise policy, policy incentives for participation would be
built into the cooperative structure; moreover, as the government
responded to members' demands with new policies, further policy
incentives for participation would be created.

Did either the corporatist or the "fully participatory social
democracy" model describe cooperative members' political participation during 1973-1977? This question cannot be fully answered
in this chapter. The corporatist and "fully participatory social
democracy" models describe decision-making patterns not only at

the local level within the enterprise but also at the national level; however, the emphasis in this chapter is upon members' participation in enterprise decisions, or "community problem solving," with reference to the relationship between members and the government only when members sought government support or placed demands upon officials. The over-all relationship between cooperative members and government officials is discussed in Chapter X. Chapter X does, however, complement one key theme of the present chapter; it points out that, when the government tried to influence enterprise decisions, it usually failed; thus the peasants' participation described in this chapter was more significant than might otherwise have been the case.

## INCENTIVES FOR COLLECTIVE POLITICAL PARTICIPATION

As mentioned in Chapter II, collective incentives such as policy benefits or public goods have in the past been considered rather weak inducements to group political organization because of the public goods dilemma: the public good cannot be denied to any member of the group, regardless of that member's contribution or lack of it to this group. More recently, however, the very large significance of many government policies or public goods in Third World nations has been thought to mitigate the public goods dilemma. This section compares the extent to which group organization brought policy benefits to peasants, first in the haciendas, then in the cooperatives, and finally in the control sites. The significance of the policy benefits in the cooperatives clearly emerges.

### Incentives for Collective Political Participation in the Haciendas

The power of decision in the hacienda was reserved almost entirely to the hacendado or his technical manager. Although by the 1960s some potential vehicles for peasant power existed, such as the unions and the electoral and party system, in most cases they were undermined by the patron. The possibility that policy benefits would result from group organization was minimal.

The control over enterprise decisions exerted by the hacendado, even on coastal estates through the 1960s, is illuminated by Greaves (1968). When a dispute occurred on hacienda El Chalán, for example, the word of the patron, Don Vicente, was law. The peasants claimed that an overseer had physically struck a worker without provocation. They protested to Don Vicente, who asserted his judgment on the case unilaterally and disdainfully:

> Don Vicente asked what the protests were, and then played the role of judge, demanding order, questioning witnesses and clarifying the facts. After some twenty minutes it was clear that the facts were very confused. . . . Don Vicente lost his patience. He launched a withering deprecation of the workers for raising serious charges when they could not agree on the facts. He had caught several workers in gross exaggerations and he angrily chastised them for slandering a man who [worked well]. . . . Then he abruptly ended the meeting, stalking out (Greaves, 1968: 160).

Furious, the peasants gathered in the union hall. There, they denounced the hacienda and decided to seek support from the Trujillo branch of FENCAP, APRA's federation of rural unions. However, when the FENCAP representative came to the hacienda, he supported the position of Don Vicente, and did nothing to encourage peasant action (Greaves, 1968: 161).

The hacendado's power over day-to-day work decisions also seemed arbitrary and excessive to Marla peasants. Greaves describes the employees' frustration at the willful decisions taken by the patron, Don Maximo, about the installation of an electricity motor:

> Rather than be without electricity, Don Maximo directed that another smaller motor be installed. The motor was connected and it was immediately apparent that it ran at too high a velocity. The noise from the generating room could be heard all over. . . . But no one was willing to point out the problem to Don Maximo since such an act would imply that Don Maximo's decision to install the motor was wrong. After two days . . . the noise had increased to a clattering racket. When I mentioned to Don Maximo that the motor made a lot of noise he assured me that this type of motor always sounded that way. The next day the motor would not start at all and the mechanic reported that the engine had suffered serious damage to the pistons, rings, crank shaft and engine block. When I mentioned to Don Maximo that it was too bad that the motor had been ruined, he replied, "Yes, they are very careless." One of the superintendents wryly commented, "there is much carelessness here; responsibility [for the motor]

lies with the employees because the decision was Don Maximo's" (Greaves, 1968: 377).

The assumption of superiority was made not only by the hacendado but also by white-collar employees. Greaves describes one such abuse by an Estrella white-collar employee in the mid-1960s:

I recall sitting one afternoon in a dusty hacienda payroll office in Peru, watching as a minor white-collar functionary assiduously ignored three hacienda workers who needed their official cards in order to visit the traveling physician. The physician came and went, the three ill workers unable to see him because the employee chose to "put them in their place," not getting around to attending them until after the doctor had left (Greaves, 1974: 8-9).

As mentioned in Chapter III, the electoral and party system and the unions were at best marginally effective vehicles for checking the hacendado's power. The significance of electoral and party activity for local peasant participation was limited for various reasons. First, only literates could vote, disqualifying roughly 60 percent of peasants from participation in 1961 (Larson and Bergman, 1969: 364-365). Moreover, the political parties themselves were not radical. In the Virú valley, APRA was allied with some members of the most powerful family in the reigon, the Ganozas; despite the fact that Virú is near Trujillo, the area of greatest APRA strength, the party did little to encourage unionization in the valley's haciendas (Chávez and Paredes, 1970: 53; Rodríguez Suy-Suy, 1965: 13; Elías Minaya, 1969a: 17-19; Greaves, 1968: 18). Only Estrella and the contiguous El Chalán were effectively unionized in this era.

Perhaps most important, the hacendados exercised considerable leverage over the peasants' votes. In Huanca, the hacienda administrator, Chaparro, was the regional leader of the Odríista party, and he served in the national Congress as the senator from Junín. The Odríista party was the most conservative of the three major parties of the 1960s, the most opposed to agrarian reform, but Chaparro cajoled Monte voters to support his candidacy. Political information to Monte residents was channeled through Chaparro to such an extent that they barely knew of other parties. Some men were also afraid that if they did not vote for Chaparro, their sabotage would be discovered, and sanctions applied. In the Virú valley, landowners distorted information about the party affiliation of candidates. Virú peasants were largely pro-APRA, but in the 1963 elections many voted for Belaúnde in the belief that he was the APRA candidate. Apparently, various Virú hacendados encouraged this perception because of their friendship with Marla's patron, who was a brother-in-law to Belaúnde.

Unions were more effective in winning policy benefits for peasants but were vulnerable to the sanctions of the hacendados. As Chapter III pointed out, only about one-third of hacienda peasants were unionized in the 1960s, and many of these were not very active. No permanent union was established in Marla or Monte because incipient union organizers were fired or bribed by the hacendados.[1] The Estrella union was successful because it was difficult for the patron to fire peasants; the hacienda produced commercial hybrid corn seed, and this seed operation required an experienced, skilled labor force. The Estrella union spearheaded a brief strike in 1962 and threatened to strike again several times.

The Peruvian unions of the 1960s were, however, limited in various ways. First, the patron often influenced leadership selection, encouraging malleable candidates (see Chapter VI). Further, the political vigor of the Virú unions was sapped by the controlling influence of regional FENCAP headquarters in Trujillo. Wages for the entire valley were typically set by negotiations in Trujillo among FENCAP officials, government functionaries, and the hacendados. Thus, a strike in one hacienda did not often result in particularly large wage increases for the peasants in that hacienda. For example, despite the 1962 strike in Estrella, eventually only a 3-percent wage increase was established for the entire valley (Elías Minaya, 1969b: 16). A public goods dilemma appeared: because wage settlements usually applied to all haciendas of the region, sites that had not struggled for a raise received the wage victory anyway.

Hence, union meetings in the haciendas were not especially significant to the outcome of a wage struggle. The meetings often merely reported the results of activities at the regional level, as in the union of the contiguous hacienda El Chalán.[2] The relevance of these gatherings was obscure to most members, who were quickly bored by the reports, as at this "typical" meeting:

[1] Peasants in both sites were emphatic on this point. For Monte, the repression and bribing are documented in the "Correspondencia del Gerente General" of hacienda Huanca, for 1947-1952 especially, in the hacienda archive in Lima. Ing. Luis Deustua of COAMA and José Elías Minaya of the Trujillo Ministry of Agriculture also emphasized the restrictions placed by the patron on peasant leadership in the haciendas.

[2] Elías Minaya (1969a: 19) and Greaves (1968: 350-351) concur that the El Chalán and Estrella unions were the most effective in the valley.

The secretary general... begins to drone forth a long list of recommendations made by the regional conference. The report has
little to do with the immediate concerns of the members and soon
they begin to drift out... by the time the report is finished no one
is listening and everyone who remains is hoping the report will
end soon so that the television can be turned on (Greaves, 1968:
282-285).

During one long but important wage battle, the El Chalán union
could not maintain the interest of its members; a dozen members at
meetings was typical (Greaves, 1968: 295).

Even with respect to issues internal to the hacienda, most peasants were not given the chance to make a significant input into the
union's decisions. Issues were discussed in the union assembly, but
not voted upon there; typically, union leaders made the final decision themselves.[3] The scant participation of most peasants in the
actual decision making was apparently favored by the union
leaders, who were typically prosperous, well-educated, and somewhat arrogant in meetings. Most union leaders considered that the
function of union meetings was not discussion of members' demands but education of members. In one El Chalán meeting, an
exasperated union leader proclaimed: "This is like your school, and
you come to listen to classes. And if you don't want to listen, then
go somewhere else to relax" (quoted by Greaves, 1968: 287).

*Incentives for Collective Political Participation
in the Cooperatives, 1973-1977*

Policy incentives for collective political participation rose in the
cooperatives. By participating in the new cooperative structures,
members were able to develop the policies they preferred on various important issues—issues that did not appear to the peasants as
"strictly business" or "minor problems of everyday life." The key
issue of the role of the enterprise director in the enterprise was a
basic one of class relations and authority structure. The common
concern with agro-industrialization reflected the peasants' efforts
to assert their vision of effective agricultural development.
Members' capacity to formulate and transmit demands to regional
authorities increased, as did the number of these demands won by
them. The vast majority of policies and demands of cooperative

[3] See Greaves (1968: 282-285). Although various important grievances were presented at the assembly, the leadership apparently did not formally adopt any.

members were forged autonomously by peasants, without compromises with technicians.

The political structures of the cooperatives were considered to be effective channels for autonomously forging enterprise policies that were favored by the members. In the 1975 survey, respondents were asked why they participated in meetings, and many emphasized the desire to make decisions. Eighty percent of Estrella and Marla respondents and 100 percent of Rachuis respondents cited the councils and/or the General Assembly in answer to the question, "Who make(s) the important decisions here?" In Estrella and Marla, another 11 percent named the councils and/or the General Assembly but also the enterprise director or the government. Only 5 percent indicated "a few top leaders," and merely 4 percent the enterprise director. Elaborated two Marla workers:

We all participate and agree what ought to be done in the enterprise—what to grow, what to buy, and the like (Q1975, 45).

At times there's no unity, and I don't like the meetings. But in general you can learn what's going on and agree about investments and planting. You vote about what you want. Sometimes too we kick out the manager (Q1975, 64).

Members also perceived the collective organizations as effective channels for resolving and transmitting demands and saw that political unity around a demand was important to resolving the concern. Of the Estrella respondents surveyed in 1975, 83 percent said that demands were made through the union, the councils, or the General Assembly; 90 percent of Marla respondents thought so. Only 4 percent of the respondents said the demands were made individually. To explain this phenomenon, many members cited the aphorism "In union lies strength." About General Assemblies, one Estrella respondent said, "We've got to go to put force behind our requests" (Q1975, 1). Members of the councils also indicated that they enjoyed council sessions and found them significant (see Chapter VI).

The effectiveness of the self-management organs seemed to be enhanced by various structural features of the meetings. Meetings were small, including no more than 100 members, except in the peasant communities, and the sites were isolated. In such cooperatives, members knew each other and could easily monitor attendance. The smallness and isolation probably encouraged political participation (Verba and Nie, 1972; Cornelius, 1973: 39-40; Olson,

1965). In most sites, fines were supposed to be charged for non-attendance; in practice, they rarely were, but they still established the expectation of participation.

Membership laws may also have stimulated participation in the cooperatives. Legally, only field workers and not white-collar employees were eligible for cooperative membership,[4] thus barring traditional leaders and suggesting an openness to the lower socio-economic strata. Although this statute was generally ignored, maximum wage laws in the cooperatives discouraged some highly skilled workers from membership. These workers resided in the cooperatives only as "contracted" workers. Although the number of contracted workers was small—5 to 10 percent in Estrella and Marla—they were concentrated in the very highest socioeconomic stratum. The zero-order correlation between economic status and cooperative membership was −.384 in Estrella and −.420 in Marla.

The impact of government laws on membership was greatest in many peasant communities. As mentioned in Chapter II, the peasant-community statute disqualified from membership those who earned most of their income outside the community or from non-agricultural occupations and those who did not live most of the year in the community. If strictly applied, this statute would have disqualified over 50 percent of peasants from membership in many communities. It was not rigorously implemented, but it was used to disqualify the socioeconomic apex in many communities. A few wealthy traders were disqualified in Patca, several businessmen and white-collar employees in Varya, and many brick makers in Agustín. The zero-order correlation between economic status and membership was −.526 in Varya, −.282 in Patca, and −.076 in Agustín. Membership laws were not applied in Monte, allowing technicians to participate in its union. The zero-order correlation coefficient between economic status and membership was only −.066 in this ex-hacienda.

The widespread use of the vote to resolve debate was also critical to making the meetings significant. The only site in which major debates were not resolved by vote was Varya (see Table V.1), and, as will be evident below, changes in political participation in Varya were much less dramatic than in the other sites. The yes/no decision format structured controversy, equalized each member's political weight, and provided concrete results to the meetings.

On the other hand, peasants wanted open debate on issues.

[4]Supreme Decree 240-69-AP, article 7.

TABLE V.1
General Assemblies in Peruvian Cooperatives, 1973-1975

| | Average number of assemblies per year[a] | Percentage of attendants who spoke | Percentage of meeting time in which top 2-3 leaders or government officials spoke | Percentage of assemblies attended by government officials | Percentage of major debates resolved by vote |
|---|---|---|---|---|---|
| IS Huanca | 4 | 30 | 50 | 100 | 95 |
| Monte | 24 | 30 | 70 | 0 | 40 |
| Varya | 8 | 40 | 40 | 0 | 10 |
| Patca | 10 | 5 | 75 | 10 | 40 |
| trella | 5 | 30 | 65 | 85 | 80 |
| arla | 5 | 20 | 65 | 85 | 80 |

SOURCE: Observations and reports for each site between 1973 and 1975. Information is less orough for Patca and Varya. Percentages are rough annual averages.
[a] Number of assemblies varies somewhat year to year.

Members seemed proud, if also awed and nervous, to offer their ideas to the group and hold its attention. Such discussion did occur in all the research sites except Patca; only in Patca did the percentage of meeting participants who spoke at a typical assembly fall below 20 percent (see Table V.1). Some Patca members grumbled that council leaders presented their own positions on agenda items at great length without seriously listening to members' comments.

What were the major political issues in the cooperatives? The most intense and almost universal concern was the establishment of a "correct" role for the enterprise director and other technicians in the cooperative, including the establishment of "correct" wages for them. (It is interesting to note that in Yugoslavia, the only other nation where self-managed enterprises were legally required to hire technicians, the issue of their role and salary was also predominant [Comisso, 1977: Chapter 7]). A second critical issue was the relationship between key socioeconomic or geographical groups in the cooperatives. In various enterprises, groups of dubious compatibility had been integrated into one cooperative, and members soon questioned the government's wisdom on these decisions, asking for a "re-structuring" of the cooperative, generally to separate the two groups. A third issue of marked concern was agro-industrialization. Members saw agro-industrialization as necessary for economic development and pressed the regional Ministry of Agriculture for funds for agro-industrial projects. To a considerable degree, average members became involved in these negotiations. A final important issue was whom to elect to the enterprise councils, a question that will be discussed in the following chapter.

Cooperative members' greatest concern seemed to be the role of enterprise directors and other technicians in the cooperative. On the one hand, members knew that technicians had agricultural expertise; many also felt that technicians could check corruption and encourage work discipline. On the other hand, they feared that a technician would try to assume the powers and prerogatives of the patron, and many also sought revenge upon the enterprise director for the abuses of the patron. Control over technicians' wages and the right to fire the director were the key means by which members could assert their power vis-à-vis the technicians.

Peasants' fears about technicians were not irrational. Most enterprise directors realized that they had to be respectful toward the peasants or else lose their jobs, but at heart they still felt innately superior to peasants. In moments of rage or intoxication, the directors often blurted out their feelings. For example, during a drinking bout, SAIS Huanca's first director called a peasant "a stupid animal"; he was fired within weeks. To hide their sense of superiority, directors were frequently reserved and terse, avoiding drinking sprees. The 1973-1976 Huanca director, for example, was considered "antiseptic," but he kept his job for three years.

In most cooperatives, members' desire for the expertise of the technicians was overwhelmed by their fears that technicians would usurp status and power. Thus, technicians' salaries were cut, and many directors were fired. The average annual salary of a director in 1974 was approximately 15,000 soles a month, or under $4,000 a year,[5] rather meager remuneration for a technician with at least

[5] The approximate salary is my calculation from the registration cards of directors at the *Segundo Conversatorio Nacional para Dirigentes y Administradores de Empresas Campesinas*, January 1974. Roughly 50 directors attended, from seven different agrarian zones. Agrarian Zone IV (south coast) was heavily represented. Declines in directors' salaries in the agro-industrial sugar cooperatives and in the major highlands wool enterprises were reported in interviews with Dr. Alberto Stewart, former head of CECOAAP, the sugar marketing agency, in Lima, March 1975; with Dr. Carlos Aramburu of CENCIRA, in Lima, October 1973, and with Ing. Luis Deustua of COAMA, in Huancayo, on his visit to several highlands SAIS in August 1973. Information on changes in salary levels in smaller enterprises is scant.

some university education working in a remote area. In the three cooperatives in this research, the record as of mid-1977 stood at six fired enterprise directors, three in Huanca and three in Marla. This record is typical; in many enterprises, even more directors were fired, such as the sugar complex Tumán where three were dismissed in one year (Agut, 1975: 511).

The new assertiveness of peasants toward technicians and directors was apparent to most observers:

> For years, the worker lived in a system in which the technicians were never at fault, and every sanction was applied on the workers; it was always the workers who suffered. Now the workers have the power and they are vindictive; they want to throw the blame for all the problems on the technician. (an "observer," quoted in Horton, 1974: 159).

> It is very difficult to work in the cooperatives.... It is fascinating—like driving a car at 120 miles per hour...you have no security...at any moment they can throw you out.... It is definitely not work for timid men or violent men, or men with heart trouble! (a director quoted in Horton, 1974: 156).

The tension between peasants and technicians was clearly evident one night in Estrella in a conversation between the vice-president of the Administrative Council and the new director, José Prado. Intoxicated, the vice-president was both combative, letting the director know that Estrella didn't want him, and insecure, referring frequently to his position in the cooperative, as if it gave him a right to speak. The director was uncomfortable; he succeeded in avoiding a confrontation, but he was terse and evasive:

Vice-Pres.: Excuse me, Engineer, that there was no council session today. It was the president's birthday. I am the vice-president.

Director: That's okay. We can have the meeting tomorrow.

Vice-Pres.: Engineer, I want very much to talk with you.

Director: We are going to talk. We're going to work together so that Estrella progresses.

Vice-Pres.: To progress, if that's what's important, Engineer, we need to plant beans, because the price of beans is very good. Excuse me, Engineer.

Director: Yes, we'll plant beans. Also, we're going to plant less tobacco.

Vice-Pres.: But the tobacco crop has come out really well.

Director: But the costs are very high. We're going to have to study this.

Vice-Pres.: Well, you analyze it, you analyze it nicely.

Director: Yes.

Vice-Pres.: Excuse me, Engineer, but you know that all the council members didn't want a director. We don't know you.... Everything was fine, we were fine before you came.

Director: Yes, I know. I was the administrator of a hacienda near here. I even had a little piece of land in the valley.

Vice-Pres.: I know my letters. I'm not educated like you, Engineer, but I know my letters. And the president, he does too, he speaks well. He's a good person.

Director: Yes.

Vice-Pres.: I am forty-five years old. I watch the tobacco ovens. You're an Engineer, you're the patron.

Director: No, I'm not the patron. I'm the enterprise director.

Vice-Pres.: What do you think of this hacienda Estrella?

Director: We must put into operation some of the land that's not being fully utilized. But look, it's late now, why not go to bed? We are going to talk about all this.

Vice-Pres.: I'm sorry, Engineer, but I'm the vice-president of the Administrative Council. ...(He leaves, awkwardly hugging the director, who reluctantly permits the brief hug.)

For various reasons members' wages were not the subject of intense debate. Although in most sites there was a consensus that wages should be raised as much as possible, during most of the period of this study, the government was seeking to limit wage increases. Members recognized that some salary increases were semi-illicit in nature; thus increases were often discussed primarily in the Administrative Council and only tacitly approved by the members. However, members' wages were an important issue in some circumstances, particularly when the dominant group in the cooperative were not the salaried "workers" themselves; in these cases, workers organized through unions to press wage demands.

The only potentially key economic issue not discussed in the assemblies was the agrarian debt. At first, cooperative members were not aware of the extent of the debt obligation. Then, just as word about the debt spread, inflation jumped, reducing the significance of the debt and the saliency of the issue.

Proponents of corporatist models for Velasco's new political structures contend that even decision making at the local level was compromised by the influence of officials and technicians in cooperative meetings. In fact, however, although officials and technicians attended General Assemblies in major sites (see Table V.1), they were rarely outspoken and even more rarely influential. For example, government officials and of course the directors themselves were usually opposed to the dismissal of the directors, but they were fired anyway. SINAMOS often supported the candidacy of one particular peasant over another, but without success; for example, in Estrella in 1973, SINAMOS was against the recall of the Administrative Council president, but the recall was approved by majority vote. In Huanca, the Ministry of Agriculture tried without success throughout 1977 to unite the workers and members in the SAIS behind the candidacy of any new manager.

There were, however, some years in some sites when technicians were influential. Of all the sites visited over the five years of the study, technicians played the largest role in Huanca. They were active in the union of the SAIS ex-haciendas because they were not prohibited from membership and leadership positions, as they were in the formal Huanca cooperative. Along with members of the Marxist CCP, the technicians encouraged the workers to demand a greater share of power and profits in the SAIS. (In contrast to the thrust of critiques of self-management, technicians were most influential in a union.) As the conflict between members and workers worsened during 1976 and 1977, technicians were caught up in the battle and to some extent compelled to take sides. In other sites, technicians seemed to influence decisions only when they had won the respect of enterprise members and when their arguments were solid—as was often the case in Estrella by 1975.

The following sections elaborate the various political issues that emerged in the research sites. These descriptions indicate the importance of enterprise decisions to members, and the peasants' capacity to resolve many concerns effectively through the political organs of the cooperative, if peasants were united and active. In short, policy benefits were available to peasants upon their active and collective political participation.

*SAIS Huanca.* Of the three research enterprises, SAIS Huanca was the most politically active. The role of enterprise technicians was an important issue in galvanizing members' political vigor. Moreover, as a major national enterprise, the SAIS had considerable political clout even in Lima, and it was able to advance demands to Lima officials with some success. Further, as will be discussed with respect to Monte, the conflict between comuneros and trabajadores was serious; resolution of the problem seemed likely, but not certain, in 1977.

As elsewhere, Huanca members were suspicious of technicians' ambitions and resentful of their relatively high salaries. Throughout 1972-1977, top technicians were fired and their salaries reduced. The first Huanca director was fired in early 1973 for insulting a council member; the second was fired in early 1976 amid charges of corruption. As a very large enterprise, Huanca also originally employed some sixteen technicians in the Development Division; about half of these men either were fired or resigned because of low salaries, and by mid-1973 the division included merely eight men, a number that did not increase.[6] Reductions in salaries and benefits were massively approved in three General Assemblies in late 1972 and early 1973. The salaries of the manager, the assistant manager, and Development Division technicians were reduced about 25 percent (McClintock, 1975b: 260-265; Montoya, 1974: 96-97). Benefits such as the use of enterprise vehicles were cut sharply. Subsequently, technicians' wages were not allowed to rise, signifying a large reduction in real terms because of the skyrocketing inflation. Between 1974 and 1977 the director's salary stayed almost the same and the average worker's salary nearly doubled.[7] Moreover, as in many large cooperatives,[8] technicians were often replaced from the ranks of Huanca peasants themselves, who, it was apparently hoped, would be less arrogant even if perhaps less knowledgeable. Further, whereas the number of "top technician" positions declined, the over-all number of white-collar employees increased about 35 percent (see Chapter VIII), and most of these new slots were filled by Huanca-born individuals.

The SAIS placed various economic demands upon the government. One major council initiative was an effort to export more wool in 1973-1974. The government wanted the wool to be sold

[6] See employment lists in *Jatari-Urayi*, 1973, and in the Huanca budgets for 1974-1975, 1975-1976, and 1977-1978.
[7] Figures are from the Huanca budgets for 1974-1975, 1975-1976, and 1977-1978. Enterprise director's salary was set at 32,000 soles monthly for 1974-1975, 33,000 for 1975-1976, and 32,310 for 1977-1978.
[8] See especially Middlebrook (1972: 86).

domestically in order to aid Peru's textile producers, but the price of wool was skyrocketing on the international market, and the SAIS wanted to sell abroad. Huanca united with the three other major SAIS of the central highlands to demand permission to sell wool abroad. After several meetings, the government did allow the SAIS to export 50 percent of their wool (de Zutter, 1975: 198-199).

SAIS Huanca was eager to industrialize, aspiring to manufacture its own textiles from its wool. Again, all four major SAIS of the central highlands worked together to gain government funds for agro-industrialization projects. Although the Velasco government did not accept the demand for funds for textile manufacture, it did agree to support meat-processing facilities. This agreement was subsequently undermined by the Morales Bermúdez government (see Chapter IX).

Huanca's political activities provide no evidence of co-optation or control by government officials. The Huanca councils rejected various government initiatives that conflicted with peasant-community preferences. For example, technicians in the Huancayo Ministry of Agriculture and in the SAIS felt that the peasant communities should be required to put a larger percenatge of their share of SAIS profits into "productive investments." The SAIS General Assembly never adopted any regulations on investment, however. The assembly once criticized a community's purchase of a tape recorder, but it did not prohibit even this "investment." Similarly, when Huancayo SINAMOS officials hoped to equalize and cooperativize landholdings in peasant communities, the SAIS refused to promote the program. In 1977, during the crisis over the employment of a director by the SAIS, the Huancayo ministry advocated a higher salary for the position to attract a capable technician from outside the enterprise, to no avail. The government did make one critical investment decision for the enterprise, for a large irrigation canal, but it was made prior to the establishment of the SAIS.

*Monte.* Monte was also politically active. Gradually, Monte built political unity among its two distinct socioeconomic groups and with other ex-haciendas, putting much greater weight behind its demands, and thus increasingly winning them.

The major demands in Monte concerned its relationship to the larger enterprise, SAIS Huanca. Monte resented its inclusion in the SAIS, because of the traditional conflict between workers and comuneros in the area, and because the SAIS statutes favored the peasant communities politically and economically. The workers could neither sway votes in the General Assembly nor elect representatives to key council positions. Ex-hacienda workers received less than 3 percent of SAIS profits and votes, although they did all the work in the SAIS. Workers were enraged. Said one Monte union leader, "With the SAIS, they talk of participation, but we don't get any. They decided that the Monte administrator would be promoted. We didn't even know. We don't choose the new administrator. We don't even know."[9]

To fight for a better deal for the ex-haciendas, a union was formed in October 1972. At first the union was active only in the most prosperous ex-haciendas, Monte and Loroya. The SAIS was trying to equalize wages and the number of privately owned sheep among the various ex-haciendas, and thus the ex-haciendas with the highest wages and most animals were especially hostile toward the SAIS. In June 1973, Monte leaders planned to organize politically with workers of a third ex-hacienda after a soccer game, but, when Monte lost, the plan dissolved in a drunken brawl.

Within Monte and Loroya, the union was also at first limited, oriented toward the more prosperous semi-skilled workers. The Monte union was led by its only white-collar member, the accountant Miguel Maray. Other key organizers were also semi-skilled workers. By mid-1973, about 30 men attended each Monte session; approximately two-thirds were semi-skilled workers. In May 1973, the union called an emergency meeting of the SAIS General Assembly in order to advance its demands. The most important demand concerned only the semi-skilled workers: permission for them to retain at least 25 privately owned sheep (Montoya, 1974: 58).

The members at the General Assembly voted down the union's demands. Not long afterward, the plea for union recognition was rejected by government authorities. The union leadership feared repression from SINAMOS: the police visited and questioned Maray. Rumors of treachery within the union were rampant.

But repression did not occur, and the union meetings continued, with a greater awareness by the leaders of the need to mobilize more workers behind its demands. Maray began to emphasize the need for a salary raise that, unlike the demand about privately owned sheep, would benefit not only the semi-skilled workers but also the shepherds. An increase from 50 to 100 soles per day was asked. Interested in the meetings for the first time, shepherds

[9] Interview in Monte, with the warehouse supervisor, in June 1973.

began to attend. They soon advanced new demands of special concern to them—overtime pay and holiday pay. (Unlike the semi-skilled workers, shepherds were expected to tend the animals day and night, seven days a week.) The semi-skilled workers agreed to include these demands in the union's proposals to the SAIS. Representation of the ex-haciendas on the SAIS councils—so the workers could at least know what was said if not determine votes—was also included as a new demand.

The union's drive for a salary raise was encouraged by various small victories during the last six months of 1973. A social worker who blocked a political movement among Monte women and who perhaps reported on union activities was dismissed upon the union's request. The demand for the repair of semi-skilled workers' houses was accepted. When a teacher who had been fired for raping a young girl returned to Monte, demanded his reinstatement, and vengefully denounced Maray, Monte's position on the issue was supported by the SAIS councils. A September 1973 General Assembly finally accepted the semi-skilled workers' earlier demand about sheep ownership; private ownership of a maximum of 60 sheep was allowed, with larger cash wages for those who owned under 60 and wage deductions for those who owned over 60.

Each victory strengthened the union. By March 1974, the degree of mobilization was impressive. Attendance at Monte union meetings skyrocketed from 30 percent to 75 percent of Monte men; a much larger percentage of shepherds was represented, almost as large as that of semi-skilled workers. Through the new Service Cooperative, the workers saved their share of SAIS profits to use as a strike fund if necessary. By March 1974, they had collected roughly $2,500, a significant sum for such a union. Monte also finally won the support of the contiguous ex-hacienda with which it had previously fought, as well as the support of the ex-haciendas in the SAIS.

The mobilization of the ex-haciendas worried the SAIS Administrative Council. The president wanted to maintain SAIS harmony and feared a possible strike. Despite the manager's opposition, the General Assembly in March 1974 granted a wage increase of 60 percent, from 50 to 80 soles per day. At the June 1974 assembly, the workers were also allowed one representative on the SAIS councils, to be elected by the Service Cooperative.

The success of the ex-hacienda union stimulated new demands. Between 1975 and 1977, all the Huanca ex-haciendas were strongly behind demands for annual 50-percent wage increases and for restructuring the SAIS itself. The workers wanted at least 50 percent of the votes in the SAIS General Assembly and councils and 50 percent of SAIS profits. Of course, the comuneros did not want to give so much power and money back to the workers.

When Huanca's enterprise director of some three years was implicated in corruption charges and fired in January 1976, the conflict between comuneros and workers came to a head over the issue of the selection of a new director. The previous assistant director, Julio Melchor, was given the post as interim manager. However, Melchor had long been associated with the workers' cause; he had worked in Huanca since the early 1960s, and had many close ties in the ex-haciendas. Melchor had also been the administrator in Monte during 1972 and 1973, and had supported the unionization effort there. In the director's role, Melchor soon began to advance the workers' cause before the Huancayo Ministry of Agriculture. Angry, the comuneros in the council suspended Melchor and promoted to the manager's post Eduardo García, a veterinarian who had only joined the enterprise in 1973. García had relatively few ties to the workers, but was inexperienced and, it was widely thought, incompetent. At this point, the conflict between workers and comuneros became a battle. Bridges were destroyed and sheep stolen and killed. The workers wanted Melchor and a restructuring of the SAIS; the comuneros wanted García and, at most, minimal changes in the SAIS structure.

According to all reports, both sides took their grievances to the Ministry of Agriculture and asked the ministry to intervene.[10] The intervention took place on June 1, 1976, but it had relatively little impact on the enterprise. With the accelerating economic crunch and political confusion of the post-Velasco period, the goal of officials in the ministry seemed to be personal survival. The intervenor's primary aim was apparently to ascend to the director's position himself, and he achieved this end by siding with the comuneros on key political issues. However, he also promoted greater participation for technicians in the SAIS assembly. He thereby alienated both comuneros and workers, and was forced to resign in early 1977. Several more months of conflict over the appointment

[10] The Administrative Council's own report is given in the *Memoria Anual* of SAIS Huanca, 1975-1976, pp. 7-9. There was agreement on this point among the various people interviewed in Huancayo in July 1977, including Juan Casas of the Huancayo CENCIRA; Miguel Candiotti, of the Huancayo Ministry of Agriculture at that time; the fired "intervenor" himself, who was back in the Huancayo Ministry; and Aurelio Osores, an ex-president of the SAIS.

of a new director and the restructuring of the SAIS ensued, with many heated meetings among comuneros, workers, and officials at the Huancayo ministry. As of July 1977, it appeared that the ministry would support García rather than Melchor as the new director, if a competent third candidate could not be found. The ministry was finally convinced, however, that the SAIS had to be restructured to give the workers a much larger share of votes and profits, and it took up the issue with the Lima Ministry of Agriculture.[11]

Some restructuring of the SAIS in favor of the workers may well occur. The structural change would attest to the strong political mobilization of the workers behind the demand, a much stronger mobilization than the more dispersed comuneros had achieved. The comuneros also lacked the power to threaten SAIS production. The actual merits of the case seem ambiguous. On the one hand, as the workers did almost all the work in the SAIS, it could be said that they deserved most of the profits and power. On the other hand, the average comunero was less well-off than the average worker, in part because haciendas had stolen peasant-community land in the past, and some measure of redress seemed just.

*Estrella.* Estrella was also politically vigorous and quite successful in resolving key political issues. It was the only one of the three research cooperatives to resolve successfully the conflict between the two major groups originally in the cooperative, and the only one to achieve a viable relationship with its director.

At its inception, CAP Estrella had included two distinct socioeconomic groups, the ex-sharecroppers (feudatarios) and workers. The ex-sharecroppers were generally more prosperous than workers; they held their own private parcels and did not work for the cooperative, which they had joined only on expectations of profits and legal security for their own plots. The ex-sharecroppers were the majority, however, and through 1973 they were also more mobilized than the workers, turning out in larger numbers for meetings. When the vice-president of the Administrative Council, Tomás Torres, a very wealthy ex-sharecropper, denounced the pro-worker president for raising his own salary, two General Assemblies were held; the ex-sharecropper majority was able to recall the president, and as a result Torres rose to the position in mid-1973. The new ex-sharecropper leadership was notoriously cor-

---

[11] This conclusion, like most of the material in this discussion of the conflict over the new director, is based on the interviews cited in the previous footnote.

rupt. It tried to evade workers' demands as much as possible by endlessly postponing General Assemblies.

Increasingly outraged, workers started to organize in late 1973. The Estrella union was revitalized and began to meet once a month. The cooperative's education committee was also galvanized; it successfully advanced projects for a library and a new sports stadium, as well as numerous social activities that provided funds for the workers' cause. In the few General Assemblies that were held, the workers angrily confronted the ex-sharecropper leadership. They asked Torres to open the cooperative's books to the assembly, a demand supported by the SINAMOS official in attendance. The demand was granted. Worker participation in the assemblies jumped; whereas only about 20 percent of Estrella workers attended the General Assembly in early 1973, and 50 percent in late 1973, by 1974 around 75 percent did.

In late 1974, the workers took up their problem in Trujillo with the Ministry of Agriculture and SINAMOS. Other cooperatives had suffered the same problem, and the concern was transmitted to Lima. Finally in 1975, an official decision to separate ex-sharecroppers from the cooperative was made for Estrella and other enterprises in similar plights. In April 1975, only workers were invited to the General Assembly for new council elections. They elected workers to the council and, for the first time, Estrella enjoyed committed leadership.

Under considerable pressure from the Ministry of Agriculture, the new Administrative Council hired Estrella's first director, José Prado. Prado was chosen for the job primarily because he was known and liked by Pedro Vásquez, the cooperative's truckdriver and an Administrative Council leader during 1975-1977. Prado was an effective director. From a relatively humble background, educated in a provincial university, Prado would not have been considered qualified as the administrator of an enterprise of Estrella's size in the 1960s. Perhaps in part for this reason, he was respectful toward workers, as suggested by his conversation with the Administrative Council vice-president quoted above. Prado did not allow his friendship with Vásquez to develop into an exclusive political alliance. He was careful to distribute considerable amounts of Estrella's produce to everyone, an important symbol of his commitment to the entire enterprise.

Prado helped the cooperative economically. He devoted great attention to the analysis of potentially lucrative investment and production options for Estrella. He worked hard, getting out into the fields morning and afternoon to check cultivation, and willing to "get his hands dirty," as the peasants put it. Prado's hard work set a good example that was increasingly followed.

Perhaps most important, Prado did not try to influence community decisions that were beyond his sphere of competence and responsibility. Although Vásquez had some wheeler-dealer proclivities, Prado was indebted to him and did not try to check this. The director stayed out of decisions about the admission of temporary workers into the cooperative. However, on issues within his competence, he was influential, promoting for example the cultivation of sugar cane in Estrella. On a wage issue in 1975, he was also influential, encouraging an increase in benefits rather than wages on the grounds that the increase in benefits would mean more financially as it would not be subject to social security deductions. At the union meeting where Prado advanced this argument, discussion ensued for some 45 minutes, with at least ten workers raising various points. Finally, in a vote by hands, Prado's position won, 45 to 15. On the whole, Prado's stands seemed sound. Thus they won support but, as this example indicates, not without questioning analysis by members.

Prado's success was symbolized by the salary increases approved for him. He won a 20 percent raise in 1976 that put his salary at 30,000 soles a month. Although this raise did not compensate for inflation, and his salary was less than that paid to administrators in the haciendas, it was the highest in the valley at the time.[12]

Why was Estrella able to establish a viable relationship with a director? First, Prado was actually chosen by Estrella leaders; he was a relatively known quantity. Second, Prado was more of an equal in the community than was the case elsewhere; his background was modest, and Estrella members were prosperous. Also, Prado was committed and sensitive.

During 1976 and 1977, Estrella was rather quiet politically; the key issues had been resolved. The major concern was economic advancement, and particularly the development of a processing

---

[12] The skyrocketing inflation of 1975-1977 and the deteriorating value of the Peruvian currency impede analysis of the real meaning of these salary levels. Data on salary levels for administrators in the haciendas is scant. Chávez and Paredes (1970: 95-96) report that in 1970 the Marla administrator earned 22,000 soles a month. Given that inflation between 1970 and 1976 was over 150 percent, a salary of 30,000 soles in 1976 was well below a salary of 22,000 in 1970. Information on the salaries of managers in the valley other than managers in Estrella and Marla was provided by Nestor Rojas Bueno of CENCIRA, in Trujillo, July 22, 1977.

mill for its sugar cane. The cooperative was seeking investment funds for the mill from the government and private sources; however, by this date funds were scarce and the outcome of Estrella's effort was uncertain (see Chapter IX).

*Marla.* Marla was less vigorous politically than Huanca or Estrella. Perhaps because of the members' previous experience with a particularly abusive patron (the "Don Maximo" mentioned above), Marla was preoccupied by efforts to fire all enterprise directors. The peasants enjoyed nothing so much as mimicking the technicians. One older peasant, a mechanic with a reticent air and crouched posture, came alive whenever he mimicked the arrogant manners and bowlegged walk of one Marla director. Although members succeeded in firing the directors, they seemed to have limited political will on other issues, such as the conflict between two geographical sectors in the enterprise and agro-industrialization.

Three directors had been dismissed from Marla as of July 1977. The first was fired in 1972 on the grounds that he could not maintain discipline. More resistance was expected to the firing of the second director, both from the Ministry of Agriculture and from residents who suspected corruption in Marla offices and thought the director could block it. Thus, to be rid of the administrator, several council leaders devised a plot to show his incompetence. They stole into the warehouse, removed the asparagus fertilizer, and substituted plant-killer. A week later the asparagus crop died, and members accused the administrator of being so ignorant that he didn't know plant-killer from fertilizer. In an emergency General Assembly in early 1973, the director was dismissed, and a law suit was launched against him.

Over the long run, however, the members' plot proved unwise. The loss of the asparagus crop damaged Marla financially, and the Ministry of Agriculture became concerned about Marla's liquidity. The ministry argued that a new director would solve Marla's problems. Marla, however, was happy with the performance of Ramón Tagle as "administrator"; of peasant stock, Tagle had considerable agricultural experience, but only a secondary-school education, and thus could not qualify as a director by the Ministry of Agriculture's criteria. Finally, Marla was threatened with loss of its bank loan if it did not hire a new director with a one-year contract.

Under this pressure, Marla did hire a new director in June 1974. But he was intensely disliked, considered a "brute," "snobbish," and "elitist." He was dismissed at the end of his contract. Another director was hired in 1976, but he was criticized for opposite reasons—for laxity and incompetence. He was paid only 20,000 soles a month or less than half the 1970 administrator's salary in real terms (Chávez and Paredes, 1970: 95-96). He too departed at the end of his contract.

In contrast to Huanca and Estrella, Marla was troubled not by a cleavage between two socioeconomic groups, but by a cleavage between two geographical sectors. The conflict was not resolved, either by compromise, as appeared likely in Huanca, or by separation of one group from the cooperative, as in Estrella. Divided by a river that could not be crossed by vehicle or horse in the rainy season, when it required almost two hours to reach one bank from another, Marla residents perceived themselves as either "northern" or "southern" bank residents. All the cooperative meetings and functions took place on the northern bank. The residents of the southern side resented their travel burden. In part because they were less likely to participate in Marla activities than northern bank members, the southern bank residents were also more skeptical of collaboration.

The division between Marla's geographical sectors was evident at General Assemblies. On many issues, the positions of southern bank residents won. A paradox thus emerged: in the center of the enterprise, northern bank residents tended to be most knowledgeable and interested in the cooperative and to be elected as leaders, but the General Assembly was dominated by southern bank residents allied with some skeptical northern bank residents. Their most important victory was the defeat of a motion by council leaders for the installation of modern housing. The southern bank residents opposed the proposal because it implied their moving to the northern side and probably transferring their private animals from their backyards to a cooperative.

The result of southern bank domination was an increasing disinclination of the council leaders to call meetings. A more appropriate resolution to the problem would have been to locate new social services and hold half the assemblies in the southern bank, but such a proposal was not made forcefully by southern bank members. They seemed eager to divide the cooperative, but yet did not push this option strongly either.

Like Huanca and Estrella, Marla was eager to industrialize, and hoped to persuade the Trujillo Ministry of Agriculture to allocate to the enterprise an asparagus-canning factory that the patron had built in the 1960s. The Ministry of Agriculture rejected Marla's proposal, however, arguing that the factory had been an economic disaster for the patron and that there was no evidence that it would be otherwise for the cooperative; the Ministry suggested that another kind of canning factory, able to can various products, might be more viable.[13] Moreover, Marla was in considerable economic difficulty and payment for the factory would have been difficult. Over all, Marla did not seem as successful as Huanca or Estrella in building support for agro-industrialization among its members or in negotiating solutions with authorities.

*Patca and Varya.* The SAIS peasant communities perceived new funds and resources as the major potential benefit of the SAIS and wanted to win as large a share of these benefits as possible. In this effort, Patca was more successful than Varya. Among the reasons for Patca's greater success was its unity; Patca put its entire political weight behind its requests to the SAIS.

Patca's General Assemblies approved the allocation of SAIS profits, petitions for loans, and other benefits. Typically the leaders reported on allocations that the SAIS might make for Patca, implying that Patca's adoption of the SAIS's priorities would benefit the community. Debate in Patca was limited, and this frustrated some members, but decisions were made effectively. Patca allocated its share of SAIS profits fruitfully—in a new weaving center, additions to the school, and a cooperative store. Patca also issued many requests to the SAIS and won more benefits than the average community from the SAIS: use of ram studs, aid with new infrastructure developments, use of SAIS equipment, and visits from SAIS technicians.

Patca also ventured various claims against other entities. The peasants launched a law suit against a mining company that had ceased to operate in the community but had refused to grant Patca rights to the hydroelectric power from the river running first through the company's land and then through Patca. Patca won the suit and, as of 1977, was beginning an electrification project with SAIS funds. The community was also involved in a land dispute with a contiguous community, a dispute that one side "won" only to be re-challenged a few months later by the other.

Of all the research sites, Varya was the least successful in formu-

[13] Interview with José Elías Minaya, of Trujillo Ministry of Agriculture, in Trujillo, July 22, 1977.

lating and resolving demands. The failure resulted, at least in part, from conflict between the community center and outlying regions. Varya's center was surrounded by eight distinct hamlets, most of which were over two hours' walk from the center. About one-third of Varya's families lived in the center, and two-thirds in the outlying hamlets. The hamlet residents resented the distance that their children had to travel to school and wanted their own schools. They also grumbled that SAIS technicans devoted all their attention to the center. In addition, the center and the hamlets were severely divided over the allocation of SAIS profits. The center wanted a road to link it to the railroad to Huancayo. But a poor road already tied several hamlets to a second thoroughfare to Huancayo; hamlet residents preferred that this road be repaired.

During 1973 and 1974, meeting after meeting was held to discuss the allocation of SAIS profits. Debate was long and diffuse. Frequently, entirely different proposals would be made, such as investment in an irrigation system, the school, or the church. No vote was ever taken. As of May 1975, Varya's share of the SAIS profits was still in the bank. Varya was also unable to develop formal requests for other benefits from the SAIS.

Varya successfully resolved some issues, however. In particular, the futility of the 1973-1974 debates alerted many peasants to the inadequate leadership of the community. Although peasants had tried and failed to depose the mayor earlier, by 1974 more peasants were mobilized against him, and a new mayor was chosen who seemed to be sincerely interested in Varya's advancement.

In part because of the leadership change, Varya grew more politically mobilized in 1976 and 1977. Rather than choosing one project from the various options, the community granted some funds to all. The road to the railroad advanced, the second road was repaired, school additions were begun, and a cow cooperative was considered. However, these advances on so many fronts were facilitated by the ascendance of a Varya man to the vice-presidency and then presidency of the Huanca Administrative Council during 1975-1977.

*Incentives for Collective Political Participation*
*in the Control Sites, 1963-1975*

The incentives for collective political participation in the control sites, especially Virú, were more limited than in the cooperatives. In Virú, most key policies were decided by superior regional authorities, not by the community. In contrast, as a peasant community, Agustín established new political organizations that helped it to resolve at least some community concerns.

*Virú.* In the 1960s, the important decisions in Virú were made not by all community members but by a few wealthy families. The most critical policy concerned irrigation, because the village was totally dependent on irrigation. During the 1960s, wealthy landowners established and dominated an "irrigation committee," which consistently allocated disproportionate shares of water to the landowners' farms (Elías Minaya, 1969: 11). APRA was also led by prosperous families and did not try to change water allocation policies or the extremely unequal land distribution in the village (Rodríguez Suy-Suy, 1965; Elías Minaya, 1969; Chávez and Paredes, 1970). In the 1970s, land and water distribution became more equal, but by government mandate rather than by community action.

Although in the 1960s major economic policy decisions were not made by the villagers, some less basic decisions were, largely because of Belaúnde's policy of allowing municipalities to elect their own mayors and to call open meetings (*cabildos abiertos*). Although wealthy landowners tended to win Virú's elections, the elections fostered political interest. Several meetings were effective in pressing demands upon the community leadership. In 1968, for example, Viruñeros thought that a community official had stolen the town's electricity generator, and they staged a massive meeting to demand its return. The generator was returned. In 1970, the community was upset by evidence of the corruption of its priest. Again, Viruñeros turned out heavily for a meeting and demanded that the priest leave. The priest did finally depart.

Under Velasco, however, Virú and other rural municipalities lost their control over local affairs. Mayors were once again appointed by the regional capital, and the role of Virú's mayor was rather patronal (see Chapter VI). As Virú rejected peasant-community status, it was not required to hold any meetings. During my research, no meetings were scheduled by community residents.

Government agencies failed to spur participation. The only active agency in Virú was a housing renovation organization. Officials visited Virú once every few months to hold a meeting. The meetings were entirely directed by officials and offered information only, not debate. The agency drew up plans for modern but small and compact houses in the community, apparently without tapping community opinion. The housing plans did not meet Viruñeros' approval, and eventually had to be given up.

*Agustín.* In considerable part through the new peasant-community structures, Agustín peasants became more politically active in the 1970s and were able to achieve new policies that favored the socio-economic majority in the community, the comuneros, over the minority, the brick makers. Since the early 1960s, comuneros were upset by the brick makers' digging large pits into fertile earth to get clay for bricks. The pits prevented agriculture in the area and were dangerous because they were easy to fall into at night. The brick makers not only typically failed to restore land devastated by their excavations but also wanted more land, arguing that a large area was owned by the church, which was controlled by the brick makers. The comuneros argued that the land belonged to the community.

The brick makers dominated Agustín in the 1960s in part through devious strategies and the manipulation of political party contacts in Huancayo (Alberti, 1974: 125). With the new community structure, however, the brick makers' position eroded; the peasant-community statute disqualified many brick makers from participating in meetings. Subsequently, many were requalified semi-illicitly, but still the weapon of potential disqualification strengthened the comuneros' position. The vote was also used more rigorously, consolidating the comuneros' advantage as a majority. An Administrative Council opposed to the brick makers was elected, and immediately upon inauguration the council launched the struggle to regain the disputed land (Alberti, 1974: 189-190). The Administrative Council president pursued the suit against the church vigorously, and in 1973 won back the land. A new community center was built on the recovered lands.

Brick making continued, but in a restricted area. The brick makers submitted quietly to the comuneros' political dominance. Even after their requalification as community members, they often did not bother to go to Agustín meetings. They knew they had little to gain there. The comuneros also recognized that the brick makers contributed greatly to the prosperity of Agustín and did not try to frustrate the industry further.

Several other important issues were taken up by Agustín peasants. The councils promoted several projects—a day care facility, a road to the high-altitude grazing lands, and the community center. At General Assemblies, peasants demanded a voice in the election of the mayor, who, as in Virú, was again appointed by regional authorities. In the final months of 1973, residents applied political pressure for the removal of their mayor. The mayor was removed, but amid considerable uncertainty about his replacement.

## CHANGES IN ATTITUDES TOWARD POLITICAL PARTICIPATION

As cooperative members became aware of the new incentives for collective political participation, their attitudes toward it became more favorable. Cooperative residents were more positive toward political union in 1974 than in 1969, and they felt more politically efficacious. At first, the peasants' attitudes resembled idealistic exhortations, but by 1975 they were expressed with greater assurance. Such attitudes were also more equally distributed among all socioeconomic strata in the cooperatives. By and large 1975 attitudes continued to prevail in 1977, although a degree of skepticism was evident in Marla, where policy benefits had been limited.

Attitudes toward political union were much more positive in 1974 than in 1969. Table V.2 reveals responses to an item about political union in 1969 and 1974. Asked whether to improve the life of the people in the place, everyone should unite, or each person should solve his own problems, 75 percent of the respondents opted to unite in 1974, versus 49 percent in 1969. The biggest jump was registered in Monte—from 36 percent choosing to unite in 1969 to 80 percent in 1974. Attitudes toward political unity also became more positive in the control site Agustín, but the percentage difference is not as large as in the cooperative sites. In contrast, attitudes toward political unity in Virú were more negative in 1974 than in 1969.

A second item tapping attitudes toward political unity asked respondents how they would stop a bad or unjust action by community authorities. Because the item was open-ended and the political structure had changed over the five years, the coding of the item was slightly distinct in the two time periods. Also, the only available data for the 1969 survey apply to the entire sample of eighteen communities, not just my research sites.[14] However, the responses

[14] Data were not at Cornell but at the Instituto de Estudios Peruanos, and were kindly given me by Dr. Giorgio Alberti in May 1975. I am not sure exactly how the entire 1969 sample would compare with my subset on the item. The 1969 sample included many more peasant communities than my own, especially around Cuzco, which tend to be radical (Handelman 1975a). It also included several prosperous ex-haciendas in the Chancay area. On specific items, of the entire 1969 sample, 62

TABLE V.2
Attitudes Toward Political Unity, 1969-1974[a] (%)

| | N | Unite | Each alone | Both, depends | Don't know, no answer, other |
|---|---|---|---|---|---|
| Cooperatives, 1974 | 229 | 75 | 24 | 1 | 1 |
| Haciendas, 1969 | 176 | 50 | 46 | 1 | 4 |
| Monte, 1974 | 79 | 80 | 19 | 0 | 1 |
| Monte, 1969 | 58 | 36 | 59 | 0 | 5 |
| Estrella & Marla, 1974 | 150 | 73 | 26 | 1 | 0 |
| Estrella & Marla, 1969 | 118 | 57 | 39 | 1 | 3 |
| Quasi-control & control, 1974 | 184 | 61 | 35 | 4 | 1 |
| Quasi-control & control, 1969 | 253 | 61 | 36 | 1 | 3 |
| Agustín, 1974 | 94 | 63 | 36 | 1 | 0 |
| Agustín, 1969 | 153 | 49 | 46 | 1 | 4 |
| Virú, 1974 | 90 | 59 | 33 | 7 | 1 |
| Virú, 1969 | 100 | 73 | 25 | 0 | 2 |
| AIS Communities, 1974 | 93 (men only) | 87 | 12 | 1 | 0 |

[a] Item read: "To improve the life of the people in this place, some say, 'everyone should unite'; others say 'each person should solve his own problems.' What do you think?"

to the item do suggest large attitudinal changes. Table V.3 shows that almost half the 1969 sample (49 percent) said they could do nothing to stop the bad or unjust action, or didn't know or gave no answer. In the cooperative sites in 1974, this percentage was cut almost in half. Further, whereas only 16 percent of respondents said they would try to "unite the community" in 1969, almost double that percentage gave this answer in 1974. "Protest through the General Assembly or union" can also be considered to involve political unity; including answers to this item, we find that the percentage proposing a collective strategy more than doubled that of 1969.

To cooperative members, "political unity" largely signified the

percent chose "to unite" on the political unity item, versus about 54 percent in my sites in 1969, and of the entire 1969 sample, 51 percent gave an answer to the political efficacy item, versus about 48 percent in my sites. Thus Table V.3 is probably conservative with regard to the amount of change. The pattern of responses for control sites versus haciendas was presumably similar with regard to this item as to others, with the control sites more enthusiastic about unity in 1969 than the haciendas.

## TABLE V.3
### Attitudes toward Unity as a Means of Political Efficacy, 1969-1974[a] (%)

| | Unite community | Protest through the General Assembly or union | Alert and unite the Vigilance Council | Recall bad leaders | Speak personally with top community authorities | Protest before superior officials | Vague, other answer | Nothing, don't know, no answer |
|---|---|---|---|---|---|---|---|---|
| Cooperatives, 1974 (N = 229) | 29 | 12 | 9 | 2 | 4 | 15 | 7 | 27 |
| Quasi-control and control, 1974 (N = 184) | 19 | 2 | 0 | 4 | 15 | 10 | 13 | 38 |
| SAIS Communities (N = 93, men only) | 18 | 51 | 1 | 38 | 10 | 11 | 1 | 6 |
| All sites, 1969 (N = 1581) | 16 | 3 | 0 | 0 | 9 | 9 | 13 | 49[b] |

[a] Percentages of specific recourses spontaneously cited in response to the item, "If the authorities of this place wanted to do something bad or unjust, what could you do to prevent it?" Percentages sum to over 100 as some respondents gave more than one answer.

[b] 36% said "nothing," and 13% "don't know" or gave no answer.

capacity to make collective demands if a community leader or government official should move against the cooperative, or if the enterprise should want something from the government, such as restructuring the cooperative or more credit. A typical comment in response to our probes about political unity was, "We would all join together and make our demands." The statement was usually made enthusiastically, at times with a grand gesture. Many peasants emphasized that unity would bring results. One young woman said, "to negotiate at all, it's necessary to join together" (Q366). A Monte semi-skilled worker said, "Now, we know how to weigh more before the authorities" (Q331). Explained a schoolteacher: "Before, you had to make your demands personally.... Now you have to make them as a group, to exert greater pressure" (Q342).

Cooperative residents' positive attitudes toward political unity were based in part on confidence that policy benefits would be shared among all members. They linked individual gains to community gains. For example, Estrella, Marla, and Rachuis respondents were asked: "Some people say that what's good for the community is good for me. Others say that what's good for the community may not be good for me. What do you think?" Overwhelming majorities—97 percent in Estrella, 88 percent in Marla, and 92 percent in Rachuis—said "What's good for the community is good for me." The link between individual and collective gains was also indicated in respondents' comments. Said one Estrella worker, for example, "Correct, if there's something that favors the enterprise, it has to be good for me, because I'm also a part of the enterprise" (Q1975, 2).

To explore the suggestion of corporatist model advocates that political participation in the cooperative would destroy members' sense of social class, I asked the Estrella, Marla, and Rachuis peasants if they thought they belonged to a social class. Most respondents (48 percent) did not recognize the term, suggesting that there was not much class consciousness to destroy. However, a considerable number of Estrella and Marla men (39 percent) replied that yes, they belonged to the class of "member workers" (*socios trabajadores*). The respondents saw their status both as members and as workers to be important, defining the group on which political unity would be based. The men apparently perceived the status of cooperative member to define their relationship to the means of production, distinguishing themselves both from other peasants as well as from technicians. Said Lorenzo Lazo, "Yes, the class is us, the member workers. I'm not a man with a tie. I work hard. But there are others who don't work hard, they leave their offices at 11 A.M. But we work hard, day and night, in the fields" (Q1975, 1).

The 1974 survey also showed, however, that many respondents considered political unity an ideal that had not yet been reached. A considerable number of comments referred to abstract moral standards without further explanation: "Joining together, it's better." Many respondents said that the community *ought* to unite or *must* unite, implying that the actual state of unity was in the future. This type of comment was especially frequent in Monte.[15] Implicit in the exhortations of unity was the fear that other members would not participate, thus wasting the respondent's effort. This fear was explicitly mentioned by residents who chose to "solve their own problems" rather than unite. These respondents rarely suggested that the individual strategy was right, only that union was not feasible. Said a female ex-sharecropper in Estrella, "If everybody were good people, then we'd all unite, but here the people are very bad. They're all envious" (Q423).

A second key attitude relevant to participation is political efficacy. Political efficacy is the sense that the individual or the group can influence authorities, especially if the authorities do something unjust. The respondent's attitude toward both his own political competence and the system's responsiveness is tapped. Table V.4 reveals that the sense of political efficacy increased between 1969 and 1974 in the cooperatives. In all cooperative sites, the percentage difference over the five years is roughly 30 percent. Not only do more respondents choose the option that they could "do something" against political injustice, but fewer respondents express no opinion at all. Political efficacy increased in Agustín as well, but by a somewhat smaller amount, and remained the same in Virú.

Probing attitudes about political efficacy, we asked respondents for their strategies to combat the injustice. Peasants' comments suggested considerable political confidence, implying that their recourse would be quickly effective. Said one young Patca comunero (Q269), for example: "The peasants in the Assembly can make the leader see his errors." Many peasant-community members considered the problem solved by the recall procedure. As Table V.3 showed, 38 percent of the SAIS community sample said they would merely recall the bad authority.

Some 25 percent of the respondents in cooperative sites still felt

[15] See especially Q301, Q305, Q308, Q314, Q320, Q323, Q327, Q336, Q343, and Q346.

TABLE V.4
Sense of Political Efficacy, 1969-1974[a] (%)

| | N | Could do some-thing against political injustice[b] | Nothing against political injustice | Don't know, no answer, other[c] |
|---|---|---|---|---|
| ɔoperatives, 1974 | 229 | 75 | 16 | 9 |
| aciendas, 1969 | 176 | 44 | 41 | 15 |
| Monte, 1974 | 79 | 67 | 15 | 18 |
| Monte, 1969 | 58 | 36 | 36 | 28 |
| Estrella & Marla, 1974 | 150 | 79 | 17 | 5 |
| Estrella & Marla, 1969 | 118 | 49 | 43 | 8 |
| ᴜasi-control & control, 1974 | 184 | 60 | 31 | 9 |
| ᴜasi-control & control, 1969 | 253 | 51 | 40 | 9 |
| Agustín, 1974 | 94 | 60 | 36 | 4 |
| Agustín, 1969 | 153 | 42 | 46 | 12 |
| Virú, 1974 | 90 | 60 | 27 | 13 |
| Virú, 1969 | 100 | 60 | 33 | 7 |
| ᴀIS Communities, 1974 | 93 (men only) | 93 | 3 | 3 |

[a] Item read: "If the authorities of this place wanted to do something bad or unjust, what could you ● to prevent it?"
[b] Includes vague references to "something."
[c] "Don't know" and "No answer" responses were difficult for the interviewer to differentiate.

politically inefficacious in 1974. Most of these respondents, espe-cially those who said "don't know," were women. In Monte, a major-ity of women still indicated attitudes of political inefficacy. They could do nothing, they said, pointing ambiguously to their political ignorance and their submission to husbands and officials. Said one young Monte housewife, "How would it be? There's nothing to do. What would my husband say? What can we do?" (Q355).

The new attitudes toward political union and political efficacy imply a new attitude toward political participation generally. The 1969 survey did not explicitly ask respondents about their attitudes toward political participation, so I had no baseline question. I added an item that delineated both the advantages and the disad-vantages regularly attributed to participation. The item described two political authorities: "One authority had all the people in the place participate in the important decisions, wanting almost every-one to be in agreement over a decision, and thus there were many delays. The second authority did not encourage much participa-tion, and so made decisions without delays." The respondent was asked which type of authority he preferred. In all sites but Virú, solid majorities selected the authority who encouraged participation: 63 percent in Monte, 70 percent in Estrella, 71 percent in Marla, 85 percent in Patca, 91 percent in Varya, and 91 percent in Agustín. The percentage drops below a majority, to 48 percent, only in the control Virú.

The Velasco government proposed political participation not only among a collectivity but also specifically among a collectivity of equals. To what extent were the new political attitudes embraced equally by all socioeconomic strata? In 1974 in the three major cooperative sites, positive attitudes toward political union and political efficacy were on the average still slightly related to socioeconomic status, but less so than in 1969. The zero-order correlation coefficient between a positive attitude toward political union and high socioeconomic status was .018 in 1974, much lower than the .303 in 1969. The coefficient between a positive attitude toward political efficacy and high socioeconomic status was .229 in 1974, slightly lower than the .237 statistic for 1969. In the control sites, the zero-order coefficients were about the same in 1969 and 1974.[16]

## CHANGES IN COLLECTIVE POLITICAL BEHAVIOR

The new incentives influenced not only attitudes toward political participation but also participatory behavior. Because the political structure changed radically after 1969, quantitative measurement of change in participatory behavior is difficult. However, roughly measured, participation in collective political activities jumped, especially in the sites of the largest policy incentives.

One item in the 1974 survey asked respondents to recall the amount of collective political activity prior to 1969 and compare it to the amount in 1974. Specifically, the question was: "Are there more or less meetings now than before the agrarian reform?" In the three major cooperatives, 70 percent of respondents reported more meetings in 1974 and only 3 percent fewer meetings; in the two SAIS communities, 49 percent reported more meetings in 1974

---

[16] In the control and quasi-control, the correlation between positive attitudes towards political union and high socioeconomic status was .261 in 1974, versus .266 in 1969, and between political efficacy and high socioeconomic status, .378 in 1974, versus .292 in 1969.

and only 15 percent fewer.[17] In contrast, in the control sites only 38 percent of respondents said that the number of meetings had climbed.

The extent of change in collective political participation is also suggested by responses to various items in the 1969 and 1974 surveys (see Table V.5). The left half of Table V.5 provides data relevant to participation in the 1960s—possession of a voting card, political party and union membership, and community leadership. These figures can be contrasted with the extent to which respondents said they participated in the modes of participation available in the early 1970s—the General Assemblies, other kinds of meetings (such as those of unions or geographic sectors), and community leadership. These modes of political activity are too distinct from one era to the next to allow elaborate analysis. The table suggests, however, the limited political activity in the haciendas in 1969, with only 39 percent of respondents even having a voting card (not to mention actually voting) and only 7 percent perceiving themselves to have served as community leaders, and it also indicates the greater activity in the cooperatives in 1974, with 71 percent of respondents reporting General Assembly participation and 18 percent service as community leaders.

The most direct measure of change in collective participation available is a comparison of the rate of participation in General Assemblies and union meetings during 1973-1974 with the rate of participation in the union sessions of the 1960s. Over a sample of fifteen cooperatives throughout the country, attendance at General Assemblies averaged 65 percent of members (Centro de Estudios de Participación Popular, 1974-1975). Over a sample of 75 cooperatives in 1975, and using peasants' self-reports, Buchler (1975: 105) suggests approximately 65 percent participation. In my sites, by personal observation and reports of community leaders rather than by the survey, roughly 70 percent of cooperative members in major sites attended General Assemblies in 1974-1975 (see Table V.6). Attendance averaged 75 percent in Estrella and 65 percent in Marla. However, according to the hindsight of Estrella residents, attendance at union meetings prior to 1969 averaged 50 percent of workers; in contiguous El Chalán, it averaged only 40 percent (Greaves, 1968: 281-282). The General Assemblies and union sessions of the 1970s also maintained members' attention. In contrast,

---

[17] "Don't know" answers are excluded from these calculations.

TABLE V.5
Political Participation, 1969 and 1974[a] (%)

| | 1969 | | | | | 1974 | | | |
| --- | N | Have voting card | Member of political party | Member of union | Community leadership position | N | Participate in General Assemblies always or sometimes | Participate in at least two types of meetings | Community leadership |
| --- | --- | --- | --- | --- | --- | --- | --- | --- | --- |
| Cooperatives (Haciendas in 1969) | 171 | 39 | 6 | 16 | 7 | 230 | 71 | 30 | 18 |
| Monte | 56 | 42 | 2 | 2 | 5 | 79 | 62 | 6 | 8 |
| Estrella | 77 | 44 | 9 | 34 | 7 | 89 | 76 | 36 | 29 |
| Marla | 38 | 30 | 2 | 14 | 7 | 62 | 77 | 52 | 17 |
| Quasi-control & control | 253 | 52 | 5 | 3 | 9 | 184 | 68 | 29 | 14 |
| Agustín | 153 | 48 | 3 | 1 | 10 | 94 | 66 | 28 | 20 |
| Virú | 100 | 55 | 7 | 5 | 7 | 90 | 70 | 30 | 8 |
| SAIS communities (Patca and Varya) | — | — | — | — | — | 93 | 93 | 77 | 51 |
| | | | | | | (men only) | | | |

[a] See Appendix 5 for further details on items.

TABLE V.6
Attendance at General Assemblies in Cooperatives, 1973-1975

| | Average attendance (percent of members) | | |
| --- | --- | --- | --- |
| | March 1973 | March 1974 | May 1975 |
| SAIS Huanca | 90 | 90 | 90 |
| Monte | 20 | 75 | 70 |
| Varya | 30 | 50 | 40 |
| Patca | 60 | 60 | 50 |
| Estrella | 20 | 75 | 75 |
| Marla | 70 | 60 | 60 |

SOURCE: Observations and reports for each site between 1973 and 1975. Information is less thorough for Patca and Varya. Percentages are rough annual averages.

union meetings of the 1960s were constantly disrupted by a "general din of horseplay, private conversation and movement" (Greaves, 1968: 286). However, in neither time period were most women classified as "members" of the union or the enterprise, and thus their participation was low during both periods.

The level of incentives for collective participation influenced meeting attendance rates. The importance of SAIS Huanca assemblies for policy outcomes was very clear, and attendance was invariably excellent. In Monte and Estrella, where many concerns were gradually successfully resolved, attendance at meetings jumped between 1973 and 1975, and by all accounts was still rising somewhat through 1977. In Marla, attendance dropped slightly, as policy gains were limited, except with respect to firing managers. As the low level of policy incentives for participation in Varya would suggest, attendance at Varya assemblies was the lowest of the sites in 1974-1975.

The frequency of General Assemblies was greater than the legal requirement. No fixed number of assemblies was stipulated; the statute required only that the assembly fulfill its responsibilities, which necessitated roughly two assemblies per year. Over a sample of seven cooperatives throughout Peru, the frequency of General Assemblies averaged twelve times per year (Centro de Estudios de Participación Popular: 1974-1975). Over a sample of 75 cooperatives throughout Peru, Buchler (1975: 102) suggests an average of seven assemblies annually. The assembly also gathered more frequently than necessary in my sites. During 1973-1975, the assembly averaged five meetings per year in the three major enterprises—SAIS Huanca, Estrella, and Marla—and fourteen times per year in SAIS Huanca's component sites—Monte, Varya, and Patca (see Table V.7). After 1975, the amount of assembly activity remained considerable, although it rose and declined in different sites at different times. Activity was intense in Huanca in 1977 because of the conflict between comuneros and trabajadores and the dispute over the manager, but limited in Marla, where the new councils preferred not to call meetings, fearing opposition from southern bank residents.

The General Assembly convened more often than the union had. According to Estrella residents, their union gathered approximately three times a year, generally during the two to four months before a wage negotiation. The frequency of El Chalán union meetings is not specified, but sessions also seemed timed with annual wage bargaining (Greaves, 1968: 282-295).

The General Assembly complemented rather than displaced union activity. As indicated above, prior to 1969 in the three research enterprises, a union operated regularly only in Estrella. In contrast, by 1975, unions existed in all three sites. In Monte, the union was the major political organization. In Estrella, the union was the primary organization through which workers fought ex-sharecroppers and then developed wage policies. In Marla, a union was established in 1975 to assure a strong commitment to the firing of the third manager.

Perhaps even more important than increased base-level participation was participation in leadership organs. The cooperative statute required the participation of at least twelve members a year in the two councils, often over 15 percent of all cooperative members. The Administrative Council was an active, collective leadership body (see Chapter VI). In every cooperative, the Administrative Council met more often than the once-a-month requirement (see Table V.7), and at least 80 percent of Administrative Council leaders attended meetings.

The Vigilance Council was less vigorous than the Administrative Council. Attendance at Vigilance Council sessions was approximately 70 percent. The Vigilance Council met more than legally required, but not as much more as the Administrative Council. By law, the Vigilance Council in cooperatives was to meet once a month, and in peasant communities twice a month; this requirement was only just fulfilled in Estrella, Patca, and Varya, although surpassed in SAIS Huanca and Marla (see Table V.7). The role of

TABLE V.7
Types of Meetings in Cooperatives 1973-1975

| | Administrative Council | Vigilance Council | General Assembly | Other active groups |
|---|---|---|---|---|
| | Meetings per month | Meetings per month | Meetings per year | |
| SAIS Huanca | 10[a] | 2 | 4 | Education Committee |
| Monte | Not applicable | Not applicable | 24[a] | Schoolparents' Committee Women's Group |
| Varya | 2 | .5 | 8 | Barrio[a] |
| Patca | 2 | .5 | 10 | Barrio[a] Women's Group |
| CAP Estrella | 2 | 1 | 5 | Union, Eduation Committee |
| CAP Marla | 4 | 2 | 5 | Barrio[a] |

SOURCE: Observations and reports for each site between 1973 and 1975. Information is less thorough for Patca and Varya.
[a] General Assembly is union meeting. Barrio is a geographical area within the community. SAIS Huanca Administrative Council meets informally almost daily.

the Vigilance Council was not as clear-cut as that of the Administrative Council. Delegates were less politically powerful, less educated, and less prosperous than the Administrative Council members. They often lacked the knowledge and the courage to exercise the required supervision of the Administrative Council. At times, Vigilance Councilmen acted as supervisors of field work, a role which had not been assigned and which was resented by some workers.

In contrast to the General Assemblies and the councils, political activity in specialized committees and other groups was often low, as it was in other cooperatives in the early 1970s (Buchler, 1975: 108-109). The Administrative Council had to appoint an Education Committee, and could also appoint other committees—commercialization, field work, work equipment, and the like. Other new groups also burgeoned after 1961: sports associations in Estrella, local residential organizations in Marla and Varya, and women's and schoolparents' associations in Monte (see Table V.7). Absenteeism at these groups' meetings was high. Majorities of committee members appointed by the Administrative Council were not aware of their assignments. Quorums were thus rare. Bemoaned the president of one Estrella committee:

> I haven't much liked being the President of the Commercialization Committee. I've felt very frustrated. There were four members, but two never came, they weren't interested. So we didn't have a quorum, and we couldn't do anything, although we wanted to do things (Q1975, 9).

These associations generally convened much less regularly than the councils or General Assemblies. The most active groups in the major cooperatives were SAIS Huanca's Education Committee, Estrella's Education Committee, and Marla's southern bank residents' group, but even these organizations gathered only about once a month during 1973-1975. The Education Committees organized a variety of talks, assembled small libraries, arranged fiestas, and the like. Marla's southern bank organization was primarily concerned with its relationship to the cooperative as a whole. During 1975, it also built its own regional meeting hall. The other groups met sporadically. Some specialized groups, including women's groups in Monte and Marla, dissolved.

Not only did the amount of collective participation increase in the cooperatives but participatory equality across distinct socioeconomic strata did also. To compare the relationship between socioeconomic status and participation in 1969 versus 1975, I constructed indices of socioeconomic status and participation that were as similar as possible for the two time points (see Appendix 5). The relationship between socioeconomic status and participation eroded in the cooperative sites but not in the control, Virú. Across the three experimental sites, the zero-order correlation between socioeconomic status and participation fell from .472 in the sites as haciendas in 1969 to .188 in the sites as cooperatives in 1974. The drop was greater in the coastal CAPs Estrella and Marla than in Monte (from .419 to .135 in Estrella and .404 to −.147 in Marla, versus from .569 to .425 in Monte). The correlation remained stronger in Monte than elsewhere because of the lack of membership restrictions on the community's socioeconomic apex. In the control Virú, the correlations are roughly the same at the two time-points: .349 in 1969 and .312 in 1974.

## SUMMARY

Through the new self-managed cooperatives and reinvigorated unions, cooperative members were able to develop new enterprise policies and transmit new demands on the government. The new policies and the successful demands stood as clear incentives to greater political participation and unity, and encouraged more positive attitudes in these spheres. The issues at stake were much more than "strict business" to the peasants. The political activity of the research cooperatives characterized most cooperatives observed by other scholars as well.[18]

The pattern of political participation in the cooperatives clearly diverged sharply from the traditional clientelist one. The patron's traditional monopoly over key decisions was gone, and peasants could advance their concerns without interference from the hacendado's carrots and sticks. Commented one peasant: "Now we participate in the decisions. The patron never permitted us to see the balance sheet. Now at least we know" (Q1975, 47).

Neither the "fully participatory social democracy" model nor the corporatist model can be accurately applied to the questions of political participation in this chapter because the chapter examines primarily peasants' political activity and not government policy; the nature of government policy is, of course, a critical factor in the evaluation of the applicability of the models. Various relevant

[18] See especially Eguren López (1975: 111-119); Bell (1977); Scott (1977); Buchler (1975); Rubin de Celis T. (1977: 54).

points can be made here, however. The study reveals no co-optation or conciliation between technicians and peasants. Indeed,
both peasants and technicians testified to the new power of the
peasants to forge their own decisions on these matters. Contrast the
exulting comment of a Huanca peasant leader to the frustrated
complaint of a Huanca technician:

> I'm free in my decisions, except at the point when we need agree-
> ment from the General Assembly. SINAMOS doesn't intervene.
> We're free.[19]

> The peasants do what they want around here. To them, the
> technicians aren't worth anything. They don't listen to us unless
> they want to.[20]

Unions were not displaced, but rather strengthened. Indeed, the
area where the impact of the cooperatives on political participation
might be judged most disappointing was one not generally anticipated by proponents of corporatist models: the scant change in
women's attitudes and behavior, presumably because they were
usually not cooperative members.

However, although this chapter supports a description of participation *within* the cooperative as the kind of participation expected
by the "fully participatory social democracy" model, it must be
pointed out, as Chapter X will elaborate, that some government
*officials* (over whom, in contrast to *technicians*, the cooperative
members wielded no formal power) did in fact try to influence
policy making in the cooperatives, in accordance with corporatist
model expectations. Members' new political will and new political
capacity enabled them usually to block government intiatives, an
eventuality not anticipated in either model.

Although self-management was much more partial in Peruvian
industrial enterprises than in agricultural ones, the impact of the
industrial reform was in a similar direction as the agricultural.
Political activity was intense in the Industrial Communities, considerably more intense than in the enterprises before the reform.
Often joined and usually supported by the union, the Industrial
Community advanced various demands on the firm owners.[21]

---

[19] Interview with Aurelio Osores, in Huancayo, August 1973.

[20] Interview with Monte administrator, in Monte, May 1975.

[21] See in particular Alberti, Santistevan, and Pásara (1977); Stephens (1977); and
Robinson (1976). The article by Pásara in Alberti, Santistevan, and Pásara (1977)
highlights the relationship between the union and the CI. Santistevan (1977b) emphasizes the character of the CI's demands.

Workers charged that the owners were undermining the Industrial Community law, trying to avoid giving workers their legal share of power and profits. The Industrial Communities often demanded greater benefits from the enterprise. In some firms, workers' frustration at the owners' subversion of the law spiraled into a rejection of the capitalist system. In this context, the Industrial Community became to some workers an "instrument of struggle." Strikes increased sharply after 1972 to the highest levels ever in Peru and very high levels in the Latin American context generally (Stephens, 1977: 242). Although the Industrial Community at times supported the firm on some issues—such as conflicts between "its" firm and another—the over-all direction of change was to increased conflict between workers and owners, rather than to conciliation.[22]

[22] Santistevan (1977b: 293) is especially explicit on this point. He also considers the issues, such as inter-enterprise ones, on which some collaboration between the CI and the firm was evident.

# VI · *Political Leadership*

> There are no leaders, there are no individuals who will always be
> leaders. We're a group, we must be a group. We must be able to train
> someone who doesn't know much how to be a leader.
>
> (Ingenio Cruz, in Monte, 1973)

IN THE ARCHETYPAL MODE of clientelism on the hacienda,
political leadership is reserved for the patron, and in some cases for
his administrators as well. The right of the patron to exclusive
decision-making powers is not to be questioned. The patron wins
authority by birthright—his ownership of the hacienda and his
socioeconomic position. The patron may be a "good patron," providing material help to peasant clients in need; but if he is not a
"good patron," the peasant has no recourse. The patron is not
accountable to the peasants in any way: he cannot be compelled to
change his behavior at their request, and he certainly cannot be
dismissed.

In the corporatist model, leadership is no longer a prerogative of
birth. Leaders are formally elected. However, leaders are caught up
in an intricate political game. In this game, government officials or
the upper classes still hold the trump cards. Usually, these elites are
able to rig any election so that their preferred candidate wins.
Typically, this candidate is of high socioeconomic status, and is thus
more likely to hold conservative political ideas. If representative
political leaders should arise, the elites co-opt them or, if necessary,
repress them. In short, in a corporatist system, leaders are manipulated from above.

In contrast, the Velasco government's model of "fully participatory social democracy" stipulated a different kind of political
leadership.[1] Leaders were to be honestly elected to councils from

---

[1] The Peruvian model of "fully participatory social democracy" is similar in many
ways to the "radical" views of democracy that have been provided recently by various
social scientists, although it is of course unlikely that the Peruvian model was derived
from these views. The Peruvian model resembles the "diffusion of power" that
Bachrach (1967) has called for, and the "participatory democracy" which Pateman
(1970) has advanced. Both Bachrach and Pateman argue that equality of *opportunity*
for leadership is not a sufficient condition for democracy; an actual sharing of
authority is necessary.

the rank-and-file. Within the councils, leadership was to be rotated and shared to a significant extent, and men of average and lower socioeconomic status were to gain decision-making roles. Poorly educated peasants could learn political skills in their new positions. The peasants could hold the leaders accountable, questioning their activities and recalling them if necessary. The Velasco government denounced all forms of hierarchical or manipulated authority—"paternalism," "verticalism," and "false leadership by unrepresentative outsiders."[2] SINAMOS described the new model of authority as follows:

> The new structure of power is not based on the monopoly of decision making by the privileged minorities who have traditionally dominated the society, but on the contrary by the assumption of economic, political, and social power on the part of those who integrate the majority sectors, previously marginalized from the society. The working people will be the people who all the time get into their hands the administration and power of decision of all the institutions in the country.[3]

The assumption behind such ideals of authority are that the ordinary individual will more fully affirm his own capabilities by exercising leadership from time to time, and also that such an individual will have a set of insights and interests that cannot be expressed or represented by an "expert" of any kind.

Many other authority modes, including variations on the authority modes discussed above, could be delineated. However, the only other mode of considerable relevance here is "democratic elitism," the common authority pattern in the United States and Western Europe (Bachrach, 1967; Pateman, 1970: 1-44). In this mode, "democracy" refers to the political method—elections—rather than the political end of equality of power. Typically, experts with high socioeconomic positions are able to win power, but it is assumed that the skills and knowledge of those experts are requisite to com-

---

[2] "63 Preguntas y Respuestas," SINAMOS, Lima, n.d. (probably 1972), pp. 7-8; "Movilización Social: de Quién y Para Qué?", SINAMOS, Lima, n.d., pp. 22-23; "Porqué se ataca al SINAMOS?", SINAMOS, Lima, n.d., p. 17.

[3] "63 Preguntas y Respuestas," SINAMOS, Lima, n.d. (probably 1972), pp. 12 and 16. See also the Ministry of Agriculture (1974a: 53-59). This chapter of the ministry's administrative manual emphasizes the importance of delegating and sharing authority. Several words recur frequently: conferment, communication, delegation, capacitación, and responsibility. It is also stressed that sharing of authority should not imply the loss of authority.

petent policy making. Legitimacy is thus derived from the electoral process and the assumed necessity of expertise.

This chapter will assess the nature of change in authority modes after 1969. To what extent did leadership in the cooperatives turn from modes in the image of the patron to the sharing of executive authority among honestly elected individuals of average socioeconomic status? The best brief answer is: somewhat.

## INCENTIVES FOR EGALITARIAN, SHARED, ELECTED LEADERSHIP

Incentives for the honest election of leaders and the sharing of leadership among individuals of average socioeconomic status increased after 1969. The jump was great with respect to the practice of honest elections. Incentives for egalitarian leadership patterns and for sharing executive authority rose, but some disincentives also remained. Policy incentives were a key type of incentive for new leadership patterns, but other types, especially individual dignity and opportunity, were also apparent.

Incentives for honest elections were marked in the cooperative. The massive responsibilities of the Administrative Council and the huge sums at stake made critical the election of the "best man" who enjoyed majority support. Few cooperative members had sufficient funds to buy votes under these circumstances—at least after one or two years, by which time members had realized the sums in question in the cooperative. Moreover, these enterprises were small, and thus members knew each other well and were in a position to make sound evaluations of candidates.

Perhaps more important than the increase in incentives for honest elections was the decrease in disincentives to such elections. In the hacienda, these disincentives had been considerable. A hacienda peasant leader could only achieve benefits for the community by establishing some rapport with the patron. If a union leader became aggressive or for one reason or another alienated the patron, he could usually be removed from his position by threats of firing or salary cuts. Such threats were made against union leaders in many haciendas, including the research haciendas, as Chapter V documented. Pedro Paredes, Estrella's angry young man of the 1970s who tried to organize the temporary workers, had also been a frustrated leader in the 1960s, expelled from the union after trying to radicalize it.

After the demise of the patron system, the achievement of policy victories were not contingent upon the peasants' selecting the candidate preferred by government officials, in contrast to the predictions of corporatist model proponents. This is not to say that government officials paid no attention to elections in the cooperatives. SINAMOS officials often spoke up for one candidate over another, typically individuals of lower socioeconomic status. However, SINAMOS was rarely able to put any weight behind its preference.[4] To my knowledge, no policy benefit was ever made contingent upon the election of a specific candidate. The most important inducements, government loans, were controlled by the Agrarian Bank, which not only frowned on the politicking of SINAMOS but also had no preference for individuals of low socioeconomic status. No cooperative member ever said to me that the government officials had influenced, let alone "rigged," an election. On a question about elections in the 1975 survey, many members commented on the freedom of the elections. Statements such as "We can elect anyone, the choice depends on the majority," were made by some 90 percent of respondents. Explained one Marla resident, for example: "You can elect whatever worker you like, now it's not as before, when they named a leader by pointing a finger, now there are elections" (Q1975, 36).

Thus, during the Velasco era, neither the hacendado nor the government wielded the incentives or the disincentives that might have distorted electoral outcomes. The key concern of members was not if they should elect, but whom they should elect, and this decision was based on analysis of the nature of leadership responsibilities as well as on the personal needs of members.

The most critical issue for cooperative members was the selection of competent leaders and the criteria for competence. Traditionally, competence had entailed educational achievement to enable the  leader to discuss wage issues articulately with the hacendado and union federation officials and to understand documents, and it had also entailed economic status, to give the leader greater presence with the hacendado. In the Velasco era, however, the criteria for competence were more ambiguous. On the one hand,

---

[4] This was more the case in the countryside than in the pueblos jovenes (migrant settlements). Stepan (1978: 181) and Dietz (1980: Chapter 8) both report some government pressures to exclude "unacceptable" candidates in elections in pueblos jovenes. But, as Stepan (1978: 209) also suggests, such pressures were rare in the agrarian cooperatives after 1972. The only successful intervention in a non-agroindustrial cooperative during the Velasco era with which I am familiar occurred in Huando (Eguren López, 1975: 118).

education was still important. The legal regulations of the agrarian cooperative were devastatingly complex, and economic management of the enterprise called for considerable knowledge of business and of agricultural economics. Although the General Assembly had the last word on investment and production decisions, on the whole members were not highly involved in the details of business decisions, for which primary responsibility lay with the councils. Thus it was important that council members be able to understand agricultural economics. Some council posts in particular were considered to require special skills; for example, the treasurer was believed to need to know accounting. Various peasants expressed the importance of knowledge to leadership competence. This emerged in Ingenio's frustration in his role as president of the Schoolparents' Association: "I wish I knew the laws. But the laws are all so complex, always some new statute in some other book." An Estrella man made a similar lament: "It's very sad, but people who don't know much, although they want to work, they can't understand a book of sales, a book of purchases, indeed so many things. I think the leader must be trained" (Q1975, 2).

However, education was gradually becoming less important to competent leadership in the eyes of many peasants. First, opportunities to learn leadership skills were increasing. In contrast to the 1960s,[5] by the early 1970s the government developed extensive training programs for cooperative members (see Chapter X). The Ministry of Agriculture distributed many manuals on enterprise management. Further, only one-third of council members were renewed every year, providing continuity of experienced members. Thus, responding to a probe in the 1975 survey about why they thought that an individual of lower socioeconomic status could serve as a leader, many members (54 percent) responded that inadequately trained leaders could gradually learn the requisite skills on the job. Said an Estrella worker:

> It's not necessary to be trained, only to be a hard worker. For example, I have been elected Secretary General of the Union, I'm not trained, but I have the desire to work. To train myself, I can read books, attend courses for leaders, and thus be able to work for the benefit of my union (Q1975, 33).

Moreover, formal education was believed to give an individual specific expertise but not necessarily common sense; if well-

[5] See especially Handelman (1975a: 237). APRA's FENCAP tried to train peasants politically, but as Chapter II discussed, its scope was minimal. See Bourque (1971).

educated leaders failed to demonstrate common sense, members were prompted to think twice about the utility of formal education. For example, when Marla's well-educated leaders used an ill-conceived tactic to oust the manager and thus damaged the enterprise economically, Marla members began to doubt the value of formal education.

Although the significance of formal education to leadership competence was thus downplayed by many cooperative members, one caveat was often made: the leader had to be able to read and write. The need for literacy was more salient in disadvantaged highlands sites where the literacy rate was much lower. Thus, answering a 1975 item about why disadvantaged men were not elected Administrative Council president, only 35 percent of Estrella and Marla respondents but as many as 79 percent of Rachuis respondents mentioned that a leader had to know how to read and write.

The competence of leaders had also traditionally entailed wealth and high economic status. A leader was expected to help the community by providing specific material benefits. Like the patron, a prosperous peasant leader was believed to be able to benefit the community economically and to provide "insurance" in case of economic crisis. A well-to-do peasant was also generally esteemed as a man of achievement, a man who could "get things done." Although it was widely recognized that a peasant's upward mobility typically entailed machinations with the hacendado, a certain degree of dishonesty was countenanced.[6] The amount of money at stake was not massive—perhaps a percentage of union membership fees or a bribe from would-be merchants to the hacienda—and peasants felt that they had a good chance of getting some of the money back through their requests for loans or the like from these leaders.

Gradually, however, prosperity seemed less important a requisite to leadership competence. Although members continued to hope for material gains from peasants or outsiders, in many cases it seemed that these gains could be won without bestowing leadership authority upon the individual. For example, like most North American scholars, I was repeatedly approached for donations to the school or the sports stadium, for car rides, and the like by peasants, but they realized that I hoped for community acceptance

---

[6] Indeed, traditionally leaders were expected to be dishonest. The Spanish words *sabido*, or knowledgeable person, and *vivo*, or an alert, lively person, both also imply slyness and deviousness. As Alderson-Smith (1973: 18) reports: "anyone bright enough to be a good leader was too bright to be trusted." Cornelius (1975: 153) indicates a similar phenomenon in many Mexican communities.

rather than authority in return. (This was not the case with my scholarly predecessor Thomas Greaves, who was offered a managerial post in one hacienda.) A similar attitude gradually emerged in Estrella toward Tomás Torres; after 1975, gifts were extracted from him without granting him authority.

Perhaps most important, honesty became a top criterion for leadership competence to many peasants, because under the purview of the Administrative Council were all the resources of the enterprise; much more money was at stake than before. If peasants' suspicion of prosperous farmers' shrewdness were exacerbated by evidence of their corruption in leadership posts, the suspicion was often generalized to wealthy peasants as a group. The implications of the logic of an Estrella peasant in his condemnation of wealthy ex-president Torres are revealing: " Torres was only watching out for his own welfare. . . . He lifted our money, *it's for this reason* that he has four cars and a poultry enterprise; it was all robbed from the cooperative . . ." (Q1975, 17) [my italics]. Members thus turned to leaders of lower socioeconomic status who they thought had less of a history of corruption and thus, they hoped, would have less of a future of it, too.

For some peasants, not only did a prosperous background imply dubious moral values, but an average socioeconomic background implied a greater understanding of the problems of the average peasant and a greater commitment to resolving them. This sense of common purpose was important in the cooperative, where very sensitive questions with significant implications for different socioeconomic groups in the enterprise often emerged. It was thought in particular that leaders with high socioeconomic status tended to give their friends of equivalent status too great an advantage in enterprise promotion and marketing policies. Various members expressed the belief that the average man would better sympathize with the peasant majority:

> The worker knows how we suffer, he knows what work is. The well-trained and well-educated man only puts everything in his wallet (Q1975, 22).

> Let the authority not be so well-trained. Then he may work so that there's equality, so that there is respect for our ideas. In meetings with these arrogant leaders, they don't give any importance to what we say, they laugh and say that what we say isn't worth anything (Q1975, 3).

The new incentives for an egalitarian pattern of authority included not only collective policy benefits but also increased personal dignity. Previously, peasants had been treated by the patron as irresponsible, unworthy of leadership roles. Peasants were "not prepared" for authority positions, some government officials and landowners had said. In a cooperative leadership position, however, the peasant was asked to fulfill very serious responsibilities, responsibilities traditionally reserved by the landowner for himself. Members thus perceived leadership as a chance to prove their own worth to themselves and to others, especially "superior" outsiders. When members talked of election to council positions, they used such words as "rising up" and "uplift."[7] They referred frequently and with pride to their leadership titles, especially in conversations with officials.[8]

Leadership positions offered opportunities for individual upward mobility, too. Council presidents were often promoted at work, both to free time for their tasks as presidents and to make their work status commensurate with their political position. Leadership also facilitated the development of new skills that could be used subsequently to gain a better job. The perception of upward mobility as an incentive to leadership was common.[9] Leaders were also able to travel a good deal.

Incentives for sharing authority were also evident in the cooperatives. Because individual leaders were not skilled in all areas of enterprise management, it was important that knowledge be pooled. In a group, the relatively inexperienced authorities could debate proposals and presumably hammer out an effective policy. As the president of Estrella's Education Committee said: "One person alone can't solve a problem. It's better to work on it among various people, because you can look to them if you need advice" (Q418). Further, it was hoped that, by including a number of individuals in the council, extra checks against corruption would be provided.

Traditionally, however, disincentives to sharing leadership have been strong, and many remained in the cooperatives. Council responsibilities were often time-consuming; but they were usually

---

[7] See especially Q1975, 9; Q1975, 34; Q1975, 54; Q1975, 64.

[8] Note the references to the title of "vice-president" in the discussion between the Administrative Council vice-president and the manager in Estrella, quoted in Chapter V. See also Eguren López (1975: 117).

[9] See especially Q1975, 6; Q1975, 46; Q1975, 47.

rewarded not by immediate economic gains, but only by prestige and upward mobility in the long run. The president won a considerable share of the prestige, in the eyes of both members and outsiders. Many Administrative Council members thus hesitated to put in the extra time beyond council meetings that complete sharing of authority would have required.

## CHANGES IN ATTITUDES TOWARD LEADERSHIP

Although evidence on attitudes toward authority prior to the agrarian reform is less comprehensive than on attitudes in other areas, the available data suggest that, with the new incentives for an egalitarian, shared pattern of authority, attitudes toward such a leadership mode became more positive. In 1973 members embraced egalitarian, shared systems of authority somewhat tenuously and idealistically, and such a leadership system was not practiced; by 1975, however, members' espousal of such an authority system was more assured and, as the next section discusses, implemented to a greater extent in some sites. This trend was especially strong in the coastal cooperatives; evidence on these attitudes in the highlands sites is scant.

The only item about attitudes toward authority administered in the 1969 survey that could be repeated in 1974 asked whether the respondent supported or rejected the patronal authority system—i.e., the automatic assumption of leadership by patrons through birthright, and the automatic subordination of peasants through their low inherited status. The item was phrased: "Some people say that a few have been born to command and others to obey. Do you think this is true or false?" The question was asked only in the coastal sites.[10]

Table VI.1 shows a large jump in the number of respondents who rejected a patronal authority system. In Estrella and Marla, the number that explicitly disagreed with the statement "A few are born to command" rose from 10 percent in 1969 to 69 percent in 1974, the largest change registered for any item in the study. Although the question was not asked in Monte, a significant change is also likely, considering Monte respondents' answers to other sur-

---

[10] The failure to apply the item in the highlands was my error.

TABLE VI.1

Attitudes towards Patronal Authority System, 1969-1974[a] (%)

| | N | A few are born to command | May be that a few are born to command | A few are not born to command | Don't know, no answer |
|---|---|---|---|---|---|
| Estrella & Marla, 1974 | 150 | 26 | 5 | 69 | 0 |
| Estrella & Marla, 1969 | 118 | 73 | 14 | 10 | 3 |
| Virú, 1974 | 90 | 33 | 13 | 50 | 3 |
| Virú, 1969 | 100 | 65 | 8 | 25 | 2 |
| Monte, 1969 | 58 | 62 | 28 | 3 | 7 |
| Agustín, 1969 | 145 | 65 | 12 | 19 | 4 |

[a] Item read: "Some people say that a few have been born to command and others to obey. Do you think this is true or false?" Unfortunately, the item was not asked in the highlands sites in 1974.

vey items.[11] The change in the control site Virú was also considerable, but not as great as that in the cooperatives. Probed for the reasons behind their answers, most respondents' comments suggested a rational perception of the patron's demise, but also enthusiasm about his fall:

> Before, those who ordered were the mayordomos, and they treated people badly, and the patron didn't say anything. Now it's different, the cooperative is for the members (Q531).

> Before, the patron commanded his employees, and they commanded us, but in the CAP now there are ideas among all the members (Q517).

Peasants favored not only the demise of patronal authority but also the rise of elected authority in the councils. Members' desire to elect authorities rather than to await their designation from above was strong, indeed so strong that a survey question tapping this attitude seemed superfluous. In most sites the issue was rarely raised because honest elections had been instituted for several years. The question was discussed in Estrella, where the corrupt Torres gained office through various machinations and the upright Saavedra was finally elected in 1975. Returning to Estrella just after Saavedra's election, I was struck by the pervasive delight at the achievement of an honest electoral process. The following comment was typical: "Now anyone can be president, just like Lucho Saavedra. Before, they bought votes . . . but now they couldn't because it was agreed in the union not to vote for them [men allied with Torres]" (Q1975, 7).

Respondents also overwhelmingly endorsed the leadership potential of the man of average socioeconomic status. In the 1974 survey, a choice was posed between two candidates: the first—symbolizing the patron—has excellent contacts with superior authorities but is eager to help only his friends; the second—symbolizing the average man as leader—lacks contacts but wants to help the entire community. Table VI.2 reveals that large majorities of respondents preferred the authority without contacts who wants

[11] Two items are relevant. On one, Monte respondents were somewhat less positive toward egalitarian, shared authority than respondents in other sites; they were less likely to prefer an authority who was more eager to help the entire community but had fewer contacts (see Table VI.2). On the other hand, with regard to a question that seemed less reliable than most, a question about the need for exact instructions from a chief, Monte respondents revealed less sense of dependence on exact instructions than their counterparts in other sites.

TABLE VI.2
Attitudes toward the Assumption of Authority by Socioeconomically
Average Men, 1974[a] (%)

| | N | Authority without contacts who wants to help entire community | Authority with contacts who wants to help only his friends | It depends, don't know, no answer |
|---|---|---|---|---|
| Cooperatives, 1974 | 230 | 79 | 12 | 8 |
| Monte | 79 | 65 | 19 | 16 |
| Estrella | 89 | 90 | 6 | 4 |
| Marla | 62 | 87 | 11 | 2 |
| Quasi-control and control, 1974 | 184 | 79 | 15 | 6 |
| Agustín | 94 | 89 | 5 | 5 |
| Virú | 90 | 68 | 23 | 9 |
| SAIS Communities, 1974 | 93 (men only) | 85 | 12 | 3 |

[a] Item read: "Imagine an election for the Administrative Council. One candidate has excellent contacts with the authorities, but he wants to help only his friends. The second wants to help the entire community but doesn't have contacts with the authorities. Which candidate do you prefer?"

to help the entire community. The majorities were especially great in Estrella, Marla, Agustín, and the SAIS communities (between 85 percent and 90 percent), and smaller in Monte (65 percent) and Virú (68 percent). The smaller percentage in Monte reflects the larger number of "Don't know" and other similar answers (16 percent), frequently given by Monte women.

In the 1975 survey, the item about assumption of authority by the average man was altered somewhat. I felt that the 1974 item posed too easy a choice; an authority "eager to help only his friends" seemed tinged by corruption. The item was rephrased to give the patronal type of leader more appeal: "There is one authority, very well trained and with good contacts in the city, but he's very busy, he can't do so much. Then there's an authority who is not so well trained but who's going to work hard for the community, all the community. Which type of authority do you think is better?" Despite the greater attractiveness attributed to the patronal type of authority, overwhelming majorities still preferred the average man: 86 percent of respondents in Estrella, 68 percent in Marla, and 89 percent in Rachuis.

Between 1973 and 1975, coastal cooperative members gradually seemed more assured of the leadership capability of men of average socioeconomic status. In 1973, members hoped for the new system, somewhat anxiously. In the quotation at the beginning of this chapter, Ingenio Cruz frequently uses the word "must." To a similar question, Lorenzo Lazo answered, "The uneducated person can learn to lead. We *must* learn" (emphasis mine). Responding to a probe after the 1975 item, however, members seemed confident, using primarily the declarative rather than the conditional tense:

> When you work as an authority, you learn little by little, as long as you have interest in working for your community (Q1975, 84).

> The authority must have the desire to work. Training is acquired little by little; you learn (Q1975, 23).

In the "fully participatory social democracy," it was hoped not only that people of average socioeconomic status would be elected leaders but also that leadership responsibilities would be shared. To tap this dimension of attitudes about authority, the 1975 instrument included the item, "How should the relations be between authorities and the rank-and-file?" The item was open-ended. A resounding majority of respondents in the CAPs—78 percent in both Estrella and Marla—desired a shared authority system. The ideal relationship was described as "coordinated," "harmonious," "equal," "united," "understanding," "supportive." Only 11 percent of respondents in Estrella and 18 percent in Marla gave responses that could be construed as supportive of a patronal model of authority—responses such as "good treatment" or "like a good father." In Rachuis, however, respondents' preferences were divided; 50 percent wanted "united," "equal" relationships between the leader and the rank-and-file, and 50 percent "good treatment" or "patronal concern." Perhaps in part because the question was phrased in terms of the ideal—"How *should* the relations be . . . ?"—peasants' answers were usually prefaced by the words "ought" and "must." Yet, in Estrella and Marla, many responses seemed assured, elaborated quite specifically:

> There ought to be a good deal of contact and always there should be meetings to consider the problems that exist inside the cooperative (Q1975, 30).

> So that an enterprise progresses, it's very important that the relations between the leaders and the other workers be based on understanding, that monthly there's information on the cooperative's accounts and personnel (Q1975, 14).

A final measure of attitudes toward the new authority pattern was made by asking individuals who had been on a council if they liked their office. The majority was enthusiastic. Of the 33 respondents in Estrella, Marla, and Rachuis who had served or were serving on a council, 20 (61 percent) responded positively and went on to elaborate specific reasons for their enthusiasm. Another 12 percent were also positive, but not to such an extent that they provided details. Only 15 percent were ambivalent, and 12 percent negative. The leaders were proud that they had assumed new responsibilities and discharged them, although at times a note of fear at the awesomeness of their job was evident:

> I like my office, for I had great responsibilities. I had to supervise the community's affairs and see that it progressed well. I planned projects in collaboration with the peasants so that they wouldn't complain of me (Q1975, 90).

> Yes, I liked my experience. I tried to do something for the community. I supervised the construction of the stadium, the school classrooms, the houses. I learned a great deal. I also got to travel to a good number of different places (Q1975, 29).

> Yes, in the Council and the union offices you learn how to defend yourselves and how to talk, so that you can't be deceived as we were by Torres. . . . (Q1975, 17).

The small minority of frustrated councilmen complained that their duties consumed too much time or that their efforts were blocked by lack of support from the council president or the cooperative's rank-and-file.

The new authority pattern was favored by peasants at all socioeconomic levels. The zero-order correlation coefficient between socioeconomic status and rejection of the patronal authority model is only .167, and between socioeconomic status and preference for the authority without contacts who wants to help the entire community, merely .067.

## CHANGES IN BEHAVIORAL PATTERNS OF LEADERSHIP

Incentives for free and honest elections were marked in the cooperatives, and members' aspirations for such elections were by and large translated into their behavior. However, the incentives for sharing authority among individuals of average socioeconomic status were not as marked, and thus, despite the widespread expression of enthusiasm for such a leadership pattern, members wavered between the election of individuals of high and average socioeconomic status. Members of low status and women were virtually never elected. Leadership patterns thus stood between the stipulations of the "democratic elitist" model and the "fully participatory social democracy" model, moving in various directions along the line between the two models in different sites and at different times. The demise of the patronal mode of authority was clearly evident in all the cooperatives.

### Local Peasant Leaders in the Haciendas

As we know, only Estrella of the research haciendas had a regularly operating union, and thus only there did a recognized union leader emerge. This leader was Juan Lescano. Lescano held the highest socioeconomic position in Estrella, excluding the patron. He was a certified accountant and also a prosperous sharecropper who gradually bought his own farm machinery that he rented out to other peasants. Much of Lescano's prosperity was due to his rapport with the patron; it was the patron who loaned him funds for accounting school, sold him land, and, during the expropriation of the hacienda, farm machinery. Not surprisingly, Lescano's relationship with the patron and economic gains therefrom put him under fire from many peasants. However, by the criteria of the era, Lescano was an effective leader. Lescano seemed to persuade the patron to be more accommodating toward the union.[12] At the Trujillo salary negotiations, the Estrella union leaders were at the forefront of the demands for wage increases in the valley. Thus, Lescano could not be accused of selling out the union.

Union leaders like Juan Lescano were common throughout Peru. The great majority of them held high socioeconomic positions (Handelman, 1975a: 189; Tullis, 1970: 1-3, 100, 113). They had to deliver some wage gains to the peasants—they were at least minimally accountable to the unions—but their rapport with the patron, their own rapid economic rise, and their inability or disinclination to delegate authority frequently rendered them suspect of informing on and betraying the union (Greaves, 1968: 287; Tullis, 1970: 85-144; Gitlitz, 1975: 243-312). The union leader was often estranged from the rank-and-file, yet rarely recalled because of the difficulty of locating a replacement who would be accepted by the patron. Tension was thus sharp, as at El Chalán:

[12] Interviews with Juan Lescano in Estrella and the hacendado in Trujillo, February 1974.

The leaders view most of the members as ignorant and apathetic to matters of vital concern. In exasperation their manner frequently becomes openly pedagogical. . . . At the same time the general membership comes to view the leaders as over-ambitious, always ready to use their office to gain and exercise power over their fellow workers for their own ends. . . . The officers are often subjected to charges that they are spending union funds for pleasure trips (Greaves, 1968: 287).

Lescano's leadership mode does not fit any one model. It was of course not in the mode of archetypal clientelism, in which there are no peasant leaders. Nor was Lescano a "broker" in the "modern" clientelist mode because his access to powers beyond the hacienda was limited; he was dependent upon the patron for his position. Yet, in various ways Lescano affirmed a clientelist authority mode, because his leadership was modeled after that of the patron. Leadership seemed to "fall," in Estrella as elsewhere, to the man of the highest socioeconomic position, as if it were his birthright. Moreover, although peasants indicated to Lescano what they wanted as a group, Lescano put these requests to the patron alone, as they must be made in the clientelist model.

*Local Peasant Leaders in the Cooperatives*
*and Peasant Communities*

Although members rejected arrogant, patronal leaders in all cooperative sites, and moved toward the election of leaders in all sites, there was considerable variation among sites with respect to the sharing of authority and the election of men of average socioeconomic status. In general, there was a stronger trend toward sharing authority among average men in the coastal cooperatives than in the highlands SAIS.

The primary emphasis in this section is on the Administrative Council because the council was the key executive organ. In cases where non-council members wielded significant leadership powers, they are discussed, however. Some men who failed to win council posts stole into meetings anyway. Non-peasant outsiders also held important powers on some issues during some periods; Estrella's ex-patron was still a relevant figure for the enterprise until 1975, for example. By and large, however, as the 1975 survey results cited in Chapter V indicated, the council was the key leadership organ.

One method of sharing authority is through frequent elections and, thereby, the rotation of posts. This strategy was practiced in many cooperatives. Frequent elections were stipulated by law but were held more frequently than legally required in many enter-prises. The terms of the council president and vice-president were often limited to one year (rather than the legal three); the specific posts of the council members were often designated in the Assem-bly, and elections were usually held annually (rather than trienni-ally, as apparently was to happen after the first three years).[13]

Leadership was also shared in the meetings themselves.[14] The president was a prominent but not overbearing participant. He had only one vote in the council, just like other members; his only special legal prerogative was his power of decision in case of a tie. Moreover, if the president's educational background were limited, he could not sway votes on the basis of technical expertise. However, the president's words often had more weight than others' because of the status inherent in his title and also because of the greater knowledge of enterprise issues he gained with his job. The president spent more time in the enterprise offices than other council officers. In both SAIS Huanca and Estrella, the work and/or payment schedules of the presidents were altered to permit them to give several hours a day to cooperative business. Usually, the presi-dent spent at least an hour every day working with the director and an hour or so every week with government officials. Thus, the president was in an advantageous position at council meetings, but the norm remained give-and-take, as these two council members suggested:

> I really liked being in the Council. Tagle [the president at the time] was great. We decided together what to plant and what to invest. Each week we met. We agreed to give more help to members—more little plots of land, more animals, and the coop-erative store that sells cheap. We planted sugar cane for the first time (Q1975, 46).

> Yes, I like my work in the council. I have to watch the progress of the CAP, how the planting goes, how meeting attendance is. In our meetings, everyone talks. One person says that it's good to have a new tractor, another one that it's not. Often the official from SINAMOS attends, and gives suggestions, and orients us.

[13] See Supreme Decree 240-69-AP, articles 61 and 86 for the legal stipulations.
[14] I observed two formal Administrative Council meetings at length. One of the meetings was in SAIS Huanca in June 1973, and one in Estrella in May 1975. I also talked a great deal with Administrative Council presidents and observed their day-to-day interactions with other council members and managers.

He always talks in favor of the peasant. After everyone gives their opinion, there's a vote.[15]

Although over-all the trend in the background of cooperative leaders was away from individuals of high socioeconomic status, the trajectory was neither universal nor invariable and was stronger in the coastal sites than the highlands ones. Members saw the flaws of leaders of high status to be dishonesty and limited concern for other members, and the flaws of leaders of average status to be mediocre executive skills and, in less advanced sites, illiteracy. The trends with regard to leadership socioeconomic status are set forth in Tables VI.3 and VI.4.

Table VI.3 specifies the socioeconomic status of the Administrative Council president (union leader in Monte) in the experimental sites across five elections. (A sixth election was held in Huanca in 1977 for which I have no information; Marla and Estrella held only five elections between 1972 and 1977 because somewhat more than a year slipped by between elections in several cases. Elections were irregular in Monte's union.) The table indicates that individuals of high socioeconomic status were consistently chosen in Huanca and Monte, whereas in Estrella and Marla this kind of leader was replaced by an individual of average status at the third election in 1975, with a subsequent return to individuals at a somewhat higher point in the socioeconomic distribution, but not at the pinnacle.

Trends in the socioeconomic position of all members of the councils are indicated in Table VI.4. Data are available only through 1975 and are not comprehensive. However, they do point to the ascendance of men of average education and means to council positions in Estrella and Marla by 1975, a trend that endured. These trends in Estrella and Marla were apparently representative of those in many Peruvian cooperatives, at least on the coast; the grasp on top leadership by the upper stratum may even have been tighter in my research sites than elsewhere. For example, whereas of the nine Administrative Council presidents of my three major cooperatives during 1972-1975, seven (77 percent) had some secondary education, of the Administrative Council presidents who attended the Second National Conference for Leaders and Technicians of Agrarian Cooperatives in Ica (a coastal city) in 1974, only

---

[15] Interview with Mercardo Cruz Baltazar, 1974-1975 Marla Vigilance Council vice-president, in Marla, May 1975.

TABLE VI.3

Socioeconomic Status of Administrative Council Presidents, 1972-1977[a]

| | First Election | Second Election | Third Election | Fourth Election | Fifth Election |
|---|---|---|---|---|---|
| CAP Estrella | 1 (Payroll supervisor) | Pinnacle (Poultry Entrepreneur) | 4 (Warehouse supervisor) | 3 (Truckdriver) | 3[b] (Truckdriver) |
| CAP Marla | Pinnacle (Accountant) | Pinnacle[b] (Accountant) | 4 (Field worker) | 4 (Field worker) | 2 (Fieldwork supervisor) |
| SAIS Huanca | 1 (Prosperous peasant) | 1 (University student) | 1 (University student) | 1 (University student) | 1 (Secondary school teacher) |
| Monte[c] | Pinnacle (Accountant) | Pinnacle[b] (Accountant) | 1 (Office helper, former butcher) | 1[b] (Office helper, former butcher) | 2 (Carpenter) |

[a] For notes on data, see Appendix 6. Numbers are based on a scale from 1 to 10, with 1 indicating the top socioeconomic decile and 10 the bottom, in that site. Deciles divide socioeconomic rank, not site members; thus it would be theoretically possible that one decile did not include any individuals.

[b] Same individual as in the previous election.

[c] Leader is union leader, not Administrative Council president. With the exception of the "fourth election," leader also served as Monte's delegate to the CS.

TABLE VI.4

Socioeconomic Status of Council Members, 1972-1975 (%)

| | | Site population[b] | Council members | | |
|---|---|---|---|---|---|
| | | | *First election* | *Second election* | *Third election* |
| **Huanca** (N=10 at first two elections, 12 at third) | | | | | |
| | *Education* | | | | |
| | At least some secondary | 19[c] | 50 | 60 | 50 |
| | Not more than complete primary | 82[c] | 50 | 40 | 50 |
| **Estrella** (N=14 at both elections) | | | | | |
| | *Education* | | | | |
| | At least some secondary | 18 | N.A. | 43 | 21 |
| | Not more than complete primary | 82 | | 57 | 78 |
| | *Wealth* | | | | |
| | Richer than average in valley[d] | 29 | N.A. | 50 | 28 |
| | Average | 43 | | 43 | 71 |
| | Poorer than average in valley | 26 | | 7 | 0 |
| **Marla** (N=12 at second election, N=7 at third)[d] | | | | | |
| | *Education* | | | | |
| | At least some secondary | 0 | N.A. | 17 | 0 |
| | Not more than complete primary | 100 | | 83 | 100 |
| | *Wealth* | | | | |
| | Richer than average in valley[d] | 5 | N.A. | 42 | 14 |
| | Average | 25 | | 25 | 29 |
| | Poorer than average in valley[d] | 69 | | 33 | 57 |

SOURCES and explications: see Appendix 6.

[a] Data are missing for one member in Estrella at the second election, and for two at the third election. Data are missing for 6 members in Marla at the second election and for 9 at the third. Results are probably biased toward inclusion of higher SES members as I was more likely to be aware of their identity.

[b] Data on site population derive from 1973-74 McClintock survey. Figures for education are based on men only.

[c] Figures refer to Patca and Varya, as representative communities in SAIS Huanca.

[d] "Valley" refers to Virú valley, the location of the coastal CAPs.

45 percent had some secondary education.[16] Further, with regard to the occupation of Administrative Council members, whereas both Estrella and Marla were dominated by white-collar employees or ex-sharecroppers until 1975, of 28 cooperatives around Trujillo in 1972-1973, only a bare majority (57 percent) were dominated by men from such occupations.[17] Similarly, of 13 cooperatives throughout the country in 1974, only 31 percent had white-collar employees as presidents of the councils and only 21 percent had more than three white-collar employees on the Administrative Council (Centro de Estudios de Participación Popular, 1974-75).

Changes in leadership patterns will be documented through discussion of the specific experiences of the various research sites. I consider first the sites where change was greatest—Estrella and Marla—and the sites where change was less—Huanca and Monte. Finally, leadership patterns in the Huanca peasant communities are briefly described.

*Estrella.* Estrella first elected a white-collar employee, Roberto Ramírez, as Administrative Council president. Ramírez enjoyed a high socioeconomic position both from his employment as payroll supervisor and from his family's ten hectares of land, but he was considered an honest man who would handle workers' demands fairly. Suddenly, however, Ramírez's father fell ill, and to pay doctors' bills Ramírez raised his salary about 20 percent. It was said that Ramírez's move was encouraged by the vice-president, Tomás Torres, an ambitious ex-sharecropper who had become the wealthiest man in the valley through his poultry enterprise. Although as an ex-sharecropper Torres had no interest in the advancement of the cooperative, he saw the CAP as an avenue to greater personal wealth and prominence.

Torres called a General Assembly in which he condemned Ramírez's "avarice" and suggested that the president be recalled, in which event Torres would automatically assume the job. Many workers were wary of Torres, and with the support of SINAMOS, they organized a series of meetings that produced a petition to forgive Ramírez for raising his salary. However, the ex-sharecroppers all endorsed Torres and purportedly purchased the

---

[16] Author's calculation from attendance forms of CENCIRA in Lima for the "Second National Conference for the Leaders and Technicians of Agrarian Cooperatives," held in Ica in January 1974.

[17] Author's calculation from data in Elías Minaya (1973: Appendix 2).

votes of some workers. Finally, a majority approved Ramírez's re-call, allowing Torres's ascendance to the presidency.

Torres proved a corrupt and ineffectual president. He failed to fulfill leadership responsibilities, visiting the cooperative only rarely. Day-to-day leadership tasks were carried out by Juan Lescano (the treasurer and former union leader) as well as by Ricardo Letos (the president of the Education Committee, an energetic young payroll supervisor). Torres and Lescano allied to bilk the cooperative. Perhaps the most lucrative swindle was the establishment of a non-existent company headed by the ex-patron. The "company" was contracted at approximately 20,000 soles a month to provide technical advice to Estrella, in lieu of a director. In fact, the "company" provided no technical services whatsoever. The fee of the "company" was split between the ex-patron, Torres, Lescano, and perhaps a few others. Other swindles were also carried out by the president and the treasurer, although they are harder to prove. Lescano and Torres probably claimed that they paid higher prices for Estrella's purchases than they did, and that they received lower prices for Estrella's products than they did, in both cases pocketing the difference themselves.

Gradually, other members of the Administrative Council became furious at these swindles. Nervous, Lescano and Torres stalled many council meetings. When meetings were held, they tried to put the workers' representatives into secretarial roles, addressing them only with commands to "note this" or "note that." At a few meetings, workers' representatives challenged the ex-sharecroppers, but the challenges were fielded by cases of beer or threats of job demotion. Chapter IV recounted the failure of Lorenzo Lazo's confrontation with the leadership clique.

Torres and Lescano were in many ways new patrons, although "good" ones. They took large sums of money from the enterprise, but during their leadership, material benefits to workers increased. Torres was appointed "godfather" of community projects and contributed adobes for the sports stadium, beer for dances, and uniforms for athletic teams. However, when the books were opened in the General Assembly and the extent of probable corruption revealed, the members realized how small were Torres's "gifts" relative to his gains. Workers increasingly denigrated Torres and his patronal style: "Before with Torres, it was like a second patron, since he didn't attend to the demands of the workers. No matter how much I petitioned to get my membership, he paid no attention. But now it's different, you can elect whomever you want" (Q1975, 19).

As described in Chapter V, after a strong workers' protest, the ex-sharecroppers were separated from the cooperative. Reacting to what was perceived as the patronal and deceiving ways of men of high socioeconomic status, Estrella members elected three workers to the top four council posts; Lucho Saavedra, the warehouse supervisor with a complete primary education, was chosen president. The only non-worker in the top four posts was Pedro Vásquez, who became treasurer. Lucho Saavedra was considered a good president. Workers felt represented; one of the first council decisions was to launch a lawsuit against Lescano on the basis of theft, a decision that upset most of the white-collar employees and ex-sharecroppers. The cooperative progressed; sound decisions were made about production and investment, the new houses and new sports stadium were opened, and no accusations of dishonesty were made. However, Saavedra did feel somewhat uncertain of his competence, somewhat awed by the job:

> It was a great responsibility to be council president. You have to deal very evenly with all kinds of problems, not be too hard or too soft. You have to buy things, get loans, and such very carefully. All these are very difficult tasks. It was much more difficult than being a union leader; the tasks were more varied, more demanding. . . . I'd like to be president again. . . . But Pedro is doing a good job now.[18]

Apparently, Estrella members also feared that the presidency was too much for Saavedra, and in 1976 and again in 1977 they chose Pedro Vásquez for the post. Vásquez was not a white-collar employee; he had only a primary education and worked driving the cooperative's truck. However, Vásquez had much stronger family ties to the ex-sharecroppers than Lucho Saavedra and had a more authoritative personality. During 1976 and 1977 Estrella was progressing rapidly, and Vásquez was very popular. He was given considerable credit for Estrella's lucrative decision to invest in sugar cane. Probably because of his ties to various groups in the cooperative, Vásquez also tried to improve the relations between workers, on the one hand, and ex-sharecroppers and white-collar employees, on the other. The lawsuit against Lescano was dropped, in return for an anticipated "gift" from Torres of some $4,000.

---

[18] Interview with Lucho Saavedra, in Estrella, July 1977.

*Marla.* In 1972-1974, the top Marla leadership was shared among several men of high socioeconomic status, who made many decisions among themselves. The Administrative Council president was Ramón Tagle, an accountant who was also serving as the director. Bright, friendly, and honest, Tagle was well-liked. He was not a vigorous leader, however, in part because he lived not in Marla but in Trujillo. The 1973-1974 Vigilance Council president was also a man of high status, a university-educated former schoolteacher who was employed as the head worker supervisor. He was intelligent and capable, but also tense and reserved and not popular among the workers. A third leader, Carlos Otiniano, was active first as the Vigilance Council president and then as the delegate to the Virú Agrarian League. Otiniano was affable, but his obvious arrogance and ambition alienated many workers.

Although the 1972-1974 Marla leaders were honest and committed to the cooperative, their leadership record was flawed. As noted previously, they were implicated in a plot to depose the second Marla manager that damaged Marla financially. Enterprise profits were scant. Rumors of leadership corruption began to circulate.

Finally in 1974, Marla members opted for leaders of average socioeconomic status, who could hardly prove less competent than the previous high-status leadership. The 1974-1975 president held the most humble occupation of any president in the major research sites: he was an unskilled field worker, although he had completed his primary education. Much newer to politics and much less confident than Estrella's Lucho Saavedra, Marla's president was nervous and hesitant. He wanted to be responsive to members, and council meetings were much more open than in the days of Tagle's presidency, but he also seemed to resent the members, feeling that they were asking too much from him:

> This is the first time that I've assumed the role of president of the Administrative Council, but I must say that the people were wrong to elect me, because now they don't want to collaborate. I've been four months on the job, and I must continue what I've planned to do. I want to make a livestock stable, a poultry hatchery, and if possible buy the factory to can the asparagus. Now we have the budget made for the factory, but it's very expensive, it's valued at eighteen million soles. The members made a demand that, when they adjudicate the cooperative, they adjudicate the factory too, because it was a part of the enterprise. But the gov-

ernment didn't do it, so now we're trying to work things out again in Trujillo to get it. It's a lot of work and I don't get much support from other people around here (Q1975, 61).

The president was unable to win the demand for the asparagus factory or to complete any other new project. Politically, he was absorbed by the task of getting rid of a capable but arrogant director, and he was not able to improve sharply Marla's economic situation. Another field worker was elected in late 1975, but enjoyed no more success than his predecessor, for unclear reasons.

In 1976, Marla members turned once again to leaders of higher status, presumably in the hope that their greater formal education would help them find a solution to Marla's problems, or at least to win larger bank loans. A fieldwork supervisor was chosen president and several other white-collar employees were elected. Although Carlos Otiniano himself was not selected, he was close to the new president, and he was believed to be exercising considerable influence. Yet, Marla still did not progress, and the cooperative leaders were thought to be neglecting the cooperative at best and robbing it at worst. By July 1977, Marla peasants were aching to recall the president, but he refused to hold a meeting and apparently the Vigilance Council was reluctant to force an assembly. Commented one peasant: "Since last year, there have been no meetings, only to change leaders. This year, we haven't met even to see the balance sheet; the leaders don't want meetings, because it would not be to their advantage; there, we'd let them have it" (Q1977, M4).

Marla peasants' resentment of the president, Otiniano, and Tagle was much greater in 1977 than in 1974, and election of a president of average status seemed imminent. But there were few counterparts to Estrella's Lucho Saavedra in Marla; the reading and writing capabilities of an average Marla member were below those of an average Estrella member. Yet, competent leadership of Marla did not seem impossible. In the 1977 questionnaire, most respondents indicated that improving production had to be the top priority, and that it could be done by rotating the asparagus and developing new products. Other crops had grown well in the 1950s and early 1960s in Marla, and a committed leader who focused on this problem could presumably make new crops grow well again.

*SAIS Huanca.* In SAIS Huanca, leadership was more honestly elected, shared, and egalitarian than in hacienda days, but less so than in the coastal cooperatives. Elections were honest and regular, but authority was shared among individuals of average socio-economic status and based on the formal council structures to a lesser degree than in the coastal CAPs. In particular, considerable influence was wielded by Julio Melchor, the ex-hacienda workers' leader and the assistant director of the enterprise. Also, the second and third presidents, both men of high status, continued to exercise influence after their terms were over, establishing themselves in white-collar positions in the enterprise. Most SAIS presidents seemed to delegate less authority to other council members than in Estrella or Marla. By 1975, Julio Melchor, the two former presidents turned employees, and a few of the top elected leaders resembled a political clique.

The reasons for the emergence of such a leadership pattern in Huanca are not entirely clear. Individuals of high socioeconomic status were probably able to maintain authority for two reasons: first, until 1976, high-status leaders were competent and honest and gave peasants no reason to question their election; second, there were relatively few literate individuals in Huanca but enterprise responsibilities were relatively great. The rather large authority of the president vis-à-vis other council members might also have reflected the vast physical distance between members in this large enterprise, which impeded contact among council workers. Moreover, both the second and third presidents were very capable and perhaps deserved continuing SAIS leadership, especially given the complexity of the enterprise and thus the greater disadvantage of leadership rotation.

Aurelio Osores, the 1973-1974 president, is a good example of the capable, but relatively aggressive and inegalitarian leadership in the SAIS. President at roughly 28 years of age, Osores had not worked as a farmer for years. (Thus, like all other Huanca presidents, he was technically ineligible for the post.) The sixth son of the richest family in a backward SAIS community, Osores was sent to primary and secondary school in Huancayo. After graduation, Osores taught in his community for a few years and then worked as an administrative assistant in the Huancayo Ministry of Agriculture. With his Ministry of Agriculture contacts, Osores was able to help his community and was eventually elected delegate to the SAIS. At about the same time, he entered the university in Huancayo, graduating with a degree in business administration in 1976.

Despite his relatively prosperous background, Osores held leftist political views, more carefully developed than those of other cooperative leaders I knew. He articulated these views dramatically, as his article in a SAIS magazine suggests:

> We are uniting all the SAIS of the central highlands so that we won't continue to be exploited by middlemen, by anybody. Also, I want you to know that now the middleman, or the factory owner, robs us, steals from us the raw materials that we produce, for example the wool, the hides, the skins, the meat. We are so humble, saying, "Let God allow us to be rich, or to progress." We stay quiet, we remain without thinking that they take our wealth. They have money to buy milk for their dogs. How long are we going to support this humiliation? I call upon you to rise up, and like one man, support this organization. With time it will give work to peasants who now are hungry and whose children are illiterate. Brother peasant, you are not poor, only you must learn to open your eyes and to see how they humiliate you, how they exploit you. But this exploiter is not a peasant, nor a worker, nor even the government. The exploiters are the Yankees. So when the so-called World Service of Churches comes, kick them out; do not accept this humiliation, learn to rise up and don't beg, rather think, believe, and wake up.[19]

Osores worked smoothly with the other council members, but he was definitely the leader. Most of the major decisions of the SAIS council during 1973-1974 reflected Osore's opinions. For example, he favored the wage increase for workers, the hiring of more technicians from humble backgrounds, and the encouragement of new commercialization and industrialization opportunities for Huanca through economic federation. The only major issue on which Osores was not able to win approval for his position was a larger salary increase for technicians.

Osores's authority was clearly demonstrated one day, when the director entered the council office to ask for a decision on one ex-hacienda administrator's threat that he would resign unless he received a salary increase. Both the treasurer and the secretary were in the office with Osores. Osores responded that the SAIS could not make the large salary increase and that the resignation should be accepted. The two council members then suggested that the mayordomo could do the administrator's job more cheaply and just as effectively. Osores said softly that he doubted the mayordomo would be able to maintain discipline, but that a young techni-

19 "La Central SAIS," *Jatari-Uyari* (SAIS magazine), 3 (July 1973), n.p.

cian could be hired who would be inexpensive because of his inex-
perience, but still competent. The question was discussed casually
for fifteen minutes. Osores's position was accepted.

Osores's leadership at times verged on the charismatic. For example, after one SAIS General Assembly in Monte, Osores motioned
to the delegates to follow him into the ex-hacendado's house. Traditionally, no peasants except the housekeepers and the guardians
were allowed into this vast, luxurious house. Osores led the peasants through the house, and then stopped on the living room,
which was still decked out with a thick carpet and chandelier, and
began to talk to the delegates. Osores spoke dramatically for thirty
minutes or more about the potential of the SAIS. The peasants
were spellbound.

Osores was confident, but not arrogant. Despite his university
education, he was perceived by the technicians as a peasant, and he
saw himself as a peasant. In the council office, he chatted frequently
with other council members on many topics, all using the friendly
"tú" form of address. Osores carefully addressed the director as
"Doctor," while the director at times forgot the new modes of address and called Osores *hijo* (son). During the lunches between
assembly sessions, Osores ate in the large dining hall with the other
delegates, while the technicians ate together in a special alcove.

After his term in the council, Osores won a position as assistant
administrator on a SAIS ex-hacienda. The job was not the idea of
technicians who wanted to "co-opt" Osores; most SAIS technicians
resented Osores's promotion, perceiving him still a peasant. Rather,
it was the idea of Osores himself, who was both committed to the
SAIS and confident he could rise within it. He wanted to continue
to play an important role in the SAIS, and he did. He hoped to be
a unifying figure, and at various times persuaded comuneros to
accept greater salary increases for the workers. In these efforts,
Osores attended many meetings to which he held no formal right
of entrance.

Osores's successor to the presidency, Roberto Meza, was similar
in style but not in ideology to Osores. Affiliated with APRA, Meza
was skeptical of the military government from the start and, probably in part for that reason, skeptical of the SAIS as well.[20] Unlike
Osores, Meza did not seek compromise positions in the SAIS. Meza

[20] Interview with Roberto Meza at SAIS General Assembly in Monte, June 1973,
just after his defeat by Osores for the presidency that year.

believed that the SAIS should be restructured, not to give the
workers more power but to reduce its size, dividing it into smaller
cooperatives.[21] During his presidency, Meza persuaded the SAIS to
make the position as head of Huanca's Education Committee a
permanent, paid slot, and after his term this job went to Meza
himself. Aurelio Osores and Roberto Meza remained the key comunero political figures, often opposing each other, and remained so
even during the intervention of the SAIS.

In 1976, the SAIS president, one or two other council members,
and the director became implicated in corruption charges; these
men were thrown out and the SAIS intervened. The ultimate impact of this episode for leadership patterns in the SAIS was unclear.
First, as Chapter V indicated, the political conflict between the
comuneros and trabajadores was probably a more important cause
of intervention than were charges of corruption; the implicated
leaders may even have been set up. However, peasants in Patca,
Varya, and Rachuis did believe that the leaders in question had
been guilty and deserved their fate; yet, in contrast to coastal
cooperative members, very few of these respondents linked the
high socioeconomic status of the leaders to corruption tendencies.
Elections were held after the intervention, and another high-status
individual was chosen. I had known the new president in 1973,
when he was in Varya, his birthplace, after some ten years as a
secondary school teacher in Lima. Although he was older than
previous SAIS presidents, otherwise he seemed similar; to my
knowledge, he had no particular political inclinations that would
have recommended him to government officials. In Varya in 1973,
he had seemed energetic and committed, but, like both Osores and
Meza, too quick to assert authority.

*Monte.* As in the SAIS as a whole, leadership patterns in Monte did
not move far toward a shared and egalitarian mode, although
leaders were competent and honest. One reason for the limited
change was that the new laws about elections did not apply to
Monte's union. Monte did not hold elections annually, and thus did
not rotate leadership often; elections were held when there was a
consensus that they should be. Morevoer, because Monte leaders
were competent and honest, peasants did not question the wisdom
of choosing authorities of high rather than average socioeconomic
status. Yet, there was some movement toward the new leadership

[21] Interview with Roberto Meza in SAIS offices in Huancayo, July 1977.

pattern even in Monte. As Chapter V discussed, political participation was great in Monte; through participating in meetings and exercising minor leadership roles, several Monte members, such as Ingenio, were developing leadership expertise. In 1977, one of these men captured the presidency of the union, and Monte seemed to be on the road to a more shared and egalitarian leadership pattern.

The top authority in Monte during 1972-1974 was the accountant, Miguel Maray. Working for several years supervising shepherds in an isolated Huanca hacienda, Maray somehow scraped together money for a few years of secondary education and accounting courses, and he moved to Monte as its accountant in the late 1960s. Maray was everything a leader could be in the eyes of Monte residents. At 33, he was a radical political thinker, a poet, a successful athlete, a winner at Chinese checkers, and a handsome father of six children. In political meetings he was softspoken, but he knew how to make his words weigh heavily on his audience. President of the Monte union from 1972-1974, Maray was a very effective organizer. In contrast to the leaders of high socioeconomic status in the CAPs, he encouraged the participation of the poorer workers in political assemblies. In late 1973, he spearheaded the successful battle for higher salaries for the ex-hacienda workers.

Maray was a thorn in the sides of the comuneros. Perhaps encouraged by SINAMOS, the Administrative Council hoped to co-opt Maray. In February 1974, Maray was offered a promotion as the assistant administrator in a distant ex-hacienda. The council evidently believed that the move would sever Maray from his base. Maray himself was ambivalent. He thought that perhaps he could strengthen the entire SAIS ex-hacienda union by politicizing another ex-hacienda. His wife was eager for the upward mobility. But Maray also knew that the workers might consider him co-opted.

Maray realized that the decision was important and that the workers' trust in the union would depend to a large extent upon their faith in him. In several union meetings, Maray opened himself to interrogation on the issue. Groups of workers descended on Maray's house several nights a week. Most members wanted Maray to stay in Monte. Finally, however, Maray decided to accept the promotion.

In his new position, Maray did continue his political activities. He became the leader of the all-Huanca union; in this capacity he returned every so often to Monte, and gradually convinced peasants of the validity of his arguments for his departure. As the leader of the all-Huanca union, he also exerted considerable influence upon the decisions of the union in Monte.

After Maray's departure, the top leadership position at Monte fell to Basilio Ortiz, who had been "number two" in Monte's unwritten leadership ranks. Although a former butcher without any secondary education, Ortiz was promoted by the SAIS to the position of office assistant and became the only white-collar employee from a peasant background in Monte, as Maray had been. Ortiz was an adequate leader, but not the equal of Maray. Younger men with stronger educational backgrounds were gaining experience and political ambition. In a 1977 union election, an energetic young carpenter was chosen leader. No confrontation occurred, though, and Ortiz, the carpenter, and other politically active young men may work together to a greater extent than previous leaders had.

In contrast to Estrella and Marla, but like the peasant communities in Huanca, many critical decisions for Monte were made not by Monte itself but by the all-Huanca union. This union was led by individuals of extremely high socioeconomic status who resembled a clique more than the Huanca leaders. Maray, Julio Melchor, and the administrator of the ex-hacienda Loroya were the key union figures throughout 1972-1977 and the major negotiators for the restructuring of the SAIS. Thus, the union structure was by no means more conducive to the sharing of leadership among individuals of average status than was the cooperative.

*Patca, Varya, and Agustín.* Authority patterns in the three peasant communities Patca, Varya, and Agustin were less clear than in other sites for various reasons. First, rather than sharing authority in one leadership body, authority in the peasant communities was divided among several individuals, who often had distinct power bases. Varya and Agustín were both district capitals; thus, they elected an Administrative Council, but they also had a mayor who was appointed by provincial officials. Conflict between the two individuals was frequent. In both Patca and Varya, the Administrative Council president tended to be more representative of the peasant majority and to have a lower socioeconomic status than the mayor. Moreover, in Patca and Varya, delegates to the SAIS were elected as well as council leaders. Although both the Administrative Council president and the delegate to the SAIS were generally committed to the advancement of the community, the president was typically an older man, less ambitious, and shouldering community responsibilities primarily from a sense of obligation. In contrast, the delegates to the SAIS were generally younger men with grander visions of the future; and, like the mayors, they tended to be from a higher socioeconomic background than the council presidents.

Despite the complexities in the leadership patterns of peasant communities since 1969, some patterns may be discerned. The electoral system became much more regular in the early 1970s and commercial middlemen near the pinnacle of the socioeconomic distribution—men who had often dominated the community in the past—were frozen out of the elections, in part because of the disqualification statute in the peasant-community law.[22] In all the communities, council leaders had considerable responsibility for various projects funded by the SAIS—schools, electrification, community centers—and on the whole carried out these responsibilities well. However, these responsibilities were not as broadening nor as satisfying as the grander tasks of enterprise management, and presidents were rarely reluctant to give up their posts, in contrast to presidents of the CAPs and SAIS.

### Leadership in The Control Site

In Virú, no new legal structure required elections or encouraged any new authority pattern. The only village authority was the mayor, who was appointed from Trujillo. Authority remained in a patronal mode.

During approximately 1970 to 1973, the mayor of Virú was Luis Almendría. Almendría was by far the richest man in the community. Although his hacienda was expropriated by the government, Almendría retained the chicken hatchery, the most lucrative part of the enterprise. Almendría spent a quarter of his time at most in Virú and thus, needless to say, did not work hard for the advancement of the village. The only village project in evidence was beautification of the plaza.

Yet, Almendría was a "good patron" and actually seemed popular. After an earthquake damaged the entire valley in the early 1970s, Almendría brought in emergency aid from his "friend," General Torrijos, the president of Panama. Almendría also gave significant funds for the beautification of the plaza and the con-

---

[22] Long and Winder (1975) provide a detailed description of the impact of the disqualification statute on leadership patterns in another peasant community near Huancayo. The impact with respect to the disqualification of middlemen of high socioeconomic status was similar to that in my research communities.

struction of a hospital (a project designed from Trujillo). Almendría had already made his fortune from the hacienda, and there were no allegations of corruption.

In 1974 the Trujillo authorities were seeking a new mayor for Virú. Viruñeros did not try to influence the appointment. Several candidates were considered by the Trujillo officials, all of them of apparently high socioeconomic status. Finally, Tomás Torres, whom we know as the corrupt Administrative Council president of Estrella, was selected. The patronal pattern of authority in all likelihood has continued in Virú.

## SUMMARY

No one model of leadership clearly fits the Peruvian cooperatives. However, it is apparent that the patronal mode of authority was roundly rejected in the cooperatives, whereas it survived in the control village Virú. The principles and practices of honest elections and of at least some sharing of executive authority emerged. The issue of the competence of the "expert," or individual of high socioeconomic status, versus the "ordinary man" remained unresolved in most sites, however. Leadership by individuals of average status became an ideal during this period, but not an ubiquitous reality.

# VII · Society

IN THE HACIENDA, the patron links each peasant client to himself individually and obstructs solidarity among the peasants. In part to impede ties among clients, the patron may imply that friendship, in the sense of shared personal experiences, is not important. Rather, he may insinuate, the motives of friendship are ulterior: to gain economic benefits. Friendship is a calculation of mutual advantage between a superior and subordinate, a longstanding network of obligation and dependence.[1] In the hacienda, the patron is the primary source of economic benefits, and thus peasants are persuaded to compete against each other for the friendship and favors of the patron. Such a definition of friendship clearly favors the maintenance of the clientelist system.

In terms of political systems, neither the corporatist nor the "fully participatory social democracy" model addresses the nature of friendship in the new system. However, some inferences may be drawn. In a corporatist system, the survival of patronal figures would presumably signify the continuation of competition among peasants for the favors of superiors, and thus also the continuation of considerable calculation in so-called friendships. In the "fully participatory social democracy," however, friendship would be different.[2] A few wealthy individuals would no longer hold the keys to economic survival, and thus peasants would not need to cultivate them personally. Peasants would look to each other as equals for

---

[1] This type of "friendship" is common in many societies, not only clientelist ones. Solomon (1971: 124-125) suggests that mutual material assistance was a key goal of friendship in traditional China. Indeed, the American notion of friendship as "need affiliation" is atypical (Solomon, 1969: 300). For discussions of social relationships in the Latin American hacienda, see especially Foster (1967); Fromm and Maccoby (1970: 110-116); Dobyns, Doughty, and Lasswell (1971); and Williams (1969).

[2] Official discussions are scant. There are some implications for the nature of friendship in the "fully participatory social democracy" in the Ministry of Agriculture (1974a). Primarily, however, my inferences are derived from conversations with officials and their speeches.

mutual material support in times of need. The concern for material benefit would no longer be the only stimulus to friendship, however. Friendship would also mean the common enjoyment of good times, the discussion of political opinions, and the sharing of personal experiences. Secrets of a romantic or political nature would be confided without fear. Members would trust each other to be honest and sympathetic. Friendship and trust would not be restricted to small groups demarcated by socioeconomic status, age, or sex, but would permeate the entire community.

To what extent did the ideals of trust and friendship implied in the "fully participatory social democracy" take root in the cooperatives? Did bonds of sympathy grow among all cooperative members? Or did friendship continue to mean primarily the manipulation of material benefits from superiors?

## INCENTIVES FOR TRUST AND FRIENDSHIP

Incentives for solidarity increased in the cooperatives, as this section will show. Economic benefits remained an important incentive to friendship, but these were no longer so closely tied to the patron. New purposes for friendship emerged too: sharing good times and exchanging political opinions. These incentives to friendship are perhaps less tangible than some incentives discussed previously, and perhaps reflect more the departure of the hacendado than the establishment of the cooperative.

In poor nations, perhaps the most important stimulus to friendship is always to assure material security in times of crisis— emergency loans, transportation to the city in case of illness, and the provision of employment opportunities for relatives. In the hacienda, the attainment of these benefits was contingent upon close ties to the patron and was uncertain, a situation pitting the peasants against each other. In the cooperative, however, members themselves controlled the economic resources of the enterprise. Hence, they were able to insure themselves against economic emergencies through the cooperative. The change in the source of material help was frequently emphasized as critical to a new solidarity among residents:

> Before, you asked help only from the patron. Now, you seek help from other people here, and sometimes they help you (Q1975, 4).

> We help each other with whatever little thing comes up among us. Before, it was different. The patron did not permit us to collaborate (Q1975, 60).

However, socioeconomic inequalities continued in the cooperatives, and on the basis of these inequalities many clientelistic
"friendships" were built, as they had been previously with the patron. Individuals in or around the enterprises were often ten times
as wealthy as a disadvantaged peasant. Although, in contrast to the
patron, they did not enjoy a monopoly of any resource, they did
have many important things, such as farm machinery. Members felt
somewhat dependent upon these individuals; given that the survival of the military government and the fate of the cooperatives
were uncertain, members felt that some day they might need these
well-to-do families' help. Further, if these wealthy men could be
persuaded to accept the role of *padrino* (godfather, champion), they
would be able to provide significant sums for community events or
family needs. For their part, the wealthy peasants had a stake in the
maintenance of the present order, although much less of a stake
than the patron had had.[3] Thus, incentives for clientelist ties remained in the cooperatives. Bonds with wealthy individuals were
one more way in which peasants could try to obtain economic
security.

Whereas the need for material support was a traditional goal of
friendship, the desire to share good times was a rather new purpose. In the hacienda, the intense competition among peasants
rendered the enjoyment of community activities difficult. "Community" activities were often arranged by the patron, and thus did
not always fit peasants' definitions of a good time. In contrast, in the
cooperative, community events held a greater potential for enjoyment. Many activities were designed to make money for the cooperative. The events were organized by members for the entire community, and generally they agreed on the desirability of different
activities.

Another new purpose of friendship was the discussion of political
opinions. The exchange of political ideas was important because
members had to be able to evaluate the leadership capacities and
political positions of council candidates. Members felt freer to discuss politics than they had under the patron; sanctions on "incor-
rect" political opinions were not applied.

Although sharing intimate personal confidences and exchanging
advice on the solution of personal problems is a common purpose

---

[3] The relatively limited rewards to peasants with high socioeconomic status from
clientelist alliances meant that they often shunned such ties. The high-status peasants feared bombardment by requests for assistance. A similar phenomenon has
been noted in China (Solomon, 1969: 300).

of friendship, it was not salient in Peru. This kind of purpose for friendship could not be instilled by the cooperative structure.

## CHANGES IN ATTITUDES TOWARD SOCIAL SOLIDARITY

By 1974, many cooperative members came to perceive trust as an ideal they would like to realize. The rise in ideals of trust and solidarity among community residents between 1969 and 1975 was dramatic. However, trust remained defined primarily in terms of mutual economic support, and was still considered primarily an ideal rather than a reality.

The sharp increase in ideals of trust among cooperative residents is revealed in Table VII.1. In the three experimental sites, the percentage of respondents who said that they could trust other people in the place rose from 13 percent to 56 percent, versus from 13 percent to only 28 percent in the control sites. The jump in positive responses in the cooperative sites is one of the largest for all items in the survey. The change is corroborated by evidence from another item added to the instrument in the final interviewing stage; Marla respondents were asked if they felt that their attitudes toward trust had altered and, if so, why. Roughly 40 percent of these respondents reported that they had become more trusting, for various reasons.[4] Using questions from the 1969 IEP-Cornell survey, Buchler (1975: 74-75) also found a considerable increase in trusting attitudes.

Trust was perceived primarily as the assurance of material aid in a difficulty. In 1975, the responses about trust were probed in Estrella and Marla, and a majority of respondents who referred to any specific type of trust referred to loans of some variety. Although the question stipulated specifically trust in other people, the cooperative was often mentioned, because it provided loans. Other types of material support, such as help in building a house, were also cited. Commented two peasants from Estrella and Rachuis, respectively:

---

[4] The calculation is complicated by some respondents who could not articulate how their attitudes had changed. About half the respondents queried (22 of 41) said their attitudes had changed; of this group, only seventeen were able to articulate reasons for the change. Twelve respondents indicated they trusted more now, five because the patron did not permit trust before and seven for various other reasons. In contrast, five respondents said they trusted less now, for various reasons.

TABLE VII.1
The Ideal of Trust[a] (%)

| | N | Can trust | Cannot trust | Both, depends, don't know, other |
|---|---|---|---|---|
| peratives, 1974 | 229 | 56 | 40 | 3 |
| iendas, 1969 | 176 | 13 | 85 | 2 |
| onte, 1974 | 79 | 50 | 44 | 6 |
| onte, 1969 | 58 | 10 | 88 | 2 |
| strella & Marla, 1974 | 150 | 59 | 37 | 4 |
| strella & Marla, 1969 | 118 | 15 | 83 | 2 |
| si-control & control, 1974 | 184 | 28 | 65 | 8 |
| si-control & control, 1969 | 253 | 13 | 85 | 2 |
| gustín, 1974 | 94 | 28 | 67 | 5 |
| gustín, 1969 | 153 | 7 | 90 | 3 |
| rú, 1974 | 90 | 28 | 62 | 10 |
| rú, 1969 | 100 | 18 | 80 | 2 |
| communities, 1974 | 93 | 45 | 34 | 20 |

tem read: "Some people say, you can trust most people in this place; others say you can't trust
najority. What do you think?"

You can trust others, for if you don't trust it would be bad. If a person is sick, you help him. If one member asks a favor from another, he gives it—for example, a loan of money, or vegetables. We help each other out (Q1975, 24).

Here, we all know each other and you can trust. If I have a bad harvest, other comuneros will loan me potatoes until the next year, and then I'll give them back (Q1975, 76).

Members who indicated that they could not trust others in the community also tended to perceive trust in a material context. Mistrust implied suspicion of financial dishonesty and uncertainty that a loan or other favor would be repaid. As the cooperative was often cited as a source of trust, in some cases it was maligned for reneging on its obligation to help. The meaning of mistrust is perhaps best indicated by some of the incidents to which members themselves applied the word. One night in Marla, we returned to our rooms to find the kerosene lamp gone; our neighbor dropped by to explain that it was broken and he had taken it to be fixed. When we mentioned the occurrence to a mutual friend, however, he said that we shouldn't trust our neighbor; he was probably just claiming that the lamp was broken, and only wanted to use it himself for awhile. Another day, I was warned that I should not leave my car unattended on the road between Estrella and the highway; it might be stolen. I was too trusting, I was told. (But the lamp was returned and my car was never stolen.)

The material context in which community residents placed social solidarity is also suggested by their responses to another item in the survey. We asked respondents how parents can show their love for their children. Answers were similar in both the cooperative and control sites. In all communities, with regard to the father's love, the most common response (about 50 percent) was that he show his love by providing his children with an education. Another 15 percent of respondents perceived love in an even more material context, saying that the father should maintain his children economically. With regard to the mother's love, the most popular response (about 40 percent) was also practical: she should take care of them by washing their clothes, cooking, and cleaning. The second most frequent response with regard to the mother's love was that she advance the children in their studies, like the father. Only some 20 percent of all respondents emphasized the emotional dimension of love, saying, for example, that "the parent gives the child affection, and respects him," or that "the parent helps the child in his life, offering him guidance and providing him models."

However, some respondents, especially younger men, did define social solidarity more broadly. These men perceived trust as the sharing of political opinions, problems at work, or community-related concerns. Said workers from Estrella and Marla, for example:

> There's more trust this last year. Working in the fields, now everyone gives his ideas, without embarrassment. Of course, there remain a few who still don't understand (Q1975, 20).

> There is trust among friends, among the young people here. We talk before the General Assemblies, agree on what we want. But at times in the Assembly everything gets disorganized again, there's fear and we don't mention what we agreed to (Q1975, 11).

> Now we trust. Especially at work. When there's a problem, we talk and confide. Before, we couldn't do this because the patron got mad if we were talking and fired us (Q1975, 60).

Although trust was desired, it was not widely perceived to prevail at the moment. The survey item used the somewhat impersonal verb form "can one," and thus allowed positive responses to the question without requiring a direct commitment to trust by the respondent. In their comments on the question, many peasants thus exhorted other residents to trust more, or placed the achievement of trust in the future:

One has to have trust in others. One has to give his ideas to others. Before, people were more distrustful (Q1975, 70).

We can trust, when and only when we have agreement among everyone (Q1975, 55).

Further, many respondents limited the group in which they felt trust to a smaller one than the survey item specified. Peasants said they could trust their socioeconomic group, or the members whom they knew well. Commented one Estrella worker: "There's trust among the workers who are members of the cooperative. With the temporary workers, you have to be very careful; they might rob the harvests. The white-collar guys in the office, they deceive you a lot, even in love affairs" (Q1975, 1).

Yet, in comparison with comments made in the control sites, even the references to trust as an ideal represented a significant positive change in attitudes toward trust. In the cooperatives, members wanted to be proud of their neighbors. For example, when a group of Peruvian university students wrote in their report on Estrella that 75 percent of community members were alcoholics, the cooperative leadership was enraged. In contrast, residents of Virú and Agustín often made sweeping accusations of all their neighbors as lazy drunks. Generally, control site residents dismissed trust as a foolish illusion, one not pursued by the wise man.

## CHANGES IN SOCIAL BEHAVIOR

Although the rise in actual trust and friendship was not as dramatic in the Peruvian cooperatives as the growth in these ideals, a gradual behavioral change was also evident. The change was especially marked in such aspects of social behavior as mutual economic support and formal social activities that could be affected directly by the incentives of the cooperative structure; it was less marked in informal social activities. Social networks became less rigidly defined by class, but they remained strictly bound by sex roles.

The ideal of trust and friendship entailed a considerable measure of hope for economic collaboration, and strides toward realizing this goal were made. Loans among members and by the enterprise seemed to increase; members reported satisfaction with the amount of loans from the cooperative (see Chapter X). Members were also more likely to expect help from others in the community in times of need.[5] Table VII.2 shows an increase in the expectation of help in the cooperative sites as well as a dip in this expectation in the control sites. A similar trend in cooperatives was reported by Buchler (1975: 74-75). The limited amount of help indicated for the SAIS peasant communities may reflect an absolute lack of resources there.

Economic support was, however, also sought from socioeconomic superiors. As noted above, income inequalities remained in the cooperatives, and members sought relationships with socioeconomic superiors out of desire for material gain. Economic calculations were often present in the choice of *compadres* (co-parents). In Estrella, for example, the restaurant manager did not have a lease for her site and was afraid that she might be ousted, as her husband was not a cooperative member. Thus she chose as her compadre Pedro Vásquez, who ate frequently at the restaurant, in the hope that he would use his influence to let her keep the restaurant. Friendship with North American students was also cultivated with material goals in mind. I was asked many times for help in gaining scholarships to the United States or employment in Lima.

Corruption and theft did not end. Economic collaboration, both in daily work activity and in new livestock and commercial cooperatives, was difficult to implement, as Chapter VIII documents. Temptations for individual short-run gains at the expense of the cooperative were large. Stealing from other peasants had been common in most communities prior to 1969 (Stein, 1961: 212), and continued, although abated. (This is my belief, although no evidence is available.) Members complained of loss of privately owned animals, although they usually blamed outsiders. My photographs of sports teams and schoolchildren were placed in community centers, but they disappeared, presumably into the homes of individuals in the pictures.

The increase in social interaction in the cooperatives was marked not only by the rise in mutual economic assistance but also by a jump in formal social activities sponsored by the cooperatives, such as fiestas. Whereas fiestas had been infrequent in the coastal hacien-

---

[5] I consider the item to tap behavior rather than attitudes because it asks about *others'* behavior and is phrased in the declarative tense, rather than the conditional.

TABLE VII.2
The Expectation of Help[a] (%)

| | N | Much help | Some help | No help | Other (don't know, no answer, etc.) |
|---|---|---|---|---|---|
| )peratives, 1974 | 229 | 1 | 67 | 25 | 7 |
| :iendas, 1969 | 176 | 4 | 46 | 48 | 2 |
| 1onte, 1974 | 79 | 1 | 52 | 42 | 5 |
| 1onte, 1969 | 58 | 5 | 53 | 41 | 0 |
| strella & Marla, 1974 | 150 | 1 | 75 | 18 | 7 |
| strella & Marla, 1969 | 118 | 4 | 42 | 52 | 3 |
| isi-control & control, 1974 | 184 | 1 | 35 | 61 | 3 |
| isi-control & control, 1969 | 253 | 1 | 52 | 44 | 2 |
| gustín, 1974 | 94 | 0 | 47 | 52 | 1 |
| gustín, 1969 | 153 | 1 | 51 | 46 | 3 |
| irú, 1974 | 90 | 2 | 23 | 71 | 3 |
| irú, 1969 | 100 | 2 | 55 | 41 | 2 |
| S communities, 1974 | 93 | 0 | 33 | 63 | 3 |

[tem read: "Suppose you found yourself in a difficulty. How much help could you receive from
•r people of your community?"

das (Greaves, 1968: 155), they were held almost once a month in these enterprises after 1974.

The nature of the fiesta also changed sharply. Traditionally, fiestas had been extravagant, fraught with tension, and dominated by the hacendado. Men often went into debt to give a major fiesta. At the fiesta, peasants seemed to try to release aggression and escape solitude (Paz, 1961). Stimulated by alcohol, peasants would confide secrets to each other, but after a brief euphoria, the fiesta would dissolve into brawls (Dobyns, Doughty, and Lasswell, 1971: 101; Stein, 1961: 204-207). At fiestas in my research sites, fighting had been common. In Estrella and Marla, brawls occurred virtually every Sunday afternoon, when men would drink heavily In 1973, conflict was still common at Monte fiestas. During one festival, four fights occurred; one schoolteacher was hit so hard in the eye that he had to be taken to the hospital. Even when fiestas did not dissipate into violence, emotions were still tense.

In contrast, by 1973 in the coastal cooperatives and by 1975 in Monte, community parties were fun, organized by members for members. In Estrella and Marla many dances were held. Featuring live rock music, the dances engaged residents from all socioeconomic strata. Some socioeconomic divisions were evident; office employees danced a larger proportion of the evening with the university students, and white-collar men were responsible for refreshments, admission fees, and security. However, the over-all atmosphere was one of social mingling and good times. No major fights were reported. Further, the dances were lucrative for the cooperative. Through the sale of beverages and admission fees, the parties in Estrella netted its Education Committee enough money to construct a new sports stadium.

In Monte, the all-day, all-night work schedule of the shepherds prevented their attendance at parties, and thus gatherings never encompassed all strata. However, parties for the skilled workers and political leaders in the center of Monte, the SAIS offices, and in Huancayo after union meetings did become more enjoyable. The role of the Monte administrator at parties in the site gradually diminished, and conversation among workers increased. In May 1975, a Mother's Day celebration in the Huanca offices was relaxed. The event featured workers' songs, poems, and a skit that mocked the behavior of the patrons.

In the control sites, community events resembled neither the traditional fiesta of previous decades nor the friendly parties in the cooperatives. Rather, fiestas were Coney Island spectaculars. Weeklong celebrations boasted a great variety of musical bands plus other major attractions, such as elaborate costumes in Virú and bullfights in Agustín. The purpose of the events seemed to be to attract the community's migrants back into the village for a few days, and to provide general diversion. The extravaganzas were too large to stimulate new friendships among diverse sets of residents. Families and friends stayed together amid the throngs of spectators. In further contrast to the parties in the coastal cooperatives, but like the traditional fiesta, these events required large cash outlays from sponsors.

Increased social interaction was also evident in the formation of new clubs. Social clubs, sports clubs, women's groups, and youth associations proliferated. The extent of activity of the groups varied. Sports clubs were often most vigorous, organizing competitions almost every week, usually with teams from other communities. Social clubs generally operated out of a community recreation room. In Monte, the room boasted a pool table and a ping-pong set, and, in Estrella and Marla, marginally functional television sets. After 1969, political meetings were also held in these rooms.

By 1974, participation in social and sports clubs was considerably higher than in 1969. In the 1974 survey, 43 percent of cooperative site residents reported membership, versus 23 percent in 1969. Participation rose most sharply in Monte, from 35 percent to 62 percent. A social-and-sports club had existed since the early 1960s, but most men had felt excluded from it. The patron had regularly played pool there with other technicians and white-collar employees; even few skilled workers entered the club. The patron and his administrators were invariably the captains of the sports team or the presidents of the clubs. In contrast, by 1974, most skilled workers used the club facilities regularly, and even the shepherds used them occasionally, generally while they waited for union meetings to begin.

In Agustín and Virú, social and sports clubs were less active. Neither site had a facility for community social activities, although Agustín was constructing one. Only 26 percent of Agustín and Virú respondents considered themselves club members in 1974, a slight rise from 16 percent in 1969.

The cooperatives also sponsored cultural activity in the community. All the cooperative sites, including Patca and Varya, established libraries during 1972-1975. In most sites, the stock of books was meager and the library was locked much of the time, but the facility did exist. Neither Virú nor Agustín had a library.

One type of social activity was on the decline in the cooperatives, however: church attendance. Prior to 1969, the patron imported a priest for religious services about once a month in the research haciendas. Cooperative members showed little interest in the maintenance of this custom. The church seemed to be associated in members' minds with the patron himself, and they neglected the church. Both Monte and Estrella had churches, but they were used only about three times a year. In the control sites, interest in religion did not decline so sharply. The repair of the church was even a prominent concern in Agustín and Virú.

The cooperative was of course more able to influence the character of formal social activities, which it sponsored, than informal social interaction, which it did not. Whereas the cooperative invited all members to its activities, the council could not tell individuals to invite everyone to their parties nor dictate group dining in the community restaurants. Gradually, however, informal social activity seemed to increase in the cooperatives, and to integrate distinct socioeconomic strata. The prestige of cooperative leadership positions and the need to talk politics seemed especially critical to this change in several sites.

Prior to 1969, friendly conversations were atypical in the haciendas. It was reported that more conversations occurred between the patron and the individual worker than among workers themselves.[6] However, even these conversations were brief and superficial.[7] When the ex-patron returned to Monte in 1973, he walked around the community awhile, with the accountant Maray and the telephone operator a few steps behind. Although the ex-patron had said to me that these two men were his "closest buddies" in Monte, virtually no words were spoken, not even simple inquiries such as "How are you doing?" The ex-patron stayed under an hour, and made no effort to visit other families in the community. When peasants encountered each other or dined with each other, silence was common.[8] This was still very much the case in Monte as late as 1973. Peasants were especially afraid to discuss political subjects, believing that their opinions would be used against them by "informers."

Gradually, however, informal social interaction increased. After 1973, workers began to eat meals together much more frequently and to converse more at meals. By mid-1975 in Monte, a group of eight or nine semi-skilled workers had established regular lunch meetings once or twice a week. In Estrella, whereas only a few white-collar employees regularly lunched in the community restaurant in 1973, by 1975 not only white-collar employees but also workers did so. Each day, roughly three workers, usually council members, ate lunch in the restaurant.

At these lunches and at other activities, men from different socioeconomic strata seemed to interact more by 1975. At the tables of the Estrella restaurant in 1973, white-collar employees and blue-collar workers were strictly segregated, but by 1975 members of the two groups often sat together. The change was spearheaded by the rise of workers of average means to political leadership positions; when Lucho Saavedra wanted to talk with the director over lunch, he had to be accepted at the "elite table." In Marla, workers and white-collar employees regularly chatted after lunch for thirty

[6] Interview with Ing. Chaparro, in Lima, August 22, 1973; and with Ing. Pinillos Ganoza, in Trujillo, February 4, 1974. Various residents also confirmed this report.

[7] This point was emphasized by Ing. Luis Deustua of COAMA, who had worked in highlands haciendas for many years, and by José Elías Minaya, of the Trujillo Ministry of Agriculture. For elaboration on hacienda society, refer to Chapter III.

[8] See Elías Minaya (1966: 55-57) and Williams (1969: 84-85). In El Chalán, social interaction was apparently minimal, because the topic is neglected by Greaves (1968) in his detailed study.

minutes or so on the bench outside the cooperative offices. To an increasing extent, workers were also invited to the parties of individuals of higher status. For example, in Estrella in 1973, when I invited Lorenzo Lazo to come to the party celebrating the baptism of my godchild, he was kept on the sidelines of the room for several hours, accepted by the white-collar employees only after many rounds of beer had been drunk. In contrast, by 1975 the parties of my compadres were regularly attended by several blue-collar workers, especially those in positions of political leadership. Increasingly in all sites, white-collar and blue-collar men talked over cokes or beers in the small community stores. Of course, socioeconomic distinctions by no means disappeared. Although political leaders and individuals of average socioeconomic status became more friendly with white-collar men, workers of low socioeconomic status without political office were still usually excluded.

The intensity and scope of discussions increased in the cooperatives. The purpose of many get-togethers was to exchange opinions on political issues or candidates for cooperative office. Planning political strategy, for example, was the major aim of the semi-skilled workers' lunches in Monte. Members' discussions were not restrained by fears of voicing disapproval of the government. SINAMOS and the directors were the targets of many jokes (see Chapter X). These jokes were often made in the presence of outsiders such as myself, without fear. Heated political arguments were avoided, but so they are in most countries.

Personal problems were also discussed, although they were usually of a practical nature. For example, women often asked my advice on contraception. The advisability of moving to the city was another personal question frequently raised among friends. Problems in buying or selling seeds or animals were also discussed. Young girls spoke at length with each other about their romantic possibilities.

On the other hand, the sharing of intimate emotional problems still seemed rare. The kind of psychological analysis of one's family and friends common to North Americans was foreign to the peasants. The disinclination to psychological analysis was evident from difficulties in the application of some survey items.[9] Several psycho-

[9] Similar difficulties have been noted by other social scientists. The most vivid description is Fromm and Maccoby (1970: 226-336; 184-185). Patrick Brennan mentioned his problems in applying questions of psychological analysis in Peruvian urban settlements near Trujillo, and so did Christopher Arterton with regard to Mexican villages.

logical questions were dropped because they had no resonance for respondents. An inquiry into the character of the respondent's father that sought to capture possible linkages with the patron bore no fruits whatsoever. A question about the respondent's fondest memories met blank looks. Rarely did respondents refer to special shared experiences with relatives or friends.

Although friendship grew in the cooperative sites, and often crossed traditional socioeconomic lines, social networks were strictly bound by sex. Despite attention by the national media to women's status, the cooperative structure did not seem to encourage the integration of women into the social life of the community in any way.

Even formal activities sponsored by the cooperatives were clearly demarcated by sex. Women's clubs were separate from the "cooperative's" clubs. Adult women were relegated for social activity to the Mothers' Clubs that were concerned primarily with sewing, nutrition, and other aspects of homemaking. Although Mothers' Clubs operated in both Monte and Marla, they engaged little interest, sometimes attracting only four or five women to meetings. If women were involved in the Schoolparents' Association of a community, then men generally were not, and vice versa. Women were discouraged from attendance at sports events, and married women were even restricted from participation at the cooperative-sponsored parties. The men preferred to enjoy the evening joking with other men or flirting with the single girls. Many women were upset by their exclusion from the parties. Said my comadre:

> Husbands and wives can't dance together here. They can't even walk close to each other. If a man does, he will be laughed at, and the people will say he lets his wife dominate him, he's a coward. So men must spend most of their time with men. Everyone must conform. Life here is really suffocating.[10]

Women seemed to remain in a subordinate role not only within the community but also within the family. In the various controversies between husband and wife with which I was familiar, the husband appeared to be the primary decision maker. Women often desired to limit the number of their children, but were discouraged from doing so by their husbands. Several women wanted to move to the provincial city, but were unable to persuade their husbands to do so. Women often sought their husband's permission to answer

---

[10] Interview in Estrella, May 1975.

my questionnaire. Further, attitudes toward the participation of women in family decisions were not especially positive. In 1974, only about 65 percent of respondents in the cooperative sites said that "much" importance was given to the wife's opinion in a family problem or that they "always" conversed with their mate about important problems.[11] The 65 percent figure is only approximately 15 percentage points higher than in 1969, about the same degree of change as in the control sites.[12] Given that the survey items specify only that the wife be consulted and that her opinion be given importance, not that she play an equal role in family decision making, the responses to this survey item suggest a distinctly subordinate role for women in the family.

Participating less in the political and social activities of the cooperative, women's attitudes and behavior remained more individualistic than men's. As Table IV.9 showed, the zero-order correlation coefficient between the male sex and collaborative attitudes toward site residents was quite strong (.337) in the cooperatives, although the correlation was about the same as in 1969 and in the control sites. On various specific items about social solidarity, women's attitudes were consistently more negative than men's. Of 84 female respondents in the cooperatives, 43 percent felt that others can be trusted, versus 63 percent of the male respondents; 26 percent did not believe that others envied hard work, versus 56 percent of the male respondents; and 64 percent believed that others would provide "much" or "some" help in a difficulty, versus 70 percent of the male respondents.[13] The percentage differences were smaller in Agustín and Virú (McClintock, 1976: 420).

## SUMMARY

The clientelist mode of "friendship" was gradually being undermined in the cooperatives. With the demise of the patron, incentives to seek friendship with him in order to win economic security

---

[11] The two survey items were phrased, "When you have an important problem at home or at work do you talk with your mate about the problem?" and "To handle a family problem, is what your wife (or yourself, if woman) says very important, of little importance, or of no importance?" This second item may sometimes have been incorrectly phrased to women; the 1969 questionnaire was not explicit on the phraseology for women.

[12] See McClintock (1970. 422) for a comphrensive breakdown of the responses to these survey items.

[13] The specific items are given in Tables VII.1, VII.2, and VIII.6.

disappeared, and the disincentives to peasant-organized social events or political talks that might have annoyed the patron were also removed. For the first time, perhaps, peasants perceived trust and solidarity among themselves as a viable option, and in their survey responses they strongly espoused these ideals. The ideals were by no means completely realized; some friendships in the clientelist mode of pure calculation between two socioeconomic unequals continued, and married women were virtually segregated. However, as aspirants to a "fully participatory social democracy" apparently hoped, social trust and solidarity were increasing. To a greater extent than in the haciendas, or in the control sites, cooperative members were assuring each other help in an emergency, and were sharing good times and new thoughts, regardless of the socioeconomic status of the member.

# VIII · *Work and Economic Performance*

MOST LARGE HACIENDAS were used for the private gain of the patron rather than for national development,[1] and to this end the patron sought to maximize short-run income from his estate. Whatever concerns for peasant welfare were expressed by the patron, they were generally not reflected in income distribution figures on the estates. Income inequality on the haciendas was severe; the income of the landowner was often 100 times that of the peasant, and approximately 35 percent of the income distributed in the hacienda was taken by the patron.[2] Rather than advance the enterprise through appropriate investment, the patron tended to consume a high portion of his income (Sternberg, 1972; Paige, 1975: 170). The patron's concern to maximize his short-run income was combined, for various reasons,[3] with a disinclination to hard work. Cunning seemed more critical to economic success than long hours at the desk or in the fields. In the past, many highlands hacendados had gained their land through illicit seizures from peasant communities or devious arrangements with individuals in the communities (Martínez Alier, 1973: 2-3; Matos Mar, 1976). In more recent decades, the hacendado's economic success typically depended more on his contacts in the commercial world than on his rational economic management.[4] Thus, especially by the 1950s and 1960s, the

[1] The economic operations of haciendas are discussed by Feder (1967); Pearse (1970); Dorner and Kanel (1971); Barraclough (1973: 3-31); Tai (1974: 35-41); Greaves (1968: 46-80, 425); and Paige (1975). Of course, differences among haciendas are great on this score.

[2] Documentation of ratio of income of landowner to peasant is given in Chapter III. Average percentage of enterprise income taken by the patron is cited in OIT (1975: 84). A similar percentage is given in Roca (1975).

[3] There are several other reasons besides those mentioned below. Paige (1975: 170) emphasizes that hard work would have borne most Peruvian hacendados little fruit, because of the lack of both credit and large markets, and insufficient economies of scale. Greaves (1968: 46-80) stresses the patron's concern with maintenance of an aristocratic tradition.

[4] For example, Marla was considered a potentially more lucrative hacienda than Estrella on the basis of the quality of its land, but in the 1960s Estrella was consistently more profitable. Whereas Marla's owner lost large sums when Trujillo businessmen refused to process his asparagus, Estrella's patron won considerable profits through his ties with a major agrarian university. See Greaves (1968: 339-421).

patron was rarely a full-time director of the enterprise who regularly ventured into the dirt and dust of the fields.

The patron was thus a symbol of wealth without work, of wealth gained through status and cunning, and wealth used for private rather than public purposes. The patron set this route to success as the norm throughout the hacienda. The landowner rewarded workers for their loyalty, their honesty, even their athletic abilities, but rarely for their initiative, ability, or capacity to work with other peasants. The most prestigious and lucrative jobs to which the peasant could aspire were often physically the easiest—the jobs of watchman, chauffeur, or guard. These jobs also entailed physical proximity to the patron, and thus a peasant could continue to curry favor and with some luck might amass funds to buy his own small farm. Such was the experience of Ingenio Cruz in Monte, and many ex-sharecroppers in Estrella and Marla haciendas.

The character of work norms that would replace those of the hacienda is not clearly addressed in either the corporatist or "fully participatory social democracy" models. However, inferences can be drawn. The corporatist model suggests that upper-class individuals or government officials are grouped with lower-class individuals, and that the upper-class members or officials bribe or co-opt a few of the lower-class members in order to exploit the lower-class majority. Such a process would seem to encourage the devious, individualistic strategies common in clientelist systems. It would also discourage commitment to hard collective work, whose fruits would be reaped primarily by others.

In the "fully participatory social democracy," a different vision of achievement is suggested. Economic resources would be used not for private ends but for the welfare of the group and society as a whole.[5] Success would be won not by individual cunning but by the hard work of the group. Cooperative members would neither exploit other peasants nor be exploited by the government or landowners. Rather, the workers would reap the profits from their own effort, and profits would represent a major incentive to work hard for the enterprise (Ministry of Agriculture, 1974a: 55). The solidarity of the group would grow as the socioeconomic equality of cooperative members was established, in part through the equalization

---

[5] Said Velasco: The economic growth of a society only has meaning when it recognizes... its condition as a means of justice in the society as a whole. No one creates wealth within a vacuum. The creation of wealth is social. The society makes it possible. Thus,... the creation of wealth must obey fundamentally the criteria of justice that guarantee the welfare and happiness of all men (Velasco, 1972: II, 295-296).

of wages (de Zutter, 1975: 111-129). The self-managed cooperative would involve members in the enterprise, increasing their sense of initiative and responsibility in the development effort.[6] Gradually, because of cooperative members' new commitment to vigorous collective work, economic growth would occur (Velasco, 1972b: 294-296; 310-312).

By 1973-1975, did craft remain the key avenue to success, as the proponents of a corporatist model might imply? Or did cooperative members begin to embrace the norm of hard work as a group, as government spokespeople hoped? Or did another pattern, or set of patterns, emerge?

## INCENTIVES AND DISINCENTIVES FOR COLLECTIVE WORK ACHIEVEMENT

The incentives for enterprise members' hard work as a group increased in the cooperative, but not as sharply as did incentives for new attitudes and actions in other realms. Frequently, incentives that had been anticipated to be strong inducements to collective work achievement were not fully implemented, undermined either by the government or by the peasants themselves. Such was often the case with respect to enterprise profitability and with respect to the role of the Vigilance Council, perceived as critical to checking corruption. Various other important policies, such as the system of work compensation, the ratio of private to cooperative production, and participation in on-the-job decisions, could have been designed to provide significant incentives for collaborative work achievement, but were often either unclear or unimplemented.

### Enterprise Profitability

The government assumed that profits would be a major incentive to hard work for the enterprise.[7] A good portion of the some 35 percent of enterprise income that had been consumed by the

---

[6] Declared the Ministry of Agriculture (1974a: 58-59): An efficient administration requires the delegation of authority; the responsibility ought to be shared at different levels.... Full participation of the members in the fulfillment of plans should stimulate the development of each individual member, permitting within his respective activities the exercise of his own judgments and the adoption of his own decisions.... It is necessary to delegate authority to conserve adapability within the enterprise, increasing efficiency, participation, and productivity.

[7] The subject was not discussed in great detail by spokespeople for the regime. However, Supreme Decree 240-69-AP, especially Chapter III, pays considerable attention to profits. The importance given to profits was also suggested in interviews with Ministry of Agriculture personnel.

patron would now be allocated to enterprise profits. However, this expectation frequently was not fulfilled, both because of the government's inroads into enterprise profits and because of members' desires for the immediate realization of the rewards from their work.

As subsequent sections of this chapter and Chapter X will describe, the government provided considerable economic support for most cooperatives during the Velasco era, primarily in the form of substantial loans at low interest rates; production was satisfactory and the enterprises were paying better wages. Thus, the charge that the government was exploiting the cooperatives is difficult to maintain. However, the government's economic stance toward the cooperatives was by no means entirely supportive. Some of its policies that impinged negatively upon the enterprises sharply reduced the attractiveness to members of enterprise profits versus wages. Particularly important were the uncertainties of government economic policy, especially in the marketing sphere, to be discussed in Chapter IX. Wages appeared a bird in the hand, but profits two in the bush.

Perhaps even more important, the government imposed various levies upon the profits of the cooperatives. The most burdensome of these was the agrarian debt. Because the debt was a fixed sum, not a percentage of profits, it is impossible to test exactly the significance of the debt payment to an enterprise; the percentage of profits allocated to the debt depended, of course, on the amount of profits. When enterprises earned no profits, such as Marla in various years and Huanca in 1976, they usually won postponements in debt payment. However, if the annual debt levies (typically interest charges during this period) are compared to the average annual gross profits listed in Table VIII.1, it is found that for these years the annual debt obligation was 75 percent of profits in Huanca, 22 percent of profits in Marla, and 11 percent of profits in Estrella.[8] Another approximation of the significance of the debt payment can be made by examining national debt remittances to the Agrarian Bank. In 1974, the average Peruvian cooperative member lost approximately 4,250 soles, or some $100, in debt payment.[9] After

[8] According to enterprise balance sheets, the annual debt payment due during this period was 7,366,799 soles in Huanca, 353,384 soles in Marla, and 403,244 soles in Estrella.

[9] Author's calculation from 1974 total debt repayment figure (499,234,000 soles), provided in an interview with Graciela Lituma Torres of the Agrarian Bank on July 25, 1977; this figure was divided by the number of cooperative enterprises and number of members in Table IV.4. Slightly higher figures for wealthier regions are reported by Bell (1977: 18).

## TABLE VIII.1
### Profits in the Cooperatives
#### (in current soles)

| | Year[a] | Gross profits | Profits after payment of agrarian debt/taxes and/or debt for previous losses | Profits distributed to members individually | Profit per member[b] |
|---|---|---|---|---|---|
| Huanca | 1972 | 6,332,000 | N.A. | 2,169,000 | 72,300 |
| | 1973 | 17,023,000 | 9,656,201 | 4,336,000 | 144,533 |
| | 1974 | 17,115,000 | 9,748,201 | 4,336,000 | 144,533 |
| | 1975 | N.A. | N.A. | 2,915,022 | 97,167 |
| | 1976 | (1,514,081) | (loss) | 0 | 0 |
| Estrella | 1973 | 626,400 | N.A. | 140,467 | 776 |
| | 1974 | (loss) | (loss) | 0 | 0 |
| | 1975 | 7,488,846 | 5,520,110 | 989,002 | 11,500 |
| | 1976 | 6,874,986 | 5,332,896 | 1,113,885 | 13,250 |
| | 1978 | 4,760,624 | 3,402,962 | 1,014,013 | N.A. |
| Marla | 1971 | N.A. | N.A. | N.A. | 2,250 |
| | 1972 | 116,452 | (loss) | 0 | 0 |
| | 1973 | (2,320,117) | (loss) | 0 | 0 |
| | 1974 | 3,652,712 | 627,320 | 150,216 | 1,500 |
| | 1975 | 4,944,447 | 1,679,842 | 484,348 | 5,100 |
| | 1976 | N.A. | N.A. | N.A. | N.A. |
| | 1978 | (2,789,628) | (loss) | 0 | 0 |

[a] The fiscal year varied from site to site. In Estrella and Marla, the fiscal year ended in December, but in Huanca in June. For Huanca, "1972" thus refers to the 1971-1972 fiscal year.

[b] The number of members declined in both Estrella and Marla. With the separation of the ex-sharecroppers from Estrella, the number of members fell from 181 to 86. In Marla, the number of members dipped from 112 in 1971 to 94 in 1977. The profit per member is an average in Huanca; profits are actually distributed to each community by a complex formula. (Recall that in Huanca the "member" is a community, not an individual.) Profits in the CAPs are the sums reported by the enterprise; actual distribution varied somewhat.

1975, inflation reduced the significance of the debt, but at about the same time a tax on profits of approximately 35 percent was extended to all cooperatives by Decree Law 21381; previously, this tax had applied only to the rich agroindustrial sugar cooperatives. The possibility of evading debt payment if the enterprise showed no profit and the new tax on profits made enterprise profits less attractive to members. Table VIII.1 shows the discrepancy between gross profits and profits after payments to the government in the three research enterprises.

Further, a considerable percentage of the profits remaining after debt payment and/or taxes was required to be allocated to purposes other than immediate consumption. Supreme Decree 240-69-AP mandated that, of the remaining profits, minimums of 15 percent be devoted to capital investment, 20 percent to social security and reserve funds, 5 percent to member education, and 5 percent to "cooperative development." It was further required that, after these allocations, at least 25 percent of remaining profits be invested, although in this case social service investments, such as houses and medical posts, were acceptable. Many of these allocations were wise, and frequently members chose to invest more than the required 25 percent of the bottom-line profit. However, if the member's top priority were immediate short-run gains, it is apparent from Table VIII.1 that he would gain more from a salary raise than a comparable increase in gross profits. And, as a comparison of the data in Table VIII.1 with the data in Tables VIII.2 and VIII.3 reveals, wages did increase much more sharply than profits.

However, in good years, the profit shares used for community services and for individual distribution were still large enough to interest members. As Table VIII.1 shows, an average Huanca community was receiving the equivalent of over $3,000 annually in the most profitable years of the SAIS, and the average Estrella member was receiving the equivalent of almost $250 in its most lucrative years. These lump sums were a boon sorely missed in poor years. The record of the research enterprises on profit distribution seems similar to that of other Peruvian cooperatives.[10]

---

[10] Unfortunately, many studies of the Peruvian cooperatives do not include data on profits. Some remote, poorer enterprises were unable to develop balance sheets, and delays in their publication were frequent, often because leaders feared allegations of corruption. However, in many moderately well-off enterprises, profits were quite good. Four cooperatives in Cañete showed excellent profits in 1974, distributing 8,732 soles to each member, on the average (CENCIRA, 1975: Ap-

## The Vigilance Council and Corruption

The Vigilance Council was established for the explicit purpose of discovering and stopping corruption, a traditional preoccupation in Peru. The Vigilance Council was granted the specific power to require that the Administrative Council convoke a General Assembly when it had knowledge of irregularities in the administration of the enterprise (Supreme Decree 240-69-AP, article 42). Together, the two councils included at least ten individuals; it seemed unlikely that so many leaders could be persuaded to engage in stealing from the cooperative till.

On the whole, however, the Vigilance Council did not fulfill its legal role as a check on corruption. In the cases of corruption in the research enterprises, the Vigilance Council was not particularly active in ferreting out evidence of corruption, and it rarely if ever initiated a demand for a meeting to examine the Administrative Council's practices. Why not? First, most Vigilance Council officials had less wealth and education than Administrative Council members, and thus Vigilance Council officials may have feared either that they would not be able to out-smart the top leaders in documenting machinations or that, if they did, they would suffer recriminations. Moreover, a certain degree of corruption seemed acceptable; many council members looked forward to the day when they would get a piece of the action, too. Drawing the line between the "acceptable" and "unacceptable" degree of corruption was of course difficult, and in some cases Vigilance Council members may have been persuaded to draw it more leniently by bribes.

Although in my judgment corruption was charged more frequently than it actually occurred, it did take place often enough to constitute the most significant disincentive to collaborative work achievement. None of the research enterprises was free from corruption throughout this period. Overcharging the enterprise for inputs and under-reporting the price of products, and then pocketing the difference, was the most common hoax. The most flamboyant escapades were the false "company" established by Torres and Lescano in Estrella and the purchase of a small ex-hacienda allegedly valued at half a million soles by the Ministry of Agricul-

---

pendix 1). Of the four major SAIS of the central highlands, Huanca had the lowest profits per community, because it had the largest number of communities in it (Caycho, 1977: 111). In the eight agro-industrial sugar cooperatives, distributed profits per member averaged 8,059 soles in 1972 (Bell, 1977: 18). Of the two somewhat poorer Piura cooperatives, one distributed 7,000 soles and the second 14,200 soles to each member in 1973 (Bell, 1977: 7).

ture for ten million by the 1976 Huanca president and director, the swindle that led to their departures.

## *Strategies of Work Compensation*

In most cooperatives, the base pay for field workers more than doubled between 1969 and 1975,[11] surpassing cost-of-living increases. Moreover, because the Ministry of Agriculture was trying to keep the lid on wages during this period, percentage increases for more specialized jobs, about which the ministry was less likely to inquire, often rose even more (see Table VIII.2). Further, although precise data are unavailable, there is widespread agreement among scholars and officials that income from privately owned land and animals was also increasing. After 1975, as inflation skyrocketed, it became more difficult to assess the real value of agricultural wages; Tables VIII.2 and VIII.3 indicate that the Estrella and Marla members were still faring quite well, but that Monte peasants were slipping somewhat behind. It should also be recalled that, as of 1976, the base wages were set by law in the Virú region, and Marla was often unable to meet its legal wage obligation.

Wages were thus relatively high in the cooperatives, and they were appreciated by members (see Chapter X). However, the increased wages did not constitute a great stimulus to collaborative work achievement because in most cases they were not established within the context of a clear, coherent overall compensation strategy.[12] Although wages increased, frustration remained because income distribution patterns were perceived as unfair: the correlation between hard work and high pay was far from perfect. The inequity alienated workers, as it had in the past; but now, workers could no longer be kept in line by the threat of firing or other

[11] My research cooperatives may have increased daily wages somewhat less than other enterprises. Consider some increases reported by Horton (1975a): CAP Posoconi (Puno), from 20 soles in 1969 to 40 soles in 1973; CAP Santa Barbara (Cañete), from 42 soles in 1969 to 75 soles in 1973; CAP San Nicolas (coast, near Lima), from 57 soles in 1969 to 80 soles in 1973; CAP Cerro Blanco (Cañete), from 53 soles in 1969 to 72 in 1973. Scholars William Bell and Pedro Ortiz, both of whom worked extensively in Piura, suggested that by 1974 typical salaries in that area were at 200 soles a day, and the head of the Ministry of Agriculture in Cañete reported that by 1975 salaries were also at around 200 soles there, in an interview on May 2, 1975. In the agro-industrial sugar cooperatives, wage increases were over 100 percent in various years (Agut, 1975: 516).

[12] Many of the points mentioned below are also discussed by Eguren López (1975: 98-110). Similar points are also made for the Chilean experience by Barraclough and Fernández (1974: 116-141 and 259-305).

## TABLE VIII.2
### Daily Wage Scales in Virú Valley, 1966-1979
(in current soles)

| Occupation | El Chalán | Marla | | | | | Estrella | | | | |
|---|---|---|---|---|---|---|---|---|---|---|---|
| | 1966 | 1969 | 1974 | 1975 | Mid-1977 | Mid-1979 | 1969 | 1974 | 1975 | Mid-1977 | Mid-1979 |
| Basic labor | 26 | 38 | 53 | 89 | 163 | 296 | 43 | 63 | 89 | 163 | 332 |
| Foreman | 32.5 | N.A. | N.A. | N.A. | N.A. | N.A. | N.A. | 73 | N.A. | 208 | 382 |
| Vehicle driver | 52 | N.A. | 106 | N.A. | 244 | N.A. | N.A. | 73 | N.A. | 208 | 412 |
| Tractor driver[a] | 40 to 55 | N.A. | 106 | N.A. | 244 | 312 | N.A. | 80 | N.A. | 194 | 432 |
| Irrigator | 35 | N.A. | 99 | N.A. | 194 | 490 | N.A. | 95 | N.A. | 285 | 485 |
| Watchman | 46 | N.A. | 108 | N.A. | 326 | 592 | N.A. | 126 | N.A. | 326 | 400 |
| Oven tender | — | — | — | — | — | — | — | 158 | N.A. | 295 | N.A. |

SOURCE: for El Chalán, Greaves (1968: Table VI.3); for Marla and Estrella in 1969, Elías Minaya (1969: 8), and for subsequent years, payroll records and interviews.

[a] 40 for a junior tractor driver, 55 for a senior.

TABLE VIII.3
Income Scales in Huanca, 1969-1979
(in current soles)

| Occupation | Daily wage | | | | Daily benefits | | Daily total income | |
|---|---|---|---|---|---|---|---|---|
| | 1969 | 1974[a] | 1977[a] | 1979 | 1969 | 1974 | 1969 | 1974 |
| Shepherd, Monte | 25 | 80 | 149 | 260 | 60 | 75 | 85 | 155 |
| Shepherd, marginal site | 15 | 80 | 149 | N.A. | 50 | 75 | 65 | 155 |
| Semi-skilled worker, Monte | 30 | 70 | 139 | 260 | 75 | 75 | 115 | 145 |
| Semi-skilled worker, marginal site | 20 | 70 | 136 | N.A. | 60 | 75 | 80 | 145 |
| Shepherd supervisor, Monte | 30 | 75 | 149 | N.A. | 75 | 75 | 115 | 150 |
| Shepherd supervisor, marginal site | 20 | 75 | 149 | N.A. | 60 | 75 | 80 | 150 |
| Skilled carpenter, Monte | N.A. | 87 | 161 | N.A. | N.A. | 75 | N.A. | 162 |
| Vehicle driver, Monte | N.A. | 156 | 225 | N.A. | N.A. | 75 | N.A. | 231 |

SOURCE: For 1969, wage figures are estimates from Huanca payrolls; benefits data are estimates from interviews. For 1974, 1975, and 1977 from Huanca budgets. Figures for 1979 from interviews in Monte. Daily benefits not available for 1977 or 1979.

[a] Depends on number of huacchas. Amount is reduced if more than sixty huacchas. Variations of some ten to twenty soles are frequent.

sanctions. Firing was a virtual legal impossibility; other sanctions were available to the Administrative Council,[13] but were rarely used out of fear of members' protest. The contradiction within the compensation system was thus that, although its inequities spurred resentment, strategies to control this anger were not present.

The prevalent, though not ubiquitous, pattern of wage inequality is indicated by the data in Tables VIII.2 and VIII.3. Table VIII.2 reveals that wage inequalities in Marla and Estrella were at least as great in 1974 as they had been in the contiguous hacienda El Chalán in 1966, and that these inequalities remained through mid-1977. Table VIII.3 shows that, in contrast, wage equalization was established among the SAIS ex-haciendas, some of which had traditionally been more prosperous and better-paying than others, and among most blue-collar posts, with the exception of such specialized positions as vehicle driver. However, wage equalization in the SAIS had not been sought by the SAIS leadership, nor by the Velasco government (which to my knowledge never promoted changes in wage scale patterns). Rather, it had been advanced by the ex-hacienda union leaders, who wanted to engage the shepherds in the union to a greater extent. Wage equalization among workers in other cooperatives was uncommon.[14]

Perhaps even more important was the pattern of inequality at the white-collar level. There was a marked tendency toward promoting blue-collar workers to white-collar office positions, and thereby increasing the total number of such jobs, especially in Huanca and Estrella.[15] Although the salary increases for white-collar positions during this period were small relative to those for blue-collar posts, for an ex-blue-collar worker the salary at the white-collar level represented a major raise.

[13] Supreme Decree 240-60-AP, article 66, section j.

[14] Data on wage scales are rarely reported, probably because enterprises were trying to hide the extent of wage increases at the blue-collar level. Unless the investigator knew of the existence of the wage scale, cooperative members generally implied that everyone received the base rate. However, Horton (1975a) includes some information on wage scales, as does Chirinos Almanza (1976), and in both studies the maintenance of wage inequalities is the dominant pattern, with some exceptions, such as CAP Posoconi (Horton, 1975a: 25.1-25.3).

[15] In Huanca, the number of white-collar positions increased from about 35 in 1969 to 48 in 1974, out of some 550 SAIS employees; in Estrella, from 5 in 1973 to 7 in 1977, out of 86 employees; and in Marla, the number of white-collar positions stayed the same (8), but the number of members dropped from 112 to 94. (Source for three enterprises: payroll records.) Similar trends are reported by Chirinos Almanza (1976); Horton (1975a: 4.12); and Middlebrook (1972: 86).

Wage inequalities might have been conducive to hard work if they had been related to work performance, but this was often not the case. Promotions were given not only on the basis of performance but, as in the past, for social and political reasons. Members of the Administrative Council usually reserved the power to allocate jobs and tended to promote themselves and their friends to better positions. At times promotions were made with co-optation in mind, as in Huanca with respect to Miguel Maray. In general too, when the Administrative Council selected individuals for courses in tractor-driving or enterprise management, courses that were critical to advancement to these posts, it was concerned about the long-term return on its investment, and chose young men with some education, even if they had worked only a few years in the enterprise, over older men with less education. Also important, the more lucrative jobs were typically easier, and frequently allocated as plums, maintaining the vision of hard labor as something to be avoided if possible. Jobs such as "irrigator," "watchman," and "oven tender" in Estrella and Marla might require night work and responsibility, but they allowed the worker to relax most of the time, even to doze.

Thus, for the average worker with scant education and few friends in leadership posts, the incentive to work hard was small. The hope of promotion was slim, the threat of being fired was infinitesimal, and neither wages nor profit remittances for "basic labor" were pegged to work achievement. In many cooperatives, the amount of work to be done each day was set through a work quota (*tarea*). The tarea fixed the quantity of work but not the quality: for example, a certain number of rows of beans to be "weeded" was established, but the standard of quality of the weeding was not. Workers thus completed the tarea as fast as possible in order to allocate extra time to alternative money-making pursuits.

### Private Economic Opportunity

Cooperative members were drawn away from collective work not only because of the disincentives to such work but also because of the rewards of small-scale private agricultural production. Cooperative agricultural production provided many advantages, especially the facilitation of major infrastructure development, but such production did not preclude benefits to small-scale private agricultural production. The Velasco government tended to emphasize the advantages of large-scale agriculture, perhaps without full consideration of the potential of alternative mixed modes of agricultural production (Padrón Castillo and Pease García, 1974: 86-93; de Zutter, 1975: 44-84). In some areas, an organizational hybrid of the production cooperative rather than the cooperative alone may be the most rational economic structure for agriculture.[16]

In the Peruvian cooperatives, small-scale private agricultural production was in fact very lucrative. In the highlands, sheep could be raised and potatoes cultivated; on the coast, rabbits, chickens, and cows could be kept and fruits and vegetables grown. These efforts could double or even triple the income of the cooperative member. The advantages of the family parcel of land were many. Production was easily integrated; corn was grown and then immediately fed to animals, for example. Livestock and crops could be carefully watched to prevent disease or predators without inconvenience because the plot was near the home. Family members were employed. Managerial problems and corruption were avoided. The cooperative was providing the important infrastructure.

The attraction of private production was further heightened by the fact that many prosperous private cultivators lived near the cooperative—or even in it, as in Estrella—and symbolized the upward mobility afforded by the individual agricultural entrepreneurship. Members realized that only individual effort would bring relatively great wealth. The successful ex-sharecroppers like Torres were more visible, as they sped about in their new cars, than those who had failed.

*Participation in On-the-Job Decisions*

Although, in self-management theory, participation in on-the-job decision making is considered a major incentive to collective work achievement, in the Peruvian cooperatives this type of participation was minimal. Although participation in on-the-job decisions was officially endorsed by the Velasco government, it was not vigorously promoted.[17] Indeed, the government's own organizational

---

[16] Such a modified form of cooperative seems to have been implemented successfully in the United Arab Republic. See Tai (1974). The question of the ideal economic agricultural structure can only be touched on here, however. Considerable disagreement exists on the success of production cooperatives, even in countries for which considerable data are available, such as Mexico (see Barraclough, 1975 and Senior, 1958 vs. Whetten, 1948: 212-214 and Belshaw, 1966: 22-23). With regard to the Peruvian case, Horton (1974) argues that the cooperative's economies of scale outweigh its problems only in coastal wage-labor farms and livestock enterprises, but not in highlands crop enterprises whose members were sharecroppers.

[17] The reasons for the failure to promote participation in on-the-job decisions are not clear. In all likelihood, the failure reflected problems of haste and oversight

charts suggest the maintenance of traditional work hierarchies. In the charts, the General Assembly and the councils are located above the director, but the director and work supervisors are placed above other workers (Ministry of Agriculture, 1974a: 39-47). Strategies by which workers could make on-the-job recommendations to supervisors were not spelled out. The main self-management organs, the councils, were oriented to the development of general enterprise policy, and no other committees for the discussion of on-the-job relationships and work techniques were legally required. Although such committees were established in some cooperatives, including Estrella and Marla, they rarely functioned.

Hence, in most cooperatives the traditional work hierarchy continued. The number of supervisory positions in Latin American haciendas was considered high, reaching one-third of all jobs in some cases (Feder, 1971: 122). Such a ratio seemed to prevail in SAIS Huanca both before and after the agrarian reform. For example, in a typical Huanca site, for some 45 shepherds there were approximately 17 supervisors, who in turn were set in a rigid work hierarchy, topped by the administrator and descending through the assistant administrator, two mayordomos, and 13 caporales.[18] In the coastal crop enterprises, the number of supervisors was smaller than in highlands enterprises but still seemed large relative to my assessment of need. In Estrella and Marla, one supervisor was usually designated for a group of ten to fifteen workers.

In these work groups, laborers were not encouraged to make recommendations to supervisors. Observing various tasks in the three sites, I never saw a worker making a suggestion or questioning a supervisor. The supervisor was rarely creative; he merely maintained discipline. The lack of participation in on-the-job decisions was indicated by members' answers to a survey item. As Table VIII.4 shows, only about one-third of cooperative members thought that they could regularly influence decisions about their work. Men in the control site felt more influential, probably because most of them worked independently. Of the residents of the coop-

---

rather than any conscious decision. The failure may also have been the upshot of conflict among officials over the appropriate role for the director in the reform enterprises. Interestingly too, on-the-job decision making has been a more marked feature of self-management schemes in Western European nations than in Yugoslavia, Chile, or Mexico, whose programs more closely resembled the Peruvian.

[18] Occupational data were given with payroll data for the Huanca haciendas in the Lima hacienda archive. Occupational data for 1973-1975 were given in the annual Huanca budgets.

TABLE VIII.4
Influence in On-the-Job Decisions[a]
(%, men only)

| | N | Yes, I can influence | Sometimes I can influence | No, I cannot influence | Don't know, other |
|---|---|---|---|---|---|
| Cooperatives, 1974 | 146 | 35 | 32 | 31 | 2 |
| Monte | 52 | 31 | 37 | 27 | 3 |
| Estrella | 56 | 50 | 30 | 18 | 2 |
| Marla | 38 | 18 | 26 | 55 | 0 |
| Control and quasi-control, 1974 | 93 | 77 | 13 | 4 | 5 |
| Virú | 45 | 93 | 5 | 0 | 2 |
| Agustín | 48 | 63 | 20 | 8 | 8 |

[a]Item read: "Do you feel that you can influence decisions about how your work in ———— goes?" Only men are included as most women work independently.

erative sites, Estrella men were most confident of their influence, probably because more Estrella men were work supervisors, usually of eventuales. Cooperative members at times expressed frustration at their lack of participation in on-the-job decision making: "Before, you received orders from the caporales, and now you do, too, it's the same. You must fulfill the obligations and requirements of your task" (Q484).

### Changes and Exceptions to the Pattern of Incentives for Collective Work Achievement

Gradually, both government officials and many cooperative members realized that collective work achievement was not being sufficiently encouraged in the enterprises, and that, if the current confused system of rewards and sanctions continued for too many years, the cooperatives would collapse. Moreover, especially in enterprises where members' incomes had increased largely because of private economic production, it became apparent that the cooperative was the goose that laid the golden egg: it provided the infrastructure and facilitated the credit that made possible the lucrative private economic production. Thus, in 1975 and 1976, when the government began to encourage cooperatives to think about their work systems, some enterprises were responsive. To a certain extent members themselves had undermined potential incentives for collective achievement, and hence to a certain extent they also had the capacity to re-establish these incentives.

In Estrella and some of the other more economically successful coastal enterprises—not in Marla—members tried to build incentives for collective work achievement through new "internal work codes."[19] A model code had been drawn up by CENCIRA, but was revised by the Estrella Council before it was taken to the assembly, debated, modified, and finally approved in 1976. In most members' eyes, the new code made the system of work compensation more just and more rational. Although as Table VIII.2 showed, considerable wage inequalities remained between specialized and "basic labor" jobs, the criteria for promotions were regularized and set so as to reward hard collective work; a system of ranks was established taking into account not only efficiency, punctuality, and initiative

---

[19] No quantitative assessment of the number of enterprises implementing a work code is available. In interviews on July 22, 1977 in Trujillo, both José Elías Minaya of the Ministry of Agriculture and Nestor Rojas Bueno of CENCIRA and, on July 25, 1977 in Lima, Roberto Masuda Matsuura of the Ministry of Agriculture indicated that "some" or "a few" enterprises had implemented the code, and that "many" had formally approved it without actually implementing it.

but also "achievements on behalf of the cooperative."[20] When the ranks of job candidates were considered equal, the more senior individual was to be given preference,[21] thus providing some hope of promotion for the older, less well-educated member, at least for posts such as watchman and tractor driver. Moreover, all salary increases were required to be approved by the General Assembly, thus providing little grounds for members' fears that raises for the president or his friends might be made unilaterally or covertly.[22] Hard day-to-day work was encouraged by downplaying the tarea system in favor of the regular eight-hour day, and prohibiting unauthorized private work during these hours.[23] Absences, tardiness, insobriety, negligence, and the like were discouraged by docking daily pay and profit remittances.[24] Although formal channels for on-the-job participation were not established, mutual consideration and respect between supervisor and worker, and the supervisor's "listening to the complaints and requests" of workers, were emphasized as important norms.[25] There was, however, no attempt to strengthen the Vigilance Council or to take other legal measures against corruption.

The new incentives for collective work achievement established in Estrella and some other cooperatives during 1975-1976 had been operative in Monte and the other ex-haciendas of the SAIS since the inauguration of the cooperative. Monte is thus an exception to much of the discussion in this chapter. (Monte's experience is not representative because the implementation of most of these incentives was made by the SAIS comunero leaders, not Monte members themselves.) Wages were raised and equalized in Monte to a significant degree. Sanctions against work irresponsibility (such as fines levied for lost sheep) and against excessive private work (operationalized as pay reductions for owning more than 60 huacchas) were retained. Promotions remained a thorny issue, however, as many workers felt that these decisions were made for political purposes, and should have been placed under their own jurisdiction

---

[20] "Reglamento Interno de la CAP...[Estrella]," article 56. Note too that most cooperative members did not want an equalization of wages. One survey item asked whether all the people in the site should receive the same income, because they all work hard, or whether they should have different incomes, because some jobs require more skills and knowledge than others. Merely 33 percent of the cooperative site respondents preferred income equality; only in Monte did a majority of respondents opt for equality. This percentage was barely higher than in Agustín and Virú; in these control sites, 21 percent of respondents chose income equality. Complete wording of item is given in Appendix 8, Part 1B, number 65.

[21] Ibid., article 59.     [22] Ibid., article 31.     [23] Ibid., article 151.

[24] Ibid., article 152.     [25] Ibid., article 143.

not that of the SAIS leadership. Ex-hacienda workers were also angry that their profit share was small relative to their work contribution, despite the fact that during the 1972-1975 period the loss in profits was well compensated by the increase in wages.

## CHANGES IN ATTITUDES TOWARD COLLABORATIVE WORK

Perhaps because of the weakness of the new incentives for collaborative achievement during the first years of the new enterprises, post-reform attitudes toward economic cooperation were more ambivalent than attitudes toward cooperation in other spheres. On the one hand, responses to the item asking directly about attitudes towards collaborative work were more positive in 1974 than in 1969. However, the meaning of the increase is brought into question by respondents' comments about this item, as well as by their answers to other items in the survey.

The increase in cooperative members' positive responses to the survey item on collaborative work is indicated in Table VIII.5. The table shows that the proportion of respondents in the cooperative sites who preferred to work with other people rose considerably more than in the control sites during this period. Monte, where incentives for collaborative work had been most implemented as of 1974, registered the biggest jump. However, although the change in the cooperative sites is significant, the absolute percentage of respondents with positive opinions toward collaborative work is smaller than the percentage with positive attitudes toward cooperation in other spheres.

Moreover, the peasants' comments qualified their commitment to cooperative work. To an even greater extent than with respect to collaboration in other spheres, peasants emphasized that cooperative work was as yet only an ideal. Cautioned men from Estrella and Monte:

> Yes, we will achieve collaborative work, when and only when we are united and we understand each other and there is no mistrust (Q469).

> It seems better to me to work united, but without the envy we often have now (Q349).

These comments suggest that, in answering the survey question, members' hopes barely triumphed over their fears of envy and deception. These fears were voiced by the respondents who said

TABLE VIII.5
The Ideal of Collaborative Work[a] (%)

| | N | Prefer to work with others | Prefer to work alone | All the same, or it depends | Don't know, no answer, other |
|---|---|---|---|---|---|
| Cooperatives, 1974 | 229 | 46 | 44 | 4 | 6 |
| Haciendas, 1969 | 177 | 14 | 81 | 5 | 1 |
| Monte, 1974 | 79 | 51 | 38 | 3 | 9 |
| Monte, 1969 | 58 | 15 | 76 | 7 | 2 |
| Estrella, 1974 | 88 | 42 | 42 | 7 | 7 |
| Estrella, 1969 | 79 | 12 | 85 | 3 | 0 |
| María, 1974 | 62 | 45 | 53 | 0 | 2 |
| María, 1969 | 40 | 14 | 81 | 6 | 0 |
| Quasi-control & control, 1974 | 184 | 23 | 65 | 5 | 6 |
| Quasi-control & control, 1969 | 253 | 12 | 84 | 3 | 1 |
| Agustín, 1974 | 94 | 26 | 57 | 5 | 12 |
| Agustín, 1969 | 153 | 12 | 83 | 4 | 1 |
| Virú, 1974 | 90 | 20 | 73 | 6 | 1 |
| Virú, 1969 | 100 | 13 | 84 | 2 | 1 |
| SAIS communities, 1974 | 93 (men only) | 65 | 33 | 0 | 1 |

[a] Item read: "In general, do you prefer to work in collaboration with others or alone?"

they preferred to work alone; about 60 percent of these peasants in the major research sites cited the need to avoid problems and conflicts or people's envious and deceptive character as reasons for preferring individual work.[26]

Further, in a follow-up probe asking the reasons for preference for collaborative work, most respondents in the three cooperatives (60 percent) offered the blunt, pragmatic statement that collaborative work was easier, going more rapidly.[27] The member seemed to have in mind the extensive acreage of his specific enterprise, and was dismayed at the thought that he might have to cultivate it all by himself. Some respondents' comments did suggest a more thoughtful commitment to collaborative work, however. Approximately 30 percent mentioned social advantages, such as "we help each other." Another 12 percent of respondents gave thoughtful variations on the theme, "Among more people there are more good ideas and knowledge." Commented a SAIS community member and a Marla worker, respectively:

> Working in union is better to produce more for everyone. At times, alone, we can't work well because we don't have economic resources (Q258).

> Working with others is better, because in a group there's more interest, and among several people you can collect good ideas about how the work ought to be done (Q514).

The disinclination to collaborate economically is also suggested by responses to a third survey item, about the use of enterprise profits. Applied only in the coastal CAPs and the two SAIS communities, the item asked if respondents would prefer that more enterprise profits be devoted to the use of the entire community or to the use of each member.[28] In both Estrella and Marla, over 70

---

[26] Survey item reads, "You said that in general you prefer to work by yourself. Why?" Less than 20 percent of respondents preferred individual work because of its advantages rather than because of the disadvantages of collective work; this small minority of peasants typically said "I can be my own boss" or "Everyone works harder if it's for his own pocketbook." (Calculations are based on excluding "don't know" responses.) Comprehensive information on responses to the item is provided in McClintock (1976: 455).

[27] The probe, asked of 103 respondents in the three major experimental sites, 23 in the control sites, and 58 in the SAIS communities, all of whom said they preferred to work in collaboration with others, was simply to affirm the respondent's statement and ask: "Why?" A full report of the answers to the probe is given in McClintock (1976: 453).

[28] Complete wording of the item is given in Appendix 8, part 1B, number 50.

percent of respondents preferred that more profits be given to the individual member. In the two SAIS peasant communities, over 85 percent preferred that more profits be allocated to the entire place, probably reflecting the fact that profits were actually allocated this way in these sites, and had proven useful in the development of community infrastructure.

Attitudes toward hard work generally—whether in a collaborative or individual mode—did not become significantly more positive over the five years. As Table VIII.6 shows, the percentage of respondents who believed that others would respect hard work increased only slightly in all sites.[29] Most respondents still believed others would envy hard work. With regard to a second item about hard work, respondents also indicated little change in their desire for work achievement. Unfortunately, the question was not appropriate to the setting of the cooperative enterprise, because it specified a work context with a patron. The item presented two employment opportunities, one with a patron who demanded hard and regular work but paid well, and the other with a patron who demanded less work but paid less.[30] The percentage of respondents who preferred to work hard for more pay rose only slightly, from 30 percent to 42 percent in the cooperative sites and from 37 percent to 45 percent in the control sites.[31]

## CHANGES IN COLLABORATIVE WORK BEHAVIOR

As we have seen, the extent to which incentives for collective work achievement were implemented varied considerably among enterprises and over time; where and when these incentives were greater, members demonstrated greater collaborative work behavior. Among the research enterprises, collective work achievement was low in Marla throughout the period of the study; low in Estrella (although not as low as in Marla at the same time) during 1972-1974

[29] Buchler (1975: 80) finds a somewhat greater increase in the respect for hard work in his sites—from 14 percent in the entire IEP-Cornell sample to 35 percent in his sites—but the increase is still not as large as that with respect to political or social attitudes within the enterprise.

[30] Complete wording of the item is given in Appendix 8, part 1A, number 39.

[31] The rise in the cooperative sites reflects almost entirely a large jump in Monte, from 35 percent preferring to work hard for more pay to 70 percent. It is not clear, however, that the rise in the preference for the hard work alternative was the result of new work incentives in SAIS Huanca, because geographic region was important in the distribution of responses. The percentage increase was considerable in all highlands sites and nil in all coastal sites for both cooperatives and controls.

TABLE VIII.6
The Fear of Envy[a] (%)

| | N | Others envy hard work | Others respect hard work | Hard work isn't worth the trouble | Don't know, no answer, other |
|---|---|---|---|---|---|
| Cooperatives, 1974 | 229 | 55 | 26 | 7 | 12 |
| Haciendas, 1969 | 177 | 66 | 12 | 2 | 21 |
| Monte, 1974 | 79 | 44 | 24 | 17 | 15 |
| Monte, 1969 | 58 | 71 | 10 | 2 | 17 |
| Estrella & Marla, 1974 | 150 | 60 | 27 | 3 | 9 |
| Estrella & Marla, 1969 | 119 | 63 | 13 | 2 | 22 |
| Quasi-control & control, 1974 | 184 | 71 | 17 | 1 | 12 |
| Quasi-control & control, 1969 | 253 | 68 | 19 | 2 | 11 |
| Agustín, 1974 | 90 | 68 | 18 | 0 | 14 |
| Agustín, 1969 | 153 | 73 | 11 | 2 | 14 |
| Virú, 1974 | 90 | 73 | 17 | 1 | 9 |
| Virú, 1969 | 100 | 61 | 28 | 2 | 9 |
| SAIS Communities, 1974 | 93 | 76 | 17 | 0 | 6 |

[a]Item read: "If you work very hard, what would other people in this community think of you?"

but high thereafter; moderately high in Monte during 1972-1975, but falling somewhat subsequently. It is difficult to be certain of the representativeness of this pattern of collective work achievement, but it does not seem unrepresentative.[32]

*Marla.* By and large, Marla members had limited faith in the economic viability of their enterprise and were thus not committed to its economic development. The members were aware of the need to rotate asparagus production and plant new, more lucrative crops; however, they had not been able to translate this knowledge into action. Although evidence of leadership corruption could have been gathered at various times—it seemed probable that government loans for new farm machinery were ending up in leaders' pockets, given the amount of loans for this purpose and the continuing deterioration of the machinery—members were reluctant to act too hastily against the leaders, who were of high socioeconomic status. In the years when Marla did turn a profit, members always allocated the largest percentage possible to individual distribution rather than cooperative investment.[33]

Marla members devoted less time to enterprise work than members in Estrella or Monte. The tarea system prevailed, and most men worked only about four hours in the morning for the enterprise, approximately 60 percent of the hours worked in 1969. The time was transferred to work on private land and animals.[34] The average Marla member's private production provided approximately another 50 percent of the member's salary, not as much as in many cooperatives, because economic shortcomings in the en-

---

[32] This generalization is based on interviews with government officials, especially Ing. Luis Deustua, of COAMA; Rodolfo Masuda Matsuura, of the Lima Ministry of Agriculture; José Elías Minaya, of the Trujillo Ministry of Agriculture; the head of the Cañete Ministry of Agriculture; Miguel Candiotti, of the Huancayo SINAMOS. It is also based on interviews with social scientists, including Christopher Scott and Manuel Manrique, who investigated coastal rice cooperatives; and William Bell, who studied Piura cooperatives. Caballero (1976: 70) and Caycho (1977) indicate that other large highlands enterprises were also demonstrating considerable collective work achievement, and Horton (1974) suggests the same. In general, on the other hand, smaller coastal crop enterprises like Estrella and Marla were encountering difficulties (Caballero and Tello, 1976: 23-25; Horton, 1974 and 1975c). As in Estrella, however, collaborative work achievement in some of these enterprises may have gradually improved.

[33] From Marla's balance sheets.

[34] Because private production was semi-illicit in all cooperatives, all figures on its extent and remuneration are approximate.

terprise as a whole—breakdowns in the irrigation system, plagues, and the like—affected private production too. On a 1974 question about the quantity of work for the enterprise, more members in Marla (26 percent) admitted to working less after the agrarian reform than in any other site.[35]

Marla residents also avoided most other collaborative ventures. Proposals for cooperatives for members' private livestock were regularly rejected. However, a cooperative store did operate successfully, suffering only a few small thefts from store managers.

*Estrella.* From 1972 to 1975, corruption was rampant among Estrella's ex-sharecropper leaders, and members hesitated to put too much effort into the enterprise. But, they hoped that these leaders would be recalled, and never gave up completely on the enterprise. Members worked roughly seven hours a day in 1974, about one hour less than they were supposed to, and one hour less than in the late 1960s. Members devoted much more time to private parcels and livestock, but generally before and after the enterprise day, with much of the work done by other family members. Between 1969 and 1975, almost one-third of all Estrella workers gained ownership rights to small parcels, typically a little more than one hectare, and the number of privately owned animals multiplied about five times. The average Estrella member earned roughly the equivalent of an entire second salary through private production.

In 1975 and thereafter, enterprise profits skyrocketed and members' commitment to the enterprise did also. Council members devoted considerable effort to production decisions; discussion of these decisions was relatively widespread, and most members seemed involved in the decisions and eager to help prove them sound ones. In 1973, tobacco had been planted for the first time; not only was the crop lucrative, but it provided considerable employment for members' daughters. The work on the tobacco crop was of a high quality; in 1975 and 1976 Estrella won the "gold leaf" from the tobacco company for the best quality tobacco in the Trujillo region. At about the same time, it was decided to plant sugar cane. Even after the fall of sugar prices, the crop was a money maker for Estrella, where the members earned less than the traditional agro-industrial sugar enterprises and where the fields were excellent for cane. In the 1977 interviews, almost all Estrella members indicated that they knew about and enthusiastically sup-

---

[35] Full details on the item and responses are in McClintock (1976: 462).

ported the sugar cane decision. Members' endorsement of these innovative production policies was further indicated by their allocation of 40 percent of their bottom-line profits to investment,[36] instead of the required 25 percent.

At the same time, the number of hours the members worked for the enterprise returned to the usual eight hours, and the quality of the work was higher than ever before. Members retained their private production alternatives, but almost all this work was done off-hours or by relatives. Members attributed the marked increase in collective work achievement to a new realization of its profitability, the work code, and the example set by the director, a very conscientious individual.

As in Marla, however, Estrella residents were still dubious about other collaborative ventures, and proposals for cooperatives for members' private livestock were similarly defeated. Also, as in Marla, only a cooperative store was attempted; as of 1977, the store was a big success.

*Monte.* Through 1975, collaborative achievement remained high in Monte. The pre-1969 work schedule was maintained; in the 1974 survey, 84 percent of respondents reported working the same amount before and after the reform; only one respondent reported working less. Because of the pay cuts implemented by the SAIS leaders for individuals owning more than 60 sheep, the number of sheep owned by the average Monte worker dropped, and thus likewise the amount of time devoted to their care.

To a certain extent, however, the good work record in Monte reflected only the norms and sanctions imposed by the SAIS leaders. Some Monte workers complained that they had to work too hard, that the SAIS leaders were rigid disciplinarians. These complaints became more bitter after 1975 as salary increases failed to accelerate as they had in the past. Ex-hacienda workers wanted a voice in the major production and investment decisions made in the SAIS, especially when these leaders' decisions appeared to have been unwise. Although Monte workers continued to put in their hours for the enterprise, they seemed to be taking a greater share of the production for themselves, consuming more milk or marketing more wool on the sly.

Yet, perhaps because of the high degree of political solidarity in Monte as well as the SAIS regulations, a spirit of community work

---

[36] From Estrella's enterprise balance sheets, 1975 and 1976.

achievement prevailed in this ex-hacienda throughout this study. As Monte workers sheared sheep or packed wool, they seemed to work together in a more easygoing way than in Marla or Estrella. *Faenas* (collaborative work projects) were held almost once a month. Houses were renovated, the volleyball stadium improved, the cemetery repaired, and construction of hot water baths begun, all through faenas. (In contrast, faenas were not established in the coastal cooperatives.) Monte workers also contributed to the success of Huanca's Service Cooperative, which initiated credit operations, a store in each ex-hacienda, and various other projects.

*Patca and Varya.* The record of the SAIS peasant communities on collective work achievement is mixed. On the one hand, peasants were working harder than before, according to their answers to the 1974 survey item; of all the research sites only in Patca and Varya did a considerable percentage (28 percent) say they were working harder, and very few respondents said they were working less. It was also reported that peasants were lavishing less time and money on the traditionally extravagant highlands fiestas. Moreover, community members were interested in limited kinds of cooperative work, such as the faena; the number of faenas increased sharply in Patca, and stayed at their traditionally high level in Varya.

On the other hand, fearful Patca and Varya peasants rejected or undermined most efforts at more formal cooperativization. Land cooperativization programs promoted by SINAMOS were successfully opposed. During 1971-1974, SAIS communities used their shares of Huanca's profits primarily for public works projects and cooperative marketing ventures; in 1975, when it was mandated in the General Assembly that the profit shares be allocated to more production-oriented investments, such as cooperative livestock stables, Varya and many other peasant communities balked.[37]

Some peasant communities, including Patca, were more receptive to collaborative economic ventures, but the record of these attempts was only fair. For several years, the SAIS funds for cooperative ventures in Patca were considered boondoggles. During 1973 and 1974, Patca's cooperative store lost over $4,000, and at least five store managers were fired for putting their hands into the till, but Patca members voted to retain the store. Some peasants

---

[37] Information for 1971-74 from interviews and *Jatari-Uyari*, March 1975; information for 1975-1977 from interviews and a massive untitled volume providing economic data for 1974-1975 and 1975-1976, p. 236.

hoped that the store would eventually be honestly managed and would sell products to Patca more cheaply; others seemed to think that not "their" money but "SAIS" money was being lost, and apparently hoped that one of their relatives would eventually be employed by the store and they would thus gain a piece of the action. Finally, in 1975, sound management was gained for the store, and it became a major symbol of the potential of cooperative ventures to other peasant communities. But, the possibility of renewed corruption did not seem too distant, given the failures of other collaborative efforts in Patca due to corruption. In 1974, peasants decided to market their potato harvest collectively, renting a truck and choosing a member to drive it to Lima with the potatoes. All the proceeds from the sale of the potatoes were lost; the driver of the truck claimed they had been stolen, but he was not believed.

Moreover, although faenas increased in most communities of SAIS Huanca, not all individual sites participated eagerly in SAIS-wide faenas. In 1971 and 1972, the SAIS asked that each community send delegates to work on the new irrigation canal or the new highway, whichever project was closer geographically. At least ten of the twenty-nine communities did not comply. Most who did comply complained that the effort was poorly organized and that the food was bad. In the General Assembly, the SAIS delegates agreed that any community that did not work on one of the projects would not receive its profit share. In 1974 and 1975, almost all communities participated, but with little enthusiasm. Finally, in 1977 peasants had to be persuaded to contribute to the faena through a daily wage.

*Agustín and Virú.* Change in work behavior was minimal in the control sites. Cooperative work efforts were rejected. However, peasants were apparently working somewhat harder by 1974.

In both Agustín and Virú, production remained strictly private. Cooperative efforts, such as a transportation cooperative and a livestock cooperative in Agustín and an agricultural service cooperative in Virú, were dead or dormant in the mid-1970s. The only kind of cooperative work project in which peasants participated was the faena, and these were held only in Agustín, not in Virú. During 1973-1975, Agustín comuneros built a municipal center, renovated the plaza, and refurbished the church tower through faenas. Community funds were devoted to non-risk, non-controversial projects, primarily of the beautification variety.

However, many residents of the control sites had increased their work effort since the agrarian reform. Answering the 1974 survey item about their work effort before and after the reform, rather large percentages of respondents (38 percent in Agustín and 27 percent in Virú) said that they were working harder in 1974 than in 1969. Especially in Virú, the increase seemed to reflect the agrarian reform. Under the reform law, poorly utilized lands could be expropriated, and this clause apparently frightened some prosperous cultivators into working harder. A considerable number of poorer peasants may also have been working harder because of new ownership rights to previously rented land.

## ECONOMIC PERFORMANCE OF THE COOPERATIVE ENTERPRISES

The extent of collective work achievement was, of course, reflected in the economic performance of the enterprises. (The correlation is by no means perfect, however: weather is always an important factor in agriculture; government credits were generous during the 1973-1975 period; and members who devoted more time to private production could often hire temporary workers in their stead.) The sharp variations in the degree of members' commitment among cooperatives and in one cooperative over time were thus evident in the economic statistics for the cooperatives. Accordingly, economic performance was stable in Huanca; better in Estrella, especially after 1974; and more-or-less stable in Marla, until 1976, when it began to deteriorate sharply.

Together, the performance of the three research enterprises averages from approximately mediocre to good, and this record seems representative. Throughout Peru, most enterprises were performing as well or slightly better economically as cooperatives than they had as haciendas.[38] The other large, well-capitalized livestock enterprises of the central highlands were generally doing better than before, and somewhat better than Huanca (Horton, 1975a: 162-166; Caycho, 1977: 92-144; Caballero, 1976: 52). The

---

[38] The most comprehensive report is Horton (1974, 1975a, 1975b, and 1975c). Twenty-three cooperatives were studied in all three major regions of the country, primarily in 1973. Although Horton's study is a rather early one and examines cooperatives at only one point in time, I believe it is the best effort to assess production patterns, because it is the only major one to examine *total enterprise* production, not aggregate production of one crop in a region or the nation. Aggregate studies of this type cannot consider the impact of production innovation into nontraditional crop lines.

traditionally most lucrative enterprises, the agro-industrial sugar enterprises, were producing considerably more sugar (Roca, 1975: 42). Production also improved somewhat in many cotton enterprises (Horton, 1974: 103-116; CENCIRA, 1975a: Appendix 1; Rubin de Celis T., 1977: 36). The final major crop of the coastal cooperatives, rice, fared less well; production apparently fell somewhat since the late 1960s (Rubin de Celis T., 1977: 36). The generally solid performance of these coastal export cooperatives is also suggested by the increase in the value of agricultural exports from $143 million in 1969 to $274 million in 1974, an increase beyond inflation (Fitzgerald, 1976: 65). Note too that the maintenance of production in these enterprises is no mean achievement, because the average yields per hectare for sugar cane and rice are well above world averages and at least twice as much as Latin American averages, and yields for cotton are also above average.[39] On the other hand, production may have declined in the majority of smaller, traditionally poorer highlands crop enterprises (Horton, 1975b: 40-41; Caballero, 1976: 52).

Overall, the Peruvian agricultural product, to which the cooperatives contributed about half, grew approximately 7.8 percent in 1970, 3 percent in 1971, 0 percent in 1972, 2.4 percent in 1973, 1.8 percent in 1974, and 1 percent in 1975, for an average annual rate of +2.7 for the six years,[40] versus an average annual rate of −1.3 for the four years 1965-1968.[41] Table VIII.7 also indicates moderate gains since 1969 in the production of the nation's principal agricultural commodities, both with respect to commodities produced almost entirely on coastal cooperatives (sugar cane, cotton, and rice) and those produced in various regions and enterprise modes (wheat, corn, potatoes, coffee, wool, pork, and various other meats). Unfortunately, no data specifying production trends in the cooperatives versus private enterprises are available.

In general, the performance of the cooperatives thus seems satisfactory, especially considering that by the conventional wisdom agrarian reform is expected to create short-term economic dislocations. However, more dramatic economic results had been hoped

[39] FAO (United Nations Food and Agricultural Organization), *Production Yearbook*, Vol. 29 (1976), pp. 89-126.

[40] Figures for 1970-1974 are from *Latin America Economic Report*, *3* (April 11, 1975), 54. Figure for 1975 is from *Informativo Politico*, No. 40 (January, 1976), 23. Figures vary somewhat. Cabieses and Otero (1977: 210) suggest greater gains, and *Business Latin America* (September 29, 1976) smaller.

[41] My calculation is from Cabieses and Otero (1977: 210).

TABLE VIII.7
Production of Principal Agricultural Commodities, 1960-1976

| Product | Year | Area (thousands of hectares) | Production (thousands of metric tons) | Yield per hectare (kilogram/hectare, in thousands) |
|---|---|---|---|---|
| Sugar | 1961 | 47 | 7,288 | 155 |
| | 1966 | 54 | 8,463 | 158 |
| | 1972 | 48 | 8,612 | 176 |
| | 1975 | 57 | 9,000 | 158 |
| | 1976 | 55 | 8,792 | 160 |
| Cotton | | | | |
| (Branch) | 1960 | 252 | 362 | 1.4 |
| | 1965 | 238 | 357 | 1.5 |
| | 1970 | 144 | 248 | 1.7 |
| | 1976 | 98 | 165 | 1.7 |
| Rice | | | | |
| (Unshelled) | 1960 | 87 | 358 | 4.1 |
| | 1965 | 75 | 291 | 3.9 |
| | 1972 | 110 | 482 | 4.1 |
| | 1975[a] | 117 | 456 | 3.9 |
| | 1976 | 133 | 570 | 4.3 |
| Potatoes | 1960 | 233 | 1,145 | 4.9 |
| | 1965 | 251 | 1,568 | 6.2 |
| | 1968 | 251 | 1,526 | 6.1 |
| | 1972[a] | 300 | 1,750 | 5.8 |
| | 1975[a] | 317 | 1,950 | 6.2 |
| | 1976 | 256 | 1,667 | 6.5 |
| Corn | 1960 | 253 | 339 | 1.3 |
| | 1965 | 342 | 557 | 1.6 |
| | 1970 | 382 | 615 | 1.6 |
| | 1975[a] | 370 | 456 | 1.2 |
| | 1976 | 385 | 726 | 1.8 |
| Beans | 1960 | 37 | 37 | 1.0 |
| | 1965 | 45 | 41 | .9 |
| | 1968 | 61 | 48 | .8 |
| | 1976 | 63 | 50 | .8 |
| Coffee | 1960 | 76 | 32 | .43 |
| | 1965 | 93 | 48 | .52 |
| | 1970 | 113 | 65 | .58 |
| | 1975[a] | 128 | 75 | .59 |
| | 1976 | 121 | 65 | .54 |
| Grapes | 1960 | 7 | 47 | 6.6 |
| | 1965 | 8 | 55 | 7.0 |
| | 1970 | 10 | 56 | 5.5 |
| | 1976 | 11 | 64 | 6.0 |

TABLE VIII.7 (Continued)
Production of Principal Agricultural Commodities, 1960-1976

| Product | Year | Area (thousands of hectares) | Production (thousands of metric tons) | Yield per hectare (kilogram/hectare, in thousands) |
|---|---|---|---|---|
| Pork, mutton, lamb, and goat meat | 1972[a] | — | 73 | — |
| | 1973[a] | — | 79 | — |
| | 1974[a] | — | 81 | — |
| | 1975[a] | — | 84 | — |
| Wool (greasy basis) | 1972 | — | 8 | — |
| | 1973 | — | 9 | — |
| | 1974 | — | 9 | — |
| | 1975 | — | 9 | — |

SOURCES: *Estadística Agraria: Perú 1960 a 1976,* Ministry of Food and Agriculture. Most of the calculations were drawn from Deustua (1979). Yield per hectare may not seem accurate on the basis of figures provided because of rounding.

[a] Source for these figures is USDA Agricultural Situation Report for Peru, January 1976. Discrepancies between these figures and Ministry's figures may be due to different bases of calculation.

for by the Velasco government and by proponents of self-management, especially because considerable credit was given to the agricultural sector (see Chapter X). More dramatic results were also economically necessary because Peru's population growth rate surpassed its agricultural growth rate, and per capita demand for food was rising. In 1974, about 25 percent of Peru's imports were accounted for by food, versus 15 percent in 1972.[42]

This discussion of the performance of various kinds of cooperative enterprises brings the analysis of this chapter full circle, indicating the close links between enterprise performance, incentives for collective work achievement, and actual work achievement. In larger, more prosperous enterprises, with more capital and greater economies of scale, members were able to realize greater increases in profits and wages that encouraged their commitment to the enterprise.[43] In contrast, in smaller, poorer enterprises with less

[42]*Latin America Economic Report and Andean Times* (November 15, 1974), p. 177.

[43]This argument was first made by Horton (1974), although he categorizes enterprises by region and type of labor more rigorously than I do. Horton's argument is summarized in n. 16 above.

capital and fewer economies of scale, members realized smaller increases in profits and wages that were insufficient to build commitment to the enterprise. Accordingly, enterprises that were prosperous in 1969 usually continued so, whereas enterprises that were poor also continued so. However, the pre-reform economic condition was not the only factor in post-reform success. Estrella was a relatively poor coastal enterprise by the standards of Horton (1974) and Caballero (1976), but it weathered a difficult transition period to become vastly more productive in the mid-1970s than it had ever been before, and approximately as lucrative as major coastal cotton enterprises.

As a major enterprise, Huanca has maintained relatively comprehensive economic statistics, and the stability of production in the enterprise before and after the reform can thus be well documented.[44] In a sheep-raising enterprise, key production indicators include the percentage of lambs born to the number of sheep impregnated and the number of pounds of wool per sheep.[45] Ratios of 80 percent lambs born to sheep impregnated and nine pounds of wool per sheep would be considered good in the United States or Australia (Barnard, 1962: 47 and 79). During the 1960s, the average ratio of lambs born to sheep impregnated was about 78 percent in Huanca; under the SAIS, the figure was 70 percent in 1972, 77 percent in 1973, 75 percent in 1974, 68 percent in 1975, and 74 percent in 1976. The average number of pounds of wool per sheep was 6.40 in the 1960s, in comparison to 5.80 in 1972, 6.60 in 1973, 6.55 in 1974, 5.82 in 1975, and 6.21 in 1976. However, it was generally believed that the production of wool and mutton was virtually as good as it could be under the arduous conditions of the cold, dry Peruvian highlands. The major concern during this period was the construction of a vast irrigation canal, which it was believed would improve the yields of beef and milk from cows, yields that were very poor in Huanca, as they had been traditionally.[46] Canal construction was completed in the late 1970s.

[44] Data for the SAIS are from the *Memoria Anual*, an annual publication of production and income figures. The *Memoria Anual* 1975-1976 gives all figures for 1973-1976. Data for the haciendas are from the "Correspondencia del Gerente General" in the Lima hacienda archive.

[45] Total number of sheep is not a good indicator; most agricultural economists argue that these enterprises already graze too many sheep.

[46] Interviews with the assistant manager of Monte, with Huancayo Ministry of Agriculture officials, and Peace Corps volunteers in Huancayo. Milk yields were below five liters per cow daily, versus at least fifteen liters in the United States.

Evaluation of the economic performance of Estrella and Marla is more difficult, as it is for smaller cooperatives throughout Peru (Horton, 1974: 165). Pre-reform economic data for these enterprises are not available.[47] For most post-reform years, only income data, not production statistics, have been provided, but income data are an inadequate guide to economic performance because they are of course affected by price swings beyond the control of the enterprise. However, production statistics would not be a good guide either, because so many cooperatives changed their product mixes. Indeed, a key to economic success in these enterprises at an intermediate degree of capitalization—i.e., ones that could alter capital equipment without massive economic dislocation—was to modify the product mix at the right time. Thus, my evaluation of economic performance in these two CAPs is based primarily on interviews with enterprise employees, directors, government officials,[48] and Estrella's ex-hacendado, as well as the study by Greaves (1968).

Estrella fared rather well in the 1960s, continued to fare moderately well in the early 1970s, and then took off in 1975. Traditionally, most of Estrella's land had been planted in corn and sorghum (corn feed for animals). Then in 1962, through an agreement with the major agrarian university, Estrella began to specialize in commercial hybrid seed corn, which proved lucrative (Greaves, 1968: 345-349). In the 1970s, this agreement ended, but with the help of government loans Estrella launched sugar cane and tobacco cultivation. The quantity and quality of Estrella's production were excellent, putting Estrella in a very solid economic position despite declining sugar prices. The extent of Estrella's success is suggested by the fact that enterprise income for the mere 1975-1976 biennium exceeded the total assessed value of the enterprise at its adjudication (compare data in Tables VIII.1 and IV.3). The enterprise withstood the vicissitudes of severe drought in late 1977 and early 1978, showing a profit even in the difficult 1978 fiscal year. During my 1979 visit, every indication was for a superlative economic performance that year.

---

[47] It is unlikely that figures on yield per hectare have ever been kept. None of the studies on the valley in the 1960s (Chávez and Paredes, 1970; Elías Minaya, 1966; Elías Minaya, 1969) includes any such statistics. No such figures were evident in the CAP offices.

[48] I have paid special attention to the opinion of Dr. José Elías Minaya, who studied the Virú haciendas in 1966 and 1969 for the Cornell-IEP team and is currently employed in the Ministry of Agriculture in Trujillo, making occasional visits to Estrella and Marla.

Of the three research enterprises, Marla was the poorest upon adjudication, with less land and less capital per member. In 1970, the enterprise was bankrupt. During the 1960s, Marla's ambitious hacendado had built a factory for canning asparagus, but the project had failed, apparently because of inadequate capitalization and antagonism with a rival Trujillo company (Greaves, 1968: 376-384). The failure was a disaster for the enterprise as a whole; debts had accumulated, and the patron had not bought necessary new capital equipment, which was in poor condition in any case because of the patron's own negligence (Greaves, 1968: 375-376). Thus, Marla did not have as good a capital stock as Estrella upon adjudication. Although the government provided Marla with credit for new farm machinery purchases, it was insufficient, especially given a certain degree of slippage from corruption. The loss of Marla's asparagus crop in early 1973 added an extra debt burden to the CAP; even when Marla was able to operate in the black in 1974 and 1975, rather large sums had to be allocated to debt repayment (see Table VIII.1). The distribution of profits to members was thus low, reducing morale and interest in production decisions. Thus, in turn, the quantity and quality of production fell in 1976. The drought in late 1977-early 1978 hit Marla hard, and the 1978 fiscal year ended in a loss. During my 1979 visit, the enterprise was reviving somewhat. Whereas it had not been able to meet its payroll many times in 1978, moderate salaries were again being paid. Yet, salary levels were well below those in Estrella (see Table VIII.2). Overall, Marla's economic performance was sporadic, and never strong enough to sustain the enterprise beyond one crop disaster or a bad credit year—in other words, an economic situation rather similar to that of the 1960s.

No data are available on the economic performance of the control sites or the SAIS peasant communities.

## SUMMARY AND CROSS-NATIONAL ANALYSIS

The work attitudes and behavior that prevailed in the hacienda endured in the cooperatives to a greater extent than other social and political orientations. Especially in poorer enterprises, members perceived no good reasons to trust the economic viability of the cooperative, and did not demonstrate such trust. In these sites, like the hacendados before them, cooperative members seemed to try to exploit the enterprise for their own private purposes. Government loans were at times perceived as windfalls, and corruption was not checked, in part because members harbored hopes for a piece of the action one day for themselves. Cunning was still considered more critical for economic success than hard work and production initiatives. The vicious circle of poor economic performance → relatively low wages and profits → skepticism of cooperative work → limited collective work achievement → poor economic performance could not be broken.

In some cooperatives, however, there was considerable achievement through collective work. Members demonstrated initiative and responsibility as they worked hard for the development of their enterprise. A strong initial resource base was an important advantage in establishing key incentives to cooperative work, namely high wages and profits. However, political and social solidarity were also critical, especially to impede corruption, and to facilitate the establishment of rational compensation strategies and an appropriate role for private economic alternatives in the enterprise.

Collaborative economic achievement requires trusting other members and leaders with all one's income, and is perhaps an ultimate test of peasant solidarity. It is thus not surprising that change in the direction of cooperative work was slower and more tenuous than change in other spheres. The incentives conceived for collaborative work achievement in the Peruvian enterprises were undermined in part by the peasants themselves, to a considerably greater degree than incentives in other realms, suggesting that a reform government must attend with particular care to the pattern of incentives for work achievement established in the enterprise. This conclusion is also supported by cross-national analysis. Such analysis indicates that the Velasco government was not alone in its assumption that a particular organizational structure would stimulate collective work achievement, and concomitantly in its disregard of the importance of strong material incentives.

Reform governments in Chile and Cuba also encountered difficulty in stimulating collective work achievement. Although the structure of the enterprise was different in these two countries, both the Allende government and the Castro regime apparently failed to give sufficient attention to the need for direct material incentives in galvanizing collective work achievement. The Chilean situation was most directly parallel to the Peruvian. Although the Allende government tried to support the rural cooperatives in its price and credit policies (Winn and Kay, 1974: 155), clear disincentives to collective work achievement were established, and never rectified by the beleaguered Popular Unity government.[49] As in the Peruvian cooperatives, wages were not pegged to the amount of work given to the enterprise, and private economic opportunities beckoned. Thus, peasants turned to work on their private plots. Figures on agricultural performance under the Allende government are inadequate, but it appears that production was at best stable, reflecting an increase in production from private land, including such goods as chicken, pork, milk and eggs, but a decline in production from cooperative enterprises, including such goods as fruit and tobacco (Barraclough, 1975: 10-13; Marchetti, 1975a: 287-369). As in Peru, the failure of the self-managed cooperatives to stimulate agricultural production significantly was disappointing to the Allende government.

In a distinctive organizational context, the Castro government also failed to increase collective work achievement, especially during the 1960s. Fidel Castro and Che Guevara hoped that Cubans' attitudes toward work achievement would become altruistic—that they would work hard not out of fear of economic sanctions or hopes of personal reward but out of selfless desires to advance national development. In the government-guided enterprises, material incentives were downplayed and "moral" incentives emphasized. The apparent result was a crisis in tardiness and absenteeism; in August 1970, approximately 20 percent of the work force was absent on an average day (Bonachea and Valdes, 1972: 375). Agricultural output dipped (Mesa-Lago, 1974: 56-58). During the 1970s, the emphasis on moral incentives had to be withdrawn; new laws monitoring work attendance were implemented to prevent "loafing."

In contrast, collective work achievement was stimulated in both Yugoslavia and China. Although the structure of the enterprise differed in these two countries, with relatively full implementation of self-management in Yugoslavia and considerable government guidance in China, in both cases incentives for collective work achievement were clear; in China and perhaps in Yugoslavia too, it was widely emphasized to the individual that his or her advancement would be linked to the advancement of the group as a whole (Riskin, 1971; Unger, 1978). In Yugoslavia, enterprise profits were a much more significant stimulus to work than in Peru; profits

---

[49] These disincentives are emphasized by Lehmann (1973:389-397); Marchetti (1975a: 287-406) and by Barraclough and Fernández (1974: 262-265). The work of these scholars is the main source for the subsequent statements on Chilean agricultural production.

often accounted for about 10 percent of the worker's total wage (Wachtel, 1973: 182). Considerable wage differentials with respect to skill and work achievement and intense debate about these differentials presumably also encouraged hard work (Comisso, 1977; Wachtel, 1973). The clear link between work achievement and income would seem to be one reason for the sharp increase in industrial production in Yugoslavia after the introduction of self-management in the 1950s, as Chapter II mentioned.

Clear incentives to work achievement were also established in China. A careful system of work points was instituted in cooperatives to encourage extra effort and work on more arduous tasks; the work-point system and each peasant's work contribution were frequently discussed by cooperative members (Printz and Steinle, 1973: 82-83; Unger, 1978). Work on private pursuits was checked by cutting the grain allotments of peasants with high absenteeism (Unger, 1978: 596). In part as a result, agricultural production increased sharply in China after 1961, especially in grains (Stavis, 1974b; United States Government, 1975).

The success of other governments in encouraging collective work achievement is difficult to evaluate. In Mexico, production in the cooperatives was generally somewhat below that on private land, but the difference seemed to reflect primarily greater government support for the private enterprises (Senior, 1958: 191-193). In Tanzania, the impact of cooperativization on collective work achievement is particularly difficult to assess because the recent cooperativization effort was not very extensive, and because it coincided with a severe drought (Feldman, 1975; Hill, 1973).

Cross-national analysis of collective work achievement patterns suggests that the establishment of self-management is not in itself sufficient to promote hard work for the enterprise. The nature of profit allocation, the character of upward mobility opportunities, the strategies of work compensation, the stance toward private economic pursuits, and the like are very important enterprise policies that must be carefully designed within the broad structural context of self-management if collective work achievement is to be encouraged.

Part Three · *THE SELF-MANAGED COOPERATIVES IN THE NATIONAL ECONOMY AND POLITY*

# IX · *Cooperative Members and Peasant Outsiders*

> The problem of combining the autonomy of the self-managed enter-
> prise with the interests of the wider community is one of [our] main
> concerns.
>
> (Hunnius, 1973:288, discussing Yugoslav self-management)

IN THE CLIENTELIST SYSTEM, the hacienda peasant was separated not only from other peasants in his own community but also
from those outside it. The severe land shortages in Peru and the
sharp income discrepancies among distinct peasant strata set the
stage for conflict. Vitriolic battles over land and water rights occurred frequently between peasant communities and haciendas, as
well as among two or three communities, and among two or three
haciendas.[1] Theft was common.[2] Conflict between peasant community members and hacienda workers was especially intense,
given the historical tensions between the two groups, and these
tensions were often fanned by the patron, who feared cooperation
among different peasant groups just as he feared cooperation
among peasants within the hacienda. In such a context, peasants
rarely sought contacts with other peasants outside their community,[3] and peasant federations were weak, hampered by government repression, landowners' sanctions, leadership opportunism,
and the suspicions of many peasants.[4]

In the "fully participatory social democracy," solidarity across
distinct peasant strata was intended to rise. Unity and cooperation

[1] On the disputes between peasant communities and haciendas, see Martínez Alier
(1973). Disputes in Huanca are documented in the *Correspondencia del Gerente General*
for Huanca in the hacienda archive in Lima. On disputes between communities, see
Paige (1975: 188). According to one survey cited by Paige, 73 percent of the peasant
communities were involved in some kind of land dispute that had been taken to
court; some of the suits had been active for forty years.

[2] See Paige (1975: 188) and Stein (1961: 19). Stein reports that at times half of all
a community's crops were stolen.

[3] This point is emphasized by Stein (1961: 183). It is also indicative that many
major studies do not mention contacts between peasants of the research site and
other sites; examples include Adams (1959); Alberti (1974); Greaves (1968).

[4] The weakness of peasant federations is described in detail in the second section
of this chapter.

among all kinds of peasants was to develop.[5] Cooperative enterprises were to collaborate with each other; richer coastal peasants were to collaborate with poorer highlands peasants; cooperative members were to collaborate with the temporary workers in their enterprises; and, in the highlands, ex-hacienda workers were to collaborate with comuneros. Such integration was to be achieved primarily through the National Agrarian Confederation (CNA), whose structure was briefly described in Chapter II. Politically, the CNA would achieve peasant solidarity by giving all peasants the opportunity to express their concerns, then by analyzing them, and finally by winning some solutions to them.[6] Integration was also to be encouraged through the establishment of economic federations, or Central Cooperatives, that would promote both agricultural economic growth through economies of scale in marketing, accounting, and the like and would advance economic equality through appropriate investment priorities and profit redistribution (Horton, 1974: 59-60; Ortiz, 1973; Supreme Decree 240-69-AP, Title 6).

In contrast, proponents of the corporatist model believed that these federations were to be the primary structures through which the Peruvian state would control and tax peasants. The primary purpose of the CNA was to channel peasant political activity through an organization basically supportive of the government, thereby checking the growth of the Marxist Peruvian Peasant Confederation (Valderrama, 1976). In the CNA itself, concerns of rank-and-file peasants would not be expressed, because wealthy peasants would be favored in its composition, and any dissident leaders would be co-opted by SINAMOS (Palmer, 1973: 157). Moreover, the state would constantly seek its own economic aggrandizement, and Central Cooperatives or any other such organizations were likely to be subordinated to the purposes of the state rather than the peasants.[7]

Did alienation among peasant groups diminish after 1969? Did the CNA or Central Cooperatives provide new incentives for solidarity among peasant groups? The answer to both these questions is no, but generally not for the reasons suggested by proponents of corporatist models.

[5] See the preamble to Decree Law 19400 and various officials' speeches in Confederación Nacional Agraria (1974).

[6] *Ibid.*, and Chapter II of the CNA statute, and peasant's speeches in Confederación Nacional Agraria (1974).

[7] See articles in various issues of *Sociedad y Política*, especially Portocarrero (1973).

## DISINCENTIVES TO SOLIDARITY AMONG DISTINCT
## PEASANT STRATA AND ENTERPRISES

Chapter II emphasized that self-management theory has yet to develop any kind of consensus on appropriate self-management organs at the national level and that, in part for this reason, these organs emerged very slowly in Peru. So much attention had been devoted to the possible "conciliation of classes" and so little to the relationships among distinct socioeconomic strata within the peasant class that many leftists were surprised and dismayed to realize that the self-managed cooperatives were perhaps even exacerbating hostility among individual enterprises and peasant strata.[8]

It was thus with limited theoretical guidelines and also rather late in the Velasco era that concerted attention was given to the development of federations that might ameliorate the tensions among peasant strata and approximate self-management at the national level. The delay in the establishment of these institutions was unfortunate for several reasons: first, cooperative members had already made a commitment to their enterprises; second, rival political cliques within the Velasco government were consolidated, increasing the probability that any new organization would be caught up in these rivalries. Ultimately, although various federations were active, they failed to achieve their proclaimed aims.

### Self-Managed Cooperative "Islands"

If the individual cooperative is an "island" of workers' control in stormy political and economic seas, incentives for political or economic collaboration across peasant enterprises and strata are scant. In such a case, structural change has occurred at the level of the enterprise, but not beyond it, and there is no reason to expect change in any relationships beyond the enterprise.

Politically, the Peruvian cooperatives were islands of peasant power in a tempestuous political ocean where the potential for the aggregation of peasant interests and for attention to these interests by the government was uncertain. Real political power was perceived to reside in the enterprise, and members wanted to maximize that power. Enterprise autonomy was critical to political

---

[8] See for example Jaime Llosa, "Reforma Agraria y Revolución," *Participación*, 2 (August 1973), 48, and the speech of the Minister of Agriculture upon the anniversary of the Agrarian Reform Law, *El Comercio*, June 24, 1973. A journalist who was close to Velasco, Pierre de Zutter, embraced the temporary workers' cause in frequent columns in the newspaper *Expreso* during 1973.

power, and so members sought to prevent encroachments by the government and by other peasants. Members particularly feared encroachments by disadvantaged peasants who were perceived to be seeking admission into the cooperative, or, even worse, various changes in its structure. Cooperative members wanted to maximize not only the power of their enterprise vis-à-vis the outside but also their own individual power within the enterprise. Each peasant desired to increase the weight of his voice within the cooperative, and thus wanted to limit the number of members in the enterprise.

Moreover, economically, the Peruvian cooperatives were first established as islands of self-management in an ocean of a competitive market economy. The cooperative was thus ipso facto in competition with other enterprises selling the same product; in agriculture, these enterprises were likely to be near each other and to feel the competition keenly. Most Peruvian agricultural enterprises sold their products not directly to the consumer but through middlemen. These intermediaries included large private and cooperative firms as well as peasants, such as prosperous coastal ex-sharecroppers and wealthy comuneros. Only these intermediaries held the necessary storage, transportation, and/or processing facilities, and thus the middlemen were able to squeeze producers economically, in many cases leaving them with less than one-third of the selling price of the good (Rubio Correa, 1977: 299; Caballero and Tello, 1976: 6; Durham, 1977: 20-21). The interest of middlemen was thus opposed to the interest of producers. Further, each cooperative or community was pitted against the others, trying to get the best deal from the intermediary. Enterprises were tempted to undersell their product to maximize volume or win an inside track with the middleman; to undersell goods without loss to themselves cooperative members could seek more work out of their eventuales for a lower wage.

However, in the long run, it was in the interest of each cooperative enterprise to assume as many of the functions of the middleman as it could. If the enterprise could invest its profits into trucks or tractors, storage warehouses or processing facilities, it could expect to make this equipment available to nearby enterprises at a good profit. Further, if a nearby enterprise were in economic difficulty, the prosperous, growing cooperative was tempted to see the other's problems as an opportunity to squeeze it even more—if the failing enterprise could not possibly afford a new harvesting machine but was about to lose an entire crop because its machine had broken down, the nearby enterprise with such a machine to spare could charge a handsome rent. Moreover, the desire of each cooperative to achieve a dominant position in a region was predicated upon making profits that could be reinvested, and once again the cooperative was tempted to eke these profits out of cheap labor by eventuales.

## The National Agrarian Confederation (CNA)

The CNA was unable to play an integrative role among Peruvian peasants for various reasons. The organization was launched near the end of 1974 with strong encouragement from leftists in the Velasco government, including Leonidas Rodríguez Figueroa.[9] It was widely realized by that time that the agrarian reform had benefited primarily wealthier peasants on the ex-haciendas rather than the most disadvantaged comuneros. In building the Agrarian Leagues and the CNA, these leftists hoped to redress the skewed benefits of the agrarian reform program by assuring strong representation of comuneros in the CNA. Ultimately, in contrast to the predictions of proponents of corporatist models, the CNA gave greater representation to comuneros than to any other peasant stratum (approximately 75 percent), considerably more than it gave to cooperative members (some 20 percent).[10]

---

[9] On this general, see Pease García (1977: 152 and 245). His involvement in the CNA was affirmed in interviews with CNA, SINAMOS, and ministry officials, and was also indicated by the fact that the CNA appointed Rodríguez Figueroa as its political adviser after he was forced into retirement in October 1975. See also Béjar (1976: 120-123) on the establishment of the CNA.

[10] My only data for the base Leagues are as of September 1974, but there is no reason to think there was any change in CNA composition. At that time, of the 1,644 base organizations, 73 percent were from the poorest type, the peasant communities, although they constituted only about 40 percent of the rural population, versus 3 percent from the richest type of organization, the associations of direct cultivators, although they made up roughly 24 percent of the rural population (SINAMOS, 1975: 4). Cooperative enterprises were more or less proportionately represented, with 19 percent of the CNA's base organizations and about 23 percent of the agrarian population (SINAMOS, 1975: 4). Cuzco, the most politically radical area, was well represented, with 13 Agrarian Leagues—more than any other department except Ancash (SINAMOS, 1975: 4). The 1974-1975 Leadership Board was also weighted against the wealthy independent coastal farmers and in favor of the less prosperous peasant communities. According to information derived from interviews with CNA leaders, SINAMOS and Ministry of Agriculture officials, and from *El Comercio*, October 5, 1974, of the eleven members of the CNA Board, eight (73 percent) were from peasant communities, two (18 percent) from cooperatives and one (9 percent) from independent coastal farms. According to the same sources, the leaders themselves were, however, much better educated than the average peasant;

Allied with leftists in the Velasco government, the disadvantaged peasants made a large number of important demands. However, the calls of the CNA were rising at a time when the power of the leftist group within the government was falling, and thus many of the CNA's concerns were rejected by the government as a whole. Moreover, because of the preponderance of comuneros in the CNA, many of its demands were at best of interest only to them, and at worst antithetical to the interests of cooperative members. Thus, the CNA failed to provide policy incentives for participation and solidarity among the peasantry as a whole due to both the government's rejection of its political initiatives and the bias of these initiatives in favor of disadvantaged peasants. Some of the responsibility for the failure also seemed to lie with the cooperative members themselves who, alienated by the preponderance of comuneros in the CNA from the start, never pressed their requests within the federation, and thus never initiated bargaining processes within it.

The one CNA priority that both won government support and did not alienate cooperative members was the acceleration and intensification of the agrarian reform. Along with SINAMOS, the CNA supported land invasions of unexpropriated haciendas, and soon thereafter government expropriations increased (see Chapter II). The CNA also advocated the re-legitimization of rural unions, primarily on the grounds of their importance in not-yet-expropriated haciendas, and this request finally became acceptable to the

---

two (18 percent) had some university education and five (45 percent) some secondary education. However, in contrast to the urban intellectual leaders of the 1960's peasant federation (Handelman, 1975a: 136), the CNA leaders were raised in agricultural communities and worked in them most of their lives. The president for 1974-1976 was a small farmer from a peasant community in the high jungle with some secondary education; he had worked as a school teacher and post office employee in the region.

For later years, information on CNA composition is available only for the Leadership Board, derived from *El Campesino*, No. 115 (1/3/77). In early 1977 the well-known leftist leader from the radical Cuzco delegation, Avelino Mar Arías, was elected president. Of the other 10 leaders, 4 were from highlands peasant communities, 1 from a jungle "native" community, and 1 was a landless peasant. Including the radical Avelino Mar from Cuzco, at least 7 of the 11 leaders, or again about 70 percent of the board, had peasant-community origins. There were again 2 board leaders from cooperatives, but only 1 from a prosperous coastal area (the second was from the jungle region). There was one presumably prosperous member from a Service Cooperative near Arequipa.

government in early 1975.[11] The CNA also asked that the landholding limits be reduced to approximately 10 hectares on the coast and 15 in the highlands,[12] and in late 1975 the limits were reduced, but not so dramatically, to approximately 50 hectares on the coast and 30 in the highlands, in Decree Law 21333. However, the exact amount of the CNA's influence on these initiatives is difficult to evaluate because they were also advanced by leftists in SINAMOS and the Ministry of Agriculture.[13]

In contrast to the acceleration of the agrarian reform, other CNA priorities failed to win full government endorsement and also alienated cooperative members. The CNA consistently supported the principles of Social Property.[14] Social Property was virtually anathema to most cooperative members who wanted neither greater wealth redistribution nor increased state regulation, and despite some efforts by leftist officials to promote Social Property in the countryside, especially for the agro-industrial sugar cooperatives, the movement ended under the Morales Bermúdez administration.

The CNA was particularly critical of the cooperatives' restrictive stance toward temporary workers. At the inaugural congress, the Commission on Peasant Enterprises demanded "just" and "equal" treatment for "peasants without land" and the incorporation of temporary workers into the enterprises.[15] In many regions of Peru, including the Virú valley, the Agrarian Leagues soon began to work with SINAMOS and the Ministry of Agriculture to promote the admission of eventuales into the cooperatives. Temporary workers who had been employed by the CAPs for years were identified and encouraged to petition cooperative councils. Finally, the CNA's concern was endorsed in Decree Law 21334 of December 1975, requiring one permanent worker for every five irrigated hectares,

[11] The motion was first made by Commission #8 at the CNA inaugural congress (Confederación Nacional Agraria, 1974), but rejected in subsequent debate (*La Crónica*, October 2, 1974, p. 4 and *Latin America, 8* (October 11, 1974)). Discussion continued thereafter, however. The demand was advanced again in 1975 at the General Assembly of Delegates in Cuzco (*La Crónica*, April 28-May 2, 1975) and finally accepted by the government (Torres y Torres Lara, 1975: 61-63).

[12] See *Latin America, 8* (October 11, 1974), 319.

[13] Interviews with officials in SINAMOS and the Ministry of Agriculture, especially Ing. Luis Deustua of COAMA in Lima, May 1975. Ing. Deustua served as a liaison official between the Ministry and the CNA. See also Valderrama (1976: 117-122), and Chapter II above.

[14] See Confederación Nacional Agraria (1975: 7-8).

[15] See Confederación Nacional Agraria (1974: "Acuerdos de la Comisión No. 11").

but by this time the government was shifting to the right and the decree was not implemented.

Nor did the CNA win any support from coastal cooperative members in its proposals on agricultural price policy. CNA leaders proposed sharper price increases in potatoes, produced largely by comuneros, but not in sugar or rice, produced largely by coastal CAP members.[16] (The price of potatoes had remained stable between early 1970 and early 1974, despite considerable inflation.[17]) The government did raise prices for agricultural products in 1975 and 1976, but the price of the potato actually climbed somewhat less than the price of most products (see Chapter X).

The CNA's initiatives on these fronts might have been accepted more readily by cooperative members if the CNA had taken a stronger stand on issues of special concern to the cooperatives, such as the agrarian debt. Debt payment was a major concern of cooperative members, and it was opposed by many government officials as well; thus, reduction of the debt would have been an excellent demand for the CNA to advance strongly. However, the CNA wavered, taking different positions on the debt, but never very strong ones.

The initial CNA congress recommended a five-year moratorium on agrarian debt payment.[18] However, subsequently the demand was not strongly advanced. The CNA's vice-president indicated he would back a new debt scheme whereby prosperous cooperatives would pay more, but struggling communities less.[19] Finally the CNA accepted the principle of the debt, but argued that it must be allocated to a rural development fund rather than the ex-hacendados.[20] Such a fund implied the transfer of funds from the cooperatives to poorer communities—not exactly what the cooperatives had in mind. In any case, as we know, the government did not accept any of the CNA's proposals about the debt.

---

[16] Interviews with the vice-president of the CNA, in Lima, on June 1, 1975, and with Ing. Luis Deustua of COAMA, in Lima, on June 2, 1975.

[17] Compare the "Peru: Agricultural Situation, Annual Report," of the United States Department of Agriculture, for February 5, 1971, Table IV, with the same report of February 4, 1974, Table 8. The trend continued through 1978, (see Avances de Investigación, No. 7 (February, 1979), p. 17).

[18] Confederación Nacional Agraria (1974: "Acuerdos de la Comisión No. 7," section 6).

[19] Interview with vice-president of the CNA, in Lima, on June 1, 1975.

[20] *Informativo Político*, No. 45 (June, 1976), p. 23.

Various other CNA requests might also have won some support from cooperative members and engaged them in the organization, but met only a limited response from the government. The CNA argued that cliques of officials in most government agencies— including SINAMOS, which had been so engaged in the birth of the CNA and which purportedly controlled the federation—were "counterrevolutionary."[21] The CNA asked for the power to review the activities of officials and dismiss them if necessary, and recommended that more individuals of peasant origin be given official posts.[22] The government did respond somewhat to the peasants' concerns. A CNA representative was included on the board of a re-organized Agrarian Bank.[23] Some SINAMOS officials were dismissed, including 300 in the Lima Agrarian Zone.[24] To assure greater employment of citizens from peasant backgrounds in state agencies in the future, the government agreed to provide full scholarships to all successful university applicants of peasant origin.[25] Yet, these actions were merely government concessions on specific problems, not a comprehensive program for peasants' accountability over officials. Peasants did not gain legal and structural mechanisms that assured them a role in the selection and dismissal of government officials.

[21] Consider the report of Commission #3, point #33, in Confederación Nacional Agraria (1974). The Commission attacks SINAMOS for the following reasons:

1. That SINAMOS is essentially an organization of support to the social mobilization of the workers, but that this support is not given in many cases in agreement with the vital needs of the peasantry;
2. That the problems of capacitación are being treated in a very superficial and deficient form;
3. That inside SINAMOS are officials with traditional political perspectives who want to plant their ideas and methods into the Revolutionary Process;
4. That the officials of SINAMOS do not identify themselves with the Revolutionary Process;
5. That officials of SINAMOS, especially in the zonal offices, are contracted and fired in agreement with the criteria of the traditional political parties;
6. That very few young people of peasant origins, despite knowledge and experience, have access to work in the public agencies, including SINAMOS.

[22] Confederación Nacional Agraria (1974: "Acuerdos de la Comisión No. 3"). See also *La Crónica*, October 1, 1974, p. 4, and *Latin America*, *8* (October 11, 1974), p. 319.

[23] *El Campesino*, September 16, 1975, p. 3; and Decree Law 21227, article 17.

[24] Interview with Dr. Miguel Candiotti of Huancayo SINAMOS, in Huancayo, May 6, 1975.

[25] Letter from Ing. Luis Deustua, of COAMA, March 18, 1976. On the demand, see *Boletín Informativo* (CNA pamphlet), *2* (March, 1975), p. 15.

Various CNA concerns were totally rejected by the government. The CNA repeatedly asked that the daily *El Comercio* be allocated to the CNA, as the newspaper reform law had promised, but it never was. A new law for peasant communities was due as of 1973, and various proposals were debated throughout 1973-1977; but the final CNA draft was rejected in May 1978.[26] Perhaps most important was the rejection of the CNA's proposals in the areas of marketing and agro-industrialization. The CNA was aware that the government's plans for central cooperatives were moving at a snail's pace. Arguing that the intermediary too often exploited the peasant, the CNA advanced a plan for the gradual phasing out of the middlemen. "Committees of Agricultural Producers" would be established, with the CNA itself playing a key role; more information would be distributed to peasants about prices to impede deception by middlemen, and peasants would be encouraged to form cooperatives to agro-industrialize and market their products themselves.[27] Although the plan was considered the CNA's most important project for 1975,[28] it was vetoed by the government. In November 1975, in Decree Law 21169, the government advanced new marketing proposals that by-passed the CNA.

The rejection of so many of the CNA's demands by the government and the bias of these demands toward more disadvantaged peasants made the organization fall far short of the vision of it in the "fully participatory social democracy." However, the CNA did not emerge as a corporatist organization either. Clearly, its design was corporatist: it was functionally based, hierarchically ordered, licensed by the state, and intended to be non-competitive within its functional sector. However, the CNA did not play the political role stipulated for it in the corporatist model. As indicated above, its peasant constituents were predominantly leftist, who were at first favored by the "progressives" in the government but later proved difficult to manipulate or co-opt. The Morales Bermúdez government vigorously opposed the election of Avelino Mar as president in 1977, but could not stop it.[29] The only way the government could deter the CNA, it finally decided, was to decapitate the organization—which it did in June 1978.

Nor did the CNA play the pre-emptive or defensive role antici-

[26] *El Comercio*, May 13, 1978, p. 5.

[27] See the "Reglamento: Comités de Productores," CNA, Lima, 1975.

[28] Interview with vice-president of the CNA, in Lima, on June 1, 1975.

[29] See *Latin America Political Report*, *11* (February 4, 1977), 36-37, and *11* (March 11, 1977), 75, and also *Informativo Político*, No. 53 (February 1977), 24-25.

pated in the corporatist model. Although some officials may have hoped that the CNA would check the political rise of the Marxist Peruvian Peasant Confederation (CCP), it did not. The CCP grew.[30] It did not become a major national force, however; its strength was centered in a few regions, primarily Piura, Andahuaylas, and Cajamarca, and the organization was virtually unknown in Virú and many other areas. The CCP was weakened by internal ideological conflict; its position on the nature of class conflict in Peru did not seem clear.[31] Increasingly, the two organizations worked together and shared members; by 1978, it appeared that the two federations might consolidate.[32]

## Central Cooperatives and State Marketing Agencies

The government's stance toward large-scale cooperatives was even more confused than its stance toward the CNA. As leftists promoted the CNA but then failed to win support from the government or most cooperatives, so leftists promoted large-scale cooperatives but failed to win support for them from other key actors. However, with respect to the large-scale cooperatives, the lack of support meant that the leftists' plans—for a nationwide pyramid of cooperatives of higher and higher scales, similar to the more politically oriented CNA pyramid—were never implemented at all.[33] Only the central cooperatives, or *centrales,* a "second-level" federation (the same level as the CNA's Agrarian Leagues) were ever

[30] *Latin America,* 9 (June 6, 1975), 175; and Pomerantz (1977: 290-301).

[31] See Pomerantz (1978: 290-301). The CCP tended to give greater support to all agricultural strata, even at times the agro-industrial sugar workers and medium-sized landowners, than the CNA. The CCP's support for Huanca's privileged ex-hacienda workers is one example. The major rallying cries of the CCP were an end to the agrarian debt and land to the tiller. Otherwise, it tended to straddle issues to avoid alienating any one stratum; see, for example, its *Confederación Campesina del Perú: Compendio sobre Asuntos Agrarios,* Lima (April 1975).

[32] See *Informativo Político,* No. 45 (June 1976), pp. 22-23; Eguren López (1975: 127-128); Chapter II, n. 25 above; and *Latin America Political Report, 12* (November 17, 1978), p. 357.

[33] Some attention was given in 1973 to the development of the PIAR (Project of Integrated Rural Settlement). The PIAR was originally set up "to delineate areas which are amenable to coherent planning and execution of land reform" (Horton, 1974: 58). Various officials hoped that the aims of the PIAR would be expanded to include responsibilities for economic development and redistribution, but this hope never neared realization (Ortiz, 1978). Central cooperatives are formally within a PIAR, but the PIAR lacked visible functions after hacienda expropriation. A National Peasant Organization, *Central Campesina Nacional,* was also envisioned by some officials, but as of 1977 it was still in very initial planning stages.

seriously promoted, and relatively few of these were established. Moreover, whereas leftists and many of the interested self-managed enterprises wanted the central cooperatives to play a large role in marketing agricultural goods, in agricultural processing, and in agro-industrialization generally, the government never fully committed itself to granting such a role to the *centrales*. With respect to marketing and agro-industrialization policy, some groups in the government seemed to support the predominance of central cooperatives, but others the predominance of the state,[34] others private firms, and perhaps even others the CNA. Definitive movement in any direction was stymied by controversy as well as by shortage of government funds.

At no time was there a coherent government policy in this sphere. The discussion of the central cooperative in Title 6 of the 1969 law is vague and does not refer to redistributive goals. The first real central cooperative was established not by the government itself but in the coastal Santa valley by DESCO, a relatively pro-government, progressive research institution, which hoped that the central cooperative would serve as a model for the nation. It was emphasized by DESCO and by leftists within the government that the central cooperatives should promote economic equality. Considerable profit distribution—pooling the profits of all enterprises in an area and then redistributing them with an eye to need—was to take place; equality was also to be advanced by centralized marketing and agro-industrialization, which would sideline private marketing and processing firms and presumably transfer their profits to the cooperative members (Horton, 1974: 59-60; Padrón Castillo and Pease García, 1974: 263-299).

However, many government officials did not want central cooperatives to play such a large role in marketing and processing. Wary officials presumably became even warier when they learned of the virulent reaction of private agencies and middlemen to the Santa central cooperative (Padrón Castillo and Pease García: 1974). Officials' worries intensified further as the opposition to central cooperatives from prosperous cooperatives became evident (Horton, 1975b: 31). Perhaps most important, as proponents of corporatist models suggested, some government officials preferred to expand

---

[34] Of particular relevance was the government's *Sistema de Producción Agropecuario* or National Production System. It was set down in Decree Law 21169 of June 1975 but of unclear significance even as of 1977. See Ortiz (1978: 97) on the general confusion of government policy in this sphere.

the role of the state rather than the role of the cooperatives in marketing and agro-industrialization.

The role of the state in marketing was never predominant, but it did gradually increase, impeding the development of vigorous central cooperatives in various cases. Several state agencies had a hand in agricultural marketing.[35] The primary agency for domestic marketing was EPSA (Public Enterprise for Agricultural Services). Throughout the period of this study, EPSA held a monopoly position in the marketing of rice; during some periods of the study, EPSA or its subsidiaries held a minority position in the marketing of potatoes, beef, palm oil, wheat, and some legume grains. Since 1974, the sale abroad of fishmeal, cotton, and coffee has been handled by EPCHAP (Public Enterprise for Marketing of Fishmeal and Oil). The state was also perceived to be active in a Social Property enterprise established for wool marketing, called *Inca Lana*. On the basis of limited evidence, these enterprises do not appear to have appropriated undue percentages of the selling price of these products to themselves.[36] However, various corruption scandals did erupt from time to time—most prominently in EPSA at the end of 1975—and in part for this reason state activity in marketing was generally opposed by peasants as well as private firms. Due to this opposition as well as a lack of funds, the activities of most state marketing agencies were centralized in Lima, thereby allowing many cooperative enterprises to escape their networks.

Thus, during 1973-1977, the economic contexts for cooperative enterprises varied. Perhaps some 20 percent of the cooperatives were obligated to market most of their major products through state agencies. Rice cooperatives were tightly tied into the state marketing network, and cotton cooperatives worked with it also, although more indirectly (CENCIRA, 1975b: 77-92; Rubin de Celis T., 1977: 45-51). About 200 enterprises, or approximately 15 percent of all cooperatives, had been organized into 28 central cooperatives, mostly in the prosperous coastal areas of Piura, Ica, and Lima.[37] A few of these, such as the central cooperative of the agro-industrial sugar cooperatives and a coffee central cooperative, put

---

[35] Data are from Ortiz (1978: 96-98) and interviews with Efraín Palti, Director of Agricultural Planning, OSPAL, Ministry of Food, July 13, 1977; and with Luis Deustua, of COAMA, July 5, 1977.

[36] This is the assessment of the World Bank missions studying the Peruvian agricultural sector in 1974-1976. Rubin de Celis T. (1977: 46-47) is more critical.

[37] List of the 28 centrales with their location was provided by the Dirección de Apoyo a las Empresas Campesinas, Ministry of the Agriculture, July 1977.

special emphasis on marketing, including export marketing.[38] A small number, including the central cooperative in Santa and in Ica, were promoting activities in such important spheres as profit redistribution, machinery pooling, input storage, and agro-industrialization projects; however, many of these projects were never fully implemented, often due to lack of funds as well as member support.[39] As of 1975, not one central cooperative had actually collected profit shares, and accordingly not one had been able to distribute profits in favor of poorer enterprises (Horton, 1975b: 31). The majority of central cooperatives were less vigorous and aspired only to facilitate the provision of services, primarily accounting services.[40] As of 1977, plans for central cooperatives had been reduced to plans for accounting centers in many areas, including the Virú valley.[41]

Approximately two-thirds of all cooperatives were neither affiliated to an active central cooperative nor obligated to a state marketing agency for the sale of most of their production. For these enterprises, the economic context changed little between 1969 and 1977. Most cooperatives bought and sold as isolated entities in a competitive market, generally with private Peruvian and non-Peruvian agro-industrial processing firms, with other cooperative enterprises, and/or individual middlemen.[42] All the disincentives to economic collaboration among various enterprises and peasant strata discussed in the first section of this chapter were thus still operative for these cooperatives.

## ATTITUDES AND BEHAVIOR TOWARD PEASANT OUTSIDERS

Without the emergence of new incentives for solidarity among peasant enterprises and peasant strata, members' attitudes and

[38] On the sugar central cooperative called CECOAAP, see Horton (1975c: 27.1-27.19) and SINAMOS (1974). On the coffee central cooperative, see *Primero Perú,* 5 (March 1977), 32.

[39] On the Santa central cooperative, see Horton (1975c: 6.1-6.7) and Padrón Castillo and Pease García (1974). On the Ica central cooperative, see CENCIRA (1975b).

[40] Ortiz (1978: 96-98) and interviews with Rodolfo Masuda Matsuura, Dirección de Apoyo a las Empresas Campesinas, Lima Ministry of Agriculture, July 25, 1977, and with Luis Deustua, of COAMA, July 15, 1977.

[41] Interview with José Elías Minaya, Trujillo Ministry of Agriculture, July 22, 1977.

[42] Caballero and Tello (1976) provide extensive information on the marketing activity of PERULAC, a milk-processing company and subsidiary of Nestlé, among Cajamarca cooperatives. An excellent general study is Rubio Correa (1977). See also Pease García (1977: 199) and Moncloa (1977: 62-66).

behavior toward outsiders remained competitive. The orientations of the 1960s by and large continued to prevail.

Evidence on peasant attitudes toward outsiders is more limited than on attitudes in other spheres because of a lack of items in the 1969 survey and the relatively factual nature of items in the 1970s interviews. This section describes the economic rivalry among enterprises and then the exploitative stance by members toward temporary workers.

As in the past, the members of peasant communities and enterprises struggled against each other for land and capital. Decades previously, Patca had fought for land rights against a contiguous community; the battle continued in the 1970s. In the 1960s, the Marla hacendado wanted his own asparagus-canning factory because he believed the Trujillo canning factory took advantage of Marla's dependence on it and undervalued its asparagus. The advantages accruing to capital remained in the 1970s, and enterprises continued to compete for profits that could be translated into capital. The rivalry is best illustrated in Estrella's relationships with other enterprises.

Estrella began its sugar cultivation in part through a loan from the agro-industrial sugar CAP Laredo, some forty-five minutes away, and was obligated to sell its cane to Laredo. Although the arrangement was profitable to Estrella, CAP members felt exploited by Laredo. They charged that Laredo underestimated the quality of Estrella's sugar, and that Laredo appropriated too large percentages of the profits for itself—two-thirds of the profits from the cane and nine-tenths of the profits from the cane by-products, according to Estrella's director. Even worse, complained Estrella members, because of the drop in sugar prices, Laredo was in debt and had not paid Estrella some 27 million soles due to it. Finally, Estrella peasants complained, Maniche (a Peruvian-run subsidiary in Trujillo of Ford Motor Company) charged outrageous prices for transporting the cane from Estrella to Laredo.

Angry at their subordination to CAP Laredo and the private firm Maniche, by 1976 Estrella members were eagerly planning the construction of a sugar mill. A North American firm, Reyes, was contracted for a feasibility study. Estrella was too small to support a mill by itself, however, and its members hoped that its mill would be used by the other enterprises in the valley, many of which now planted cane. Estrella members also hoped to agro-industrialize by canning the fruits and vegetables of the Virú CAPs. As of 1977, Estrella still lacked the funds for either a sugar mill or a canning factory, but its ambitions were clear. The place of poorer Virú

CAPs like Marla in these designs was also clear: they were to be subordinate to Estrella, primary producers dependent upon processor, as Estrella had been upon Laredo.

Similar tensions emerged between two cooperatives in the coastal Chancay valley, Huando and Torre Blanca, observed during my 1977 visit. Huando was somewhat larger than Estrella, economically successful and well-known throughout Peru for its vigorous political activity; Torre Blanca was a small, struggling enterprise some twenty minutes away. Both cooperatives produced oranges and processed some of the fruit into marmalade. In 1976, however, Torre Blanca's processing equipment broke down, and there was no money to repair it. Huando offered to process the oranges, but, Torre Blanca peasants alleged, Huando delayed in processing the fruit for some six months until it all rotted. Then Huando refused to pay Torre Blanca any money. Of course, Huando peasants had a different story, and the truth of the matter could not be learned.

In this context of economic rivalry among enterprises, members were tempted to perceive eventuales, the most disadvantaged peasant stratum, as a group that could be used to the advantage of the enterprise. Members wanted this group to remain subordinate and dependent, to provide a pool of cheap labor ready to work whenever the enterprise, not the eventual, saw fit. Eventuales were thus very important to the enterprise. Legally, they were hired for a maximum of three months, generally to work on a particular harvest, and thus their number in any one enterprise would vary according to its type of products and the agricultural season. However, many eventuales were in fact illicitly on the payroll all year, year after year. In a very hypothetical "average" cooperative, eventuales did about one-third the total amount of enterprise work.[43] As of 1977, Estrella was employing some 125 eventuales on the average, or more eventuales than permanent members, whereas Marla was employing about 50, or about 60 percent the number of permanent members. In Huanca, eventuales were employed primarily in the shearing season, and thus constituted a mere 15 percent of the labor force on the average.

Unfortunately, the 1969 survey contained no items on attitudes

---

[43] In eight rice CAPs, temporary workers contributed about 51 percent of the work (Caballero and Tello, 1976: 39). In eight agro-industrial sugar CAPs, temporary workers constituted about 17 percent of the labor force (Roca, 1975: 12). OIT (1975: 87, 100, 110, 114, 117) found the percentage of eventuales to permanent members about 300 percent in a Piura CAP; 30 percent in an Ica CAP; 55 percent in one Puno CAP and 12 percent in another; and 48 percent in a Cuzco CAP.

of permanent workers toward eventuales, and thus it is impossible to assess trends in these attitudes. When questioned about helping the temporary workers, members recognized the plight of the eventuales, and were often sympathetic: "The temporary workers have no social security, if they get sick they get no help, they have to pay out of their own pocketbooks" (Q1975, 59). However, most members were unwilling to translate their sympathy for the eventuales into any action on their behalf. When I probed members about helping the temporary workers by one key act—admitting them into the cooperative—members' faces hardened. The most common answer was, "Yes, eventuales are admitted into the cooperative whenever they have fulfilled the requirements and there is an opening." It was a rather stock reply, one that put the responsibility on the cooperative and not on the member himself. A minority, but a minority that included many cooperative leaders, was more adamant, typically arguing that if the CAP was to include more members, it should be given more land, or that poorer people are poor because they haven't worked hard. Only about one-third of the members said that temporary workers had a right to be admitted; these members had often served more recently as eventuales themselves, or had relatives employed in the cooperatives as eventuales.

Eventuales were discriminated against economically. Income differences are difficult to calculate because they were to a large extent differences in benefits rather than base pay and because temporary workers did not work regularly, or if they did, did so illicitly. However, I estimate that a permanent worker's income was about twice that of a regularly employed eventual.[44] In Marla and Estrella, eventuales and members received the same base wage, except in later years when the government decreed rather high minimum wages and the cooperatives felt they could not pay such wages to temporary workers. However, the members received holiday bonuses, profit remittances, decent housing, private plots, and enterprise-grown food and fodder—none of which the temporary worker received, and which constituted approximately a second income for the member. Moreover, temporary workers were closely

[44] In eight sugar CAPs, a permanent laborer averaged almost four times as great a monthly income as a regularly employed eventual (Roca, 1975: 12). According to OIT (1975: 87, 100, 114, 117), a permanent laborer averaged six times as much as an eventual in a Piura CAP; five times as much in an Ica cotton CAP; and one and one-half times as much in one Puno CAP and eight times in a second, but it is unclear if in these CAPs the eventual was regularly employed. See also Bell (1977: 15).

supervised, required to put in a full eight-hour day, and assigned the most physically onerous tasks. Although evidence is limited, it seems that the eventual was making about the same real income in the cooperative as he had in the hacienda, but that of course implied a widening gap between him and the permanent laborer (Roca, 1975: 15; OIT, 1975: 87, 100, 110, 114, 117).

Temporary workers were also segregated socially. Coastal cooperative members, who were almost always fluent in Spanish and usually literate, looked down upon highlands-born eventuales who were often neither fluent in Spanish nor literate. Eventuales did not play on the permanent workers' athletic teams nor participate in community fiestas or meetings. At community stores and bars they were sometimes treated rudely. The huts of temporary workers were isolated from the rest of the community. The social subordination of the eventual on Estrella and Marla in the mid-1970s seemed similar to that on El Chalán in the mid-1960s:

> In the evenings the light of the television flickers through the windows of the union hall; the nomads [eventuales] timidly peek through the barred windows to see the proletarians [permanent laborers] enjoying the entertainment from the benches inside. On Saturdays [the eventual noted] the raucous celebration, the high consumption of costly beer and the evident swagger . . . (Greaves, 1968: 189-190).

These economic and social differences were maintained by the refusal of the cooperative members to admit eventuales into the enterprise, despite a pre-1969 law, still in force after 1969, that they be admitted if they worked more than three months for the enterprise, and despite Decree Law 21334 of late 1975 stipulating one member for every five hectares in the enterprise. By either of these laws, many more temporary workers should have been admitted into the cooperatives, especially in Estrella.

Members went to considerable lengths to prevent the admission of eventuales. When eventuales began to organize a union in Estrella in late 1973, many of the organizers were fired by the Administrative Council, thus frightening the other eventuales and resulting in the dissolution of the union. When SINAMOS, the Ministry of Agriculture, and the CNA joined together in 1974 and 1975 to compel the admission of more temporary workers into the cooperatives, members devised various strategies to block the outside pressure. The enterprises set up stringent entrance requirements, many of which had not been in force previously. Satisfaction of military service obligations and "good conduct" certificates from the police were required. At most 50 percent of the candidates could fulfill such requirements, and even after fulfillment, candidacies were carefully reviewed by the council, resulting in long delays. Few new members were ever admitted in the three research cooperatives, or in cooperatives.[45]

One caveat should be made about the validity of the calls by government agencies and the CNA for the admission of eventuales into cooperatives on the grounds of equity. It is not clear that the entrance of more temporary workers into the cooperatives would have equalized incomes among the entire Peruvian peasantry. As Caballero and Tello (1976: 40-42) point out, forced admission might have increased the number of members but would probably have decreased the number of temporary workers employed. In many cooperatives, especially prosperous ones like Estrella, more temporary workers were being employed in the mid-1970s than in the 1960s, thus giving more landless laborers the opportunity for some income. (The percentage of eventuales who were relatives of members also increased, however.)

The rivalry among enterprises was clearly perceived by the cooperative members. Answers to questionnaire items about help from outsiders and collaboration among enterprises changed little during the 1969-1977 period. Peasants were asked in both 1969 and 1974 if they could expect any help from outsiders in an emergency. In both years, only about 15 percent of respondents in Estrella, Marla, and Monte expected any such help, a very small percentage that was about the same as—indeed, slightly less than—in the control sites.[46] A second item inquiring about change in relationships with outsiders was asked in 1977 in five sites: "Do you think there

[45] Internal documents of the cooperatives—membership lists in Estrella and Marla and the annual budget in Huanca—indicate the following trends in membership: the total number of members dropped from 112 in Marla upon its adjudication to 94 in 1977. In Estrella, the number declined from 181 at its inception to 86 in 1977; however, Estrella's original membership included at least 86 ex-sharecroppers who were subsequently ousted from the CAP, and thus the number of non-feudatario members in Estrella was about the same in 1977 as upon the date of adjudication. In Huanca, the number of permanent workers stayed about the same; there were 94 workers in Monte in 1973, 92 in 1974, and 95 in 1977. On the representativeness of my research cooperatives in their reluctance to admit temporary workers as permanent employees, see Scott (1977: 22-23); Bell (1977: 8-9), and Stepan (1977: 223-224).

[46] Exact wording of item is given in Appendix 8, part 1A, no. 33. See McClintock (1976: 497) for comprehensive information.

is more or less collaboration now with other [communities and/or ex-haciendas, as applicable], than there was in 1970?" In four of the five sites (Estrella, Marla, Patca, and Rachuis), not one respondent said that collaboration was greater. Only in Varya, where peasants were working with other communities on the construction of a new road for the area, did respondents report considerable collaboration. In both Estrella and Marla, the majority of respondents said that collaboration was less—in Estrella, the majority was overwhelming (95 percent). In Patca and Rachuis, most respondents said that there was no collaboration, but that there had been none before either. Few respondents reported many close friends in nearby sites: no more than 13 percent of respondents in any of the cooperative, control, or SAIS community sites said that they had more than three friends in nearby sites.[47]

Especially revealing were members' comments on the follow-up probe to the 1977 item asking why there seemed to be more or less collaboration with other sites now than in 1970. In these comments, members perceived distinct interests for distinct cooperatives, saw competition among them, and did not really question this state of affairs. Said Estrella and Marla peasants, for example:

> There is collaboration in some things, as in technical aspects or orientation, but other kinds of help aren't given, because now each cooperative has to care and watch out for its own interest (Q1977, E15).

> The cooperatives couldn't care less if other cooperatives are going well or badly, each one looks to its own progress. It's as in Estrella, they're progressing well now (Q1977, M5).

Moreover, in booming Estrella, members realized how well they were doing, and were delighted that they had won economic superiority in the valley. Self-satisfied members repeatedly mentioned to me Estrella's large new sports stadium or its prize tobacco production and then asked me eagerly, "Which do you think is the best cooperative in the valley?" It was virtually a rhetorical question. Recall that at a party welcoming me back to Estrella in 1977, the president Vásquez began by naming all Estrella's achievements since my 1975 departure, and then toasted everyone with exhilaration: "By our own efforts! By our own efforts!"

Whereas Estrella felt itself the winner of this competition, Marla

---

[47] Exact wording of item is given in Appendix 8, part 1B, no. 31. Comprehensive information on responses is given in McClintock (1976: 495).

felt itself the loser; Marla members seemed disappointed, but resigned to the new order. Sighed one member: "Each cooperative looks after its own problems, there's no help among us. Other cooperatives of the valley are better than Marla, and we have to suffer the consequences" (Q1977, M2).

Various items in the 1974 survey went beyond the items mentioned above in capturing aspirations about relationships with outsiders rather than just perceptions, but unfortunately were not asked in 1969 and thus no analysis over time was possible. One such item asked about members' support for nearby miners during a strike. Respondents were asked whether they would replace the striking miners, to earn good salaries; whether they would stay outside the conflict; or whether they would help the miners. Although in no site did as many as 10 percent of respondents indicate they would try to take the miners' jobs, nor did a majority in any site offer to help the miners, despite the fact that no specific kind of help or sacrifice was required. Moreover, the percentage of respondents opting to help was higher in the control sites than in the cooperative sites.

A second such item asked members if a site should sacrifice a bit to help poorer communities develop. Such a request required more from the respondent than did the previous item—"sacrifice" in contrast to "help"—and members were more reluctant to take up this challenge.[48] Few respondents in the ex-haciendas wanted to sacrifice for poorer peasant communities (See Table IX.1). The percentage was greatest (38 percent) in Monte, where political collaboration with poorer ex-haciendas was winning policy benefits for members. I repeated the item in the 1975 survey, to test the impact of the CNA and the Agrarian Leagues, which was not yet operating in the Virú valley during the initial survey. The percentages willing to sacrifice rose, but only slightly, from 5 percent to 11 percent in Estrella and from 24 percent to 32 percent in Marla. The larger percentage in Marla in part reflected its vision of itself as a "poorer nearby community."

## ORIENTATIONS TOWARD OFFICIAL FEDERATIONS AND CENTRAL COOPERATIVES

In the 1960s, agrarian federations did not achieve many policy benefits, thus alienating peasants from the federations, and in turn

---

[48] This item also seemed more reliable than the previous one. The phenomenon of striking miners seemed too remote to many coastal respondents.

TABLE IX.1
Solidarity with Poorer Nearby Communities, 1974[a] (%)

| | N | Will sacrifice for poorer nearby communities | Does not want to sacrifice | Don't know | No answer, other |
|---|---|---|---|---|---|
| Cooperatives, | | | | | |
| 1974 | 230 | 21 | 65 | 9 | 5 |
| Monte | 79 | 38 | 34 | 24 | 4 |
| Estrella | 89 | 5 | 87 | 0 | 9 |
| Marla | 62 | 24 | 73 | 3 | 0 |
| Quasi-control & control, 1974 | | | | | |
| Agustín | 94 | 10 | 86 | 3 | 1 |
| Virú | 90 | 16 | 78 | 4 | 3 |

[a]Item read: "Here we have two authorities with distinct characteristics. One authority says that this community is richer than other near-by communities, and we ought to sacrifice a bit so that these other places can develop. The second says that we here aren't so rich, and it's most important to continue improving life here. Which authority do you prefer?"

weakening the federations and reducing further the possibility of policy benefits. This vicious circle continued in the 1970s.

During the 1960s, the most active federation nation-wide was APRA's FENCAP, but it was often clientelistic in style (see Chapters II and V). It claimed a mere 87 base affiliates in the late 1960s (Bourque, 1971: 178). Some coastal enterprises with unions participated in FENCAP—Estrella was one—but there was limited interest in FENCAP by the 1970s. In the highlands, FENCAP was known by few peasants, and taken seriously by even fewer (Handelman, 1975a: 145-150). Other peasant federations such as the FDS (Federación Departamental de Campesinos) of the Communists and Belaúndistas and the FSC (Frente Sindical de Campesinos) of the Christian Democrats and the Cáceres family, prominent in certain regions of Peru, also seemed clientelistic in style (Dew, 1969; Handelman, 1975a: 124-154). Various federations emerged in the Huancayo region, including FEDECOJ (Department Federation of Junín Communities) and the "Federation of Communities on the Right Side of the Mantaro River," but the federations were weak (Tullis, 1969: 198-200; Handelman, 1975a: 124-154). By the 1970s, neither peasants, technicians, nor my research assistants seemed to remember any of these federations. Peasants were skeptical of them:

[peasant village leaders] suspected the motives of peasants from other comunidades. . . . Several village leaders suggested that officials of the departmental peasant federation were using that organization solely for the benefit of their own communities and were indifferent to the needs of other comunidades. It was difficult for peasant federations to function effectively in such an atmosphere. Until village leaders share a broadly based sense of common destiny, any campesino federation will be limited (Handelman, 1975a: 149-150).

Peasants viewed the CNA and its Agrarian Leagues as they had these previous federations. In Estrella, Marla, and the Huanca peasant communities, most members were uninformed, disinterested, and critical. Even as of 1977, majorities or near-majorities had not heard of the CNA (technically the pinnacle of the federation),[49] although by that year most had heard of the Agrarian Leagues, the second-level components of the federation. Of 77 respondents evaluating the league in Estrella, Marla, Rachuis, and Patca in 1977, only 19 percent said that it had ever done anything positive, and the majority of these respondents were in Patca, where the league had just played a role in resolving a boundary dispute. Peasants criticized the leagues for doing nothing in their community or cooperative or for only politicking. Even delegates to the leagues were cynical toward them, participating primarily with an eye to personal advantages of a clientelist nature. They were excited by the travel, the lavishness of the meetings, by the government officials' respect for the peasants, and by the job opportunities. Explained Carlos Otiniano:

> You go, you travel a lot, you make friends. You talk, and if you talk well, SINAMOS may choose you for a position. For example, one fellow from the Virú Agrarian League makes 7,000 soles a month for a league position in Trujillo. The delegate from the peasant community near Virú has a position in Lima at 17,000 soles a month.[50]

Although the cooperatives had various concerns that might have been advanced in the leagues or the CNA, such as an end to the agrarian debt or higher prices for agricultural products, they did

[49] In 1975, only about 30 percent of Rachuis and Patca peasants had heard of the CNA, and still in 1977 only 55 percent of Estrella and Marla respondents had heard of it.

[50] Interview with Carlos Otiniano, a 1973-1974 delegate, in Marla, May 28, 1975.

not seem to consider promoting these requests. Talking with Estrella and Marla delegates to the Virú Agrarian League, I could not interest them in a discussion of CNA demands. I asked Lucho Saavedra about the demand to reorganize the Agrarian Bank, for example; he did not respond. Overall, cooperative members still did not seem to see common political interests with other peasants.

Given members' cynical attitudes toward the CNA and its Agrarian Leagues, it is not surprising that members did little to advance these federations. Although at the height of Agrarian League activity in 1975, cooperative members did participate regularly in meetings, by 1977 the government was no longer supporting the leagues to any degree and thus material particularistic benefits were no longer an attraction of participation. In all three cooperatives, peasants lacked the will and the means to continue the leagues' activities, and they were barely operating at this time. To the degree that the leagues did function, they seemed enmeshed in rather traditional types of activity; the only major undertaking of a league in the two research areas during 1976-1977 was to arbitrate Patca's boundary dispute.

One important exception to the pattern of cynicism toward politically oriented federations was Monte. As Chapter V discussed, Monte was an enthusiastic and active participant in the CCP-affiliated union of the ex-haciendas, which for a time spanned not only Huanca but the other ex-haciendas of the central highlands SAIS as well. However, the impact of the CCP was not only to bring ex-hacienda workers together but to divide them from the comuneros, thus shedding doubts on the over-all effectiveness of the CCP.

The stance of cooperative members toward large-scale cooperatives was more varied than their stance toward the politically oriented federations. Members' attitudes typically depended upon the economic rank of the enterprise in its region. In the Virú valley, for example, ascendant Estrella was most opposed to the central cooperative, whereas Marla was positive toward it. Of 17 Estrella respondents to a 1977 query about the value of a central cooperative, 15 were negative. These members feared that in a central cooperative, they would have to make economic sacrifices for poorer cooperatives like Marla. Said one Estrella worker: "It's possible that a central cooperative would help, but how would it really be, since now the other cooperatives are worse than we are, and why should we join up with them?" (Q1977, E17).

In contrast, by 1977 Marla members thought that they could gain from a central cooperative. However, they were aware that other cooperatives had reasoned that Marla would weigh the central co-operative down, and Marla members failed to question or protest the other cooperatives' logic: "No, I don't think a central coopera-tive could help out, because the members don't know much about it and the other cooperatives don't want to help Marla anyway" (Q1977, M5).

Given these attitudes, it is not surprising that no central cooperative had been established in the region by 1977.

The major Huancayo SAIS were initially more positive toward a central cooperative than the Virú CAPs, but government policy ultimately dissipated their enthusiasm. During 1973-1975, SAIS leaders strongly believed that the four SAIS of the central highlands could progress by uniting and developing their own pro-cessing plants and marketing facilities.[51] Knowledge of the plans for a central cooperative was limited among most Huanca peasants. Yet, during this period integration seemed to be working—comuneros and workers were both making some gains from the SAIS and appeared to be moving toward conciliation, and the four SAIS of the central highlands had won the right to export more wool by making their demand together. Thus the peasants who did know about the plans for the central cooperative seemed to back it.

In November 1974, the four SAIS eagerly formed the Central de Empresas del Centro del Perú. Although the central cooperative was initiated with government support, the cooperative leaders had more ambitious aims than the government apparently anticipated. Central cooperative leaders wanted to establish their own textile factory to add to the value of their wool. Huancayo officials, however, vetoed this project; they wanted to develop a Social Property enterprise to process wool.[52] In due course such an

---

[51] Said Aurelio Osores, the 1973-1974 Huanca president, in his introductory words to the SAIS magazine, *Jatari-Uyari*: "With the *Central* of the SAIS, we will construct a great regional power, the powerful force that begins in the fields and ends in the factory. In this moment, when unemployment is tremendous, when there is no land to work, we must think about creating new sources of work, taking advantage of what we have—that is to say, the value added of our prime materials that ought to stay with us.... I ask you to leave behind envy and egoism; to defeat the enemies, the Yankee, the middleman and ignorance, whose product is misery, we must construct an alliance with our brother peasants and workers of the other SAIS and cooperatives who have developed their consciousness" (*Jatari-Uyari, 3* [July 1973]).

[52] Interviews with Huanca technicians, August-September 1973 and May 1975. See also Beatriz Bissio, "Nace la Inter-SAIS," *Correo*, November 25, 1974; de Zutter (1975: 210-220); and Caycho (1977: 133-139).

enterprise, Inca Lana, was established. The decision dissipated the impulse of the four SAIS to develop a strong central cooperative.[53] One of the key leaders in the effort left for a lucrative position in Inca Lana. Moreover, the four SAIS were again in heated competition with each other over wool sales to Inca Lana. Thus, although the central cooperative was to develop a meat butchery and refrigeration facility,[54] progress on this front slowed. By 1976, it had ground to a halt; the Morales Bermúdez government had decided that EPSA should have a role in beef marketing, and, although this role was primarily only setting prices for the sale of beef in Lima, the government was no longer supporting the Huancayo central cooperative and withdrew a promised loan of 400 million soles for its meat butchery and refrigeration facility.

## SUMMARY

The new federations established under Velasco failed to provide sufficient incentives for solidarity among Peruvian peasants. Neither the political federation, the CNA with its Agrarian Leagues, nor the larger-scale economic organizations, the central cooperatives, were able to modify the traditional skepticism of peasants toward institutions beyond their own enterprise or community. Why did these federations fail? The most important reason would seem to have been the limited support for them from the government. Although the government did not control the CNA as corporatist model proponents contended, it did not respond creatively or positively to its concerns, as it should have in a "fully participatory social democracy." Government policy was even more detrimental to the development of economic federations; there was no clear policy on who was to have power in the critical areas of marketing and agro-industrialization—whether it was to be the central cooperatives, the state, or private agriculturalists. Few central cooperatives ever gained power in this area and thus never had a real opportunity to win significant economic gains for members.

Another reason for failure was the belated interest in these federations by the government. The dynamic of rivalry among enterprises and arrogant postures by many cooperative members

---

[53] Interviews with Aurelio Osores and Julio Melchor of SAIS Huanca, and Juan Casas Casas of CENCIRA, in Huancayo, July 8-11, 1977.

[54] See de Zutter (1975: 210-220); and *El Comercio*, February 15, 1975 and November 19, 1975.

toward disadvantaged peasants had already been set in motion, with isolated self-managed enterprises solidly established, when the movement toward federations was initiated. With respect to the CNA, one specific mistake may also be cited: cooperative members should have been given greater representation, more in line with their real economic and political power in the country; cooperative members might then have become more involved in the development of the political demands of the CNA, and the CNA might not have become the association of comuneros to the virtual exclusion of cooperative members. Attachment to organizations previously active in the countryside, such as FENCAP, did not hamper the development of the new federations because so few peasants had been enthusiastic about the 1960s organizations.

Without new and stronger federations, the cooperatives remained islands in stormy economic and political seas, and members were unconvinced of the potential value of aggregating peasant political demands or of integrating peasant political demands or of integrating economically. An attitude of competition among enterprises and peasant strata prevailed, and behavior was competitive as well. As with respect to work achievement in many cooperatives, the vicious circle of peasant skepticism toward outsiders→ weak federations→skepticism toward outsiders was not broken. Over all, change in enterprise relationships with outsiders was scant, moving toward the pattern implied in neither the corporatist nor the "fully participatory social democracy" model.

Nor did the pattern of relationships between Industrial Community members and outsiders move in any one clear direction.[55] As in the agrarian cooperatives, members wanted to maintain their new prerogatives for themselves, and often resisted the efforts of temporary workers in the firm to become CI members (Santistevan, 1977b: 304). However, CI members were in many respects a more homogeneous group than CNA peasants, and thus there was a greater consensus among CI members about their key concerns. Whereas some peasants had held their cooperatives for years, others had seen barely any signs of agrarian reform. Most industrial workers in large enterprises were in a similar position vis-à vis the industrial reform: they had gained the Industrial Community, but this organization provided them limited power. Industrial workers were more united in their desire for a radicalization of the In-

[55] This paragraph draws heavily upon Santistevan (1977a), as well as upon Stephens (1977) and Alberti, Santistevan, and Pásara (1977).

dustrial Community law, and worked together toward this goal for a year or so in their federation, CONACI. However, CONACI proved even more threatening, more quickly, to many groups in the government than the CNA did, and the government's efforts to manipulate CONACI and the entire labor federation movement were more vigorous (see Chapter X). Thus, although the labor federation movement was soon politically splintered, the reasons for the factionalization would seem to lie heavily upon the government, perhaps even more heavily than the reasons for the divisions among the peasantry.

# X · *Cooperative Members and the Government*

> We don't know whether we will have a new life or just a new patron, the government which has expropriated the hacienda to form the cooperative.
>
> (Peasant quoted by Gall, 1971:287)

> By encouraging the forces of change and the desires of the masses you might set loose forces beyond your control, ending in a revolution which could be your enemy.
>
> (Che Guevara, quoted in Hellman and Rosenbaum, 1975:73)

THE IMAGES of the Velasco government advanced in the corporatist and "fully participatory social democracy" models were described in Chapter II. In the corporatist model, the government is perceived as controlling and monitoring citizens' political activity and aiming to co-opt or pre-empt radical mobilization that might impede the development of a "harmonious organic social whole." In contrast, in the "fully participatory social democracy," the government was to support political participation and decision making, never imposing its own policy preferences (Delgado, 1973: 263-285; Velasco, 1972b: 271-289). "When the common man and the public servant meet, there is neither servant nor served, but two men pledged to the same revolutionary task."[1] Whereas in the corporatist model, peasant support for the government could be opportunistic at best, the "fully participatory social democracy" model implied that the government's help for peasants' own political efforts, as well as its provision of considerable economic benefits and "policy goods" in response to these efforts, would encourage support for the regime among the peasantry. As Chapter II also discussed, neither model adequately described the role of the Velasco government: various factions with various ideas about the role of the government struggled against each other, creating a kaleidoscope of changing government action and policy.

This chapter delineates in greater detail than Chapter II the actual character of government action and policy in the coopera-

---

[1] "Movilización Social y SINAMOS," SINAMOS, Lima, n.d., back cover.

tives, and seeks to assess the overall impact of the government and its policies upon peasants' support for the regime. (Peasants' support for the regime is not an exact equivalent to "loyalty to the nation" or the political system as a whole, the orientation of greatest concern to political culture analysis, but in politically unstable countries like Peru, it seems one of the few available indicators of this orientation.[2]) The major issue emerges as: why, despite the fact of significant policy benefits for cooperative members during the Velasco era and a year or so beyond, did the government fail to win political commitment from these peasants?

## INCENTIVES FOR PEASANT LOYALTY TOWARD THE GOVERNMENT

The agrarian reform was the most substantial effort of the Velasco government. Land redistribution was combined with increased investment, greater credit, and gradually also improved prices for the reformed agricultural sector. Most cooperative members were better off than ever before.

Cooperative members were generally pleased by the agrarian reform program. In Estrella, Marla, and Huanca peasant communities, members' evaluation of their cooperatives was positive (see Table X.1), and in most other cooperatives I visited, it seemed positive as well. Monte workers viewed the SAIS negatively, indeed so negatively that I deleted the item from the questionnaire to avoid members' suspicion of my research group; however, very few ex-haciendas had been adjudicated into a SAIS on such unfavorable terms as Monte had been, and thus Monte peasants' views were not representative.

The primary reason for members' positive assessment of their cooperative was the perception that their standard of living had risen via the cooperative. Many members said that the cooperative paid better, provided better facilities, gave easier loans, or improved work conditions (see Table X.2). Members also cited the political changes in the cooperatives as an important improvement,

[2] Considerable effort has been devoted to the development of survey items that distinguish between "system affect" and "incumbent affect." See especially Muller and Jukam (1978). However, in situations such as the Peruvian, it is recognized that the peasant has historically been skeptical and suspicious of the national political system (see Chapter III). Attitudes toward the traditional political system are thus not an indicator of loyalty toward the new system that the military government was ostensibly trying to establish.

TABLE X.1
Evaluation of the Cooperatives[a] (%)

| | N[b] | Cooperative helps a lot | Cooperative helps some | Cooperative helps other sectors of community | Cooperative does not help |
|---|---|---|---|---|---|
| ...operatives, 1974 | | | | | |
| Estrella and Marla | 154 | 18 | 62 | 0 | 20 |
| Estrella and Marla, men only | 85 | 23 | 64 | 0 | 13 |
| ...IS Communities, 1974 | | | | | |
| Patca and Varya | 91 | 12 | 71 | 7 | 10 |

[a] Answers to the item, "Do you think that the CAP/SAIS helps a lot to improve the way of living the people in this place, helps some, or doesn't help at all?"
[b] Not applicable, don't know answers, etc. have been excluded.

although less frequently than the economic improvements. It was the demise of the patron that most pleased these members:

> Now there are no longer the patrons who abused us and punished us (Q1975, 64).

> You can't fire the members. You don't have to work so much, although now we work harder than last year. We participate in the decisions. The patron never permitted us to see the balance sheet. Now at least we know (Q1975, 47).

In general, the cooperative was supported by the government's economic policies. Perhaps most important to the enterprise was the increase in loans from the government. The amount of loans granted by the Agrarian Bank jumped roughly 350 percent in current soles, from about 4 billion soles in 1968 to almost 15 billion in 1975, an increase much greater than inflation.[3] Interest rates on loans were also lower; in the 1960s, a typical annual interest rate was 20 percent, whereas from the early 1970s through July 1976 it was only between 7 and 12 percent for the short-term credit and between 9 and 13 percent for long-term credit.[4] Moreover, increas-

[3] Figures are from *Informativo Político*, No. 45 (June 1976), 32.
[4] On 1960s rates, see Greaves (1968; 416). Information on 1970s rates from Marla and Estrella balance sheets and from interview with Graciela Lituma Torres, Agrarian Bank, July 13, 1977.

## TABLE X.2
### Positively Evaluated Features of Cooperatives[a] (%)

| | N[b] | More money (profit shares, better salaries; easier loans, etc.) | Better work (easier tarea, no firings, etc.) | Better facilities (new houses, easier transportation, etc.) | More individually owned animals | More union and equality | More technical help | Other |
|---|---|---|---|---|---|---|---|---|
| Cooperatives, 1974 | | | | | | | | |
| Estrella and Marla | 84 | 90 | 35 | 44 | 18 | 24 | 8 | 18 |
| SAIS Communities, 1974 | | | | | | | | |
| Patca and Varya | 90 | 70 | 0 | 57 | 0 | 8 | 52 | 4 |

[a] Item read: "You think the SAIS/CAP helps in some ways? Why?"
[b] Only applicable respondents. As some respondents gave more than one answer, percentages do not always add to 100.

ing percentages of the loans were allocated to the cooperatives.[5] Whereas large enterprises (mainly haciendas) received approximately 52 percent of Agrarian Bank loans in 1968, and the owners of medium-size or small farms 48 percent, in 1974 large enterprises (mainly cooperatives) won 77 percent of the loans and the owners of medium-size or small farms only 23 percent (Eguren López, 1977: 248). Moreover, whereas in 1970 about 40 percent of Agrarian Bank loans was allocated to the cultivation of export crops such as sugar, cotton, and coffee that are primarily grown in the cooperatives, by 1974 this figure had risen to approximately 45 percent.[6] There was some effort to direct loans to cooperatives in poorer regions of Peru, however; such impoverished departments as Puno, Cuzco, and Cajamarca increased their percentages of the total loan allocation.[7]

All my research enterprises won considerable funds from the government during the Velasco era.[8] Huanca was one of the largest loan beneficiaries in the nation, winning some 300 million soles for a vast irrigation canal. In 1973 alone, Estrella received 8.6 million soles and Marla 4 million, primarily in both cases for farm machinery purchases and new crop cultivation. Both Estrella and Marla also sought and won non-government loans from private agro-industrial firms and CAP Laredo.

The government's own investment and support projects for agriculture also increased during the Velasco era. The budget for the most relevant institution, the Ministry of Agriculture, multiplied about eight times in current soles between 1967 and the 1975-1976 biennium, advancing from ninth to fourth among Ministry allocations and from 3 percent of the national budget to 7 percent.[9] The ratio of public investment in agriculture to gross agricultural product climbed from an average of .026 in 1965-1968 to .049 in 1972

[5] One of the reasons for this shift was that private banks were declining to lend to cooperatives. However, over-all, the availability of loans to smaller enterprises like Estrella and Marla was considered greater, according to my interviews in such cooperatives. See also OIT (1975: 148-150) and Greaves (1968: 416), who cites the difficulties of the Virú enterprises in obtaining any loans.

[6] *Marka*, 2 (February 19, 1976), 14.

[7] *Ibid.*

[8] For Huanca, see *El Comercio*, August 19, 1974, and its *Memoria Anual* for 1973-1974, pp. 12-14; for Estrella and Marla, see 1973 enterprise loan documents.

[9] Contrast 1967 budget figures provided by Gomez (1969: 32) and figures for 1975-1976 budget in Decree Law 21057, Title II. The Ministry of Agriculture's average budget percentage under Belaúnde is provided by Bayer (1975: 22). See also OIT (1975: Table 65).

(OIT, 1975: 145). Of the budget allocations at the national level for central ministry operations, approximately 15 percent was destined for land adjudication and general support for peasant enterprises; somewhat more than 15 percent to irrigation projects; about 7 percent to conservation and reforestation; another 7 percent to other projects; and most of the remainder (about 50 percent) to personnel and administration.[10] The cooperative enterprises thus had a good share of total ministry expenditure; the funds for land adjudication and support for peasant enterprises of course fell to them, as did some of the money for irrigation projects.[11]

The impact of the government's pricing policies for agricultural products upon cooperative members is more difficult to assess. A policy of low food prices was begun under Belaúnde and continued for most of the Velasco era.[12] From 1969 to 1974, the index of food prices rose only at the same rate as the cost of living generally (Fitzgerald, 1976: 67). The ostensible purpose was to impede inflation and help the urban poor. However, the food most affected, the potato, was cultivated primarily by the poorest highlands peasants, and the low prices for potatoes hurt this group (Webb, 1975: 117-120). The damage was less severe than might be assumed, though, because the poorest highlands peasants consumed most of their potato harvest; for the potatoes they did market, they were usually not paid the government's price anyway, but yet lower prices set by middlemen (Rubio Correa, 1977: 335). The impact of the low prices of potatoes, rice, sugar, and livestock products upon cooperative members was also a more complex issue than might be assumed. In theory, cooperative members had a common interest in higher prices for agricultural products. However, in practice most enterprises produced only one of the staples. Thus, usually cooperative members condemned price increases in any food they did not produce. Price increases in staples were seen as a major

[10] Data for 1975-1976 budget from Rodolfo Masuda Matsuura, Dirección de Apoyo a las Empresas Campesinas, Ministry of Agriculture, provided in Lima, July 25, 1978. For 1973-1974 budget, see OIT (1975: n.p.).

[11] Although the aim of most irrigation projects was to bring new coastal land into cultivation and thus provide acreage for landless peasants, some of the projects were to improve existing irrigation systems. Thus the "Chao-Virú-Moche-Chicama" project would improve installations on the Virú River and help Estrella and Marla, for example. For description and evaluation of these irrigation projects, see Eguren López (1977: 252-254) and Moncloa (1977: 69-70). It is widely believed that the large irrigation projects have been too costly, and that smaller ones and/or conservation/reforestation efforts would be more cost-effective.

[12] See *Latin America Economic Report*, 2 (November 15, 1974), 177.

component of inflation, and inflation was an intense concern. Indeed, among respondents who criticized the government in the 1974 survey, about 90 percent cited inflation as a problem that the government should have solved. Many more respondents mentioned inflation than any other difficulty.[13]

In late 1974 and early 1975, the government became increasingly concerned that low food prices were discouraging domestic production and encouraging food imports, hence hurting the balance of payments, and food prices were increased. The average rise in the price of eight foods for which data are available was almost 90 percent during the approximately two years between late 1973 or early 1974 and January 1976,[14] a rise greater than inflation. The price increases were more favorable to cooperative members than to the poorest peasants; the prices of items produced to a greater extent by cooperatives, such as beef and milk, climbed more than the price of potatoes.[15]

Not all government policies were supportive of the cooperative members. The government's failure to encourage central cooperatives and discourage avaricious middlemen may have hurt the cooperatives. Moreover, the government was requiring reimbursement for the land redistribution to cooperative members. During the Velasco era, the great majority of cooperatives paid only the interest on this debt; even this interest payment was a considerable sum for many enterprises (see Chapter VIII). The total amounts due seemed gargantuan. The average CAP owed about 21 million soles and the average SAIS about 27 million, plus another 60 percent in interest, to be paid over 20 or 30 years.[16] SAIS Huanca owed approximately 145 million soles, Estrella 9 million, and Marla 4 million, plus interest. Although many peasants were not aware of the size of the debt at first, as they learned about it, they became angry:

> If we are owners, like the government says, why do we have to pay for the land? These lands were ours years ago, too (Q200).

[13] For details on the survey item and responses, see McClintock (1976: 590).

[14] The price data are derived primarily from the reports of the United States Department of Agriculture entitled, "Peru: Agricultural Situation, Annual Report," of February 4, 1974, and January 19, 1976. The data are described in detail in Appendix 2.

[15] Calculation from data in Appendix 2.

[16] Author's calculation from "Reforma Agraria en Cifras," a serial publication of the Ministry of Agriculture. Calculation was made from the November 30, 1974, issue.

The agrarian debt is a nightmare for the communities. The hacendados have exploited us for a long time, but they're not the bosses any more, so we should not pay (Q1975, 71).

However, as Chapter II mentioned, no inflation clause was included in the debt law. Thus, by 1977, the debt meant little to most cooperatives and was expected to mean even less soon.[17] At its 1975 and 1976 profit levels, an enterprise like Estrella could pay its entire debt in little more than two years. As inflation reduced the significance of the debt, however, the government extended a 35 percent tax on profits to the CAPs.

The overall economic impact of the agrarian reform and the government's agricultural policies was positive. Most cooperative members felt they had progressed economically since 1969. Table X.3 shows the majorities of respondents in Estrella, Marla, and the Huanca communities who considered themselves better off in 1974 than five years before. In my own return visits to the research cooperatives, I assessed their economic progress first-hand. Between 1973 and 1977, I noted remarkable advancement in all sites—more advancement than the peasants themselves indicated. In 1977 in both Estrella and Marla, I saw new schools and new housing; the new facilities were much larger and more modern. Whereas the bicycle had been the common peasant vehicle in 1973, by 1977 many cooperative members were whizzing about on motor scooters. Despite Monte members' complaints about the negative impact of the SAIS and the government on peasants' well-being, I witnessed dramatic economic progress there. In 1973, there were many children of secondary-school age residing in Monte and attending its school, which was authorized only at the primary level; by 1977, almost all these children were in secondary school in Huancayo, a considerable expense that their families could now afford. Nutrition also improved markedly.

The agrarian reform program and the agricultural policies of the military government thus provided reasons for peasant loyalty to the regime. A further reason may have been the character of the officials themselves. The issue of patronal behavior by officials was a very important one to peasants, as the first quote at the beginning of this chapter revealed. Although change in the attitudes and behavior of officials is difficult to measure, my observation suggested that on balance government ministers in the agrarian

---

[17] For discussion of this fact, see *The Andean Report*, 3 (March 1977), 48.

TABLE X.3
Perceived Quality of Life, 1969-1974[a] (%)

| | N[b] | Better-off now than 5 years ago | The same | Worse-off now than 5 years ago |
|---|---|---|---|---|
| ...operatives/haciendas | | | | |
| Estrella & Marla, 1974 | 123 | 51 | 20 | 29 |
| Estrella & Marla, 1969 | 118 | 42 | 33 | 25 |
| Monte, 1974 | 71 | 11 | 56 | 32 |
| Monte, 1969 | 44 | 18 | 61 | 20 |
| ...asi-control & control | | | | |
| Agustín, 1974 | 74 | 42 | 49 | 9 |
| Agustín, 1969 | 129 | 29 | 52 | 19 |
| Virú, 1974 | 87 | 15 | 28 | 57 |
| Virú, 1969 | 92 | 37 | 27 | 36 |
| IS Communities | | | | |
| Patca & Varya, 1974 | 90 | 56 | 37 | 7 |

[a] Item read: "Five years ago, the people of this place were better-off, about the same, or worse-off ..n now?"
[b] Not applicables, don't know, etc., have been omitted.

sector—like the new enterprise directors—were less patronal than their predecessors. The norm of an egalitarian posture was assumed by Velasco himself, who, when a peasant knelt before him to ask a favor during a highlands meeting, asked the peasant to rise and then, when the peasant did not, knelt down with him (Pease García, 1977b: 231). Especially at gatherings where the new behavioral norms for officials could be monitored, government personnel approached peasants with respect, and peasants often spoke warmly of this new demeanor.[18] Moreover, although officials did often promote policies over peasant opposition, they were also frequently compelled to withdraw these policies, as the next section discusses.

Egalitarianism was reinforced by a reduction in the objective status of officials. Salary levels declined from the 1960s.[19] By Decree

[18] Said Lucho Saavedra in an interview in Estrella in May 1975: "I ate right at the same table with government ministers. I slept in the same room with them. They listened to us."

[19] Interview with Luis Deustua of COAMA in Lima, July 3, 1977. Ing. Deustua worked for the government before and after 1968. See also Ortiz (1978: 91-92).

Law 21058, the maximum salary in all government ministries was fixed at 40,000 soles a month in 1974-1976, or approximately $10,000 a year.[20] Officials at somewhat lower rungs in the bureaucracy, such as an agronomist in a provincial office of the Ministry of Agriculture, earned under $4,000 per year.[21] Moreover, more individuals from humble backgrounds were employed—in part because of the increase in government jobs.[22] Government scholarships for all successful university applicants of peasant origin promised that the number of such officials would increase further in the future.

These reductions in the socioeconomic position of officials may have had some drawbacks. Many technicians, especially agronomists, left Peru for lucrative posts elsewhere (Ortiz, 1978: 91-92). Still, the professional qualifications of technicians at the middle and upper ranks were higher in the 1970s than the 1960s (Cleaves and Scurrah, 1976: 19-21). Some poorly paid officials were probably more tempted by supplementary part-time work opportunities and by fraud than in the past. However, though abuses existed in the Velasco era, I doubt they were more numerous than in the 1960s.[23]

## DISINCENTIVES TO PEASANT LOYALTY TOWARD THE GOVERNMENT

Although the policies of the Velasco government toward the agrarian cooperatives were generally favorable, this fact did not weigh very heavily with members. Cooperative members were pleased with the new agrarian structures, but saw the government as trying to violate them. Three fatal flaws of Peruvian officialdom can be distinguished: severe political oscillation and confusion; unaccountability and intrusiveness; and inability to link official benefits or sanctions to peasant support for the government.

One of the most important disincentives to peasant support for

---

[20] As Cleaves and Scurrah (1976: 21) point out, some officials evaded this stipulation by negotiating special contracts of the consulting variety, but the total number of such arrangements was small.

[21] This figure is a rough average calculated from the salaries of officials interviewed in these cities.

[22] Exact information on the number of officials from peasant backgrounds is not available. My evaluation is based primarily upon my own observation.

[23] This is also the opinion of Peter Cleaves, a scholar of Peru's agricultural bureaucracies, expressed in Houston in November 1977. On abuses in the 1960s, see Gomez (1969: 63-64).

the government was the uncertainty caused by the intense political struggle within the government. As Chapter II described, agencies were created and then destroyed, laws came and went, policy priorities emerged and disappeared. In such a context, peasants could not feel secure that their new economic gains would endure. Moreover, the constant zigs and zags of policy confused peasants, wasted resources, and, because peasants had limited impact on the policy changes, reminded them of the distance between the new system and the "fully participatory social democracy."

Cooperative members were most alienated by the policy zig to the left during 1973-1975. Most cooperative members wanted their enterprises to remain in the mode of their adjudication and felt threatened by the calls from government agencies for the radicalization of the agrarian reform program. SINAMOS, the CNA, and to some extent the Ministry of Agriculture had sought both the admission of temporary workers into the cooperatives and the transformation of the cooperatives into Social Property, an enterprise mode that most cooperative members perceived as socialistic and hostile to their interests. Yet, none of these initiatives was implemented; thus, the support of cooperative members was damaged needlessly, and without any gains in support from the disadvantaged peasants, who were never helped.

Even in many peasant communities there was fear of the policies of the Peruvian left. During 1972-1975, SINAMOS was encouraging the development of a more radical version of the peasant community statute. Recall that this statute disqualified commercial middlemen from membership in the community and called for the equalization of landholdings in the community. The law was vague, however, and during 1973 the Huancayo SINAMOS was encouraging peasant communities to adopt a stricter program of disqualification of village commercial elites and land equalization, called the Community Enterprise system. The program might well have increased the participation and wealth of peasants from the lower and middle income ranks of the community (Long and Winder, 1975; Roberts, 1975). But, threatened prosperous comuneros and commercial elites opposed the program and campaigned against it, calling it an attempt by the government to control the communities (Alderson-Smith, 1973: 28-31; Roberts, 1975). Other peasants either believed the middlemen, or were afraid to act against them. Said one Agustín peasant: "It's said they're going to try to cooperativize the land, and the great majority are not in agreement, because they say it will eliminate what they have worked for and what their children will inherit.... Most people will take up guns and let the blood flow if they try to equalize all landholdings here."[24]

Uncertainty was created not only by policy changes over time but also by the contradictory directives of distinct agencies and from within the same agency. The two most important agencies in the countryside during the Velasco era, SINAMOS and the Ministry of Agriculture, were frequently at odds. In general, the ministry tended to favor the economic consolidation of the enterprise, preferring the maintenance of traditional work patterns and the election of well-educated peasants to top positions in the cooperative. In contrast, SINAMOS sought further radicalization of the cooperatives, showing less concern for short-run economic gains and more interest in the devolution of power and wealth to lower strata within the cooperatives. As Chapter VI discussed, SINAMOS often spoke in favor of the election of candidates of lower socioeconomic status to cooperative positions. The most serious clash between the two agencies was with respect to the employment of directors in the cooperatives. SINAMOS officials frequently criticized enterprise directors as remnants of the hacienda owners and advised peasants that they could run their cooperatives without directors. Thus, SINAMOS tended to encourage the firing of directors, whereas the ministry usually struggled for their retention.

An excellent example of the confusion was the fate of the effort of the Huancayo SINAMOS to advance the Community Enterprise system. As indicated above, the Community Enterprise system was intended to be a relatively radical revision of the peasant community statute. Although most SAIS Huanca communities rejected the program, two did not; one of these was Patca. When Patca began to develop its Community Enterprise code, however, Huancayo officials had no real idea of what the system was to be like. Moreover, the Huancayo SINAMOS was asked to slow down its work on the program until a new peasant community statute was developed in Lima. (This revised statute was due in 1973 but became the object of bureaucratic struggle and has not emerged to date.) Thus, when Patca finished its draft of a Community Enterprise code and forwarded it to SINAMOS, SINAMOS was at a loss. Only after some three months did SINAMOS return its comments to Patca. The suggestions could not be deciphered by Patca's leaders. Patca members were annoyed that SINAMOS should play any role at all in the policies of its own community, and were frustrated by the red

[24] Interview with gobernador of Agustín, in Agustín, August 1973.

tape. The comuneros let the new code lie. One Patca peasant expressed the community's frustration: "The laws are too complicated, and by the time you have one law figured out, they've changed it to a new one. It's not worth the effort."[25]

A second major disincentive to peasant support for the government was the unaccountability and intrusiveness of the government. "Unaccountability" refers to the fact that officials were not subject to popular election or recall and that most major decisions were made by Velasco's inner circle and were rarely intended to be subject to change by popular action. "Intrusiveness" refers to the fact that many officials tried to implement initiatives in the cooperatives that had been rejected by members. Clearly, hermetic decision making and intrusive actions are not features of a "fully participatory social democracy." Although enough officials were skeptical of "rule-from-above" and manipulation that official initiatives spurned by peasants were rarely implemented, peasants could not be certain when the balance among officials might be tipped toward the more interventionist group.

The style of many military officers accentuated the image of the government as command-oriented and hermetic. Officers continued to wear their military uniforms in all public appearances and to maintain a physical distance from civilians. General Velasco himself was considered a quintessential military leader: "authoritarian and frank, secure of his rank, that situated him above his team; knowing his men and their weaknesses well, shrewd and bold" (Pease García, 1977: 231). These same traits characterized many generals who headed ministries, and they frustrated civilians:

> Barandiarán [one minister of agriculture] can be characterized as impulsive, to say the least. In more than one occasion his abuse of his authority upset ministry employees. Beginning in 1970, he established an "inspection" branch which initiated military practices in civilian offices . . . All the employees felt controlled, supervised in their every movement, threatened constantly by sanctions (Ortiz, 1978: 81).

The government's unaccountability and intrusiveness created a wide gap between its "fully participatory social democracy" rhetoric and reality, a gap that confused and disillusioned peasants already upset by the government's oscillating policies. Grumbled one white-collar employee from Estrella: "It's better when a government is

---

[25] Interview with Patca comunero, in Patca, October 1973.

elected by democratic vote,... not like the government of Velasco that has taken power and supervises everything. They talk about democracy but it's all talk, nothing else" (Q1975, 29). Replying to the same question about the worst features of the Velasco government, another Estrella peasant said: "... everything was false..." (Q1975, 26).

Cooperative members were angry at the government's attempts to rule by decree. Complained an Estrella worker: "Now with the military guys you have to do what they tell you" (Q1975, 28). When in 1977 I asked Lucho Saavedra why he thought Velasco had fallen, he replied, "Velasco believed he was omnipotent."[26] The angriest attacks on the government, made in the privacy of the home or over beer in the cooperative restaurant, invariably emphasized the government as an intrusive patron: "Now the government is the owner of everything!" "The government is the new patron." A popular sardonic joke asked: "SINAMOS Or 'con amos'?" ("Without masters? Or with masters?") With a vehemence that satisfied the group of friends around him, an Estrella leader responded to a SINAMOS inquiry about one of Estrella's decisions: "SINAMOS can't tell us what to do. This is our place."[27]

Peasants wanted to be able to hold the government accountable through elections. The 1975 survey asked, "What kind of government do you think is best? Would you like to have elections, as before?" Of the 60 Estrella and Marla respondents, 53 percent said they would prefer elections; 13 percent did not want them; 6 percent felt they were a good idea but not very practical; and 27 percent were undecided or vague. In Rachuis, where very few men had ever voted, about half the peasants wanted elections. Explained one cooperative member: "It's better to have elections for a government; in this way the voice of the people is understood, and the leader is the representative of the majority of the people" (Q1975, 2).

The rumors about the corruption of certain members of Velasco's inner circle, particularly Tantaleán, had reached some cooperative members, and elections were emphasized as a way to inhibit abuses: "It's better to choose officials through elections, because appointing them from the top, this way leads to abuses, and they all take advantage of the system to extract good profits"

[26] Interview, in Estrella, July 1977.
[27] Comment by president of Estrella's Education Committee, which I overheard, in December 1973.

(Q1975, 7). Some peasants drew the logical parallel between the wisdom of elections within the cooperative and within the nation: "In whatever case that an authority or a government is elected via elections, it's better because the leader enjoys the support of the people" (Q1975, 53).

Government agencies encroached on cooperative members' prerogatives with respect to various issues. On almost all of these policy concerns, the agencies promoted their designs strongly enough to be considered intrusive, but not strongly enough to implement them. (Perhaps it could be said that they had the worst of both worlds, torn between assertiveness and responsiveness and in the end neither assertive nor responsive.) Policy with respect to the admission of temporary workers into the cooperatives is one important example. So were various Ministry of Agriculture policies oriented to the maintenance of productivity in the cooperatives: the encouragement of investment over consumption, cooperative over individual production, and the employment of enterprise directors.

For most of the period covered by this study, the ministry tried to limit wage increases in the cooperatives so that enterprise profits would be available for investment purposes. As Chapter VIII indicated, however, the ministry failed because of strike threats in some enterprises and devious tactics in others. The ministry's attempts were viewed as a serious violation of members' rights. The comment of one infuriated Estrella man was typical:

> Here in Estrella you don't see any type of government help. The past year, for example, the Councils and the union agreed to a 20 percent salary increase, but the guys from SINAMOS and the Ministry of Agriculture came to protest, saying we shouldn't increase our salaries until we saw the enterprise balance sheet. But when the balance was done and some profits came they didn't say go ahead, they'd made a mistake, they didn't say anything (Q1975, 2).

Ministry officials also encouraged cooperative production, apparently in the belief that the economies of scale of cooperative production were critical. Many ministry officials recommended a law that would link cooperative members' wages to the actual hours worked for the enterprise. In contrast, most peasants preferred either a combination of enterprise and private work or private work alone. The ministry, as we have seen, was only partially successful in this. No new laws were enacted. Although few larger cooperatives were subdivided, in most sites the number of members with private parcels and livestock increased and the number of hours worked for the enterprise dipped. Many peasants felt that the government had betrayed them by promising that they would be "owners" and then not allocating them private parcels. Lorenzo Lazo's accusation was typical: "The government says that we're owners, but the CAP didn't want to give me even a little piece of land. Finally they gave it to me, but only after a struggle" (Q1975, 1).

The ministry was also perceived as intruding into the cooperative's decision making by trying to enforce the requirement that the enterprise employ a director. When it became apparent that many cooperatives were evading this requirement, the ministry was able to get the Agrarian Bank on its side and threaten recalcitrant enterprises with loss of their bank loans if they did not hire administrators. Many cooperatives did hire them—but then soon fired them. The ministry developed new requirements, such as minimum one-year contracts for the director and prohibition of the departure of one administrator before the arrival of his replacement.[28] However, these requirements were never incorporated into a national decree, and were implemented in only a few regions. As a result, the number of enterprises with administrators did not increase after 1974 (see Chapter II).

In most cases the director could not guide the cooperative as effectively as many officials had hoped. The administrator could not advance his designs too vigorously for fear that he would be fired by members or that his salary would be cut. Moreover, as salaries for administrators fell, the positions ceased to attract qualified and authoritative agronomists. By 1977, almost all directors in the Virú valley came from provincial universities and had not completed their course of study. These directors often could not persuade peasants that their higher education was worth more than the peasants' experience.

The anger of many peasants at what they perceived as government meddling was expressed by a leader in one Cajamarca SAIS, who pinpointed SINAMOS as the culprit, perhaps accurately and perhaps not:

SINAMOS only created confusion, destroying what was left of the enterprise with the hacienda, and setting a bad example. They promised aid and capacitación, but they didn't come

[28] See, for example, the Trujillo Ministry's policy on directors in its mimeographed regulation *Directiva Administrativa* 001-DEPC-DGPA-73.

through. They broke down work discipline, and people didn't want to work. It was their fault too that land was invaded and divided among many people who now have the land.... And it was their fault too that many permanent workers were hired, allied to the former leaders, until there were almost 400 employees, when at the most 200 are necessary, and it became impossible to pay everyone. The workers didn't want to work and there was no respect. Also, they got four administrators named, one for each ex-hacienda in the SAIS, who didn't know anything about administration. When the situation had become impossible, some of the SINAMOS guys left, and we kicked out the others. Now we've begun to organize our own enterprise little by little, the people trust us, and we're all learning... (quoted by Caballero and Tello, 1976: 32).

A third major disincentive to peasant support for the government was the absence of any concrete benefits linked to such support, or any specific sanctions against disloyalty. The government wielded few effective carrots or sticks for mustering peasant support or, at least, compliance. The agrarian reform itself came as a "gift fallen from the sky," in the expression of Béjar (1976: 158). Land expropriation was determined primarily by the size of the holding, with expropriation priority going to larger, more prosperous enterprises, rather than by peasant pressure. Loan and credit decisions were reserved for the Agrarian Bank, a relatively conservative institution that regarded its loan criteria as apolitical and rarely if ever bent these criteria to support redistributive or fiscally lenient initiatives by SINAMOS or the Ministry of Agriculture. Other incentives to peasant support for the government were scant. Given the shifting sands of political power within the regime, political pull with one official was not a significant inducement; too often, the official lost his influence overnight. Especially in later years, government agencies were too resource-scarce to offer even minor carrots such as transportation and office help. Indeed, as suggested above, the typical field official was meagerly reimbursed, which made him susceptible to peasants' bribes; in contrast to conventional practice, the prosperous peasant frequently offered juicier carrots to the official than vice versa. In addition, all government agencies employed some officials who opposed the regime and who thus could not serve as political transmission belts between the military leaders and the peasants.

The military government did not seem to realize fully the importance of building peasant loyalty. As Pease García (1977: 232-237) suggests, some government quarters may have preferred that, when peasants enter the national political arena, they passively spectate rather than applaud. Neither SINAMOS nor CENCIRA devoted serious effort to the question of what support for the government would entail. Talks by CENCIRA instructors were criticized as vague, abstract, and either apolitical or conservative (CENCIRA, 1973b: 2; Confederación Nacional Agraria, 1974: "Acuerdos de la Comisión No. 5"; CENCIRA, 1975c).

These various shortcomings of the Velasco regime seem related to a critical political decision of the government, its decision to eschew a Velasquista political party or the "no-party thesis." As discussed in Chapter II, the decision clearly revealed the reluctance of the military to ally with civilians, to consider even the terms of eventual national-level elections, or to "dirty itself in politics generally," as Velasco himself saw it. But it also indicated the other characteristics of the government discussed above. As Béjar (1976: 140-163) points out, a Velasquista party would have been caught up in the same political struggles that were ravaging most other institutions. Could the young intellectual leftists of SINAMOS and the anti-Communist "toughs" of "the Mission" be effectively united in one party? The answer has to be no, especially if the party were unable to offer many inducements for affiliation—as was the case in the later Velasco years. Thus, a pro-government party would probably have resembled the weak and divided reformist party in Bolivia, the MNR (National Revolutionary Movement), not the relatively strong and coherent Mexican party, the PRI (Institutionalized Revolutionary Party). The no-party thesis of Velasco may have been more a result than a cause of the regime's difficulties.

The practice of intervention that emerged during the Morales Bermúdez administration is also a prism of these various shortcomings of the military government. "Intervention" was the term applied to the assumption of ultimate authority in the enterprise by a Ministry of Agriculture official, the "intervener," usually on the grounds of gross financial irregularities.[29] As of July 1977, 21 enterprises—primarily wealthier ones such as the agroindustrial sugar cooperatives—had been intervened.[30] The interventions were a dramatic indication of the policy oscillations in the military government. Intervention obviously contradicted the ideals of the

[29] The law on intervention was Decree Law No. 21815, issued in March 1977.

[30] Interview with Rodolfo Masuda Matsuura, Dirección de Apoyo a las Empresas Campesinas, Ministry of Agriculture, in Lima, July 25, 1978.

"fully participatory social democracy," and showed how quickly a new administration could move against the self-management policy of earlier years. Perhaps, too, intervention affirmed the validity of cooperative members' insecurity and uncertainty about government policy. Of course, the intervention also demonstrated once again the intrusive tendencies of many officials.

We described earlier the intervention in SAIS Huanca in 1976. The reasons for the intervention were not clear. Perhaps the government's purpose was to respond to the requests of peasants; perhaps to mitigate conflict between the trabajadores and comuneros; perhaps to end financial scandals; perhaps to check the influence of the CCP among the ex-hacienda unions.

All these concerns may have prompted the intervention, or none of them. What were the results of the intervention? A year later, as Chapter V described, the conflict between the two SAIS groups seemed to be moving toward a resolution, but this outcome did not seem to have been significantly affected by the intervener. Economic viability also appeared to be restored, but this improvement could have been spearheaded by a regular director. The influence of the CCP was not checked. Over-all, the effect of the intervention seemed to be a minimal one that primarily illuminated the limited will and resources of the government: the choice of a new director for the SAIS was complicated, as the intervener sought to win the post for himself. Because the enterprise wielded juicier carrots for the intervener than did the government, the intervener was unlikely to implement government directives for the SAIS against the peasants' will, even if such directives had been issued by the Ministry of Agriculture. Thus, the intervention frightened and confused peasants[31]—as usual; but, as usual the government's bark was greater than its bite.

## ATTITUDES TOWARD THE GOVERNMENT

The shortcomings of the Velasco government were more apparent to cooperative members than were the advancements made under the regime. Given that the major policy benefits were allocated in a political vacuum, without significant links between government and peasant, cooperative members rarely credited the government

---

[31] Attitude of Huanca comuneros is evident in the 1977 questionnaires. The evaluation of the Ministry's action is based on the 1977 interviews with officials and peasant leaders mentioned in Chapter V.

for these steps. Any tendency to credit the government was checked by the recurrent attempts of officials to modify the features of the cooperatives most liked by members: their higher wages and increased benefits, and their political independence. For these reasons, members felt they could not rely on the government as an ally, and typically credited themselves for their advancement. Recall once again the exuberant cry of the Estrella president: "By our own efforts! By our own efforts!"

Table X.4 reveals the relatively skeptical attitudes toward the government among peasants. Support for the government dipped between 1969 and 1974. Although the decline reflects not peasant support for Belaúnde versus Velasco, but for Velasco in his honeymoon period versus Velasco after five years in office, it was still ominous. Of the sites where the item was applied, the drop was sharpest in Marla, where economic development was the most limited and where the government was perceived as particularly meddlesome in its demands for the employment of a director. As of 1975, support of the government had plummeted further in Marla, but stayed about the same in Estrella, the increasingly more successful cooperative.[32] The question was too sensitive to apply in Monte; however, Monte was of course angry about its adjudication in the SAIS, and the percentage of members negative toward the government would certainly have been larger than in the coastal CAPs. By cross-national standards, peasant support for the government in Peru was low. For example, in *The Civic Culture*, Almond and Verba (1965) found that the national government was believed to "improve conditions" without the qualification of "sometimes does, sometimes does not" by over 60 percent of respondents in the United States, Great Britain, Germany, and Italy, and even by 58 percent in Mexico (1965: 48).

The relatively strong support for the government in the control site Virú is also indicated in Table X.4. Indeed, only in Estrella by 1975 was peasant endorsement of the government as high as it was in Virú, with 64 percent of the respondents in both cases saying that the government helps at least "more or less." Table X.5 reveals that more residents of Virú than of Estrella or Marla cited the agrarian

---

[32] In 1975 in Marla, 64 percent of the respondents thought that the government did not help, versus 36 percent in 1974. In 1975 in Estrella, a slightly higher percentage than in 1974 said the government did not help (30 percent versus 25 percent), but a considerably greater percentage than in 1974 said it helped at least "more or less" (64 percent versus 36 percent). The number of "don't knows" in Estrella, rather large in 1974, declined by 1975.

TABLE X.4

Peasant Support for the Government, 1969-1974[a] (%)

| | N | Government helps | Government helps more or less | Government does not help | No answer | Don't know, other |
|---|---|---|---|---|---|---|
| Cooperatives/haciendas | | | | | | |
| Estrella, 1974 | 88 | 13 | 32 | 25 | 3 | 27 |
| Estrella, 1969 | 79 | 33 | 25 | 27 | 0 | 15 |
| Marla, 1974 | 62 | 7 | 40 | 36 | 3 | 15 |
| Marla, 1969 | 40 | 50 | 11 | 22 | 3 | 14 |
| Monte, 1974 | — | — | — | — | — | — |
| Monte, 1969 | 58 | 40 | 19 | 21 | 0 | 21 |
| Control & quasi-control | | | | | | |
| Virú, 1974 | 90 | 24 | 40 | 33 | 0 | 5 |
| Virú, 1969 | 190 | 40 | 32 | 19 | 0 | 5 |
| Agustín, 1974 | — | — | — | — | — | — |
| Agustín, 1969 | 153 | 41 | 23 | 21 | 1 | 14 |
| SAIS Community | | | | | | |
| Rachuis, 1975 | 27 (men only) | 4 | 56 | 37 | 0 | 4 |

[a] Item read: "Do you think that in general what the government does helps to improve conditions in the country?"

TABLE X.5
Positively Perceived Actions of the Government[a] (%)

| | Agrarian reform | More equality, social justice | More loans, technical help, or economic development | Better education | Other specific type of help | Ot |
|---|---|---|---|---|---|---|
| Cooperatives, 1974 | | | | | | |
| Estrella and Marla (N = 58)[b] | 33 | 22 | 33 | 24 | 10 | |
| Control, 1974 | | | | | | |
| Virú (N = 41)[b] | 57 | 16 | 38 | 37 | 22 | |

[a] Item read: "You think that the government is doing some good things. What?" Percentage not add to 100 as some respondents gave more than one answer.

[b] These are the respondents citing positive actions by the government.

reform as a "good thing" being done by the government. Why would approval of the Velasco regime be greater in Virú, where by their own report (see Table X.3) fewer peasants thought themselves better-off in 1974 than in 1969? The answer would seem to lie in the relatively limited government intervention in the village. The political confusion of the Velasco era did not impinge upon Virú. The agrarian reform in Virú had merely promoted the devolution of land and water rights from absentee holders to the ex-share-croppers. Ownership was individual, and the Ministry of Agriculture did not pay great attention to the management of private land.

Table X.5 also indicates the rather small number of cooperative members who cited positive actions by the government. In 1974, considerably more Estrella and Marla respondents cited negative actions of the government than positive ones. (One hundred four-teen cited negative actions, 58 positive actions.) Agrarian reform, economic aid, and improved education were most frequently mentioned as the major achievements of the Velasco era. The high cost of living was the overwhelming "winner" of the contest for the worst government action.[33] In 1975, the similar questions "What do you like most about what's happening in the country's politics?" and "What do you like least about what's happening in the country's

[33] Details on the negative actions cited by respondents are provided in McClintock (1976: 590).

politics?" were asked, and the results were also similar. As in 1974, more respondents cited negative actions than positive ones; 70 cited negative actions, 48 positive. Of the 48 respondents who mentioned something they liked, the most common statement (19 percent) was "now there are no longer the patrons."

The style and form of the peasants' responses to these questions are revealing. Peasant responses often seemed modulated and uncertain. The peasants seemed to weigh various features of the government, trying to summarize the meaning of the mixed bag of government actions, without great success. Such a comment was given by a Marla member: "Now we're participating in the decisions. There is no patron who is the owner of the entire hacienda. There's more liberty in participation. [But] the salary is low and the cost of living high" (Q1975, 47).

Another Marla member's response suggests the confusion and uncertainty about government policy that was common among peasants. In this case, the peasant's meaning is not entirely clear; he slips back and forth between the general and the specific and cites one negative action when various other such actions might also have been on his mind: "There have been changes, the patron was kicked out, and the enterprise passed into the hands of the members, but in reality we're not owners of anything, and we're worse off. The government should be concerned about the workers and promote order and justice, for the director is very abusive, and they ought to sanction bad directors" (Q1975, 54).

The distance between the government's rhetoric and its action as well as the disparity between the goals of different groups of officials were also frequently criticized by peasants. The aftermath was confusion:

In reality, about what's going on here in the government, I don't know anything. At times they say they're going to give us this or do that, and they promise things, but they haven't given it, at least until now. There really isn't any help, they don't even want to increase the salaries. SINAMOS was against an increase so, if those guys are from the government, then the government isn't helping the peasantry (Q1975, 34).

The agrarian reform has equalized the situation of the peasantry, there's free participation, and the oligarchy is gone. [But] there are many bad officials who are doing wrong to the revolution, as in the case of EPSA (Q1975, 83).

There are good laws but they are not always applied (Q1975, 62).

Whereas during the Velasco era an attitude of skepticism tempered by uncertainty and some lingering hopes prevailed among cooperative members, by 1977 during the Morales Bermúdez administration and the economic crisis, skepticism had turned to loathing. As one analyst found in a trip across the nation, "not one citizen had a good word" for the Morales Bermúdez government.[34] Such was also the case in the research sites, where not one peasant said that the government was helping to improve national conditions and only one said that it was helping "more or less," in contrast to 76 who answered that it was not helping. Sixty-nine respondents, or 90 percent, said that the government of Velasco had been superior to that of Morales Bermúdez. Peasant criticism was intense and wholesale, roundly denouncing the military and charging it with forgetting and abandoning the peasantry; especially in the peasant communities, the criticism had a traditional ring to it, recalling the denunciations of the 1960s recorded by Handelman (1975a). Some representative comments follow:

> Military men are always the same, although with Velasco there was greater support for the agrarian reform; now things are different because they have forgotten the cooperatives and the peasants (Q1977, M16).

> All military men are alike, they fill their pockets with money and it's the people that have to suffer the consequences (Q1977, E4).

## ACTION TOWARD THE GOVERNMENT

Cooperative members' skepticism toward the government was evident in their subversion and evasion of most government initiatives. The new political capacity of the cooperative members was used not only to advance various peasant demands upon the government, as Chapter V showed, but also to block government demands upon the cooperative. As members perceived the self-managed enterprise to be the only secure political and economic resource available to them, its autonomy became a major issue of conflict. The battle was not drawn on a national scale because it was only truly initiated when an official came to the cooperative armed with a new statute; the battle was not sought by the cooperative members themselves, who wanted to cultivate their gardens. Ultimately, given the greater

---

[34] Bernard Margueritte, "Hot Summer in Peru," *The Christian Science Monitor* (September 8, 1977), p. 27.

political capacity of the cooperative members than the government officials, indicated heretofore, the cooperative members appeared to win this contest.

The intense struggle between the government and the cooperative at the local level did not entail active peasant partisanship at the national level. Perhaps because of the remoteness of most agrarian cooperatives, few peasants were committed to national pro-government or anti-government efforts. Their disinterest in the CNA as well as the CCP was noted in Chapter IX. Cooperative members rarely marched for the government; with grave consequences to the Velasco government, they did not march for it during a February 1975 political crisis. Agrarian reform posters or photographs of Velasco were rarely seen in cooperative offices. Nor, however, were many cooperative members anti-Velasco activists. SINAMOS was the target of most opposition—a considerable number of SINAMOS offices was destroyed and some agents lynched—but it is doubtful that many peasants were involved. Even during the nation-wide July 1977 strikes, cooperative members played a limited role. The major concern of Estrella members during the one-day general strike was what to do with their milk before it went bad. (The director decided to make cheese.) Peasants did sympathize with the strikers, however; when I asked the reason for the strikes, most peasants said simply, "I'm sure it's because they don't have enough to eat." But few cooperative members were active in the strike movement.

The remarkable capacity of cooperative members to check government initiatives has been mentioned at previous junctures in this study, when appropriate. By recalling these instances, indicating several others, and detailing the subversive strategies, this section emphasizes how frequently and how successfully members undermined government directives.

Cooperative members evaded government efforts to promote greater equality in the countryside. When rather high regional minimum wages were set in 1976, cooperatives frequently did not pay these wages to temporary workers, only to the members. Earlier, when temporary workers had been encouraged to apply for admission into the cooperative by government officials, members had devised all kinds of new requirements for admission and processed applications slowly. When wealthy middlemen were to be disqualified from community membership in accord with the peasant community statute, community leaders protected those intermediaries whom they liked. Lists of community members and their property would be "lost" or falsified. No government official had the time to track down exactly how much time an intermediary spent out of the village. When programs for the equalization or cooperativization of livestock were initiated, animals were hidden in remote nooks, and peasants lied to officials to protect their neighbors.[35] Profit redistribution schemes of the central cooperatives were ignored.

The government's efforts to improve agricultural production and investment were also subverted. Statutes requiring the cultivation of 40 percent of enterprise lands in basic foods (panllevar) were not respected. In many areas, enterprise lands were subdivided, private production increased, and the number of hours worked for the enterprise declined. Although the Ministry of Agriculture was able to persuade most sites to hire directors, it could not stop them from firing them, and this sanction enabled members to influence the action of directors.

Although the ministry tried to check wage increases during the Velasco era, it rarely succeeded. Even if the ministry threatened the enterprise with loss of credit if it raised salaries, members doctored the cooperative's books and got their raise in one way or another. Exorbitant overtime pay was common. Members would claim more overtime than they worked, and would charge overtime at several times the regular wage. In one sugar cooperative, workers were receiving more overtime hours than existed in the month.[36] The elevation of routine jobs to "specialized skill" status was also common. For example, tending the tobacco ovens, an undemanding task, earned double-rate pay in Estrella. Another technique was the reclassification of the tarea so members could perform two or three "daily" work quotas and thus receive two or three "daily" wage allocations. The higher wages also enabled the cooperatives to pay less money to the state (see Chapter VIII).

The government's attempts to build political support and enhance its economic strength in the countryside also failed. It was apparently intended by some officials that the CNA would enhance support for the government and counter the CCP, but it did not. Efforts to co-opt political leaders almost invariably backfired, as in the case of the promotion of Miguel Maray in Huanca. Later, when Huanca was intervened and CCP activity in its ex-haciendas was to

[35] This was the case in my sites and is also mentioned by Bourque and Warren (1978:24).

[36] Interview with Ing. Luis Deustua, of COAMA, in Trujillo, November 1973.

be stalled, a Monte peasant reported to me, with a smile: "Sure, we have meetings now, just as before. Only we don't write them up in the *Acts of the Union* book any more."[37] The government's attempts to enlarge its economic role in the countryside through such means as state marketing agencies were successful only in regions of rice production; most other cooperatives avoided the state's networks and marketed their goods as they preferred.

Cooperative members battled not only against government officials' policies but also against the officials themselves. Peasants were especially sensitive to the assumption of a patronal posture by technicians or officials and, although many of these individuals adopted an egalitarian posture, others did not. Many such arrogant men were publicly criticized by peasants, and some were ousted, to the glee of the peasants. Rachuis blocked the admission of a SINAMOS official into the community, and Marla compelled the transfer of a SINAMOS agent. A similar story was given by the angry Cajamarca peasant cited in the first section of this chapter, and was reported too in peasants' shouts at a Piura General Assembly, shouts protesting a government technician's efforts to annul a holiday bonus approved by the assembly: "[The members] were showing with cries... that it was the General Assembly which commands and that they were not going to have any other patron called the Agrarian Reform Ministry..." (Bell, 1977: 12).

## SUMMARY

The policies of the Velasco government toward the agrarian cooperatives that were actually implemented generally favored members. Policy benefits were not, however, allocated through coherent political channels that could link benefits to peasant loyalty to the government. Moreover, peasants worried that these advantageous policies would be changed. During the Velasco era, some plans to enhance equality and productivity were advanced by various groups of officials. The initiatives were perceived as confused and meddlesome, despite the fact that they rarely received enough backing from top elites to enable their implementation over cooperative members' opposition. Relatively secure about their political and economic capability within the cooperative, members were with good reason insecure about any such capability beyond it. Thus, traditional peasant skepticism toward the national govern-

---

[37] Interview with Monte worker, in Monte, July 1977.

ment endured. Members turned their new political solidarity into a weapon against what they considered government encroachment on "their" self-managed cooperatives. The weapon proved potent.

The reality of government action and peasant response thus sharply diverged from the patterns predicted by both the corporatist and the "fully participatory social democracy" models. Government action was too fragmented to fit either model. It was too intrusive to fit a "fully participatory social democracy" but too easily blocked by peasants to fit the corporatist design. Such effective peasant opposition was not anticipated in either analytical scheme.

A similar dynamic prevailed in the industrial sector.[38] As the government's commitment to full implementation of the Industrial Community policy wavered, and as Social Property displaced the Industrial Community as the priority government policy in the industrial sector, workers presumably felt as insecure of their gains through the CI as peasants did of their gains through the CAPs and SAIS. The confusing conflict between SINAMOS and the Ministry of Agriculture in the agrarian sphere was paralleled by a conflict drawn on similar ideological lines between SINAMOS and the Ministry of Industry in the industrial sector.

Moreover, the government's intrusiveness was even more marked in the industrial sector than in the agrarian. When industrial workers spontaneously organized their own federation, CONACI, primarily to demand fuller implementation of the Industrial Community law, the military government moved quickly to try to rechannel or reorganize CONACI along what it perceived to be less threatening lines. The government launched its own federation alongside the independent CONACI, and also initiated other federations among specific groups of workers, such as the Tantaleán-led CTRP (Revolutionary Workers' Center of Peru) among fishermen, which it tried to manipulate more feverishly than it did the CNA.

However, as in the agrarian sector, the government's efforts were largely ineffective. The strictly pro-government federations won scant support among workers; breakaway movements occurred even within the federation perceived to be most tightly controlled, the CTRP. The government was unable to check the power of

[38] This paragraph draws heavily from Stephens (1977), Santistevan (1977a) and Sulmont (1977). Strike activities of Aprista and Communist federations are discussed in *Latin America*, *9* (July 25, 1975), 225, and *Latin America*, *10* (March 26, 1976), 98.

independent, Aprista, and Communist federations, which frequently orchestrated regional strikes opposing government industrial policies. As Chapter V indicated, strike activity was very intense during this period. Ultimately too, like the peasants, the industrial workers did not stand up and demonstrate for Velasco during the critical months of 1975.

Part Four · *CONCLUSION*

# XI · *Self-Management, Reform Government, and the Peasant*

If we make mistakes, it's because we're doing something. If there are no errors, it's because nothing is being done.[1]

We cannot help being astonished by the subtlety, the intrigue of which a simple peasant is capable, when his wretched appearance might make one believe that he doesn't see beyond the muzzle of his buffalo.

Pierre Gourou, cited by Popkin (1976:431)

FROM THIS STUDY, self-management emerges as a powerful agent of change in patterns of political authority and social solidarity. In Peru, prior to 1969, hacienda peasants had long been enmeshed in a tenacious clientelist system—a system of the archetypal variety, where the patron wielded extremely great resources relative to the peasant and effectively blocked any ties among peasants. Traditionally, Peruvian hacienda peasants were cowed and atomized, fitting well into the modal image of the peasant presented by anthropologists and scholars of political culture. The Peruvian hacienda peasant did not appear to be a likely candidate for rapid dramatic development into a "new man." Yet, with the demise of the hacienda and the emergence of the self-managed enterprise, new orientations of assertiveness and collaboration emerged relatively quickly.

The Peruvian experience thus provides considerable support for the theories of Gramsci, de Man, Gorz and the recent scholarly proponents of self-management. Workplace decisions were important ones to cooperative members, involving basic questions about authority relations in particular—not just minor problems of everyday life. Whereas skeptics of self-management said that the policy would favor class conciliation, the opposite was the case; members' political consciousness and activity grew, and was often directed against technicians and bureaucrats. Unions were not displaced; to

[1] Roy Becerra, the Secretary of the Agrarian Federation of Lima, speaking at a conference on self-management, in June 1975.

the contrary, in many enterprises they were established for the first time. Unions were often the arena for the discussion of wage issues, while the self-management organs were usually the arena for the consideration of broader concerns in which members came closer to being "makers of history," in Gramsci's phrase. However, work achievement and responsibility were not encouraged in the Peruvian enterprises to the extent predicted by Gramsci and other proponents of self-management.

It must be emphasized that the power of self-management as an agent of change in Peru depended upon the particular kind of self-management that was established. As another term for "enterprise democracy" or "economic democracy," self-management is a broad concept. Different types of self-management structures would have had distinct effects. If Peruvian peasants had won only shareholding rights in the enterprise, or even parity representation with the patron on an enterprise board, the impact on the peasant's orientations would presumably have been much less. Similarly, in the mode of self-management implemented in the Peruvian countryside, the state reserved various powers to itself; in particular, the government required the enterprise to employ a technical director, and it required various kinds of debt payments and investments. If the state had put many more requirements on the enterprises, or indeed if it had actually exerted more of the powers available to it by law, again the impact of self-management would probably have been less.

However, although the Peruvian "new man" was a more participatory and trusting individual, the focus of these new attitudes was the self-managed enterprise itself. Peasants remained rather unconcerned with the fate of other peasants beyond their own enterprise, and they also continued to be skeptical of the national government. Cooperative members emerged as "group egoists," a phrase commonly used in Peru. The continuation of these traditional orientations seriously flawed the pattern of political culture change. Concern for the plight of disadvantaged comuneros and eventuales on the part of cooperative members was important to the development of a strong agrarian movement in Peru and to economic equity in the countryside, but such concern did not emerge. There was no increase in commitment to Peru as a nation, and no enthusiastic support for Velasco. This lack of support was one reason for the general's fall.

Yet, "group egoism" was an extremely rational response to the new structures established in Peru. Self-management took root only at the level of the single enterprise; no regional or national federations of self-managed enterprises were effectively developed on a broad scale. The single self-managed enterprise can provide incentives for participation and collaboration only among other members of the enterprise. If a market economy continues and the results of regional or national political efforts are uncertain, the most rational stance of the cooperative member toward peasant outsiders is competitive. Moreover, whereas to some analysts the Velasco government seemed to deserve support from the cooperative members, there were various reasons why it did not win hearty endorsement from peasants or other analysts. Although the government was not establishing a corporatist political system as its critics charged, it was also not achieving the "fully participatory social democracy" as its spokespeople claimed (see Chapter III).

This study thus indicates that the major characteristics of peasant political culture are by no means as intractable as has often been suggested. New structures incorporating significant incentives for change can be created by a government that desires to do so. Although new structures and new incentives may be subverted by traditional cultural patterns—as occurred to some extent in rural Peru—this is by no means inevitable. Rather, as strong inducements for the adoption of specific attitudes and behavior are provided, the peasant responds rationally to them. In a sequence of change somewhat different from that found in the Cuban experience by Fagen (1969), the Peruvian peasant's ideals seemed to change first; then, as the peasant became convinced that his fellows also shared these ideals and that his own new efforts toward political activity or social collaboration would not go for naught, his behavior also began to change. Although peasant skepticism of community outsiders endured in Peru, this skepticism was not illogical; in other nations, such as China, Tanzania, and Cuba, greater incentives for peasant commitment to the nation were established, and peasant attitudes in this realm did apparently change, as Chapter I indicated. The Peruvian experience thus contributes much evidence to support the image of a rational—indeed, perhaps shrewd and calculating—peasant as proposed recently by Migdal (1974), Popkin (1976), and Bates (1978).[2]

[2] It is possible that discussions of changing peasant political culture should put more emphasis on the question of whether or not peasants are too rational and calculating—whether or not their perspectives are overly short-term, constantly hedging bets and trying to maximize security. My emphasis on peasant rationality is not meant to contradict the thesis of Scott (1976) that peasants rebel with a sense of

Positive as the results of this study are for those concerned with the possibility of political culture change through self-management, they may well be disquieting to a Third World government that seeks not only peasant assertiveness and solidarity but also its own survival. The new configuration of attitudes and behavior that emerged among Peruvian peasants—in particular their new political capacity and their tendency to use this capacity against rather than for the state—was marked not only in Peru but in other Third World nations that have instituted self-management, as will be evident in the comparative analysis below. This analysis includes the Chilean and Mexican experiences, as the two most prominent Latin American cases and thus presumably the most relevant to the Peruvian, as well as the Yugoslav experience, which is the best-known and most enduring to date. The Algerian case is also similar in important respects to the Peruvian, but it will not be analyzed here because it is not as prominent and the information about it is relatively limited.[3]

There are various reasons why the Peruvian pattern of political culture change might prove common in the Third World, whereas in the First World traces of such a pattern have not been evident.[4] First, the power of self-management as a stimulus to political asser-

---

indignation and a moral desire to right wrongs. I contend that the peasant is not irrational, rather than that he is not moral. But I would side with Migdal (1974) against Scott (1976) that the peasant at least takes the possibility of success into very serious consideration before engaging in revolutionary struggle. My argument *is* intended to counter various other views of the peasantry. Wolf might suggest that the "group egoism" of the Peruvian peasant was not a rational response to the character of the political structures in Peru, but that invariably "the peasant utopia is the free village, untrammeled by tax collectors, labor recruiters, large landowners, officials" (Wolf, 1969: 294). However, the change in attitudes toward outsiders among Chinese, Cuban, and Tanzanian peasants belies Wolf's argument. The theory that peasants change their political orientation from a revolutionary perspective to a conservative one once they gain land is also countered in this study; the peasants analyzed here had never shown a strong capacity for revolution—indeed, their political demands increased after gaining land.

[3] The dynamic of "group egoism" that emerged in Peru was first identified in the Algerian case in the early 1960s. Blair (1970) analyzes in detail the problem of "group capitalism" or "little cells of socialism" in Algeria during this period. However, the problem was even more extreme in Algeria than in Peru because the amount of land transferred to the peasants was relatively small and the power of the new Algerian state, just emerging from colonial status, was also relatively weak. Traditional economic elites thus remained rather intact.

[4] The issue is rarely discussed in studies of self-management in the First World. See, for example, Garson (1977).

tiveness and social solidarity may be especially great in the Third World. The subordination of the peasant in the Latin American hacienda is by most criteria much more severe than that of a worker in an American or European firm. The demise of the patron and the opportunity for self-management represents a dramatic structural change for most peasants. As Chapter V showed, the peasant in the self-managed enterprise is particularly keen to assert his new prerogatives over technical directors or similar officials in the cooperative; he is very sensitive to any efforts by such traditionally superior individuals to "become the new patron," and often may seek redress for past abuses. Moreover, enterprises in the Third World, especially rural estates, are unlikely to be as technologically complex as those in Europe or the United States, and thus the possibility that the new self-managed enterprise can in fact be successfully run by the workers seems greater.

Whereas self-management is thus likely to have a particularly strong meaning for Third World peasants, the state in the Third World tends to be weak. The Velasco regime was not the first reform-oriented Third World government to be ridden by factions, unable to decide when to encourage popular participation and when to assert governmental authority, and unable to allocate benefits in such a way as to enhance popular support.[5] The difficulties of political mediation by the state would be particularly great with respect to the peasantry, because inadequate communication networks impede regular contact between officials and peasants in remote areas. Moreover, in many Third World nations, socioeconomic inequities and ethnic divisions among the peasantry are serious, and self-management institutions are more likely to become ensnared in these conflicts among peasant strata.

Thus, the question emerges: is self-management a dangerous policy for a Third World government without unusual capabilities? Will a new sense of political confidence and power among the peasantry inevitably place too many demands upon the state, impeding its own capacity to formulate and implement policy? Will it thus also in turn tarnish the image of the government's efficacy and undermine popular commitment to the regime? In the terms of political culture, must political assertiveness be at odds with national loyalty? Considerable support for the thesis of such a trade-

---

[5] The capacity of reformist governments in the Third World to gain strength and to institutionalize has been exaggerated because of the success of the Mexican model. See especially Huntington (1968). However, the fate of the reformist government in Bolivia between 1952 and 1964 may be more typical. See Malloy and Thorn (1971).

off could be found in this study. As Chapter I indicated, such a trade-off seemed evident in China, Tanzania, and Cuba, where loyalty to the new national leadership apparently increased more dramatically than political assertiveness. It seems clear that, if the government does not want to listen to peasant demands and try to respond to them, citizens will indeed become more frustrated and angry at the government.

Despite the evidence to the contrary, however, I will suggest here that such a trade-off between political assertiveness and commitment to the nation is by no means inevitable. The key to a successful resolution of these tensions seems to be real acceptance and attention to peasant demands by the government, entailing particularly strong efforts to explain to the peasantry why it cannot meet their demands, if in fact it cannot. Over the long run, through peasant participation and government mediation, more effective policies would be developed.[6] In other words, as I will argue in greater detail below, peasant power is not necessarily contradictory to state power because the total amount of power in the system can increase. Peasants' political self-confidence and commitment to the nation would then be mutually reinforcing, based on a positive assessment of the results forthcoming from political action.

This concluding chapter recapitulates the major points of previous chapters, and then compares the impact of self-management in rural Peru with its impact in the Chilean and Mexican countrysides, revealing a surprising similarity across the three cases. The final section addresses the issue of the inevitability of the apparent trade-off between self-management and state control. I emphasize the need for the early development of federations of single, self-managed enterprises, and the need for the government to pay them heed, once developed. I also suggest that these tensions seem to have been relatively successfully resolved in Yugoslavia, despite the predominantly Third World status of this country.

## SELF-MANAGEMENT, REFORM GOVERNMENT, AND THE PEASANT IN PERU

As noted earlier, self-management is a broad term, encompassing various kinds of structural arrangements and incentives. In the

---

[6] Throughout this chapter, I use such phrases as "effective policies," "viable strategies," and "strong government." Specific definition and precise measurement of these phenomena are difficult, and this study is not the place for such an effort.

Peruvian countryside, self-management incorporated the greatest incentives for attitudinal and behavioral change in the realms of political participation, political leadership, and friendship. It was in these areas that traditional clientelist attitudes declined most dramatically. In other realms, Peruvian self-management incorporated fewer incentives for change, and traditional attitudes and behavior endured to a considerable degree.

Especially in contrast to the hacienda, the self-managed enterprise devolved major political rights and powers to members. Each member had one vote in the General Assembly of the cooperative, which was required to meet roughly twice a year and made all final decisions. Activity in this organ was by no means confined to business trivia. The most important issues of contention in the cooperatives of this study were (in descending order of significance): 1) the establishment of a correct role and appropriate wages for technicians in the enterprise, especially the director; 2) the restructuring of the cooperative, so that the groups included in the enterprise and the relationship among them would be determined by the members themselves, not the government (as had been the case upon adjudication); and 3) agro-industrialization. Members' wages were an important concern, but typically not a point of serious dispute, as workers tended to agree on sizable increases and were usually able to overcome the resistance of government officials. Exceptions to this pattern occurred primarily when rather distinct socioeconomic groups had been formally integrated into the cooperative, and for one reason or another the largest group were not actual salaried workers in it. In these instances in particular, the salaried workers tended to organize through a union.

The significance of the opportunity to debate and resolve such important issues was not lost upon members, whose attitudes and behavior soon became more inclined toward collective political activity. In the experimental sites, the percentage of politically efficacious peasants jumped from 50 percent to 75 percent between 1969 and 1974, and the percentage of peasants with positive attitudes toward political unity increased by a similar margin over the same time span. General Assemblies and unions met more frequently than was required by law, and attendance at these meetings rose.

In the cooperatives, leadership was no longer an automatic birthright bestowed upon the patron and other individuals of high socioeconomic status. By law, council leadership was to be fairly elected and rotated, so that it would be shared among many members. For peasants, there were various important incentives to such a change in authority patterns. Honest elections to choose the best leaders were of course important for the success of the cooperative. More egalitarian and shared authority patterns gave the average peasant the chance for upward mobility and, perhaps even more significant, the chance to prove that he could discharge responsibilities that had long been deemed beyond his grasp by the patron. Sharing leadership helped the peasant to learn leadership skills on the job. Moreover, in some cooperatives, a leader of average socioeconomic status seemed more likely than a leader of high status to sympathize with the concerns of most cooperative members.

The new leadership structure incorporating these incentives had a dramatic impact on members' attitudes and behavior toward political authority. Whereas only 10 percent of experimental coastal site respondents rejected the statement "A few are born to command" in 1969, 69 percent did so in 1974. Responses to other items also indicated strong rejection of the patronal image of authority. In the cooperatives studied, elections were held regularly and conducted honestly by 1974. Ideals of egalitarian and shared authority were not fully translated into behavior, however; the incentives for such a pattern were countered by the fact that competence in leadership roles still required a relatively strong educational background—especially literacy—and in many cooperatives only a handful of peasants had these skills.

There were also new reasons for sincere friendships in the cooperatives, and considerable change in social attitudes and behavior. The patron no longer divided peasants by promising benefits to those who curried his favor; the cooperative members themselves now controlled many of these benefits (such as the keys to the cooperative's vehicle to transport a critically ill peasant to the city). The patron also no longer distorted community social activities toward his own idea of a good time. Further, in the cooperative, members felt it more important to exchange political ideas, and were also free to do so.

As a result, residents in the cooperatives embraced ideals of trust and solidarity to a much greater extent in 1974 than in 1969. The number of respondents who said they could trust other people in the place rose from 13 percent to 56 percent in the experimental sites. The respondent's expectation of help from other community members in time of need also increased considerably. Social activities such as parties and sports events were more frequent, and more relaxed than in the past. More good times and new thoughts were shared—but to a much greater extent among men than among women, and still rarely between men and women.

The Velasco government hoped that traditional work norms, emphasizing individual cunning rather than hard work as the key to economic success, would be replaced by norms favoring responsibility and collaboration. But actual change in this direction was sporadic. Although members' attitudes toward collaboration became more positive, the traditional fear that the hard worker would be the victim of envy remained strong. The extent of actual collective work achievement varied considerably among the cooperatives studied, with a tendency for it to be greater in enterprises starting with a sounder economic base. Over all, the economic performance of the cooperatives seemed neither significantly better nor significantly worse than before 1969.

The relatively disappointing results in the sphere of work highlights the need for advocates and implementors of self-management to consider carefully not only the overall political structure of the enterprise but also the specific incentives and disincentives established for collective work achievement. In the Peruvian case, as in the Chilean, there were significant disincentives to such work, primarily because of the combined effect of a poorly conceived compensation strategy, the tarea system, lucrative private economic opportunities, and the maintenance of traditional hierarchical structures on the job. In part because of government levies and in part because of corruption, enterprise profits were often not sufficiently great to counter these disincentives to collaborative effort. Gradually, the most alert government officials and cooperative members, especially the members in the more successful enterprises, became concerned and began to debate new work codes, but such discussion should have been initiated at the very outset.

Self-management really took hold in Peru only at the level of the individual enterprise. Leftist government officials encouraged the establishment of regional federations of enterprises (central cooperatives), but others in the government favored a greater role for the state in marketing and processing, areas that would have been primary ones for central cooperative activity. Confronted by political opposition and then also by an acute lack of funds, the movement toward central cooperatives stalled. Without any kind of organization to provide incentives for regional economic cooperation, the self-managed enterprises continued to operate in the context of a traditional market economy. Competition was keen, particularly with nearby enterprises because they often produced similar goods. Frequently, a prosperous enterprise with a relatively large capital endowment gained a margin of economic hegemony in its area and began to use other cooperatives in the vicinity to its own advantage. The dynamics of economic rivalry encouraged an exploitative attitude to seasonal workers in the enterprises as well; these workers were not granted the same advantages as cooperative members, and they encountered large obstacles in their quests for membership. Concern for the plight of landless rural workers and other disadvantaged peasants might have been promoted by the National Agrarian Confederation (CNA), a national-level, politically oriented federation, but the CNA failed to become a viable political force. It entered the political scene late in the Velasco period, in 1974, by which time the rivalry among enterprises had already begun; thus the CNA as well as the central cooperatives were opposed by ascendant enterprises.

Cooperative members also remained skeptical of government officials. In 1974, only some 10 percent of experimental site respondents said that the government "helps," with another 35 percent reporting that it "helps more or less"—percentages that were somewhat lower than in 1969 and somewhat lower than in a nearby control site. At first glance, these cooperative members, perhaps the primary beneficiaries of Velasco's reforms, seem ungrateful. In large part because of Velasco, these peasants were free of their patrons. With the redistribution of profits from patron to members and larger government expenditures and loans for the cooperatives, the peasants also enjoyed a higher standard of living.

However, members did not feel secure about these gains. The military government was factionalized and given to policy changes. The development and fate of the CNA and of SINAMOS reveal why members would feel insecure. Probably, some officials of the Tantaleán tendency hoped that the CNA would channel peasants into a malleable pro-government institution that would preempt the Marxist Peruvian Peasant Confederation; and probably these same officials hoped that SINAMOS would be the agency to guide the CNA toward conciliatory policies and toward frequent demonstrations of support for the government. However, other government officials, including Rodríguez Figueroa who headed SINAMOS until 1974, saw the CNA differently. While this "progressive" tendency was uppermost in SINAMOS, it encouraged the representation of the poorest peasants, the comuneros, in the CNA, and worked with the CNA as it became a vigorous, demand-making organization. These demands, especially those for the incorpor-

ation of temporary workers into cooperatives, frightened cooperative members, who began to see the government as too radical—
as threatening the gains they had just achieved. SINAMOS was
blamed for these excessively radical demands, by both the cooperative members and Tantaleán-style officials. Ultimately, in yet
another policy change by the government, SINAMOS was repudiated; later, in 1978, the CNA was also repudiated, in part because
it was on the verge of unification with the Marxist peasant confederation, which proponents of corporatist schemes had originally
expected it to pre-empt. The factionalization of the Peruvian military thus resulted in confused policy goals for many organizations
and, ultimately, short lives for these organizations.

In the peasants' view, government officials were guilty not only of
presenting conflicting messages but of doing so high-handedly.
Velasco, Delgado, and many SINAMOS officials spoke eloquently
of citizen participation in the new Peru, of official and peasant as
equals, "two men pledged to the same revolutionary task." In the
context of such rhetoric, peasants felt angry and betrayed when
officials did try to dictate to them on community decisions—when
the Ministry of Agriculture agent tried to limit wage increases or
when the SINAMOS representative tried to pool members' livestock into cooperative arrangements. Peasants asked why, if the
"new Peru" were a "fully participatory social democracy," they did
not control the hiring and firing of these officials.

Usually, given the new political unity and strength of the cooperative members, they were able to block attempts by ministry and
SINAMOS officials to intervene. The effectiveness of the peasants'
opposition invalidated the corporatist model of politics in Peru's
countryside. Yet, peasants remained angry that the government did
not carry through its promises of a "fully participatory social
democracy," and also nervous that its corporatist schemes might be
bolstered in the future if the balance of power among the military
factions were to shift. Thus, the cooperative members were always
wary of the military government.

## SELF-MANAGEMENT, REFORM GOVERNMENT, AND
## THE PEASANT IN CHILE AND MEXICO

As in Peru, self-management was an important stimulus to peasants' political confidence and activity in Chile under Allende and in
Mexico in the late 1930s and early 1940s. Moreover, as in Peru, the
new political vigor of cooperative members entailed some difficul-

ties for the state. Cooperative members saw their own enterprises as the bedrock of their new power, and opposed encroachments upon them by other peasants and/or the state. In Chile, the government was as factionalized and as torn about the correct role of the state in the countryside as it was in Peru, and could not resolve the tensions confronting it. In contrast, Mexico "solved the problem" in part by undermining the self-management institutions; fortunately for the Mexican government, peasant loyalty to the political system seemed to increase. Thus, like the Peruvian case, the Chilean and the Mexican experiences suggest that, in the context of a weak state and previous socioeconomic divisions in the countryside, self-management can be dangerous to the regime, encouraging peasants' political vigor but not their commitment to the nation. However, the discussion in this section and the next will also point to some "roads not taken" in Chile and Mexico.

The Chilean self-managed cooperatives were roughly similar in structure to the Peruvian.[7] In the great majority of cases, the patron was compelled to leave the enterprise, and the single ex-hacienda became the base of the new cooperative. As in Peru, membership was usually restricted to permanent workers in the enterprise (i.e., temporary workers and most women were excluded). Each member had one vote in a general assembly, which elected five individuals to a peasant committee for one-year terms. Until 1968, the members of the peasant committee were required to work with two officials of the agrarian reform agency (CORA) in a body called the Administrative Council. This council was responsible for most matters within the cooperative, including the preparation of a work plan and discipline problems. Although there was considerable variation across Chile's cooperatives, on balance the role of the CORA officials and the state in general seems to have been some-

[7] This discussion is based on my own visits to two Chilean cooperatives near Santiago in March 1973, and also on available secondary sources. Gazmuri (1970) studied four *asentamientos* (cooperatives established by the original Frei law) and provides survey data on the political attitudes and activity there. Whiting (1973) analyzes two asentamientos, where he lived for the bulk of a year during 1971-1972; he too carried out a survey of most members of these cooperatives. Marchetti (1975) examines in detail the political and economic course of four haciendas that became asentamientos or CERAs; the four enterprises were studied during 1972-1973, and were selected in part for their differences. Steenland (1977) traces developments in Cautín province in the south, and one enterprise there in particular, between 1970 and 1973. Lehmann (1973), Barraclough and Fernández (1974), Barraclough (1975), and Loveman (1976a) provide broader analyses, including more discussion of the politics within the Popular Unity government itself.

what greater in the Chilean cooperatives during the Frei period than in the Peruvian under Velasco (Gazmuri, 197: 149; Loveman, 1976a: 275-276). After 1968, the requirement for regular CORA participation in internal administration of the enterprise was eliminated. The Popular Unity government was divided by the question of what agrarian structure would be most effective in the countryside, and particularly by what role for the state would be most appropriate. As a result, enterprise structure varied considerably. In many cases, expropriated farms never gained a clear legal status and were technically responsible to a government "intervener." However, these interveners apparently often suffered the same vicissitudes as the directors in Peru.

In many cooperatives, the new self-management structures encouraged considerable political awareness and activity. As in Peru, the issues addressed by cooperative members were not business trivia, but such concerns as the relationship between the enterprise and technicians or officials and, especially in the later Allende years, access to agricultural machinery and supplies. For example, at the General Assembly described below, workers were heatedly engaged in a discussion of the most suitable mode of agricultural production. The president, a former trade union activist, opposed a division of the cooperative's land into individual plots, but a government official in attendance favored such a division:

> [The] government functionary . . . entered the debate. He suggested that it would be better to divide the farm so that lazy workers would have to work as hard as more conscientious workers. The assembly's president told the functionary, "Stop right there, comrade. It would be better if you do just what you are assigned to do here. Let us organize this reformed farm as it seems best to us." The assembly supported its president, and the functionary said nothing throughout the rest of the discussion. The debate between the group which supported the idea of the individual enterprise and the group which supported the collective *chacra* [farm] continued for two hours. Gradually various conclusions were being drawn. . . . [Finally] forty-one of the forty-nine workers voted for the system of the collective chacra (Marchetti, 1975b: 73).

Although this particular cooperative was one of the more politically conscious and active in Chile, it does not seem entirely unrepresentative. The assembly was widely perceived to be a major decision-making organ; its meetings were frequent and attendance was high, averaging 67 percent in four cooperatives in the late 1960s (Gazmuri, 1970: 144; Whiting, 1973: 62). Trade unions continued alongside the new cooperative organs; council presidents were often former union leaders. In various cooperatives, peasants acted to curtail the role of government interveners, to equalize the size of individual parcels, to take over the reserve land of the ex-patron, and to demand more machinery from regional officials (Marchetti, 1975a: 266-434; Steenland, 1977: 170-175). Real wages approximately doubled (Zammit, 1973: 128). Peasants reported, "Here, everyone is boss now" (Marchetti, 1975a: 411). Peasants' confidence and interest were also indicated by the fact that, of the respondents in a sample of two cooperatives, not one answered "I don't know" to a question about what were important problems in the area (Whiting, 1973: 65).

There is less information on the impact of self-management on other kinds of attitudes and behavior with respect to fellow cooperative members. Information on changes in social orientations in the cooperatives is particularly scant. With respect to political leadership, the available information suggests that members instituted honest elections and tried to select the "best" leaders, but by and large continued to choose leaders from high socioeconomic strata (Marchetti, 1975a: 413-415 and 1975b: 38-39 71-72, 158; Lehmann, 1973: 400-409; Barraclough, 1975: 10-17; Whiting, 1973: 24). This pattern was of course similar to the Peruvian. With respect to collective work achievement, more information is available; as Chapter VIII discussed, collective work achievement did not seem to increase in Chile, for similar reasons as in Peru.

Moreover, in Chile as in Peru, changes in the structure of the single enterprise were not accompanied by significant social and economic changes in structures beyond the enterprise. In addition, as in Peru, the new enterprise became the peasants' "port in the storm," sustaining skeptical attitudes toward peasant outsiders and government officials.

The new Chilean cooperative members did not prove any more sympathetic to the needs of peasants beyond their enterprises than their Peruvian counterparts. This problem was if anything greater in Chile than in Peru because the new cooperative members had gained a larger percentage of Chile's land while more peasants remained landless day laborers (see Table II.1). In many enterprises, members oriented their production to less labor-intensive crops to avoid employing more temporary workers (Marchetti, 1975a: 288-299). Although government officials and social scientists encouraged the admission of seasonal workers as full members, Chilean cooperative leaders argued that the enterprise could not afford more members and that in any case the temporary workers tended to "drink a lot and are not responsible" (Marchetti, 1975a: 295). Moreover, as a few years went by and some enterprises began to succeed economically while others began to fail, competition among enterprises emerged. For example, San Nicolás, a successful cooperative in the image of Peru's Estrella, refused to join the machinery pool in its area, instead fighting for and winning a third tractor for itself from the government (Marchetti, 1975a: 45).

Like the Peruvian government, the Chilean became aware of the tendency for the single, self-managed enterprise to pit its members against peasant outsiders, and the government sought new self-management structures that would not have such an effect. But the Popular Unity was not successful in this effort. Although it was an elected, civilian government, it was similar to the Velasco regime in three crucial ways: it was factionalized, its attitudes toward popular participation were ambivalent, and it was unable to use effectively the limited resources available to it. These three flaws are all suggested by one scholar of Chile's agrarian reform:

> By 1972 the state bureaucracy was increasingly unable to carry out the tasks assigned to it by those directing the various agencies, due partly to political conflicts within the system, and partly to what can only be called a breakdown of administrative authority. Organizations such as CORA are structured to control activities of their clientele, and to impose a legal order upon their own activities. The control of activities which have close connections among them is divided among numerous strata and hierarchies; officials at regional level are responsible both to the regional chiefs and to chiefs of functional divisions at national level—who may disagree about policy. Officials at the bottom may lecture the peasant clientele on the evils of excessive indebtedness or short working hours, but they do not have the means to apply rewards and sanctions for good or bad performance. Decisions at the top are taken often on the assumption that officials can more or less order the workers and peasants to do whatever the politicians and bureaucrats think is good for them, and the officials at the bottom simply cannot and do not implement these decisions; a system of institutional lying is created (Lehmann, 1973: 427-428).

The primary structure advanced by the Popular Unity to replace the single self-managed enterprise was the Agrarian Reform

Center (CERA). However, the CERA remained a provisional solution, the result of almost nine months of debate within the Popular Unity government, a result that had not satisfied anyone and that no one was thus fully committed to implementing.[8] In some respects similar to the central cooperative and PIAR schemes in Peru, the CERA was to integrate at least two ex-haciendas and was to require that 90 percent of enterprise profits be transferred to regional and national funds for redistribution and capitalization. Moreover, temporary workers, women, and teenagers were to gain most rights of membership. The previous self-management structures such as the General Assembly and Administrative Council were to continue, but their specific prerogatives vis-à-vis the state were ambiguous.

Most of the changes in the previous cooperative structure portended by the CERA were perceived by ex-hacienda members as an infringement on new rights and new powers to which they had aspired. Spurred on by the conservative opposition forces that denounced the CERAs as state farms, the peasants rejected the new structures, which were rarely implemented as planned. The peasants had some reason to be suspicious. Despite the fact that, some months before, the government had established a National Peasant Council (CNC) to transmit the opinion of the peasants to the government, the CNC had not been consulted on the CERA, and peasant participation in the CERA did indeed promise to be less significant than it had been in the previous cooperative structure.[9]

The CERA policy did not help the Popular Unity to build broader, national commitments among cooperative members. Moreover, the shortcomings of the CERA policy were only one indication of the factionalization and ambivalence toward popular participation within the Allende government, problems that seemed to become gradually more severe. Officials were so involved in the struggle for governmental power that their main effort in the countryside often appeared to be electioneering rather than resolving the real problems of the peasants (Marchetti, 1975a: 277, 419-420).

The problems of the Allende government in the countryside were particularly evident in the development of the National Peas-

---

[8] The discussion in this paragraph and the next on the character of the CERA and the politics behind its design draws heavily upon Loveman (1976a: 291-301).

[9] See especially Loveman (1976a: 295-297), and Barraclough and Fernández (1974: 201).

ant Council, the CNC. As in Peru, the government refused to cooperate with the peasant federation that it had created.[10] The Popular Unity met only six times with CNC leaders from its establishment through mid-1973, and at these sessions the government primarily informed the CNC of decisions that had already been taken (Barraclough and Fernández, 1974: 207). As stated above, the CNC was not consulted with respect to the establishment of the CERA. The government generally worked only with those provincial CNC organs whose leaders were members of the Popular Unity parties and who supported its program. The establishment of these provincial bodies was carried out by the traditional parties, each of which selected one of its traditional leaders to campaign for the position. Even in cases where leaders sympathetic to the Popular Unity were elected, when they began to carry out responsibilities—such as researching the possibilities for new expropriations and then requesting takeovers—the government often paid them no attention.

Amid the confusion and limited responsiveness of the Allende government, it is not surprising that cooperative members perceived their enterprise as an island of hope and security. Increasingly, government officials were perceived as intruders—who arrived like a sudden "rainstorm" on their island, in the words of one peasant quoted by Marchetti (1975a: 277). However, as in Peru, peasants favored evasiveness to open dissent; during meetings with officials, "[peasants'] heads are nodded in agreement, so that the long-winded officials will depart soon, after which new rules are circumvented and bent by a peasantry seeking to pursue their interest in their own way" (Lehmann, 1973: 427). Few cooperative members supported Allende. In many areas, particularly those where the agrarian reform had been implemented by the Christian Democrats, many peasants favored the Christian Democratic party; in other areas, espcially the south, the radical MIR had often spurred the agrarian reform and won support (Loveman, 1976a: 288; Whiting, 1973: 42; Steenland, 1977).

It is more difficult to assess the impact of self-management in Mexico than in Peru or Chile. No survey data are available on peasants' attitudes and behavior prior to the reform, but presumably their attitudes toward collective political activity and solidarity

---

[10] My description of the shortcomings of Popular Unity interaction with the CNC is based largely on Loveman (1976a: 285-287); Barraclough and Fernández (1974: 202-213); and Marchetti (1975: Vol. 1, 420-426).

were not too negative, for a considerable number of peasants participated in the Mexican Revolution (1910-1917). By the accounts available, it seems that self-management encouraged peasant unity and enhanced peasant political capacities for peaceful struggle.[11] Yet, as peasants were becoming more politically assertive, the Mexican government was becoming stronger and more unified. The government decided that the peasants' political activity was a threat to its own position, and moved to undermine the self-management structures.

In Mexico, agrarian cooperatives were called *ejidos*, and their members *ejidatarios*. Although sometimes formed directly and exclusively on the base of an expropriated hacienda, they more often developed on the base of a peasant village to which the lands of an expropriated hacienda were added. The first ejidos emerged after the revolution, during the 1920s, but in very small numbers; it was not until the presidency of Lázaro Cárdenas (1934-1940) that the government began to encourage the development of ejidos. At the time the law regulating the structure of the ejido was introduced, in 1925, self-management had not emerged as a specific school of thought. In fact, however, the ejidos incorporated most key features of self-management. The patron was assumed to have left the enterprise. Ultimate authority in the ejido was to reside with the Ejido Assembly, which elected three members to an Ejido Comissariat and three or more to the Vigilance Council, for two-year terms. The Ejido Comissariat was to be the executive organ with primary responsibility for the progress of the cooperative, and the Vigilance Council was to check that the commissariat behaved correctly. In other words, the division of responsibility among the two executive organs paralleled that in Peru. The original ejido law required that the ejido allocate 10 percent of its income to a common fund for agricultural machinery and the like, and another 5 percent for taxes. Although ejidos were generally not required to employ a technical director, as in Peru, or to include officials on their execu-

---

[11] My discussion of Mexican cooperatives draws on my own visits to several ejidos in Morelos in August 1977, and various secondary sources. Unfortunately, regions closer to Mexico City, especially La Laguna, Morelos, and Puebla, are overrepresented in the literature. The major studies by Senior (1958), Wilkie (1971) and Restrepo and Eckstein (1975) focus on ejidos in La Laguna. Ronfeldt (1973) provides a detailed analysis of the political struggles of one major ejido in Puebla from 1910 to 1969. One of the studies that provides considerable detail on ejidos in various regions is Simpson (1937); unfortunately, it was written at an early stage in the Mexican agrarian reform process.

tive council, as was originally the case in Chile, they were expected to review a plan for the ejido's production formulated by the government's Agrarian Department; to approve the plan or return it to the department with the ejido's recommendations for revision; and, if the plan were approved, to follow it.[12] The requirement to employ a technical director did apply to some ejidos with major industrial facilities.

In the new ejidos, political activity was intense. The major concerns of ejido members corresponded to those of their counterparts in Peru and Chile. In some areas, hacendados remained nearby and tried to influence events in the ejidos; considerable energy was then devoted by ejidatarios to the consolidation of their position vis-à-vis the hacendados or their representatives. For example, the ejido Atencingo devoted most of a decade of political struggle, from 1938 to 1947, to win real control of a large sugar mill that, while technically the property of the ejidatarios, continued to be run by its former managers and manipulated in the interest of its former owner (Ronfeldt, 1973: 33-67). Hacendados frequently promoted their candidates in ejido elections; the incumbent leadership usually denounced the hacendados' interference to government authorities (Simpson, 1937: 471-474). Because Mexican peasants generally fought hacendados more violently and over a longer period of time than Peruvian and Chilean peasants, the focal point for change in the peasants' orientations toward authority seemed to be victory over the hacendado, rather than victory over enterprise technicians.

Selection of the best leader was also a major concern in many ejidos, and was frequently linked to tensions among district socioeconomic strata in the cooperative, as in Peru. For example, according to Simpson (1937: 355-374), the ejido Tapilula was split between the two groups, "The Rich" and "The Agrarians," who struggled for control of the commissariat, which entailed control over cooperative funds and the distribution of parcels in the ejido. This conflict degenerated into armed attacks on some ejidatarios by others. After the ejido Atencingo finally won control over the sugar mill, a battle for political leadership ensued for several years between the ejidatarios who had led the battle and the managerial

---

[12] The most specific discussion of ejido structure available to me was Simpson (1937). He cites the original Law of Ejido Patrimony of 1925 and its revisions through 1934. Some of the provisions mentioned in my text may thus have been modified subsequently.

staff, many of whom had collaborated with the previous leadership. Although the ejidatario group won this battle quite easily, some years later a struggle for ejido leadership ended in the assassination of the leader of the rebel group. The frequency of violence in leadership struggles spurred the following comment by a scholar familiar with Mexico before and after the revolution; the comment is also an important assessment of change in peasants' political orientations:

> Although it is regrettable that the ejido communities apparently waste much time and energy in politics and internal discussions, and although it is to be deplored that often the game of politics is played to the tune of popping pistols and violence and bloodshed of all sorts, yet, surely the present situation—pistols, politics and all—is to be preferred to the apathetic hopelessness of these same people only a few years ago. Violence, though death is sometimes its fruit, may be a sign of vitality, an indication of upsurging energies. Ejidatarios quarreling and intriguing among themselves, even ejidatarios "electing" their Administrative Committees with shotguns instead of ballots, are at least men with something to plan for, something to fight over, and not slaves and peons, landless, hopeless, and helpless. Out of competition and conflict there may come integration, unity and order; out of the sodden impotence of peons tied in debt slavery to the hacienda, the only issue possible was stagnation and death (Simpson, 1937: 352).

Ejidatarios were also concerned about their route to agricultural development. In many ejidos, controversy arose as to whether to work the land individually or collectively, and whether to move toward crop specialization and agro-industrialization or to diversify crop production and limit agro-industrialization. In most cases, it was decided to divide the ejido up and work the land individually, but also to work together on some kinds of industrialization, such as road construction projects, the acquisition of machinery and vehicles, and the establishment of more favorable marketing arrangements for the ejido as a whole (Simpson, 1937: 313-315, 470-479; Restrepo and Eckstein, 1975: 283). There were some exceptions to this pattern, primarily large export enterprises such as Atencingo. The government feared that dividing an agro-industrial enterprise such as Atencingo into small plots would reduce the cultivation of sugar cane, which the government desired for its foreign exchange value. As of 1969, the government was still effectively blocking Atencingo's desires for subdivision of the enterprise.

These political issues engaged peasants, and their stance toward collective political action within the ejido seemed positive during the 1930s, and at times through the 1940s and even into the 1950s. The accounts of the La Laguna region as a whole by Senior (1958) and of one ejido—San Miguel—in that area by Wilkie (1971) indicate that general assemblies convened frequently, attendance was high, and debate was informed and lively. In San Miguel, peasants met two or three times a month in the Ejido Assembly, with virtually 100-percent attendance. Comments Senior:

> One remembers hundreds of meetings in which men and women vibrated with a new dignity and determination to work hard and make a success of the "land which is ours." One recalls the mixed meetings of ejidatarios, private owners, urban businessmen, and government officials into which the former day-workers came armed with facts and figures, presenting well-reasoned arguments for their position, with calmness and determination (Senior, 1958: 195).

With respect to the effect of self-management on other kinds of attitudes and behavior toward fellow ejidatarios, less information is available. As noted above, most ejidatarios preferred private to collective cultivation of the land, but this preference may have reflected primarily government and market incentives for private cultivation (Whiting, 1977). (As noted above, the case of Atencingo, where the government discouraged parcellization, was an exception.) The selection of political leaders was by bullet rather than ballot more frequently than in Peru or Chile; the socioeconomic status of the leader also seemed to be less of an issue than in Peru or Chile, perhaps because during this era the educational and economic backgrounds of the Mexican peasants varied less widely.

Social solidarity within the ejido increased markedly.[13] In many cooperatives, members worked together on the construction of a school or a health center. Sports activities increased and parties were held more frequently. Friendships grew.

As in Peru and Chile, however, the ejidos were islands of peasant economic and political power in stormy seas, and the main concern

[13] The discussion in this paragraph is based on the description of Octlán and Remedios by Simpson (1937: 307-315; 413-415), of San Miguel by Wilkie (1971: 40), and of various other ejidos in the La Laguna area by Senior (1958: 196-199).

of many cooperative members was to protect their own ship. Ejidatarios refused to open the enterprises to new members; very few temporary workers ever gained admission—even when they were the sons of members.[14] Temporary workers were relegated to the most back-breaking jobs, and kept at a marked social distance. Again as elsewhere, competition among ejidos often became intense.[15] For example, the ejido San Miguel became dissatisfied with what it saw as the high cost and poor quality of the cotton fiber produced at the cotton gin of a nearby ejido, and struggled to build its own gin. In 1948, the gin was built, and was soon processing the cotton of 13-odd neighboring ejidos, at a solid profit for San Miguel. However, in the 1970s, these other ejidos began to complain about the quality of San Miguel's processing and no longer wanted to send their cotton there; San Miguel suddenly found itself in financial straits. Over all, successful ejidos such as El Manantial and San Miguel during the 1950s and 1960s resembled San Nicolás in Chile and Estrella in Peru: over time, the relatively small group of cooperative members became an elite, working primarily at supervisory tasks themselves and gaining considerable economic advantage from the work of temporaries and from capital installations.[16]

Moreover, the assertive ejidatarios were much more interested in advancing their concerns to the government than in singing their thanks for the agrarian reform. The concerns advanced by the ejidatarios were generally well-founded. In the 1920s and 1930s, the Mexican government was ridden by conflict, agrarian reform laws were subject to change, and peasants felt insecure.[17] The typical peasant community had to spend five years struggling with the bureaucracy to win adjudication of an ejido (Simpson, 1937: 447). At times, just after the ejidatarios had planted their first set of crops, local officials would decide to re-allot land. Many important issues about the legal structure of the ejido remained muddled for

[14] The split between ejidatarios and temporary workers in Mexico has been well documented. See Landsberger (1973: 84) and Senior (1958: 180-181) on the Laguna region generally. Information on specific ejidos is provided by Wilkie (1971: 92-98)—on San Miguel—and by Restrepo and Eckstein (1975) on El Manantial and also San Miguel.

[15] The role of the cotton gin in San Miguel's rise and fall is recounted in Wilkie (1971: 60-61) and Restrepo and Eckstein (1975: 290-299).

[16] See Wilkie (1971) and Restrepo and Eckstein (1975: 282-299).

[17] The points in this paragraph are drawn primarily from Simpson (1937: 375-481), Senior (1958: 126-137), and Landsberger (1973: 80-81).

years. Credit was inadequate, as was technical assistance. In such a context, it is not surprising that cooperative members pressured—and even staged demonstrations—for greater credit allocations and a reorganization of the Ejidal Bank. Demands for the adjudication of factories to ejidos were at times made via strikes. In 1940, with the end of the Cárdenas administration and the decline of government support for the ejidos, opposition to the government became more pronounced; in the La Laguna region, a rival agrarian federation, the Central Union, was launched against the government's National Peasant Confederation (CNC).

As elsewhere, cooperative members tended to praise themselves for their successes and blame the government for their failures. When San Miguel was prospering because of its cotton gin, members attributed their success to their own business acumen; when it was failing because of its cotton gin, members claimed that the Ejidal Bank was unfairly transferring cotton to other gins for processing (Restrepo and Eckstein, 1975:292-293). One very successful ejido, Octlán, sang "songs to the glory of *their* ejido"—not to the government that had expropriated the hacienda lands (Simpson, 1937: 313). There was a tendency to exaggerate the capacity of a single ejido to advance entirely on its own. Said one ejidatario to a social scientist about the Ejidal Bank, for example: "They've talked a lot but they haven't done much. And besides, there's too much red tape about getting a loan. What we are going to do as soon as we can, is establish our own bank right here in our village and then when we want to borrow money we won't have to wait six months to get it" (quoted by Simpson, 1937: 480).

Although the similarities among the Peruvian, Chilean, and Mexican experiences with self-management are marked, there are also some differences—especially with respect to their denouements. Mexican officials always seemed more determined to keep a hand in the operation of the ejidos, even during the apex of self-management in the Cárdenas era. The peasants themselves may also have tended to look more often to the government to resolve internal conflicts, such as leadership disputes—or at least this is suggested by the hundreds of letters from ejidatarios to officials cited in Simpson (1937). Thus, when the government turned to the right after Cárdenas and apparently became sufficiently worried by the vehemence of ejidatarios' demands that it decided to exert greater control over the ejidos, it had a certain basis for such action.

Gradually after 1940, self-management in Mexico was undermined by the increasing strength of the Institutional Revolutionary

Party (the PRI) and the Ejidal Bank.[18] Collective political participation diminished as clientelistic relationships were established by PRI officials with ejido leaders. Party officials provided ejido leaders with benefits, such as advice on crop cultivation or money for the construction of new facilities in the ejido, in return for the leader's delivering the ejido's votes to the PRI and helping the PRI with its political recruitment tasks. Because the government wanted to keep reliable leaders in power, PRI officials looked the other way when ejido leaders evaded the requirement for periodic leadership rotation. Rather than providing an institutional channel for peasant demands, the Mexican peasant confederation, the CNC, often worked primarily to co-opt rival peasant leaders who did voice peasant concerns. The Agrarian Bank also played an important role in consolidating government control in the ejidos. By the 1950s, if an ejido were to get credit from the bank at all, it generally had to accept strict stipulations on what crops would be produced, which technicians would be employed, what kinds of fertilizers and technology would be used, and how the harvest would be sold (Restrepo and Eckstein, 1975:187).

Yet, as in Tanzania, Cuba, and China, the government apparently convinced peasants that it was working in their best interest. By and large, the Mexican economy did well in the 1940s, 1950s, and 1960s, and the government provided enough support for the ejidos that members were generally satisfied. Lavish benefits to individuals who agreed to work with the PRI also helped to curry favor. Moreover, the regime became adept at evoking the symbols of its revolutionary heritage to cultivate support. Although many peasants remained without land, hope lingered that they would get it. Thus, in word and deed, most Mexican peasants seemed to support the government. The vast majority of peasants said that the goals of the Mexican Revolution had not been forgotten (Landsberger, 1973: 90). A large majority of the peasantry voted for the PRI (Reyna, 1971; Ames, 1970).

## SELF-MANAGEMENT AND THE NATION

We return now to the question posed at the beginning of this chapter: Is self-management a dangerous policy for a Third World

---

[18] Most of the points in this paragraph and the subsequent one are not the subject of controversy. Useful discussions include Martínez Vázquez (1975: 154-186); Restrepo and Eckstein (1975); Adie (1970); Anderson and Cockroft (1966); Landsberger (1973); and Whiting (1975).

government whose authority may not be fully established? Is there an inevitable trade-off between the confidence and power that the self-managed enterprise gives its members on the one hand, and the loyalty and control that a Third World government needs to promote development of the nation as a whole, on the other? Although this study provides evidence that such a trade-off has occurred in numerous cases, it has also hinted at "roads not taken" by the governments in question—roads that might avert this trade-off or contradiction.

Various scholars analyzing self-management experiences from theoretical perspectives have concluded that enterprise economic autonomy and members' power are at loggerheads with state economic planning and government control.[19] However, these analyses tend to be based upon the conventional definitions of the terms in question, as well as on the assumption that the total amount of power in a political system cannot grow. Thus, although on the basis of conventional definitions, logic would dictate that peasant power is at odds with governmental power, a perception of power as variable in absolute as well as relative terms alters this logic considerably.[20]

Consider the situation of a strong self-managed enterprise within a weak national political system. Such an enterprise may be able to resolve its own concerns effectively, and rapidly unite its members behind important demands to be pressed on regional or national authorities. But a weak state, a state paralyzed by conflict or without resources of its own, will not be able to respond to these demands. Gradually, the members of the once-vigorous enterprise will be-

[19] See, for example, Stepan (1978: 228), whose emphasis is upon the political side of the equation and is focusing on Peru, and Milenkovitch (1971) and Comisso (1977), who stress the economic trade-offs in Yugoslavia.

[20] The concept of power as an entity that can be increased has been emphasized by Frederick W. Frey. Frey (1970) distinguishes concentration of power (the comparison of power capabilities among all members in a unit) from the amount of power, defined as the actual number of power relationships or linkages in a unit, divided by the number of possible linkages in the unit. Developed and underdeveloped political systems have also been distinguished by some scholars "in terms of the level or degree of absolute power which the system is able to mobilize. Some systems that may or may not be stable seem to operate with a very low margin of power, and the authoritative decision makers are close to being impotent in their capacity to initiate and consummate policy objectives" (Pye, 1966: 43). See Huntington (1968: 1 2) for implications of a similar conceptualization of power. Conceptualization and measurement of power are key issues for a set of social scientists that includes Dahl, Hunter, Mills, Wolfinger, and Bachratz; a useful collection of their work is Hawley and Wirt (1968).

come apathetic as their demands are not met. Whatever the hopes of an enterprise, in today's context it cannot survive as an island; its development is inextricably related to that of the economy as a whole. As we have seen, a principal concern of many self-managed agrarian cooperatives is agro-industrialization and the establishment of new marketing arrangements—issues related to the national pattern of development. And Third World agrarian enterprises are usually dependent, at least in the short run, on fertilizers, insecticides, and other inputs that have traditionally been imported. No matter how effective the mobilization of power within the enterprise, this power may mean little if it is not reinforced beyond the enterprise.

We may consider also the situation of a government that appears strong by conventional criteria: its leaders seem united, it has established coherent plans for national development, it has initiated new political and economic organizations that have enrolled considerable numbers of citizens. This would not be the first time that a scholar has pointed out that such strength may prove an illusion. Can a national development plan be viable if it does not take into account citizens' desires? Even more important, in the Third World context in particular, can such a plan be implemented without citizen support? Moreover, as the Peruvian and Chilean cases clearly showed, government-sponsored organizations can be created and citizens can be brought into them, but these structures become meaningless shells if the government does not respond to citizens' concerns. Authoritarian leaders may seem powerful as they issue decree after decree, but when crisis comes, no one defends them and political collapse is often sudden.

Real governmental power in the Third World today—the power not only to issue plans but to execute them, the power to enhance the quality of life for the largest numbers of citizens, the power to endure—may come through a process of sincere negotiation between citizens' groups and the government. Through meaningful interchange, both citizens' groups and the government may come to understand the needs and constraints of the other. Exchanging views honestly and searching for "maximizing" solutions may not be easy, but it has been successfully done in different nations at different times.[21]

---

[21] My discussion here touches on very general questions of political theory and personal political beliefs; it is intended not as a comprehensive treatment of the topic, but rather as a suggestion of "paths not taken." My point has also been made

The danger presented by self-management to the Velasco, Allende, and Cárdenas regimes was not the fault of self-management per se, but was rather a reflection of the inability of these governments to follow through with the movement toward participation that they themselves had initiated. To establish commitment to the nation rather than just the enterprise, the government had not only to create economic and political federations of single self-managed enterprises but also to respond to the concerns of the new federations so that they could develop significant incentives for attitude and behavior change.

But this did not take place. The Peruvian and Chilean governments backed away from peasant political federations almost as soon as they had been created. The members of self-managed enterprises did not trust these federations to aggregate their interests effectively because, in fact, they were never given an important role in policy making. Although the aggregation of peasant interests by these federations was a difficult task because of the distance among distinct socioeconomic strata within the peasantry, the task was not impossible. Had government officials in Peru really worked with the CNA and had sought viable solutions to the problems of cooperative members and comuneros, new policies might have evolved that would have attracted these distinct peasant groups to the CNA. Marketing, agricultural prices, and labor-intensive agricultural development emerge as policy areas in which the CNA might have helped to design innovative schemes that would have benefited both cooperative members and comuneros. If the CNA had been able to develop such policies, cooperative members would have had a much more sympathetic view of the comuneros and of the government. Similarly, in Chile, if the government had worked with the CNC, its policies might have improved, and distinct peasant groups might have lost some of their skepticism towards each other and the government. The design of the CERA and the procedures for land expropriation stand out as examples of such policies. If the Mexican government had negotiated with the Central Union (the CNC's rival in the La Laguna area), viable new policies toward the Ejidal Bank might well have emerged.

---

by Pye (1966: 77): "An important but often overlooked function of open and competitive political articulation is that of creating in the minds of the public a better appreciation of the distinction between the plausible and the possible." Examples of such successful articulation, negotiation, and problem resolution may be found in Peterson (1977) on Swedish politics and Meisner (1978) on Chinese politics. A similar process seems to have occurred in Yugoslavia, as will be discussed below.

The governments also undermined the development of larger-scale economic federations. In Peru, the government favored the growth of the state's role in the critical areas of marketing and agro-industrialization, and thus limited the scope and meaning of the central cooperative. The Chilean government hedged on the question of the character of the CERA, especially on the extent of peasant participation within it, and ultimately was unable to develop CERAs in the countryside. The Mexican government promoted the authority of the Ejidal Bank and the CNC, impeding the emergence of any economically oriented federations of self-managed enterprises. Some of the difficulty in the development of economic federations in Peru and Chile lay in bad timing; if the regional organizations had been established at the same time as the single cooperatives, the more successful enterprises would not have resented the federations as drains on their wealth and intrusions on their property.

The Yugoslav experience with self-management provides some evidence that these hopes for the resolution of the problems of self-management through more rather than less self-management are not just optimistic visions. Although the tensions that emerged with respect to self-management in Peru, Chile, and Mexico also emerged in Yugoslavia, Yugoslavia appears to have moved toward their successful resolution.

Is Yugoslavia sufficiently similar to the Latin American nations that its case is relevant? My answer is yes. Although Yugoslavia has played a much larger role in international power politics than most Third World nations, its internal socioeconomic structure and political dynamics as of the early post-World War II era, when self-management was initiated, were characteristic of Third World nations. Just before World War II, annual per capita national income was only about $65, or less than one-third that of France and less than one-eighth that of the United States; about 75 percent of the population worked in agriculture; and almost half the population was illiterate (Rusinow, 1977: xviii). Ethnic conflict was intense, especially between the economically ascendant Croats and Slovenes and the politically ascendant Serbs. In part as a result, governments had been unstable.

Begun in the early 1950s, self-management in Yugoslavia has undergone various transformations. What is commonly referred to as "Yugoslav self-management" is the model that prevailed between the 1965 "liberalizing" reforms and the adaptations introduced in the 1974 Constitution and the 1976 Law on Associated Labor.

There are several important distinctions between Yugoslav self-management and the Peruvian, Chilean, and Mexican versions: In Yugoslavia, self-management was implemented primarily in industry rather than agriculture. Two leadership organs were established: the Workers' Council, including about 35 members elected by all employees, and the Management Board, the executive body including approximately nine members plus the enterprise director, and elected by the Workers' Council. Finally, the enterprise director was stronger in Yugoslavia than in the Latin American countries; members did not play as large a role in the selection of the director as in Peru, and it was much more difficult for them to dismiss the director (Blumberg, 1969: 205; Hunnius, 1973: 279). However, despite these structural differences, between 1965 and the early 1970s, a similar dynamic emerged in the Yugoslav self-management experience as in the Latin American cases: participation and solidarity were increasing among the members of the single enterprise, but were not extended beyond the enterprise.

Although the enterprise director was a more significant figure in the Yugoslav enterprises than in the Latin American ones, and at times dominated decision making in the firm, the great majority of Yugoslav workers found their participation in the enterprises to be significant, and their political activity was considerable.[22] Key debates often involved the position of workers vis-à-vis white collar technicians: salary differentials, allocation of profits to investment or consumption, and reimbursement for overtime work. Gradually, the number of issues on meeting agenda grew. Although unions were not important in the Yugoslav system, the practice of the strike was; short strikes were often initiated to bring wage grievances to the fore, and then subsequently resolved in meetings or at times with just the director alone. The new structures engaged workers. They were interested and informed about enterprise decisions in comparison to their counterparts in Western Europe (Riddell, 1968: 63); they participated in elections for the Workers' Council at the extraordinarily high rate of approximately 90 percent (Pateman, 1970: 93), and their leaders held more and more council meetings—up from an annual average of 17.1 in 1950 to 24.3 in 1960, about three times the legal requirement (Supek,

---

[22] My discussion of political activity within the Yugoslav self-managed firm is drawn from Comisso (1975 and 1977); Blumberg (1969); Supek (1975); Pateman (1970); Shabad (1978); Hunnius and Ramirez (1973); Adizes (1971); Kavčič, Rus, and Tannenbaum (1971); Whitehorn (1974); Riddell (1968); Kolaja (1965); Sachs (1975a); and Garson (1974).

1975: 9). Social activity and friendship also seemed on the rise in the self-managed firms (Sachs, 1975b).

With respect to commitment to the nation as a whole, however, the record of self-management was not as positive. The 1965 decentralization program entailed a dramatic movement toward a market economy, and thus also more competition among enterprises and, especially given Yugoslav tradition, more conflict among wealthy Croats and less advantaged groups.[23] Self-managed firms competed against each other for credit, and often sought to establish market monopolies. Willingness to admit new workers into the enterprises was limited despite unemployment rates as high as 7 percent or more. Income inequalities among regions—regions that were closely identified with specific ethnic groups—became more severe between 1952 and 1968 (Denitch, 1976:143). Ironically, however, it was not the disadvantaged groups that became most frustrated, but the wealthy Croats, who argued that the government's tax and investment policies were *too* favorable to the less developed areas. Croatia seemed on the verge of a declaration of secession in 1971.

Although the specific context of Yugoslav self-management between 1965 and 1971—the predominantly market economy combined with a series of complex and preferential tax and investment policies—may have exacerbated Yugoslavia's traditional ethnic conflicts, in some respects self-management was a source of basic legitimacy for Tito's government, which helped it to weather the 1971 crisis. As Denitch (1976) shows, by the late 1960s self-management was perceived by majorities of key citizen groups as the core of the Yugoslav system, and as a particularly positive contribution to it.[24] For example, majorities of student and worker samples stated that "Self-management is the proper direction for the development of our society." Large majorities also thought that socialism was impossible without self-management, and that self-management meant the "management of the means of production by the working class" or "participation of citizens in decision-making in all aspects of life and work of the community." Attitudes toward self-management were most positive among the young and, signifi-

---

[23] My information on competition among firms and emerging inequalities is based on Adizes (1971: 218-225); Garson (1974: 42-43); Blumberg (1969: 213); Wachtel (1973); and Byrd (1975: 28). Milenkovitch (1971: 167-186) and Rusinow (1977: 245-307) discuss the revival of Croatian dissidence.

[24] This argument, and the survey results reported in this paragraph, are drawn from Denitch (1976: 149-206).

cantly, among the workers, who presumably had the most intimate knowledge of it.

The widespread favorable view of self-management as an underlying principle of the Yugoslav nation as a whole would thus seem to have helped President Tito rally support for various important modifications in the self-management system in the early 1970s. The Croatian challenge was suppressed by removing key secessionist leaders from top political positions. Subsequently, according to available sources, prolonged debates ensued among President Tito and top leaders of the political party, the League of Communists (LCY), with respect to improving the self-management structure and the political system generally; proposals, counterproposals, and compromises were made.[25] Ultimately, the new 1974 Constitution and the new 1976 Law on Associated Labor emerged, designed at least in part to encourage solidarity beyond the single enterprise. The enterprise itself was divided into Basic Organizations of Associated Labor (BOALs), and asked to work to a greater extent with the representatives of other BOALs, as well as representatives of the region and the LCY. Three "chambers" were established, one each for the BOALs, the region, and political organizations such as the LCY; delegates were elected at the communal, republic, and federal levels. The decision-making powers of these chambers seem significant. Although some analysts have speculated that the League of Communists might regain the large powers of communist parties elsewhere, this has apparently not occurred, in part because the values of the LCY members themselves are not in line with such a monopolization of political power by the LCY.

Various other direct steps were taken to check the economic rivalry among firms that had fanned the flames of conflict between Croats and other ethnic groups. It was feared that, amid the competition for technological ascendance and credit, professional directors and bankers were promoting "economistic" goals at the expense of other aims, and thus the power of the directors and bankers was curbed. In the BOALs, enterprise directors were subject to a more rigorous electoral system, in which candidates were proposed to the workers' council by a commission including an

[25] The discussion in this paragraph and the next draws heavily from Rusinow (1977: 308-347) and Wilson (1978). Unfortunately, however, the information available to me on the politics of this period is incomplete. Evaluation of the exact amount of give-and-take by President Tito and top LCY leaders with respect to citizens' opinions is impossible. It is also hard to assess the character of popular attitudes toward the purge of Croat leaders.

equal number of representatives from the enterprise and from a communal assembly; managerial staff were prohibited from positions on the workers' councils; and the banks were significantly more responsible to the BOALs. The "persuasive" role of the LCY within the BOAL was also enhanced.

The effects of these changes in the self-management structures upon attitudes and behavior in Yugoslavia are not yet clear. In one of the few reports available in English, Wilson (1978) suggests that secessionist tendencies have dissipated, and that political activity within the BOALs and the chambers is vigorous, with technicians retaining somewhat more influence than stipulated in the new laws, and the LCY gaining some influence but by no means dominating activity.

The significance of Yugoslavia's experience with self-management must be interpreted cautiously. The new self-management structures are young, and questions about the role of the LCY in the BOALs and about the ultimate impact of the structures on Yugoslavs' attitudes and behavior cannot yet be definitively answered. For the purposes of this study, it would be helpful to know more about the process by which the new self-management system was discussed and established, in order to assess whether or not there was any significant responsiveness by top leaders to expressed popular concerns. There are major differences between the Yugoslav case and the Peruvian or Chilean: President Tito wielded greater authority than did President Velasco or President Allende at similar critical moments, and Tito's power was based on both a solid grasp of a dominant political party and on his own charismatic personality. However, as Denitch's data indicate, Tito's authority and the government's capabilities in general were enhanced by popular respect for Yugoslavia's self-management principles. The same opportunity to bolster national authority via self-management was lost by Velasco and Allende, but the Yugoslav experience suggests that it did indeed exist.

At a minimum, the Yugoslav experience shows that many Yugoslavs believe self-management may fit the needs of a Third World nation. In Yugoslavia, it has not been necessary to resort to Mexico's drastic curtailment of self-management principles to enable the survival of the nation or the government. There has apparently been widespread recognition among Yugoslavs that self-management is relatively untried and it may be necessary to adapt specific self-management structures at times. Yugoslavia has earnestly sought solutions to the tensions generated by self-management at the level of the single enterprise, and has apparently succeeded in encouraging simultaneously both enterprise members' political power and their loyalty to the Yugoslav nation and political system.

Yugoslavia may thus have moved toward the resolution of tensions generated by self-management structures, a movement that Peru was not able to achieve. Yet, if all the obstacles to the development of self-management in Peru are taken into account, the extent of interest in and commitment to the process of experimentation with self-management seems more noteworthy than the ultimate failure of this process. By 1974 and 1975, there was a significant number of officials and peasants, such as the peasant leader quoted at the beginning of this chapter, who sought to advance such potentially viable variations on the theme of single-enterprise self-management as the CNA, the central cooperatives, and Social Property. For some of these individuals, self-management had spurred a new sense of pride and hope, hope for what could be done even within the Peruvian context. The context was difficult; the "progressive" group within the military government was always weak and was becoming weaker. Ultimately, time ran out on this group altogether.

Nevertheless, a dynamic of change was initiated in Peru that may have made the possibility of a "next time" significantly greater. And, next time, with a greater understanding of the tensions generated by single-enterprise self-management, the possibility seems greater that new self-management structures overcoming these difficulties will be established.

# Appendix 1

## RESEARCH METHODOLOGY

### Site Selection

The five major sites were selected almost entirely on the basis of the availability of the 1969 attitudinal data collected by IEP and Cornell. I reapplied the survey in the only three ex-haciendas in the 1969 study, with the exception of those in the Chancay region that were to be studied by Dr. Giorgio Alberti of IEP. With respect to the control sites, Virú was the only town in the valley that had been studied in 1969, and thus there were no alternatives to it. In the Huancayo region, however, three peasant communities had been surveyed in 1969. Agustín was chosen largely because it was more accessible.

I did exercise discretion in the selection of the three minor sites, the three peasant communities in SAIS Huanca. Of the 29 SAIS communities, Patca and Varya were selected to provide maximum diversity within the SAIS. The text in Chapter IV describes the differences between Patca and Varya. The third community, Rachuis, was investigated only briefly in 1975. I decided to go to a new community to expand my knowledge of the SAIS. Rachuis was selected because it is relatively backward and thus more representative of rural Peru, and also because its attitudes toward the SAIS were considered typical. Access in Rachuis looked favorable as well, because my research assistant had friends there.

### Field Strategies and Research Access

Since I hoped to replicate some aspects of the 1969 study, I wanted my field strategy to be as similar to the IEP-Cornell team's as possible. Interviews with the head 1969 investigators, Professor William Whyte of Cornell and Dr. Giorgio Alberti of IEP, increased my knowledge of their work. I gained further understanding of the work from interviews with Professor Juan Rodríguez Suy-Suy, field coordinator in the Virú Valley research, and Dr. José Elías Minaya and Manuel Ortiz, field interviewers in 1969.

In both the 1969 and 1974 studies, Peruvian university students were employed as research assistants. The 1969 team used about six assistants in each site. I worked with two assistants in each site, one man and one woman. A total of seven assistants was employed through the course of the 1973-1974 field work. One assistant, Rodolfo Osores Ocampo, worked not only in both regions during the 1973-1974 research, but also again in

Estrella, Marla, and the highlands sites in 1975 and 1977. For both the 1969 and 1973-1974 studies, interviewers received considerable training. In 1973, interviewers practiced the questionnaire implementation with each other. During the pre-test of the questionnaire and in roughly 20 percent of the sample interviews, I was present at the administration of the questionnaire, checking for the quality and consistency of delivery and coding over time and among different interviewers. I also visited and briefly queried some 10 percent of the respondents subsequent to the interview, to ensure that the questionnaire had been correctly administered.

My research assistants and I spent more time in each major site than did the 1969 team. The longer residence in the sites reflected our greater interest in the structure of the cooperative and in peasant behavior. Further, whereas rapport with the peasants was relatively easy to develop in 1969, by 1974 it was difficult, and the extra time helped us to establish the same level of collaboration in the community that the 1969 group achieved. As in many Latin American countries, anti-Americanism increased in Peru between 1969 and 1974. In the cooperative sites, we were asked to submit evidence of our university affiliations (in my case, the Universidad del Centro of Huancayo), as well as research proposals. We avoided any association with the government.

Ultimately, my research group seemed to receive as much cooperation as the 1969 team. The statistics on respondents' collaboration with the interviewers indicate similar rapport levels in 1969 and 1974 (McClintock, 1976: 668). The refusal rate for interviews was negligible in both studies. In 1974, several residents on the sample list rejected the interview at first, but we returned to them after several more weeks in the community and were accepted in all but one case.

*Questionnaire Construction and the Validity of Responses*

The 1969 and 1974 survey instruments differed substantially in content. My questionnaire included only about 30 percent of the 1969 items, primarily the questions on sociopolitical attitudes. These items were worded in exactly the same way in the two survey instruments. I added a number of questions designed to probe these attitudes more deeply and also to ascertain opinions about the cooperatives. Although the 1974 questionnaire is shorter than the 1969 instrument, the more complex character of the items about the cooperatives and the more probing orientation of my interviewers resulted in interviews of about the same length (approximately one hour).

In both 1969 and 1974, the instruments were pre-tested. In 1974, new pre-tests were made as our research group entered another kind of site or a second region. Questions were also changed slightly at these times. Generally, we became more cautious with regard to items about wealth, and less cautious with regard to items about the government and politics.

Despite the pre-testing, some questions often seemed to elicit biased responses. Not surprisingly, respondents wanted to present themselves in a favorable light. Comparison of questionnaire responses with official documents suggested, for example, that some interviewees added a year or two to their educational attainment. Respondents also depicted their roles in the community as more influential than observations indicated. At times, too, respondents were probably aware that some answers would be construed negatively by the interviewer. For example, in speaking to a female interviewer during Peru's "Year of the Woman," male respondents were unlikely to report that they "never" discussed important decisions with their wives. Biases with regard to political questions are more difficult to evaluate. On the whole, I think that the items were answered accurately. In virtually every interview, the respondent indicated some attitude that contradicted official ideology, and large numbers of respondents indicated hostility to the government (see Chapter X).

The most difficult interview task was to probe attitudes deeply. With regard to some of our key items, such as social trust, respondents often seemed to have one unqualified, black-or-white position. The items seemed to have almost too much resonance for the respondent: they did not encourage the individual to think more creatively or elaborately about the question.

*Sampling*

Some discrepancy in the establishment of the number of respondents for each site existed between the two studies. In 1969, the IEP-Cornell team aimed at a certain percentage of the total number of residents in each site. Thus, the less populous sites like Monte and Marla have a lower "N" than the more populous sites like Agustín. In contrast, I sampled a roughly similar number of respondents in each site, despite its size. Although Monte and Marla have relatively few residents, I wanted an "N" of sufficient size so that I would be able to evaluate the functioning of each cooperative from the survey data. Thus I set a rough goal of 80 respondents in each major research site, enlarged to 90 in Estrella, Agustín, and Virú because of the variety of socioeconomic groups there, and reduced to 60 in Marla because of its greater socioeconomic uniformity.

With this exception of sample target "N," sampling techniques were similar in the two studies. In the cooperative sites, the current payroll or membership list provided a sampling frame. We selected the necessary number of respondents to match the basic specifications of the 1969 sample—i.e., 2 of 3 workers on the list, but only one of each 2 workers' wives on the list.

In the control sites, accurate lists of residents were not available. Thus, we had to sketch a map of the site. From the data on the number of houses and the occupational profile of each region, we could calculate the percentage of dwellings in each area that should be contacted. The person in the house at the time of the interviewer's arrival was interviewed, regardless of sex.

In the SAIS communities, a rigorous sampling frame could not be obtained within the limits of my resources. We merely estimated the number of residents in each geographic sector and spent enough time in each to interview a proportionate number of respondents, interviewing whichever men were home at the time of our arrival. The sample was thus not random and the results of the SAIS community surveys must be interpreted with this caveat.

*Sample Weighting*

As indicated above, there was a greater variation in the number of people sampled in the 1969 sites than in the 1974 sites. However, each site had to be represented in equal proportion for the combined "haciendas/cooperatives" and "control and quasi-control" totals. For this reason, samples from sites that were underrepresented were weighted. There was also a slight weighting of samples to equalize the 1969 and 1974 samples on such criteria as age, sex, education, and occupation. In all samples, except the Marla 1969 sample, this weighting was minimal—a total difference in "N" of 2 or 3 respondents in each site. However, the original Marla 1969 sample of workers was only 19. They had to be weighted by 1.5 to bring their proportion in the sample up to the proportion in the 1974 sample. Finally, one eventual in Estrella was excluded from the combined 1969-1974 samples but retained in my 1974-only data work. This discrepancy accounts for the fact that in Estrella an "N" of 88 is usually reported in tables of 1969-1974 data, but an "N" of 89 in tables of 1974 data only. This discrepancy also accounts for the one number difference in some "N"s for the samples of the three cooperatives combined.

# Appendix 2

INFLATION RATES, CURRENCY EQUIVALENTS,
AND AGRICULTURAL PRICE TRENDS IN PERU

*Inflation in Peru, 1966-1979*[a]

| Year | Inflation Rate (%) |
|------|--------------------|
| 1966 | 8.9 |
| 1967 | 9.8 |
| 1968 | 19.1 |
| 1969 | 6.2 |
| 1970 | 5.0 |
| 1971 | 6.8 |
| 1972 | 7.2 |
| 1973 | 8.7 |
| 1974 | 16.9 |
| 1975 | 23.6 |
| 1976 | 45.0 |
| 1977 | 32.4 |
| 1978 | 73.7 |
| 1979 | 66.7 |

1969–1974 } 50.8  1969–1975 } 74.4

*Currency Equivalents*

| | |
|---|---|
| 1967-October 1975 | U.S. $1 = 38.7 soles[b] |
| 1967-October 1975 | U.S. $1 = 43 to 44 soles[c] |
| 1976 | U.S. $1 = 57.5 soles[b] |
| 1977 | U.S. $1 = 83.8 soles[b] |

[a] Figures for 1966 through 1975 from Cabieses and Otero (1977: 214), in turn from Peru's INE. Figure for 1976 from *Business Latin America*, March 2, 1977, 65; for 1977 from *Business Latin America*, March 15, 1978, 88; for 1978 from *The Andean Report*, V (May, 1979), 80: for 1979 from *Business Latin America*, February 20, 1980, 64. Slight discrepancies in inflation rate reports occur. Figures from Cabieses and Otero are derived with 1973 as the base year.

[b] IMF, International Financial Statistics (June 1978). Figures are for exchange certificates, not drafts. Figures for 1976 and 1977 are averages for the year.

[c] This was the exchange rate for the tourist in Peru at the bank. Black market exchange rate during this period was about 60 soles to the dollar.

*Agricultural Price Trends*[a]

|  | Percentage price change: from late 1973 or early 1974 to early 1975 | Percentage price change: from January 1975 or early 1975 until January 1976 |
| --- | --- | --- |
| Potatoes, white | 35 | 29 |
| Poultry, dressed | 29 | 45 |
| Corn, yellow | 95 | 12 |
| Rice, rough | 50 | 26 |
| Sorghum, grain | 100 | 12 |
| Milk, evaporated (7.8%) | 41 | 13 |
| Milk, fresh | 47 | 26 |
| ** Beef, first class | 29 | 131 |
| ** Beef, second class | 40 | 168 |
| ** Beans | 0 | 36 |

[a] All data are from the reports of the United States Department of Agriculture entitled "Peru: Agricultural Situation, Annual Report," of February 4, 1974, and January 19, 1976, except the foods marked by a double asterisk. Price trends of the foods marked by a double asterisk were calculated from data in OIT (1975: 156) and information in *La Prensa* and *El Peruano*. All foods for which comparable data are available are listed and are the ones included in the calculation of food price changes in Chapter X. The only complication in the calculation was the slight variation in the date of changed prices, indicated in the table. All items are measured by kilogram except evaporated milk, which is for 14.5 ounces. All prices are retail. Prices for the two types of milk and beef are averaged to avoid overweighting these products in the calculation.

# Appendix 3

## AGRARIAN REFORM IN PERU AND OTHER LATIN AMERICAN NATIONS

Data on agrarian structure in Latin America are inadequate and a large margin of error must be accepted for all figures.

### Peru

Data on the advance of the agrarian reform and the kinds of enterprises created, reported in Tables II.1 and IV.4, are reliable; they are from the Ministry of Agriculture (1976) and also (namely the post-1976 figures) from *Latin America Economic Report*, 1 (June 29, 1979), 196. Other figures in Table IV.4 are less reliable. The number of hectares available for agriculture is taken from the 1972 National Agriculture and Livestock Census; however, there have been wide discrepancies in the results of these censuses, and the figure is open to question. The figure for total farm families is based on the 1972 census data (see the 1977 World Bank "Peru: Agricultural Sector Survey," Annex 2, Appendix 2). It is also very much a ballpark figure. The data on the number of families and of hectares in peasant communities, private farms, and without land are extremely rough; they are based on the same sources as the previous figures, as well as on data in Horton (1974) and Van de Wetering (1973).

Sources on compensation for expropriated land are Supreme Decree 265-70-AG and *Latin America Weekly Report*, 79-04 (November 23, 1979), 37-38.

### Chile

Figures courtesy of Van Whiting. Data on the advance of the reform are from a CORA document, quoted in "Comentarios de la Situación Economica," Departamento de Economía, Universidad de Chile, Santiago, 1973. Other data are from Steenland (1974). Key figures are also confirmed by Loveman (1976: 281). See also World Bank (1978).

### Mexico

Sources are Stavenhagen (1970: 241-244); Stavenhagen (1975); and Whiting (1975). "Reforms" refer to ejidos. Information on compensation is from Flores (1967) and Whiting (1975: Part 1). Amount of land redistributed between 1960 and 1970 appears significant, but the quality of land has worsened and the number of landless laborers continues to rise (Stavenhagen, 1975). See also World Bank (1978).

### Bolivia

All figures are from Wilkie (1973: 5). Percentages seem somewhat high, perhaps because they include some colonization figures, as Wilkie (1973: 5) suggests. Evidence on compensation is from Alexander (1974: 43). See also World Bank (1978).

### Venezuela

Most figures are from Wilkie (1973: 5). Percentages seem somewhat high, perhaps because they include colonization figures, as Wilkie (1973: 5) suggests. Evidence on compensation is from Wilkie (1973: 77-80). Data on landless workers are from Kirby (1973: 209). See also World Bank (1978).

# Appendix 4

## DESCRIPTION OF ATTITUDE INDICES

### Index of Participatory and Collaborative Attitudes toward Site Residents

Five items were chosen for the index on the basis of their validity and reliability. They include: A) community sociopolitical organization; B) trust; C) community help; D) work with others; and E) political efficacy. Results of item application are reported above in the chapters. The items read:

A. To improve life here, some people say everyone ought to get together. Others say each person should solve his own problems. What do you think?

B. Can you or can you not trust the majority of people in this place?

C. Suppose you found yourself in difficulty. Would the other people in your community help you? A lot, a fair amount, or not at all?

D. In general, do you prefer to work in collaboration with other people, or by yourself?

E. Suppose the Administrative Council [or Town Council, or hacienda administration, as appropriate] here wants to do something bad or unjust. What could you do to prevent it?

The five items were dichotomized, with 1 equivalent to a "pro-collaboration" answer and 0 equivalent to an "anti-collaboration" answer, or "don't know's" and "no answer's." The average Kendall correlation coefficient of item-to-item intercorrelation for the ex-haciendas in 1974 is .294; for the control sites in 1974, .172; for the haciendas in 1969, .107; for the control sites in 1969, .087. All these coefficients are significant at the .001 level. Items with the consistently highest intercorrelations were sociopolitical organization, trust, and work-with-others:

*Average Item-to-item Intercorrelation for Each Item, by Community Type and Year*

|  | ex-haciendas 1974 | control sites 1974 | haciendas 1969 | control sites 1969 |
|---|---|---|---|---|
| sociopolitical organization (A) | .344 | .206 | .108 | .134 |
| trust (B) | .312 | .226 | .112 | .065 |
| community help (C) | .263 | .105 | .078 | .068 |
| work with others (D) | .291 | .158 | .127 | .072 |
| political efficacy (E) | .257 | .167 | .114 | .096 |

The five items were added to form the index.

*Index of Collaborative Attitudes toward Outsiders*

The only two relevant items for both 1969 and 1974 samples were attitudes toward the government and attitudes toward outsiders. Items read, "Would you say that what the government does helps improve conditions in this country?" and "[If] ... you have a problem, how much help could you get from outsiders?" For both items, a negative answer was scored as 0, a positive answer ("Yes, government helps," or "much" help from outsiders) as 2, and a moderate answer ("government helps more or less," or "some" help from outsiders) as 1. Items were then added to form index. In Monte and Agustín, where the item on attitudes toward the government was not asked, items on sacrifice for disadvantaged sites and help for striking miners were substituted.

*Index of Respondent's Own Attitudes*

Items include: sociopolitical organization (A); trust (B); work with others (D); political efficacy (E); and traditionalism ("To have a better life, should we live like our ancestors?"). Scale ranges from 0-5.

*Index of Respondent's Evaluation of Others' Attitudes*

Items include: community help (C); community collaboration; and envy of hard work. Scale ranges from 0-3. The community collaboration item reads, "When the community tries to realize a project for the advantage of its people, would you say that there is among you much collaboration, fair collaboration, little collaboration, or no collaboration?" This last item was dichotomized with "much" and "fair" collaboration receiving 1 and all other answers 0. The envy-of-hard-work item asks, "If you work very hard, what do the other people here think of you?" Of the alternative answers, 1) they would respect you 2) the work is equal for everyone 3) that it's not worth the trouble and 4) they would envy you, the first three are counted as 1 and the envy response as 0.

# Appendix 5

## DESCRIPTION OF INDICES OF POLITICAL PARTICIPATION, SOCIOECONOMIC STATUS, AND CULTURE-CONTACT

### The Political Participation Indices

Unfortunately, because of the political changes in Peru between 1969 and 1974, the political participation index must be different for the two periods.

A. The 1974 index:

| Items: | Codes: | | |
|---|---|---|---|
| Do you participate in political meetings here? | yes = 2 | sometimes = 1 | no = 0 |
| How many kinds of meetings do you participate in here? (In sierra sites, faena participation is included.)[a] | more than 1 = 2 | 1 = 1 | none = 0 |
| Have you ever been an authority in this place? How many times?[b] | more than 1 = 2 | 1 = 1 | none = 0 |
| Did you attend the last General Assembly? (Or general site meeting in Virú; not asked in Monte.) | | yes = 1 | no = 0 |

[a] Meetings mentioned include Administrative and Vigilance Councils, government talks, Schoolparents' committee, sports and fiesta committees, irrigation committees, etc. as well as all-site general meetings.

[b] Includes top community authorities as well as low-level ones, such as member of specialized committee of cooperative, President of Schoolparents' Association, top union official, and authority of area in community. Patca, Varya, and Agustín encompass "annexes" that have their own leaders and thus score especially high in this "area" category.

Is there anything
that you have tried
to do to resolve a
need or problem of
this place? (Monte
only)                                    yes = 1              no = 0

Gamma item-to-item correlation coefficients were all above .35. The items
were added; each respondent could score from 0 to 7. To gain similar
distributions in the 1974 scale and the 1969 scale, and a reasonable N in
each category, I recoded the index into 5 categories: very low = 0 and 1;
low = 2 and 3; moderate = 4, high = 5, and very high = 6.

B. The 1969 Index:

Items:

1. Do you have a voting card?
2. Do you belong to a political party?
3. Have you ever been worried about any Peruvian problem so as to
   be willing to do something about it?
4. Have you ever been worried about some problem of the village so
   as to be willing to do something to solve it?
5. Are you or have you ever been an official of this village?
6. Outside your home, when something needs to be done that requires the cooperation of several people, who usually organizes it?

Item-to-item gamma intercorrelations were all .69 or above. All items were
dichotomized with 0 = low participation and 1 = high. A respondent could
score from 0 to 6 on the scale. The scale was recoded with 3, 4, 5, 6, = 3
to insure sufficient N at the top.

*The Socioeconomic Status Indices*

Although it would have been possible that the cooperatives encouraged a
decline in socioeconomic inequality among residents and that the fall in
participatory inequality would thus be a statistical artifact, reflecting the
limited variation in the 1974 socioeconomic status, in fact this did not
happen. Socioeconomic inequality continued, although in absolute terms
most members gained (McClintock, 1976: 426-489). Thus, although the
level of variation was similar at the two time-points, scores on the 1974
index were tilted toward the upper level of the scale.

The socioeconomic status index adds indices of economic status and of
education. These two indices are strongly correlated, with zero-order coefficients above .400 in most cases. They are equally weighted in the socioeconomic status scale; at both time points, the maximum score for
economic status was 4 and, for education, 4 also. Descriptions of these
indices follow after the tables providing the scores on the indices.

Scores on Socioeconomic Status Index, 1974 (%)

| | N | 0 | 1 | 2 | 3 | 4 | 5 | 6 | 7 | 8 |
|---|---|---|---|---|---|---|---|---|---|---|
| Cooperatives | 230 | 10 | 27 | 25 | 16 | 8 | 7 | 4 | 2 | 3 |
| Monte | 79 | 22 | 30 | 19 | 19 | 3 | 5 | 0 | 0 | 3 |
| Estrella | 89 | 1 | 17 | 26 | 14 | 16 | 10 | 7 | 6 | 5 |
| Marla | 62 | 7 | 37 | 31 | 15 | 3 | 3 | 5 | 0 | 0 |
| Quasi-control and control | 184 | 8 | 12 | 16 | 18 | 16 | 9 | 8 | 9 | 5 |
| Agustín | 94 | 14 | 19 | 15 | 13 | 17 | 7 | 7 | 3 | 4 |
| Virú | 90 | 2 | 4 | 18 | 23 | 14 | 10 | 8 | 14 | 6 |
| SAIS Communities | 93 | 17 | 32 | 20 | 13 | 7 | 4 | 2 | 1 | 3 |

Scores On Socioeconomic Status Index, 1969 (%)

| | N | 0 | 1 | 2 | 3 | 4 | 5 | 6 | 7 | 8 |
|---|---|---|---|---|---|---|---|---|---|---|
| Haciendas | 177 | 20 | 23 | 20 | 21 | 7 | 5 | 2 | 2 | 2 |
| Monte | 58 | 26 | 24 | 14 | 24 | 3 | 5 | 2 | 0 | 2 |
| Estrella | 79 | 14 | 18 | 18 | 22 | 11 | 8 | 3 | 4 | 3 |
| Marla | 40 | 47 | 40 | 5 | 2 | 7 | 0 | 0 | 0 | 0 |
| Quasi-control and control | 253 | 5 | 15 | 13 | 18 | 17 | 12 | 8 | 7 | 6 |
| Agustín | 153 | 3 | 20 | 19 | 19 | 13 | 8 | 8 | 7 | 2 |
| Virú | 100 | 5 | 11 | 8 | 16 | 20 | 15 | 8 | 7 | 10 |

A. Economic Status Index

The economic status index is somewhat different for 1969 and 1974, for reasons discussed in McClintock (1976: 681). For 1974, the index includes 3 indicators; the highest possible score is 5. The items are:

1.  What is your principal occupation?
    shepherd, domestic servant, temporary worker, worker = 0
    independent farmer, merchant, skilled worker = 1
    student (secondary school or above) and white-collar employee = 2

    Occupation of wife is coded as occupation of husband if she does not earn her own income. This seems justified as the index measures wealth, not education or culture.

2.  In general, this informant is observed to be in which economic position?
    1) one of the richest persons in the community
    2) somewhat richer than average
    3) average
    4) somewhat poorer than average
    5) one of the poorest people in the community

    Coded on a range of 0 to 2, according to the prosperity of the site.

3. Possession of a house with a non-earth floor (brick, cement, or wood) was coded as 1, except in Monte. This item was not asked in Monte; Monte residents' position on the goods ownership scale was substituted with possession of two or more of the relevant items coded as 1.

For 1969, the index includes 2 indicators; the highest possible score is 4. The items are:

1. Do you own a 1) radio 2) sewing machine 3) clock 4) kerosene stove?
        Possession of 0 or 1 item  = 0
        Possession of 2 items      = 1
        Possession of 3 or 4 items = 2

2. Occupation is coded exactly as for the 1974 scale, for scores of 0 to 2.

B. Education Index

The education index is the same for 1969 and 1974, based on one item, "Have you attended school?" It was re-coded as follows:

        One year or less            = 0
        2 to 4 years                = 1
        Primary complete            = 2
        Some secondary              = 3
        Secondary complete or more  = 4

C. The Culture-Contact Index

The index is exactly the same for 1969 and 1974. It includes four items, re-coded as follows:

1. How often do you read the newspaper?
   at least once a week = 1; else = 0
2. How often do you listen to the radio?
   every day = 1; else = 0
3. How often do you travel to Trujillo/Huancayo?
   at least once a week = 1; else = 0
4. Have you lived outside this place for more than a month?
   yes = 1; else = 0

Scale ranges from 0 to 4. It was re-coded with 0 and 1 = 0 (very low); 2 = 1 (low); 3 = 2 (moderate) and 4 = 3 (high). The following distributions resulted:

Scores on Culture-Contact Index, 1974

|  | N | 0 | 1 | 2 | 3 |
|---|---|---|---|---|---|
| Cooperatives | 230 | 23 | 31 | 26 | 20 |
|   Monte | 79 | 33 | 43 | 15 | 9 |
|   Estrella | 89 | 11 | 17 | 37 | 35 |
|   Marla | 62 | 27 | 35 | 24 | 13 |
| Controls | 184 | 13 | 21 | 32 | 34 |
|   Agustín | 94 | 11 | 12 | 32 | 46 |
|   Virú | 90 | 16 | 30 | 32 | 22 |
| SAIS Communities | 93 | 42 | 17 | 33 | 8 |
|   Patca | 48 | 54 | 15 | 24 | 2 |
|   Varya | 45 | 29 | 20 | 38 | 13 |

Scores on Culture-Contact Index, 1969 (%)

|  | N | 0 | 1 | 2 | 3 |
|---|---|---|---|---|---|
| Haciendas |  |  |  |  |  |
|   Monte | 58 | 50 | 21 | 26 | 3 |
|   Estrella | 79 | 20 | 28 | 27 | 25 |
|   Marla | 40 | 36 | 41 | 12 | 11 |
| Controls |  |  |  |  |  |
|   Agustín | 153 | 28 | 20 | 29 | 24 |
|   Virú | 100 | 16 | 25 | 29 | 30 |

# *Appendix 6*

## DERIVATION OF DATA ON SOCIOECONOMIC STATUS OF COUNCIL MEMBERS AND TOP LEADERS

### *Data Sources*

All data are derived from documents and elite interviews in the sites, except population parameters, which derive from the 1974 McClintock survey.

### *Who are Council Members?*

Members of both Administrative Council and Vigilance Council are included; Administrative Council leaders tend to be higher in socioeconomic status. Number in the councils may change over time, although one number is specified in each cooperative statute.

# Appendix 7

AGRARIAN COOPERATIVE MEMBERS IN THE PERUVIAN
ECONOMY

The OIT (1975: 7-33) provides the figures cited below that indicate the
place of agrarian cooperative members in one Peruvian economy.

Income from agriculture was about 15 percent of the gross domestic
product in Peru in 1972, whereas the agricultural work force was approximately 46 percent of the entire work force. Roughly 60 percent of the
entire agricultural income was generated by agrarian reform beneficiaries,
although beneficiaries were less than 25 percent of rural farm families.

On the basis of a study of selected urban and rural areas, it was estimated
that the average income in urban regions was 4.5 times that in rural
regions. It was further estimated that the average income on the rural coast
was 2 times as much as that in the rural highlands. The income difference
between the most prosperous central section of the rural coast and the most
impoverished part of the rural highlands (Cuzco, Puno, Apurímac) was
assessed at 4:1, or $1,072 vs. $280 in 1972.

Average Annual Income for Various
Positions and Regions in Peru, 1972

|  | Dollars | Soles |
|---|---|---|
| Average family, Lima | 2,700 | 118,800 |
| Field worker, agro-industrial sugar cooperative | 2,035 | 89,540 |
| Temporary worker, agro-industrial sugar cooperative | 553 | 24,332 |
| Average family, rural coast | 846 | 37,224 |
| Average family, rural highlands | 392 | 17,248 |
| Average family, poorest areas of rural highlands | 280 | 12,320 |

It is very hard to locate the cooperative members of this study in these
income-distribution figures. My own rough estimate, considering the 1969
wage scales as given in Tables VIII.2 and VIII.3, the approximate benefits
during that period, and inflation rates during 1969-1972, is that the com-
posite Estrella Marla Monte/family had an income somewhat above that of
the "average-family, rural coast"—perhaps, 30 percent above. Comparisons are very difficult, however; in most studies, the benefits to

workers beyond daily base wages are not taken into account, and calculations of numbers of workers per family often vary.

Any comparison between the figures in Table IV.5 for average daily family income in the cooperatives must thus take into consideration these calculation uncertainties as well as the dramatic increases in wages, and particularly, in benefits between 1972 and 1975 for these sites. Figures for daily family income in the research sites in Table IV.5 include such benefits as new housing, new schools, etc. Because of these difficulties in "income" calculation, the best indication of the extent to which the research cooperatives are economically representative of the universe of agrarian cooperatives is the data in Table IV.3 on adjudication debt. It can then be kept in mind that probably over half of Peru's coastal land was adjudicated as cooperatives, and such calculations will help to place agrarian cooperative members in the Peruvian economy.

# Appendix 8

## SURVEY QUESTIONNAIRES

In this appendix, items for both the 1974 questionnaire and the shorter, informal 1975 and 1977 questionnaires are given. The 1974 questionnaire items are *not* listed as they were asked to the respondent. Rather, they are separated on the basis of their inclusion in the 1969 IEP-Cornell survey. Items in the 1969 questionnaire are listed first, and those new to the 1974 version follow. Often, however, an item in the second section followed an item in the first section in the actual interview (e.g., "Has your opinion about trust changed," followed the item about trust-in-people). It must also be remembered that some items included as formal components of the questionnaire were *not* asked in all sites, for one reason or another.

### 1. 1974 Questionnaire

A. *Items in Instituto de Estudios Peruanos and Cornell Survey Used in 1974 Survey*
1. Interviewee's sex
2. How old are you?
3. Where were you born?
4. When did you come here?
5. Have you ever lived outside this place for more than a month?
6. What is your principal occupation?
7. What is your husband's occupation?
8. Are you self-employed or employed by somebody else?
9. Apart from your occupation, do you often engage in another money-making activity?
10. Have you attended school? How many years?
11. How many live children do you have?
12. Do you have or have you had a leadership position?
13. What is the roof of your house made from?
14. What is the floor of your house made from?
15. Do you have a radio in your house?
16. Do you have a sewing machine in your house?
17. Do you have a kerosene or primus stove in your house?
18. Are you a comunero here?
19. Do you belong to a social or sports club?
20. (If applicable) How often do you travel to Trujillo?
21. (If applicable) How often do you travel to Huancayo?

22. How often do you read the newspaper?
23. How often do you listen to the radio?
24. Do you think of moving to another place?
25. Do you think that the patron (before) helps (helped) improve the people's life here a lot; helps (helped) a little; does not (did not) help?
26. To improve life here some say that everybody should get together; that each person should solve his own problems. What do you think?
27. Some have been born to command and others to obey. Do you think this is true, more or less true, false?
28. Some people say that you can trust most people here; others say that you cannot trust most people here. What do you think?
29. We should live like our elders (grandparents) to have a better life. Do you think this is true, more or less true, false?
30. We are now interested in knowing what help you think you can get from other people. Let's suppose that you have a problem. How much help could you get from relatives?
31. How much help could you get from townspeople?
32. How much help could you get from friends?
33. How much help could you get from outsiders?
34. When you have an important problem at home or at work, do you talk to your husband (wife) about it?
35. When solving a family problem, is what your wife (or your husband) says very important, of little importance, of no importance?
36. Suppose the _____ (fill in as appropriate: Town Council, hacienda administration, Administrative Council) of this community wants to do something bad and unfair, could you do something to stop it?
37. Have you worried about a local problem to the point of wanting to do something to solve it?
38. In general, do you prefer to work in collaboration with others, or alone?
39. A man needs to work and two men offer him a job. Here is what the two men were like and tell us for whom you think it would be better for the man to work. The first man is fair and pays a little more than other patrons. But he is strict and insists that his employees work hard and be always on time. He gets angry when an employee takes time off to travel or have fun. The second man pays less but he is not harsh. He understands why an employee would miss work, go on a trip, or have fun for a day or two. When he returns, he almost always continues to employ him, without saying much to him. For which of these men do you think it would be best to work?

40. Suppose you went out to find another job. Which of the following jobs would you prefer? A job where there is always a person to help you with problems that may arise, or a job where you are on your own more?
41. If you worked very hard, what would other people from around here think of you?
42. Is there divisiveness or strife between the people around here?
43. When it comes to cooperating on some project for the community, how well do the people cooperate? Would you say there is much cooperation, some cooperation, little, or none?
44. In your opinion, what do people here need most? What are the most important problems in this community, in your opinion?
45. Five years ago, people here were better off, about the same, or worse off?
46. Would you say that what the government does helps improve conditions in this country? (yes; more or less; no)
47. How long did the interview last?
48. What do you think of the informant's cooperativeness?
49. Did the informant understand the questions?

B. *Items not applied in 1969, only in 1974 Survey*
   1. Part of locality or neighborhood of respondent: close to the town center; fifteen or more minutes on foot from the town center?
   2. (If applicable) When have you spent time outside this place? (Largest place was coded if respondent had spent time in more than one place.)
   3. (If applicable) Why are you thinking of moving to another place?
   4. (If applicable) Where are you thinking of moving?
   5. In your past life, what do you remember most?
   6. How does a father show his love for his children?
   7. How does a woman show her love for her children?
   8. Some people say:
      a. that you can trust most people
      b. others say you can't trust
      Four years ago, what was your opinion on this matter?
      a. same or
      b. different
   9. (If applicable) Four years ago you thought one couldn't trust people and now you think one can. Why did you change your mind?
   10. (If applicable) Four years ago you thought one could trust people and now you think one can't. Why did you change your mind?

11. To improve life here some say that everybody ought to get together and others say each person should solve his own problems. Four years ago, what was your opinion on this matter?
    a. same or
    b. different

12. (If applicable) Four years ago you thought that each person should solve his own problem and now you think they ought to get together. Why did you change your mind?

13. (If applicable) Four years ago you thought that everybody ought to get together and now you think that each person should solve his own problems. Why did you change your mind?

14. Some are born to command and others to obey. Four years ago, what was your opinion on this subject?
    a. same or
    b. different

15. (If applicable) Four years ago, you thought that the sentence "some are born to command and others to obey" was false and now you think it's true. Why have you changed your mind?

16. (If applicable) Four years ago you thought that some were born to command and others to obey, and now you don't think so. Why did you change your mind?

17. Are you a member of a cooperative enterprise here?

18. Are you a member of a Service Cooperative?

19. (If housewife) Is your husband a member of the cooperative?

20. How often have you had a leadership position?

21. Do you regularly participate in community faenas?

22. Why don't you participate? (If answer to 21 was no)

23. Did you participate in the last meeting of _____ (specify date of the last General Assembly in the CAP or an important meeting after September 1973 in Virú [i.e. in the last 2½ months].

24. Do you regularly participate in meetings here?

25. In what type of meetings do you participate?

26. Why don't you participate in meetings here?

27. Have you been to the cooperative for SAIS movies or talks?

28. (If applicable) You have attended a (some) talk(s) at the CAP/SAIS. What was the subject matter of the talk(s)?

29. Have you attended talks given by SINAMOS or other state agencies?

30. (If applicable) You have attended a (some) talk(s) given by a state agency. What was the subject matter of the talk?

31. Do you have very close friends in nearby communities with whom you help each other out?

32. (If applicable) Generally speaking, you prefer working in cooperation with others. Why?

33. (If applicable) Generally speaking, you prefer working alone. Why?

34. Do you feel that you can influence in decisions connected with your work in _____ (interviewer inserts type of work)?

35. Imagine two sons. One is very intelligent and ambitious and he goes to Lima and puts up a shop and does well, he makes a lot of money. And he remembers you. But he is a busy man, having few friends. The other son stays here and doesn't make a lot of money, but he has friends and is always at ease. Which of the two sons would you prefer?

36. Some people say that to do a good job, it's very important that our chiefs tell us exactly what to do and how to do it. Other people say that we can usually do our job efficiently without instructions from our chiefs. What do you think?

37. Do you work harder now than before the Agrarian Reform, or not as hard?

38. (If applicable) Why do you work harder now than you did before the Agrarian Reform?

39. (If applicable) Why don't you work as hard as you did before the Agrarian Reform?

40. (If applicable) You said that nothing could be done or nothing would succeed if the Administrative Council tried to do something bad or unfair. Does that mean that there is something that could be done, but it would not succeed and would not be worth it?

41. (If applicable) What would you do to stop a bad or unfair step taken by the Administrative Council, would that be that successful?

42. (If applicable) Why is there a lot of conflict here?

43. (If applicable) Why is there little divisiveness or conflict between the people here?

44. We'll describe two leaders with opposite characteristics. We'd like you to tell us whom you'd prefer. The first leader makes everybody here participate in important decisions. He wants all the members to agree to a decision. Because of this there are many delays. The second leader does not make people participate much; he makes decisions without delays. Which leader would you prefer?

45. Here we have two leaders with opposite characteristics. The first leader says that this place is richer than neighboring ones and that we should sacrifice ourselves a little so that other places can develop. The second leader says that this place isn't that rich and that the most important thing is to continue to improve life here. Which leader would you prefer?

46. On an election to the Administrative Council, suppose you could

choose between two very different candidates. The first candidate has very good connections, but he prefers to help his friends, not you all. The second candidate wants to help all of the community, but he has no connections. Which of the two would you prefer?

47. Suppose you all lived very close to a great mining center. The mines are on strike and the company which owns the mine offered you *good salaries* to replace the striking miners. Should the peasants work in the mine, stay out of the conflict, or do something to help the striking miners?

48. In a big enterprise, which we can call "Posoconi," suppose the temporary workers struck to become members. What should the members do? (Probe: under what conditions should temporary workers be admitted to the cooperative?)

49. If you and other cooperatives or communities or former haciendas of the SAIS were faced with a common problem, how would you protest?
    a. each place or cooperative on its own
    b. through one organization, all together
    c. through one organization for the communities and another for the haciendas?

50. In the cooperative, as you know, part of the profits are directed to funds and re-investment for the common use and another part goes directly for the members' own private use. Do you think it would be better if more money were for the common use or if more money went to the members for their own use?

51. Do you feel that you participate in the important decisions of this community?

52. Before the Agrarian Reform, were there more or less meetings here?

53. Before the Agrarian Reform, were communal faenas here more or less frequent than now?

54. (If applicable) You think people here were better off five years ago. Why?

55. (If applicable) You think people were worse off five years ago. Why?

56. Do you think that the SAIS helps improve conditions here a lot, helps a little, doesn't help, or helps other places (the center, not the surrounding places)?

57. (If applicable) You think that the SAIS helps a lot or a bit. Why?

58. Is the SAIS doing some bad things? What?

59. Do you think that the cooperative helps improve life here a lot, helps a little, or doesn't help?

60. (If applicable) You think that the cooperative helps a lot or a bit. Why?

61. (If applicable) You think that the cooperative doesn't help. Why?
62. Do you think that the government does some bad things? What?
63. Do you think that the government does some good things? What?
64. Before the Agrarian Reform, were fiestas held more or less frequently than now?
65. Some people say that it's fairer when everybody has the same income because they all work hard. Others say that it's fairer if there are income differences because some jobs require more knowledge than others. What do you think?
66. Do you think that this place needs services? What services are lacking?
67. Three or four years ago, was there less or more cooperation between the people here?
68. Who makes the important decisions here? For example, are decisions made by
    a. some people, one or two or three leaders
    b. the councillors
    c. the General Assembly
    d. everybody here
    e. the government

(Marked by Interviewer)

69. Evaluation of person's appearance
70. Evaluation of person's house
71. In general, this informant is among the
    a. richest in the community
    b. somewhat richer
    c. average
    d. somewhat poorer
    e. among the poorest
    f. cannot evaluate

*2. 1975 Questionnaire*

1. Informant's sex
2. What is your principal occupation?
3. Have you attended school? How many years?
4. Economic status (Interviewer's evaluation)
5. Are you a member of the cooperative?
6. Some people say that you can trust most people here; others say that you can't trust most people here. What do you think?
    a. trust or
    b. don't trust?

Why can or can't you trust? Whom can you trust? With what sort of things can you trust others? With what can't you trust others?

7. When you have a problem, do you ask other townspeople outside your family for help? Before the Agrarian Reform, did you ask other townspeople for help? Why do you now do it more, or less, frequently?

8. Some say that what's good for the community is good for me. Others say that what's good for the community maybe isn't good for me. What do you think? Why?

9. Here we have two leaders with opposite characteristics. We would like you to tell us which of the two leaders you would prefer. The first leader says that this place is richer than nearby places and that we have to sacrifice a little so that these other places can develop. The second leader says that this place isn't so rich and that the most important thing is to continue to improve life here. Which leader would you prefer?

10. Let's suppose that the temporary workers of a large enterprise, which we can call "Posoconi," went on strike to become members. What should the members do? (Probe: under what conditions should temporary workers be admitted to the cooperative?)

11. Do you think that you are a member of a social class?

12. Do you take part in political meetings here?

13. Why do you (or don't you) participate?

14. How do you make complaints here? Why are complaints made? Are they made more frequently than before the Agrarian Reform?

15. Have you been a member of a specialized committee here? (If yes) Did you enjoy the experience? What did you do? Did you learn something?

16. Have you been a member of a Council here? (If yes) Did you enjoy the experience? What did you do? Did you learn something?

17. Was there more or less collaboration between the people here three or four years ago? Why? How is it different (or the same) now?

18. Who makes the important decisions here? For example, are decisions taken by
    a. a few persons, one or two or three leaders
    b. the Councils
    c. the General Assembly
    d. all the people here
    e. the government
    f. other

19. Do you think that the cooperative:
    a. helps improve conditions here a lot

b. helps a little

c. doesn't help

Why? What do you like most about the cooperative? What don't you like in the cooperative?

20. There is a leader who is very well trained and has good connections in the city, but he is very busy and can't do that much. There's another leader who isn't trained that well, but he is going to work hard for the community, for all the community. What sort of leader do you think is better? Why? Which is the best kind of leader?

21. Why aren't poor workers chosen here? Can anybody become President of the Administrative Council?

22. What should relations between officials and the rest of the people be like?

23. In general do you think that the government helps improve conditions in Peru?

a. yes

b. more or less

c. no

24. What do you like most about what's happening politically in the country? What do you like least?

25. What's the best sort of government? Would you like to have elections as before? What did you like about the government before? What didn't you like?

## 3. 1977 Questionnaire

There were a few slight variations in wording from the highlands questionnaire to the coastal one. They are indicated if they are of any significance.

1. Informant's sex

2. What is your principal occupation?

3. Have you attended school? How many years?

4. Economic status (Interviewer's evaluation)

5. Are there meetings here? How often?

6. Do you participate in the meetings? Always, most of the time, every so often, or never or almost never?

7. Why do you participate (or not participate) in the meetings? Do you think that they're worth it?

8. Since 1970 (1975 in the highland communities) do you think that there have been any changes in the system of production, or the system of marketing? (If yes) What kind of changes?

9. Do you think that production and marketing are better or worse now? Why?

10. Do you think that there is more or less collaboration now with other ex-haciendas (and communities, in the highlands) than there was in 1970? Why?

11. Have you heard of the CNA? (If yes) Do you think that the CNA is an organization that does positive things in the country? Why, or why not?

12. Have you heard of the Agrarian League? (If yes) Do you think that the Agrarian League is an organization that does positive things in the country? Why, or why not?

13. Do you think that the Cooperative (or the SAIS) helps to improve the conditions of life here? Why do you think this way?

14. Do you think that the government helps to improve the conditions of life here? Why? What do you think the government ought to do to help the people here?

15. What do you think of the government of Morales Bermúdez in comparison to that of Velasco? Why?

16. Research site

*Questions Asked in Coastal Cooperatives Only*

17. Has anything been done here to help the temporary workers? (If yes) What? Why has something been done (or not been done)?

18. Do you think that you are a member of a social class? Why? (Or why not?)

19. Have you been a member of a specialized committee here? Have you been a member of a Council here? (If yes to either question) Did you like the experience? What did you do?

20. Who makes the important decisions here? For example, are the decisions made by 1) a few people, one or two or three leaders 2) the Councils 3) the General Assembly 4) all the people 5) the government 6) the gerente 7) the Councils and the General Assembly 8) the Councils and/or the General Assembly and the gerente and/or the Government.

*Questions Asked in Estrella Only*

21. What do you think now of the sugar cane production? Was the decision to produce sugar cane a good one or not?

22. What do you think of Ing. Prado (the director)? What do you like about him, and what don't you like about him?

*Questions Asked in Patca, Varya, and Rachius Only*

23. Why do you think the SAIS was intervened?

# Bibliography

Abusada-Salah, Roberto
  1977 "Industrialization Policies in Peru, 1970-1976." Paper presented at the Latin American Studies Association Meeting, Houston, November, 2-5.
Acheson, James A.
  1972 "Limited Good or Limited Goods? Response to Economic Opportunity in a Tarascan Pueblo," *American Anthropologist, 74* (October), 1152-1169.
Adams, Richard N.
  1959 *A Community in the Andes: Problems and Progress in Muquiyauyo.* Seattle: University of Washington Press.
Adie, Robert F.
  1970 "Cooperation, Co-optation, and Conflict in Mexican Peasant Organizations," *Inter-American Economic Affairs, 24* (Winter), 3-25.
Adizes, Ichak
  1971 *Industrial Democracy: Yugoslav Style.* New York: Free Press.
Adizes, Ichak, and Elisabeth Mann Borgese, eds.
  1975 *Self-Management: New Dimensions to Democracy.* Santa Barbara, Calif., and London: Clio Press.
Agut, James R.
  1975 "The 'Peruvian Revolution' and Catholic Corporatism: Armed Forces Rule Since 1968." Unpublished Ph.D. dissertation, University of Miami.
Alberti, Giorgio
  1974 *Poder y conflicto social en el valle del Mantaro.* Lima: Instituto de Estudios Peruanos.
Alberti, Giorgio, and Julio Cotler
  1972 "La Reforma Agraria en las Haciendas Azucareras." Unpublished paper: Instituto de Estudios Peruanos, Lima.
Alberti, Giorgio, and Enrique Mayer, eds.
  1974 *Reciprocidad e Intercambio en los Andes peruanos.* Lima: Instituto de Estudios Peruanos.
Alberti, Giorgio, Jorge Santistevan, and Luis Pásara, eds.
  1977 *Estado y Clase: La Comunidad Industrial en el Peru.* Lima: Instituto de Estudios Peruanos.
Alderson-Smith, Gavin
  1973 "Peasant Response to Cooperativization under Agrarian Reform in the Communities of the Peruvian Sierra." Paper presented at the Nineteenth International Congress of Anthropological and Ethnological Sciences, Chicago, August 28-31.

Alexander, Robert J.
 1974  *Agrarian Reform in Latin America.* New York: Macmillan.
Alfara, Julio, and Teresa Oré
 1974  "El Desarrollo del Capitalismo en la Convención y los Nuevos
       Movimientos Politicos de Campesinos con Tierra." Unpublished
       B.A. thesis, Universidad Católica, Lima.
Almond, Gabriel A., and Sidney Verba
 1965  *The Civic Culture.* Boston: Little, Brown.
Ames, Barry
 1970  "Bases of Support for Mexico's Dominant Party," *American Politi-
       cal Science Review, 64* (March), 153-167.
Anderson, Bo, and James D. Cockroft
 1966  "Control and Co-optation in Mexican Politics," *International
       Journal of Comparative Sociology, 7* (March), 2-28.
Aramburu, Carlos
 1973  *SAIS Cahuide.* Lima: CENCIRA.
Arora, Phyllis
 1967  "Patterns of Political Response in Indian Peasant Society," *Western
       Political Quarterly, 20* (September), 645-659.
Ashford, Douglas E.
 1969  "Attitudinal Change and Modernization," pp. 147-188 in
       Chandler Morse et al. (eds.), *Modernization by Design.* Ithaca: Cor-
       nell University Press.
Astiz, Carlos A.
 1969  *Pressure Groups and Power Elites in Peruvian Politics.* Ithaca: Cornell
       University Press.
Astiz, Carlos A., and Jose Z. García
 1972  "The Peruvian Military: Achievement Orientation, Training, and
       Political Tendencies," *Western Political Quarterly, 25* (December),
       667-685.
Bachrach, Peter
 1967  *The Theory of Democratic Elitism: A Critique.* Boston: Little, Brown.
Bamat, Thomas
 1977  "Relative State Autonomy and Capitalism in Brazil and Peru,"
       *The Insurgent Sociologist, 7* (Spring), 74-84.
Banfield, Edward G.
 1958  *The Moral Basis of a Backward Society.* New York: The Free Press.
Barker, Jonathan S.
 1974  "Ujamaa in Cash-Crop Areas of Tanzania: Some Problems and
       Reflections," *Journal of African Studies, 1* (Winter), 441-463.
Barnard, Alan, ed.
 1962  *The Simple Fleece: Studies in the Australian Wool Industry.* New York:
       Cambridge University Press.
Barraclough, Solon
 1973  *Agrarian Structure in Latin America.* Lexington, Mass.: D.C. Heath.

1975 "Major Economic Problems Affecting Rural Development in Chile During the Allende Administration." Paper presented at the Second International Conference on Self-management, Cornell University, Ithaca, New York, June 6-8.

Barraclough, Solon L., and Arthur L. Domike
1970 "Agrarian Structure in Seven Latin American Countries," pp. 41-97 in Stavenhagen (1970).

Barraclough, Solon, and José Antonio Fernández
1974 *Diagnóstico de la Reforma Agraria Chilena.* Mexico, D.F.: Siglo Veintiuno Editoriales.

Bates, Robert H.
1976 *Rural Responses to Industrialization: A Study of Village Zambia.* New Haven. Yale University Press.
1978 "The Issue Basis of Rural Politics in Africa," *Comparative Politics, 10* (April), 345-360.

Bayer, David L.
1975 *Reforma Agraria Peruana: Descapitalización Del Minifundio Y Formación De La Burguesía Rural.* Lima: Centro de Investigaciones Socio-Económicas.

Béjar, Hector
1976 *La Revolución en la Trampa.* Lima: Ediciones Socialismo y Participación.

Bell, Williams S.
1977 "Unequal Redistribution: Post Agrarian Reform Differentiation in Coastal Peru." Discussion paper, Peasants Seminar, Centre of International and Area Studies, University of London.

Berger, Suzanne
1972 *Peasants Against Politics: Rural Organization in Brittany, 1911-1967.* Cambridge: Harvard University Press.

Bernstein, Paul
1974 "Run Your Own Business: Worker Owned Plywood Firms," *Working Papers, 2* (Summer), 24-34.

Bernstein, Thomas P.
1977 *Up to the Mountains and Down to the Villages: The Transfer of Youth from Urban to Rural China.* New Haven: Yale University Press.

Bienen, Henry
1967 *Tanzania: Party Transformation and Economic Development.* Princeton: Princeton University Press.

Blair, Thomas L.
1970 *The Land to Those Who Work It: Algeria's Experiment in Workers' Management.* Garden City: Doubleday Anchor.

Blanco, Hugo
1972 *Land or Death: The Peasant Struggle in Peru.* New York: Pathfinder Press.

Blau, Peter M.
1964 *Exchange and Power in Social Life.* New York: Wiley.

Blue, Richard N., and James M. Weaver
    1977 "A Critical Assessment of the Tanzanian Model of Development." Development Studies Program, Agency for International Development, Occasional Paper #1.

Blumberg, Paul
    1969 *Industrial Democracy.* New York: Schocken Books.

Bonachea, Rolando E., and Nelson P. Valdes, eds.
    1972 *Cuba in Revolution.* Garden City, New York: Doubleday Anchor.

Borgese, Elisabeth Mann
    1975 "Introduction: The Promise of Self-Management," pp. xix-xxviii in Adizes and Borgese (1975).

Bourque, Susan C.
    1971 *Cholification and the Campesino: Three Peasant Organizations and the Process of Social Change in Peru.* Ithaca, N.Y.: Latin American Studies Program, Cornell University.

Bourque, Susan C., and David Scott Palmer
    1975 "Transforming the Rural Sector: Government Policy and Peasant Response," pp. 179-219 in Lowenthal (1975).

Bourque, Susan C., and Kay Warren
    1978 "Political Participation and the Revolution: Lessons from Rural Peru." Paper presented at the Conference on "The Peruvian Experiment Reconsidered," October 1978.

Bourricaud, Francois
    1970 *Power and Society in Contemporary Peru.* New York: Praeger.

Brower, Michael
    1971 "Voting Patterns in Recent Colombia Presidential Elections." Unpublished paper, Harvard Center for International Affairs, Harvard University.

Buchler, Peter
    1975 *Agrarian Cooperatives in Peru.* Berne and Stuttgart: Paul Haupt.

Burke, Melvin, and James M. Malloy
    1974 "From National Populism to National Corporatism: The Case of Bolivia (1952-1970)," *Studies in Comparative International Development, 9* (Spring), 49-73.

Bryan, Derek
    1975 "Changing Social Ethics in Contemporary China," pp. 53-61 in William A. Robson and Bemard Crick (eds.), *China in Transition.* Beverly Hills: Sage Contemporary Social Science Issues.

Byrd, Barbara
    1975 "A Participatory Strategy for Nation-Building in the Third World: The Case of Yugoslavia." Paper presented at the Second International Conference on Self-Management, Ithaca, June 6-8.

Caballero, José Mariá
    1976 "Reforma y Reestructuración Agraria en el Perú." Working Paper, Department of Economics, Catholic University in Peru.

Caballero, José Mariá, and Manuel A. Tello
 1976  "Problemas Post-Reforma Agraria en Cajamarca y La Libertad."
   Lima: Centro Peruano de Estudios Sociales (CEPES).
Cabieses, Hugo, and Carlos Otero
 1977  *Economía Peruana: Un Ensayo de Interpretación.* Lima: DESCO.
Cárdenas, Gerardo
 1973  "La Nueva Estructura Agraria," *Participación, 2* (August), 26-32.
Caycho, Hernán
 1977  *Las SAIS de la Sierra Central.* Lima: Escuela de Administración de
   Negocios (ESAN).
Caycho, Hernán and Carlos Aramburu
 1973  *Estudio Comparado Entre Dos SAIS de la Sierra Central.* Lima:
   CENCIRA.
Cell, Charles P.
 1977  *Revolution at Work: Mobilization Campaigns in China.* New York:
   Academic Press.
CENCIRA (Center for Capacitación and Research on the Agrarian
   Reform)
 1973a *Cooperativa Agraria de Producción [Huanca] Ltda: Manual De
   Organización y Funciones.* Lima.
 1973b "Informe Del Primer Conversatorio de Dirigentes Campesinos."
   Lima.
 1975a *Los Comités de Educación de las Empresas Campesinas del Valle de
   Cañete.* Lima: Dirección de Investigación.
 1975b *Comercialización de Productos Agrícolas.* Lima: Dirección de
   Investigación.
 1975c "Análisis de las Actividades de Capacitación del CENCIRA."
   Lima.
Centro de Estudios de Participación Popular
 1974-1975 *Informes* (on various cooperatives). Lima: SINAMOS.
Cevallos, T. C.
 1965  *Informe Sobre Chawaytiri.* Lima: Instituto de Estudios Peruanos.
Chaplin, David
 1968  "Peru's Postponed Revolution," *World Politics, 20* (April),
   393-420.
Chávez, Dennis, and Pedro Paredes
 1970  "El Valle de Virú." Unpublished paper, Lima: Instituto de Estudios Peruanos.
Chinchilla, Norma Stoltz, and Marvin Sternberg
 1974  "The Agrarian Reform and Compesino Consciousness," *Latin
   American Perspectives, 1* (Summer), 106-128.
Chirinos Almanza, Alfonso
 1976  "Percepción del Campesinado y los Cambios en el Sector Rural
   del Perú." Lima: Centro de Investigaciones Socioeconómicas
   (CISE), Universidad Nacional Agraria.

Chonchol, Jacques
   1970 "Eight Fundamental Conditions of Agrarian Reform in Latin
        America," pp. 159-172 in Stavenhagen (1970).
Citrin, Jack
   1974 "Comment: The Political Relevance of Trust in Government,"
        *The American Political Science Review, 68* (September), 973-988.
Clark, Martin
   1977 *Antonio Gramsci and the Revolution That Failed.* New Haven: Yale
        University Press.
Cleaves, Peter S.
   1976a "Implementation of the Agrarian and Educational Reforms in
         Peru." Paper presented at the conference on "Implementation in
         Latin America's Public Sector: Translating Polity into Reality," at
         the University of Texas at Austin.
   1976b "Managing the Agrarian Cooperatives." Unpublished paper,
         Department of Political Science, Yale University.
   1977 "Policymaking in Peru from 1968." Unpublished Manuscript,
        Yale University.
Cleaves, Peter S. and Martin J. Scurrah
   1976 "State-Society Relations and Bureaucratic Behavior in Peru."
        S.I.C.A. Series Paper Number 6, Department of Public Adminis-
        tration, California State University, Hayward.
   1978 *Agriculture, Bureaucracy and Military Government in Peru.* Unpub-
        lished manuscript. (Cornell University Press, forthcoming.)
Clegg, Hugh
   1960 *A New Approach to Industrial Democracy.* London: Blackwell.
Cliffe, Lionel, and John S. Saul, eds.
   1972 *An Interdisciplinary Reader of Socialism in Tanzania.* Vol. I. Dar es
        Salaam: East African Publishing House.
   1973 *An Interdisciplinary Reader of Socialism in Tanzania.* Vol. II. Dar es
        Salaam: East African Publishing House.
CNA (National Agrarian Confederation)
   1974 *Congreso de Instalación de la Confederación Nacional Agraria.* Lima.
   1975 *Plan de Trabajo de la Confederación Nacional Agraria 1975-76.* Lima.
Collier, David
   1975 "Squatter Settlements and Policy Innovation in Peru," pp.
        128-178 in Lowenthal (1975).
   1976 *Squatters and Oligarchs: Authoritarian Rule and Policy Change In
        Peru.* Baltimore: Johns Hopkins University Press.
Collier, David, and Ruth Berins Collier
   1977 "Who Does What, to Whom, and How: Toward a Comparative
        Analysis of Latin American Corporatism," pp. 489-512 in Malloy
        (1977).
Comisso, Ellen
   1975 "The Role of the Yugoslav League of Communists at the Grass
        Roots Level and Recruitment of Blue Collar Workers." Paper

presented at the Second International Conference on Self-Management, Ithaca, New York, June 6-8.
1977 "Workers' Control Between Plan and Market." Draft, Ph.D. Dissertation, Yale University.

Cornelius, Wayne A.
1973 "Political Learning among the Migrant Poor: The Impact of Residential Context," *Sage Professional Papers in Comparative Politics,* Vol. 3, No. 01-037.
1975 *Politics and the Migrant Poor in Mexico City.* Stanford, Calif.: Stanford University Press.

Cotler, Julio
1969 "Actuales Pautas de Cambio en la Sociedad Rural del Perú," pp. 60-79, in José Matos Mar and William F. Whyte (eds.), *Dominación y Cambios en el Perú Rural.* Lima: Instituto de Estudios Peruanos.
1970a "Traditional Haciendas and Communities in a Context of Political Mobilization in Peru," pp. 533-558, in Stavenhagen (1970).
1970b "The Mechanics of Internal Domination and Social Change in Peru," pp. 407-444, in Horowitz (1970).
1970c "Political Crisis and Military Populism in Peru," *Studies in Comparative Internal Development, 6,* 95-113.
1972 "Bases del Corporativismo en el Perú," *Sociedad y Política, 1* (October), 3-11.
1975 "The New Mode of Political Domination in Peru," pp. 44-78, in Lowenthal (1975).
1978 *Clases, Estado Y Nación en el Perú.* Lima: Instituto de Estudios Peruanos.

Cotler, Julio, and Felipe Portocarrero
1969 "Peru: Peasant Organizations," pp. 297-322 in Henry A. Landsberger (ed.), *Latin American Peasant Movements.* Ithaca, N.Y.: Cornell University Press.

Craig, Wesley W., Jr.
1969 "Peru: The Peasant Movement of La Convención," pp. 274-296 in Landsberger (1969).

Delgado, Carlos
1973 *Testimonio de Lucha.* Lima: Biblioteca Peruana.

Delgado, Oscar
1972 "La Organización de los Campesinos y el Sistema Político," *Apuntes,* No. 25 (July), 84-106.

Denitch, Bogdan Denis
1976 *The Legitimation of a Revolution: The Yugoslav Case.* New Haven: Yale University Press.

DESCO (Centro de Estudios y Promoción del Desarrollo)
1977 *Estado y Política Agraria.* Lima.

Deustua, Luis
1979 "El Proceso de la Reforma Agraria Peruana: Un Intento de Evaluación," *Cuadernos Agrarios,* II (November), 39-48.

Dew, Edward
  1969  *Politics in the Altiplano: The Dynamics of Change in Rural Peru.*
        Austin: University of Texas Press.
de Man, Henrik
  1929  *Joy in Work.* London: George Allen and Unwin Ltd.
  1979  *A Documentary Study of Henrik de Man, Socialist Critic of Marxism.*
        Princeton: Princeton University Press.
de Zutter, Pierre
  1975  *Campesinado y Revolución.* Lima: Instituto Nacional de Cultura.
Dietz, Henry Avery
  1975  *"Becoming a Poblador: Political Adjustment to the Urban Environment
        in Lima, Peru."* Unpublished Ph.D. dissertation, Stanford Uni-
        versity.
  1978  "Bureaucrat-Client Interactions as Politics: Perceptions and
        Evaluations by the Urban Poor in Lima, Peru." Paper presented
        at the American Political Science Association Meeting, New York
        City, August 31-September 3.
  1980  *Poverty and Problem-Solving under Military Rule: The Urban Poor in
        Lima, Peru.* Austin, Texas: Institute of Latin American Studies
        Monograph Series.
Dietz, Henry A., and David Scott Palmer
  1978  "Citizen Participation under Military Rule," pp. 172-188 in John
        Booth and Mitchell Seligson (eds.), *Political Participation in Latin
        America.* New York: Holmes and Meier.
Dobyns, Henry F., Paul L. Doughty, and Harold D. Lasswell
  1971  *Peasants, Power and Applied Social Change: Vicos as a Model.* Beverly
        Hills, California: Sage Publications.
Domínguez, Jorge I.
  1976a "Political Culture in Cuba: Continuity and Change." Paper Pre-
        sented at the Latin American Studies Association, Sixth National
        Meeting, Atlanta, March.
  1976b "Cuba's Maturing Revolution," *Problems of Communism, 25*
        (January-February), 68-73.
  1976c "Revolutionary Values and Development Performance: China,
        Cuba, and the Soviet Union," pp. 20-54 in Harold Lasswell,
        Daniel Lerner, and John Montgomery (eds.), *Values and Develop-
        ment: Appraising Asian Experience.* Cambridge, Mass.: M.I.T. Press.
Domínguez, Jorge I. and Christopher Mitchell
  1977  "The Roads Not Taken: Institutionalization and Political Parties
        in Cuba and Bolivia," *Comparative Politics, 9* (January), 173-196.
Dorner, Peter, ed.
  1971  *Land Reform in Latin America.* Madison, Wisconsin: Land Eco-
        nomics, University of Wisconsin.
Dorner, Peter, and Don Kanel
  1971  "The Economic Case for Land Reform," pp. 39-56 in Dorner
        (1971).

Doughty, Paul L.
1971 "Human Relations: Affection, Rectitude and Respect," pp. 83-113 in Dobyns et al. (1971).
Durham, Kathleen Foote
1977 "Expansion of Agricultural Settlement in the Peruvian Rainforest: The Role of the Market and the Role of the State." Paper presented at the Joint Meeting of the Latin American Studies Association and the African Studies Association, Houston, November 2-5.
Eckstein, Shlomo
1970 "Collective Farming in Mexico," pp. 271-300 in Stavenhagen (1970).
Eguren López, Fernando
1975 *Reforma Agraria, Cooperativización, y Lucha Campesina.* Lima: DESCO.
1977 "Política Agraria y Estructura Agraria," pp. 217-256 in DESCO (1977).
Einaudi, Luigi R.
1972 "Revolution from Within? Military Rule in Peru Since 1968." Unpublished paper, the Rand Corporation.
Elías Minaya, José F.
1966 "El Valle de Virú." Unpublished paper, Lima: Instituto de Estudios Peruanos.
1969a "Las Haciendas y el Pueblo de Virú." Unpublished paper, Lima: Instituto de Estudios Peruanos.
1969b "Estudio Socio-Económico de la Hacienda [. . .]" Unpublished paper, Lima: Instituto de Estudios Peruanos.
1973 "Problemática Funcional de la Empresa y Alternativas para su Consolidación Económico-Social." Trujillo: Ministry of Agriculture.
Erasmus, Charles J.
1968 "Community Development and the Encogido Syndrome,"*Human Organization, 27* (Spring), 65-74.
Espinosa, Juan G., and Andrew S. Zimbalist
1978 *Economic Democracy: Workers' Participation in Chilean Industry 1970-1973.* New York: Academic Press.
Fagen, Richard R.
1969 *The Transformation of Political Culture in Cuba.* Stanford, Calif.: Stanford University Press.
1972a "Mass Mobilization in Cuba: the Symbolism of Struggle," pp. 201-224 in Bonachea and Valdes (1972).
1972b "Continuities in Cuban Revolutionary Politics," *Monthly Review, 23* (April), 24-48.
Fagen, Richard R., and William S. Tuohy
1972 *Politics and Privilege in a Mexican City.* Stanford, Calif.: Stanford University Press.

Feder, Ernest
 1971  *The Rape of the Peasantry.* Garden City, N.Y.: Anchor Books.
Feldman, Rayah
 1975  "Rural Social Differentiation and Political Goals in Tanzania," pp.
    154-182 in Ivar Oxaal, Tony Barnett, and David Booth (eds.),
    *Beyond the Sociology of Development: Economy and Society in Latin
    America and Africa.* London: Routledge and Kegan Paul.
Ferner, Anthony
 1978  "A New Development Model for Peru? Anomalies and Readjust-
    ments," *Bulletin of the Society for Latin American Studies, 28* (April),
    42-63.
Finucane, James R.
 1974  *Rural Development and Bureaucracy in Tanzania: The Case of Mwanza
    Region.* New York: Africana Publishing Corporation.
Fioravanti, Eduardo
 1974  *Latifundio y Sindicalismo Agrario en el Perú.* Lima: Instituto de Estu-
    dios Peruanos.
Fishel, John T.
 1974  "Attitudes of Peruvian Highland Village Leaders toward Military
    Intervention." Paper prepared for presentation at meetings of
    the Latin American Studies Association, San Francisco, Calif.,
    November 14-16.
Fitzgerald, E.V.K.
 1976  *The State and Economic Development: Peru Since 1968.* London:
    Cambridge University Press.
Flores, Edmundo
 1967  "On Financing Land Reform: A Mexican Casebook," *Studies in
    Comparative International Development,* Vol. III, No. 6, 115-121.
Foster, George M.
 1965  "Peasant Society and the Image of Limited Good," *American An-
    thropologist, 67* (April), 293-315.
 1967  "Introduction: What is a Peasant?", pp. 2-14 in Jack M. Potter et
    al. (eds.), *Peasant Society: A Reader.* Boston: Little, Brown.
Frey, Frederick W.
 1970  "Summary Description and Comparison of Power Structures."
    Unpublished paper, Massachusetts Institute of Technology.
Fromm, Erich, and Michael Maccoby
 1970  *Social Character in a Mexican Village.* Englewood Cliffs, N.J.:
    Prentice-Hall.
Gaitzsch, Andrea Christana
 1974  "The Meaning of the Agrarian Reform of 1969 for the In-
    dian Peasant Communities of the Peruvian Sierra." Unpub-
    lished Ph.D. dissertation, Faculty of the University of Cologne,
    Germany.
Gall, Norman
 1971  "Peru: The Master is Dead," *Dissent* (June), 281-320.

Garson, G. David
  1973  "The Politics of Workers' Control: A Review Essay," pp. 469-489 in Gerry Hunnius et al. (1973).
  1974  *On Democratic Administration and Socialist Self-Management: A Comparative Survey Emphasizing the Yugoslav Experience,* Beverly Hills, Calif.: A Sage Professional Paper.
Garson, G. David (ed.)
  1977  *Worker Self-Management in Industry: The West European Experience.* New York: Praeger Special Studies.
Garson, G. David, and Michael P. Smith, eds.
  1976  *Organizational Democracy: Participation and Self-Management.* Beverly Hills: Sage.
Gayn, Mark
  1974  "From the Village," *Problems of Communism,* 23 (September-October), 1-16.
Gazmuri, Jaime
  1970  *Asentamientos Campesinos: Una Evaluación de los Primeros Resultados de la Reforma Agraria en Chile.* Buenos Aires: Companía Impresora Argentina, Edición Torquel.
Geertz, Clifford
  1973  *The Interpretation of Cultures.* New York: Basic Books.
Gilbert, Dennis
  1977  *The Oligarchy and the Old Regime in Peru.* Ithaca, New York: Cornell University Latin American Studies Program Dissertation Series.
Gilhodes, Pierre
  1970  "Agrarian Struggles in Colombia," pp. 407-452, in Stavenhagen (1970).
Gitlitz, John S.
  1975  "Hacienda, Comunidad, and Peasant Protest in Northern Peru." Unpublished Ph.D. dissertation, University of North Carolina.
Goldrich, Daniel, Raymond B. Pratt, and C. R. Schuller
  1970  "The Political Integration of Lower-Class Urban Settlements in Chile and Peru," pp. 175-214 in Horowitz (1970).
Gomez, Rudolf
  1969  *The Peruvian Administrative System.* Boulder: The University of Colorado.
Gonzalez, Edward
  1974  *Cuba under Castro: The Limits of Charisma.* Boston: Houghton Mifflin.
Gorz, André
  1973  "Workers' Control Is More Than Just That," pp. 325-343 in Hunnius et al. (1973).
Gramsci, Antonio
  1975  "Selected Writings from *L'ordine nuovo* (1919-1920)," pp. 221-233 in Horvat et al. (1975).

1977 *Selections from Political Writings (1910-1920)*. New York: International Publishers.

Greaves, Thomas C.
1968 "The Dying Chalán: Case Studies of Change on Four Haciendas of the Peruvian Coast." Unpublished Ph.D. dissertation, Cornell University.

Greenberg, Edward S.
1975 "The Consequences of Worker Participation: A Clarification of the Theoretical Literature," *Social Science Quarterly, 56* (September), 190-209.

Grindle, Merilee
1977 *Bureaucrats, Politicians, and Peasants in Mexico: A Case Study in Public Policy*. Berkeley: University of California Press.

Guillet, David
1979 *Agrarian Reform and Peasant Economy in Southern Peru*. Columbia: University of Missouri Press.

Hagen, Everett E.
1962 *On the Theory of Social Change*. Homewood, Ill.: The Dorsey Press.

Handelman, Howard
1975a *Struggle in the Andes: Peasant Political Mobilization in Peru*. Austin, Texas: University of Texas Press.
1975b "The Political Mobilization of Urban Squatter Settlements," *Latin American Research Review, 10* (Summer), 35-72.

Harding, Colin
1975 "Land Reform and Social Conflict in Peru," pp. 222-253 in Lowenthal (1975).

Hawley, Willis O. and Frederick M. Wirt (eds.)
1968 *The Search for Community Power*. Englewood Cliffs: Prentice-Hall.

Hill, Frances
1977 "Experiments with a Public Sector Peasantry: Agricultural Schemes and Class Formation in Africa," *African Studies Review, 20* (December), 25-41.

Hilliker, Grant
1971 *The Politics of Reform in Peru: The Aprista and Other Mass Parties of Latin America*. Baltimore: Johns Hopkins.

Hirschman, Albert O.
1965 *Journeys Toward Progress*. New York: Anchor.

Hopkins, Jack W.
1967 *The Government Executive of Modern Peru*. Gainesville: University of Florida.

Horowitz, Irving Louis, ed.
1970 *Masses in Latin America*. New York: Oxford University Press.

Horton, Douglas E.
1974 *Land Reform and Reform Enterprises in Peru*. Report submitted to the Land Tenure Center and the International Bank for Reconstruction and Development, June.

1975a "Land Reform and Group Farming in Peru." IBRD Department of Development Economics, Studies in Employment and Rural Development No. 23.

1975b "Land Reform and Reform Enterprises in Peru." IBRD Department of Development Economics, Studies in Employment and Rural Development No. 24.

1975c "Peru Case Study Volume." IBRD Department of Development Economics, Studies in Employment and Rural Development No. 22.

Horvat, Branko
1975 "An Institutional Model of a Self-Managed Socialist Economy," Vol. 2, pp. 307-327 in Horvat et al. (1975).

Horvat, Branko, Mihailo Marković, and Rudi Supek, eds.
1975 *Self-governing Socialism.* White Plains, New York: International Arts and Sciences Press, Inc. Two volumes.

Huberman, Leo, and Paul Sweezy
1964 "Peaceful Transition from Socialism to Capitalism," *Monthly Review, 15* (March), 569-590.

Huizer, Gerrit
1972 *The Revolutionary Potential of Peasants in Latin America.* Lexington, Mass.: Lexington Books, D.C. Heath and Co.

Hunnius, Gerry
1973 "Workers Self-Management in Yugoslavia," pp. 268-278 in Hunnius et al. (1973).

Hunnius, Gerry, G. David Garson, and John Case, eds.
1973 *Workers' Control: A Reader on Labor and Social Change.* New York: Random House.

Hunt, Shane
1975 "Direct Foreign Investment in Peru: New Rules for an Old Game," pp. 302-349 in Lowenthal (1975).

Huntington, Samuel P.
1968 *Political Order in Changing Societies.* New Haven: Yale University Press.

Hurtado, Hugo
1974 *Formación de las Comunidades Campesinas en el Perú.* Lima: Ediciones Tercer Mundo.

Hyden, Goran
1975 "Ujamaa Villages and Rural Development in Tanzania." Paper presented at the Second International Conference on Self-Management, Cornell University, Ithaca, New York, June 6-8.

Ingle, Clyde R.
1972 *From Village to State in Tanzania: The Politics of Rural Development.* Ithaca, New York: Cornell University Press.

Inkeles, Alex
1969 "Participant Citizenship in Six Development Countries," *American Political Science Review, 63* (December), 1120-1141.

Inkeles, Alex, and David H. Smith
  1974  *Becoming Modern: Individual Change in Six Developing Countries.*
        Cambridge: Harvard University Press.
Jaquette, Jane S.
  1971  *The Politics of Development in Peru.* Ithaca, New York: Cornell
        University Latin American Studies Program Dissertation Series.
Kaufman, Robert R.
  1974  "The Patron-Client Concept and Macro-Politics: Prospects and
        Problems," *Comparative Studies in Society and History, 16* (June),
        284-308.
Kavčić, Bagdan, Veljko Rus, and Arnold S. Tannenbaum
  1971  "Control, Participation and Effectiveness in Four Yugoslav
        Industrial Organizations," *Administrative Science Quarterly, 6*
        (March), 74-86.
Kiesler, Charles, A., Barry E. Collins, and Norman Miller
  1969  *Attitude Change: A Critical Analysis of Theoretical Approaches.* New
        York: Wiley.
Kirby, John
  1973  "Venezuela's Land Reform: Progress and Change," *Journal of
        Inter-American Studies and World Affairs, 5* (May), 205-220.
Klarén, Peter
  1973  *Modernization, Dislocation, and Aprismo.* Austin: University of
        Texas Press.
Klein, Ralph
  1963  "The Self-Image of Adult Males in an Andean Culture." Unpub-
        lished Ph.D. dissertation, New York University.
Knight, Peter T.
  1975  "New Forms of Economic Organization in Peru: Towards
        Workers' Self-Management," pp. 350-401 in Lowenthal (1975).
  1976  "Social Property in Peru: The Political Economy of Predomi-
        nance," *Economic Analysis and Workers' Management, 10* (Fall,
        1976).
Kolaja, J.
  1965  *Workers' Councils: The Yugoslav Experience.* London: Tavistock.
Kramer, Daniel C.
  1972  *Participatory Democracy: Developing Ideals of the Political Left.* Cam-
        bridge, Mass.: Schenkman.
Kuczynski, Pedro-Pablo
  1977  *Peruvian Democracy Under Economic Stress: An Account of the
        Belaúnde Administration, 1963-1968.* Princeton: Princeton Uni-
        versity Press.
Landsberger, Henry A., ed.
  1969  *Latin American Peasant Movements.* Ithaca, N.Y.: Cornell Univer-
        sity Press.
  1973  "The Limits and Conditions of Peasant Participation in Mexico:
        A Case Study," pp. 63-96 in William P. Glade and Stanley R. Ross

(eds.), *Encuesta Política: Mexico.* Austin: Institute of Latin American Studies, University of Texas.

Landsberger, Henry A., and Tim McDaniel
1976 "Hypermobilization in Chile, 1970-1973," *World Politics, 28* (July), 502-541.

Lane, Robert E.
1974 "Notes on a Theory of Democratic Personality," pp. 422-436 in Gordon J. Di Renzo (ed.), *Personality and Politics.* New York: Anchor.

Langton, Kenneth P.
1975 "Situations, Psychological Dispositions, and Learning in Understanding the Decision to Participate Politically." Paper prepared for delivery at the Annual Meeting of the American Political Science Association, San Francisco, California, September 2-5.

La Palombara, Joseph
1965 "Italy: Fragmentation, Isolation, and Alienation," pp. 282-329 in Pye and Verba (1965).

LaPiere, Richard T.
1934 "Attitudes versus Actions," *Social Forces, 13,* 230-237.

Larson, Magli S., and Arlene G. Bergman
1969 *Social Stratification in Peru.* Berkeley, California: Institute of International Studies, University of California.

Leeds, Elizabeth R.
1972 "Forms of 'Squatment' Political Organization: The Politics of Control in Brazil." Unpublished M.A. Thesis, University of Texas at Austin.

Lehmann, A. David
1973 "Agrarian Reform in Chile 1965-1972." Unpublished Manuscript, Cambridge, England: Institute of Development Studies.

Lemarchand, René, and Keith Legg
1972 "Political Clientelism and Development," *Comparative Politics, 4* (January), 151 and 166.

LeoGrande, William M.
1978 "Political Participation in Cuban Local Government: The Organs of People's Power." Paper presented at the Annual Meeting of the American Political Science Association, New York, New York, August 31-September 3.

Lerner, Daniel
1963 *The Passing of Traditional Society: Modernizing the Middle East.* Glencoe, Ill.: Free Press.

Lewin, R.
1973 "Matetereka," pp. 189-194 in Cliffe and Saul (1973).

Lewis, Oscar
1963 *Life in a Mexican Village: Tepoztlán Restudied.* Urbana: University of Illinois.

## 396 • Bibliography

Linz, Juan J.
   1970   "An Authoritarian Regime: Spain," pp. 251-283 in Erik Allardt
          and Stein Rokkan (eds.), *Mass Politics: Studies in Political Sociology*.
          New York: The Free Press.
Llosa, Jaime
   1973   "Reforma Agraria y Revolución," *Participación, 2* (August), 48-53.
Lockhart, James
   1968   *Spanish Peru 1532-1560*. Madison: University of Wisconsin Press.
Long, Norman, and David Winder
   1975   "From Peasant Community to Production Co-operative: An
          Analysis of Recent Government Policy in Peru," *Journal of Devel-
          opment Studies, 12* (October), 75-94.
Lopreato, Joseph
   1967   "How Would You Like To Be a Peasant?" pp. 419-437, in Jack M.
          Potter et al. (eds.), *Peasant Society: A Reader*. Berkeley: University
          of California.
Loveman, Brian
   1976a  *Struggle in the Countryside: Politics and Rural Labor in Chile,
          1919-1973*. Bloomington: Indiana University Press.
   1976b  "The Transformation of the Chilean Countryside," pp. 238-296,
          in Arturo Valenzuela and J. Samuel Valenzuela (eds.), *Chile: Poli-
          tics and Society*. New Brunswick, N.J.: Transaction Books.
Lowenthal, Abraham F., ed.
   1975   *The Peruvian Experiment*. Princeton: Princeton University Press.
          Also "Peru's Ambiguous Revolution," pp. 3-43.
Malloy, James M.
   1974   "Authoritarianism, Corporatism and Mobilization in Peru," pp.
          52-84 in Pike and Stritch (1974).
   1977   *Authoritarianism and Corporatism in Latin America*. Pittsburgh: Pitts-
          burgh University Press. Also "Authoritarianism and Corporatism
          in Latin America: The Modal Pattern," pp. 3-22.
Malloy, James M., and Richard S. Thorn, eds.
   1971   *Beyond the Revolution: Bolivia Since 1952*. Pittsburgh: University of
          Pittsburgh Press.
Malpica, Carlos
   1968   *Los Dueños del Perú*. Lima: Ediciones Ensayos Sociales.
Mangin, William
   1965   "Mental Health and Migration to Cities: A Peruvian Case," pp.
          546-565 in D. B. Heath and R. H. Adams (eds.), *Contemporary
          Cultures and Societies of Latin America*. New York: Random House.
Mankiewicz, Frank, and Kirby Jones
   1975   *With Fidel: A Portrait of Castro and Cuba*. New York: Ballantine.
Mansbridge, Jane J.
   1973   "Town Meeting Democracy," *Working Papers for a New Society, 1*
          (Summer), 5-15.
Marchetti, Peter
   1975   "Worker Participation and Class Conflict in Worker-Managed

Farms: The Rural Question in Chile—1970 to 1973." Unpublished Ph.D. dissertation, Yale University. Two vols.

Marshall, Dale Rogers
1971 *The Politics of Participation in Poverty.* Berkeley: University of California Press.

Martínez Alier, Juan
1973 *Los Huachilleros del Peru.* Madrid: Reudo Ibérico, and Lima: Instituto de Estudios Peruanos.

Martínez Vázquez, Victor Raúl
1976 "Despojo y Manipulación Campesina: Historia y Estructura de dos Cacicazgos del Valle del Mezquital," in Roger Bartra, et al. (eds.), *Caciquismo y Poder Político en el México Rural,* Mexico City: Siglo Veintiuno Editores.

Mathiason, John R., and John D. Powell
1972 "Participation and Efficacy: Aspects of Peasant Involvement in Political Mobilization," *Comparative Politics, 4* (April), 303-329.

Matos Mar, José
1969 *La Tenencia de la Tierra en una Micro-Region del la Costa Central.* Lima: Instituto de Estudios Peruanos.

Matos Mar, José, ed.
1969 *La Oligarquía en el Perú.* Lima: Instituto de Estudios Peruanos.
1976 *Hacienda, Comunidad Y Campesinado en el Perú.* Lima: Instituto de Estudios Peruanos.

McClelland, David C.
1967 *The Achieving Society.* New York: Free Press.

McClintock, Cynthia
1973 "The School-Community Communications Program of Boston's Model Cities: An Evaluation of Citizen Participation in School Reform." Unpublished paper, Department of Political Science, Massachusetts Institute of Technology.
1975a "Socioeconomic Status and Political Participation in Peru: The Impact of Agrarian Cooperatives, 1969-1975." Paper presented at the Annual Meeting of the American Political Science Association, San Francisco, September 2-5.
1975b "Sharing the Benefits of Cooperative Agricultural Enterprises with Outsiders in Peru: The Political and Economic Impact of SAIS Cahuide," *Economic Analysis and Workers' Management, 9,* No. 3-4, 249-273.
1976 "Structural Change and Political Culture in Rural Peru: the Impact of Self-Managed Cooperatives on Peasant Clientelism, 1969-1975." Unpublished Ph.D. dissertation, Massachusetts Institute of Technology.
1977 *Self-Management and Political Participation in Peru, 1969-1975: The Corporatist Illusion.* London: A Sage Professional Paper in Contemporary Political Sociology.
1980 "Velasco, officers, and citizens: The Politics of Stealth." Unpublished manuscript, George Washington University.

## 398 • Bibliography

Mehnert, Klaus
 1975   "What Do They Really Think of Mao?" pp. 431-434, in Joel Coye
        and Jon Livingston (eds.), *China Yesterday and Today*. New York:
        Bantam.
Meisner, Mitch
 1978   "Dazhai: The Mass Line in Practice," *Modern China, 4* (January),
        27-62.
Mesa-Lago, Carmelo
 1974   *Cuba in the 1970's: Pragmatism and Institutionalization.* Albuquer-
        que: University of New Mexico Press.
Middlebrook, Kevin Jay
 1972   "Land for the Tiller: Political Participation and the Peruvian
        Military's Agrarian Reform." Unpublished B.A. thesis, Harvard
        College.
Middlebrook, Kevin Jay, and David Scott Palmer
 1975   *Military Government and Political Development: Lessons from Peru.*
        Beverly Hills, Calif.: A Sage Professional Paper.
Migdal, Joel S.
 1974   *Peasants, Politics and Revolution: Pressure toward Political and Social
        Change in the Third World:* Princeton: Princeton University Press.
Milenkovitch, Deborah D.
 1971   *Plan and Market in Yugoslav Economic Thought.* New Haven: Yale
        University Press.
Ministry of Agriculture
 1967   *Boletín de Estadística Peruana 1964.* Lima: Dirección General de
        Reforma Agraria y Asentamiento Rural.
 1970a  *Proyecto [Enterprise Huanca]: Datos para Adjudicación [and] Datos
        para el Desarrollo.* Lima: Dirección de Comunidades Campesinas.
 1970b  *Plan Nacional de Desarrollo,* Vol. 2. Plan Agropecuario, Lima:
        Dirección de Comunidades Campesinas.
 1971   "El Marco Institucional de la Reforma Agraria Peruana," in *Semi-
        nario Latinoamericano de Reforma Agraria y Colonización.* Chiclayo,
        Peru.
 1972   *Opiniones y Actitudes de los Presidentes de las Comunidades Campesinas
        del Departmento de Lima.* Lima: Dirección de Comunidades Cam-
        pesinas (March).
 1973a  "Adjudicación del PIAR 'Virú-Chao'." Agrarian Zone III
        (January).
 1973b  *Distribución de Ingreso Anual Promedio por Regiones para el Ambito
        Rural.* Lima: Dirección General de Reforma Agraria y Asenta-
        miento Rural.
 1974a  *Manual de Administración para las Empresas Campesinas del Area
        Reformada.* Lima: Direccion General de Produccion Agraria.
 1974b  *Manual para la Formulación de Planes de Explotación y de Desarrollo
        de Empresas Campesinas.* Lima: Dirección General de Producción
        Agraria.

1974c "Empresas sin Administradores Nombrados en el Sistema de Ley." Lima: Dirección General de Producción Agraria (December).

1976 "Reforma Agraria en Cifras." Lima: Dirección General de Reforma Agraria y Asentamiento Rural (September).

Moncloa, Francisco
1977 *Perú: ¿Que Pasó? (1968-1976).* Lima: Editorial Horizonte.

Montoya, Rodrigo, *et al.*
1974 *La SAIS Cahuide y sus Contradicciones.* Lima: Universidad Nacional Mayor de San Marcos.

Moreira, Neiva
1974 *Modelo Peruano.* Buenos Aires: La Línea.

Muller, Edward N., and Thomas O. Jukam
1977 "On the Meaning of Political Support," *American Political Science Review, 61* (December, 1977), 1561-1595.

National Institute of Health
1971 "Informe de los Estudios Dietéticos Realizados en Talhuis, Pucara, Cullpa-Cochas Chico, Chongos Bajo, Acopalca y Laive," Lima: Institute of Nutrition and COMACRA.

Nie, Norman H., G. Bingham Powell, Jr., and Kenneth Prewitt
1969 "Social Structure and Political Participation: Development Relationships," *American Political Science Review, 63* (June and September), 361-73 and 808-32.

Nie, Norman H., Sidney Verba, and John Petrocik
1976 *The Changing American Voter.* Cambridge: Harvard University Press.

North, Liisa
1966 *Civil-Military Relations in Argentina, Chile, and Peru.* Berkeley: Institute of International Studies, University of California.

1979 "Perspectives on Development Policy and Mass Participation in the Peruvian Armed Forces," The Wilson Center Latin American Program Working Paper #22.

Obradović, Josip
1970 "Workers Councils in Yugoslavia: Effects on Perceived Participation and Satisfaction of Workers," *Human Relations, 23* (October), 459-471.

O'Brien, David J.
1975 *Neighborhood Organization and Interest-Group Processes.* Princeton: Princeton University Press.

OIT (Organización Internacional del Trabajo)
1975 *Estudio Sobre Ingresos de los Trabajadores Rurales en el Perú.* Lima: OIT.

Olson, Mancur
1965 *The Logic of Collective Action.* Cambridge, Mass.: Harvard University Press.

Ortiz Vergara, Pedro
  1973  "PIAR." Lima: CENCIRA.
  1978  "El Proceso de la Reforma Agraria Peruana." Unpublished manuscript, University of Venezuela at Alto Barinas.
Overseas Development Council
  1975  *The U.S. and World Development: Agenda for Action 1975.* New York: Praeger.
Padrón Castillo, Mario and Henry Pease García
  1974  *Planificación Rural, Reforma Agraria y Organización Campesina.* Lima: DESCO.
Paige, Jerry M.
  1975  *Agrarian Revolution Social Movements and Export Agriculture in the Underdeveloped World.* New York: The Free Press.
Palmer, David Scott
  1973  *'Revolution from Above': Military Government and Popular Participation in Peru, 1968-1972.* Ithaca: Cornell University, Latin American Studies Program Dissertation Series.
  1974  "Social Mobilization in Peru," pp. 45-73 in Leila A. Bradfield (ed.), *Chile and Peru: Two Paths to Social Justice.* Kalamazoo, Mich.: Western Michigan University, Institute of International and Area Studies.
Palmer, David Scott, and Kevin Jay Middlebrook
  1976  "Corporatist Participation under Military Rule in Peru," pp. 428-454, in David Chaplin (ed.), *Peruvian Nationalism: A Corporatist Revolution.* New Brunswick: Transaction.
Pásara, Luis
  1977  "Communidad Industrial y Sindicato," pp. 189-240 in Alberti, Santistevan, and Pásara (1977).
Pateman, Carole
  1970  *Participation and Democratic Theory.* New York: Cambridge University Press.
  1976  "A Contribution to the Political Theory of Organizational Democracy," pp. 9-30, in Garson and Smith (1976).
Payne, Arnold
  1968  *The Peruvian Coup d'Etat of 1962: The Overthrow of Manuel Prado.* Washington, D.C.: Institute for the Comparative Study of Political Systems.
Paz, Octavio
  1961  *The Labyrinth of Solitude.* New York: Grove Press, Inc.
Pearse, Andrew
  1970  "Agrarian Change Trends in Latin America," pp. 11-40 in Stavenhagen (1970).
Pease García, Henry
  1977a "La Reforma Agraria Peruana en la Crisis del Estado Oligárquico," pp. 13-136 in DESCO (1977).

1977b *El Ocaso del Poder Oligárquico: Lucha Política en la Escena Oficial, 1968-1975.* Lima: DESCO.

Perez-Stable, Marifeli
1975 "Cuba's Workers 1975: A Preliminary Analysis." Paper presented at the Latin American Studies Association, Sixth National Meeting, Atlanta, March.

Peterson, Eric A.
1977 "Interest Group Incorporation in Sweden: A Summary of Arguments and Findings." Paper presented at the Annual Meeting of the American Political Science Association, Washington, D.C.

Philip, George
1976 "The Soldier as Radical: The Peruvian Military Government, 1968-1975," *Journal of Latin American Studies, 8,* Part 1 (May), 29-51.
1978 *The Rise and Fall of the Peruvian Military Radicals, 1968-1976.* London: Athlone Press of the University of London.

Pike, Frederick B., and Thomas Stritch, eds.
1974 *The New Corporatism.* Notre Dame: University of Notre Dame Press.

Pinelo, Adalberto J.
1973 *The Multinational Corporation as a Force in Latin American Politics: A Case Study of the International Petroleum Company, Peru.* New York: Praeger.

Pomerantz, Phillis Reva
1978 "Public Policy and Societal Change: Agrarian Reform and Conflict in Peru." Unpublished Ph.D. dissertation, the Fletcher School of Law and Diplomacy.

Popkin, Samuel L.
1976 "Corporation and Colonialism: Political Economy of Rural Change in Vietnam," *Comparative Politics, 8* (April), 431-464.

Portocarrero, Felipe
1973 "La Coyuntura Económica: Conciliación y lucha de clases," *Sociedad y Política, 1* (May), 4-20.

Powell, John D.
1970 "Peasant Society and Clientelistic Politics," *American Political Science Review, 44* (June), 411-425.
1971 *Political Mobilization of the Venezuelan Peasant.* Cambridge, Massachusetts: Harvard University Press.
1972 "On Defining Peasants and Peasant Society," *Peasant Studies Newsletter, 1,* No. 3, 94-99.
1974 "Peasants in Politics." Unpublished manuscript, Center for International Affairs, Harvard University.

Pratt, Cranford
1976 *The Critical Phase in Tanzania 1945-1968.* Cambridge, England: Cambridge University Press.

Pratt, Raymond B.
  1968  "Organizational Participation, Politicization, and Development:
         A Study of Political Consequences of Participation in Community
         Associations in Four Lower Class Urban Settlements in Chile and
         Peru." Unpublished Ph.D. dissertation, University of Oregon.
Printz, Peggy, and Paul Steinle
  1973  *Commune: Life in Rural China.* New York: Dodd, Mead.
Pye, Lucian W.
  1962  *Politics, Personality, and Nation-Building: Burma's Search for Identity.*
         New Haven: Yale University Press.
  1965  "Introduction: Political Culture and Political Development," pp.
         3-26 in Pye and Verba (1965).
  1966  *Aspects of Political Development.* Boston: Little, Brown.
  1968  *The Spirit of Chinese Politics.* Cambridge: M.I.T. Press.
Pye, Lucian W., and Sidney Verba, eds.
  1965  *Political Culture and Political Development.* Princeton: Princeton
         University Press.
Quijano Obregón, Aníbal
  1971  *Nationalism and Capitalism in Peru.* New York: Monthly Review.
  1975  "La 'segunda fase' de la 'Revolución Peruana' y la lucha de clases."
         *Sociedad y Política, 2* (November), 4-19.
Redfield, Robert
  1953  *The Primitive World and Its Transformations.* Ithaca, N.Y.: Cornell
         University Press.
Restrepo, Iván, and Salomón Eckstein
  1975  *La Agricultura Colectiva en México.* Mexico: Siglo Veintiuno Edi-
         tores.
Reyna, José Luis
  1971  "An Empirical Analysis of Political Mobilization: The Case of
         Mexico." Unpublished Ph.D. dissertation, Cornell University.
Riddell, Davis S.
  1963  "Social Self-Government: the Background of Theory and Prac-
         tice in Yugoslav Socialism," *British Journal of Sociology, 19,* 46-75.
Rigby, Peter
  1977  "Local Participation in National Politics: Ugogo, Tanzania," *Af-
         rica, 47,* No. 1, 89-107.
Riskin, Carl
  1971  "Incentive Systems and Work Motivations: The Experience in
         China," *Working Papers, 1* (Winter), 27-92.
Roberts, Bryan
  1975  "Center and Periphery in the Development Process: The Case of
         Peru," pp. 77-106 in Wayne Cornelius and Felicity Trueblood
         (eds.), *Urbanization and Inequality: Latin American Urban Research,*
         Vol. 5, Beverly Hills, Calif.: Sage Publications.
Robinson, Richard D.
  1976  *The Peruvian Experiment: The Theory and Reality of the Industrial*

*Community.* Report submitted to the Tinker Foundation via the Center for International Studies, Massachusetts Institute of Technology.

Roca, Santiago
1975 "The Peruvian Sugar Cooperatives: Some Fundamental Economic Problems, 1967-1972," in J. Vanek (ed.), *Self-Management in Peru.* Program on Participation and Labor-Managed Systems, Cornell University, Ithaca, New York.

Rodríguez Pastor, Humberto
1969 *Caqui: Estudio de Una Hacienda Costeña.* Lima: Instituto de Estudios Peruanos.

Rodríguez Suy-Suy, Juan
1965 "El Pueblo de Virú." Unpublished paper, Lima: Instituto de Estudios Peruanos.

Rogers, Everett M.
1969 *Modernization Among Peasants: The Impact of Communication.* New York: Holt, Rinehart and Winston.

Ronfeldt, David
1973 *Atencingo: The Politics of Agrarian Struggle in a Mexican Ejido.* Stanford: Stanford University Press.

Rubin de Celis T., Emma
1977 *Las CAPs de Piura y sus Contradicciones.* Piura: Centro de Investigación y Promoción del Campesinado.

Rubio Correa, Marcial
1977 "Problemas de Comercialización Agraria," pp. 257-342, in DESCO (1977).

Rusinow, Dennison
1977 *The Yugoslav Experiment 1948-1974.* Berkeley: University of California Press.

Sachs, Stephen M.
1975a "Implications of Recent Developments in Yugoslav Self-Management." Paper presented at the Second International Conference on Self-Management, Ithaca, New York, June.
1975b "The Impact of Workers' Self-Management Upon the Social Responsibility of the Enterprise." Paper presented at the Conference for a Relevant Social Science, March.

Samoff, Joel
1974 *Tanzania.* Madison, Wisconsin: The University of Wisconsin Press.

Santistevan, Jorge
1977a "El Estado y Los Comuneros Industriales," pp. 105-188 in Giorgio Alberti, Jorge Santistevan, and Luis Pásara (eds.), *Estado y Clase: La Comunidad Industrial en el Perú.* Lima: Instituto de Estudios Peruanos.
1977b "La Comunidad Industrial y los Comuneros," pp. 291-340 in Giorgio Alberti, Jorge Santistevan, and Luis Pásara (eds.), *Estado*

*y Clase: La Comunidad Industrial en el Perú.* Lima: Instituto de Estudios Peruanos.

Schmidt, Steffen W., James C. Scott, Carl Lande and Laura Guasti, eds.
1977 *Friends, Followers, and Factions: A Reader in Political Clientelism.* Berkeley: University of California Press.

Schmitter, Philippe C.
1974 "Still the Century of Corporatism?" pp. 85-131 in Pike and Stritch (1974).
1975 *Corporatism and Public Policy in Authoritarian Portugal.* London: A Sage Professional Paper.

Schonfeld, William R.
1975 "The Meaning of Democratic Participation," *World Politics, 28* (October), 134-158.

Schram, Stuart R., ed.
1973 *Authority, Participation and Cultural Change in China.* London: Cambridge University Press.

Schurmann, Franz
1978 *Ideology and Organization in Communist China.* Berkeley: University of California Press.

Scott, Christopher
1974 "Los Trabajadores Eventuales en la Agricultura Costeña." Unpublished paper (January), Lima: CENCIRA.

Scott, James C.
1972 "Patron-Client Politics and Political Change in Southeast Asia," *American Political Science Review, 66* (March), 91-113.
1976 *The Moral Economy of the Peasant.* New Haven: Yale University Press.

Scott, Robert E.
1965 "Mexico: The Established Revolution," pp. 336-395 in Pye and Verba (1965).

Senior, Clarence
1958 *Land Reform and Democracy.* Gainesville, Florida: University of Florida Press.

Shabad, Goldie
1978 "Strikes in Yugoslavia: Implications for Industrial Democracy." Paper presented at the 1978 Annual Meeting of the American Political Science Association, New York.

Shanin, Theodore
1966 "Peasantry as a Political Factor," *Sociological Review, 14* (March), 5-27.

Simpson, Eyler N.
1937 *The Ejido: Mexico's Way Out.* Chapel Hill: University of North Carolina Press.

SINAMOS
1972 *Diagnóstico Socio-Económico Preliminar del Area Rural Peruana.* Lima: Dirección General de Organizaciones Rurales.

1974 *Red de Instituciones Externas Relacionadas con las Cooperativas Agrarias de Producción Azucarera.* Lima: Centro de Estudios de Participación Popular.
1975 *La Confederación Nacional Agraria: Información Básica.* Lima: Dirección General de Organizaciones Rurales (January).

Singelmann, Peter
1975 "The Closing Triangle: Critical Notes on a Model for Peasant Mobilization in Latin America," *Comparative Studies in Society and History, 17* (October), 389-409.

Skinner, B. F.
1953 *Science and Human Behavior.* New York: Free Press.

Solomon, Richard H.
1971 *Mao's Revolution and the Chinese Political Culture.* Berkeley: University of California Press.

Spalding, Karen
1974 *De Indio a Campesino: Cambios en la Estructura Social del Perú Colonial.* Lima: Instituto de Estudios Peruanos.

Stavenhagen, Rodolfo
1970 *Agrarian Problems and Peasant Movements in Latin America.* Garden City, N.Y.: Doubleday Anchor. Also "Social Aspects of Agrarian Structure in Mexico," pp. 225-270.
1975 "Collective Agriculture and Capitalism in Mexico: A Way Out or Dead End?" *Latin American Perspectives, 2* (Summer), 146-163.

Stavis, Benedict
1974a *People's Communes and Rural Development in China.* Ithaca, New York: Rural Development Committee, Center for Institutional Studies, Cornell University.
1974b *Making Green Revolution: The Politics of Agricultural Development in China.* Ithaca, New York: Rural Development Committee, Cornell University.

Steenland, Kyle
1974 "Rural Strategy under Allende," *Latin American Perspectives, 1* (Summer), 129-146.
1977 *Agrarian Reform under Allende: Peasant Revolt in the South.* Albuquerque: University of New Mexico Press.

Stein, William W.
1961 *Hualcan: Life in the Highlands of Peru.* Ithaca, N.Y.: Cornell University Press.

Stepan, Alfred
1978 *The State and Society: Peru in Comparative Perspective.* Princeton: Princeton University Press.

Stephens, Evelyne Huber
1977 "The Politics of Workers' Participation: The Peruvian Approach in Comparative Perspective." Unpublished Ph.D. dissertation, Yale University.

Sternberg, Marvin J.
  1972  "The Latifundista: The Impact of His Income and Expenditure Patterns on Investment and Consumption," *Studies in Comparative International Development*, 7 (Spring), 1-18.
Stevens, Evelyn P.
  1977  "Mexico's PRI: The Institutionalization of Corporatism?" pp. 227-258 in Malloy (1977).
Strasma, John
  1974  "Agrarian Reform in Peru and Chile," pp. 93-110 in Leila A. Bradfield (ed.), *Chile and Peru: Two Paths to Social Justice.* Kalamazoo, Mich.: Western Michigan University, Institute of International and Area Studies.
Sulmont, Denis
  1977  "Labour Conflicts and Popular Mobilization: Peru 1968-76." Paper presented at the Seminar on Third World Strikes, Institute of Social Studies, The Hague, September 12-16.
Supek, Rudi
  1975  "Problems and Experiences of Yugoslav Workers' Self-Management." Paper presented at the Second International Conference on Self-Management, Cornell University, Ithaca, New York, June 6-8.
Swansbrough, Robert H.
  1975  "Peru's Diplomatic Offensive: Solidarity for Latin American Independence," pp. 115-130, in Ronald G. Hellman and Jon Rosenbaum (eds.), *Latin America: The Search for a New International Role.* New York: Halsted.
Taylor, Charles Lewis, and Michael C. Hudson
  1972  *World Handbook of Political and Social Indicators.* New Haven: Yale University Press.
Thaxton, Ralph
  1977  "The World Turned Downside Up: Three Orders of Meaning in the Peasants' Traditional Political World," *Modern China, 3* (April), 185-228.
Thiesenhusen, William C.
  1974  "Chile's Experiments in Agrarian Reform: Four Colonization Projects, Revisited," The Land Tenure Center, University of Wisconsin, Madison.
Thorndike, Guillermo
  1976  *No, Mi General.* Lima: Mosca Azul.
Thorp, Rosemary
  1977  "The Post-Import-Substitution Era: The Case of Peru," *World Development, 5*, Nos. 1/2, 125-136.
Thorp, Rosemary, and Geoffrey Bertram
  1978  *Peru 1890-1977: Growth and Policy in an Open Economy.* London: Macmillan.

Tornquist, David
  1973 "Workers' Management: The Intrinsic Issues," pp. 374-394 in Hunnius et al. (1973).
Torres y Torres Lara, Carlos
  1975 *La Empresa de Propiedad Social, el Modelo Empresarial Peruano.* Lima: Asesorandina.
Townsend, James R.
  1974 *Politics in China.* Boston: Little, Brown.
Trimberger, Ellen Kay
  1978 *Revolution from Above: Military Bureaucrats and Development in Japan, Turkey, Egypt, and Peru.* New Brunswick: Transaction.
Tullis, F. LaMond
  1970 *Lord and Peasant in Peru.* Cambridge, Mass.: Harvard University Press.
Ulmer, Melville J.
  1973 "The Yugoslav Experiment: A Socialism of Sorts," *The New Republic, 169,* (August 18 and 25), 13-16.
Unger, Jonathan
  1978 "Collective Incentives in the Chinese Countryside: Lessons from Chen Village," *World Development, 6* (May), 583-602.
United States Government
  1975 "China: A Reassessment of the Economy." A Compendium of Papers submitted to the Joint Economic Congress of the United States.
Urdanivia Ginés, José
  1954 *Una Revolución Modelo [del] Ejército Peruano.* Lima: Editorial Castrillón Silva.
Valderrama, Mariano
  1976 *7 Años de Reforma Agraria Peruana.* Lima: Pontificia Universidad Católica del Perú.
Valdez Angulo, Enrique
  1974 *El Sector Agrario.* Lima: Ministry of Agriculture (May).
Valenzuela, Arturo, and J. Samuel Valenzuela, eds.
  1976 *Chile: Politics and Society.* New Brunswick, New Jersey: Transaction Books.
Vanek, Jaroslav
  1970 *The General Theory of Labor-Managed Market Economies.* Ithaca and London: Cornell University Press.
  1971 *The Participatory Economy.* Ithaca, New York: Cornell University Press.
  1975 "Introduction," pp. 11-36, in Vanek (1975).
Vanek, Jaroslav, ed.
  1975 *Self-Management.* Harmondsworth: Penguin Education
Van de Wetering, H.
  1973 "The Current State of Land Reform in Peru," *LTC Newsletter,*

University of Wisconsin-Madison Land Tenure Center (April-June).

Van Velzen, H.U.E. Thoden
1973 "Staff, Kulaks and Peasants," pp. 153-179, in Cliffe and Saul (1973).

Velasco, Juan Alvarado
1972 *La Voz de la Revolución.* Two vols. Lima: Oficina Nacional de Informaciones.
1974 "Plan Inca." (Independence Day Message to the Nation, July 28, 1974.) My citation is from *Correo,* July 29, 1974.

Verba, Sidney
1965 "Conclusion: Comparative Political Culture," pp. 512-560, in Pye and Verba (1965).

Verba, Sidney, and Norman H. Nie
1972 *Participation in America: Political Democracy and Social Equality.* New York: Harper.

Villanueva, Victor
1969 *¿Nueva Mentalidad Militar en el Peru?* Lima: Mejía Baca.
1973 *Ejercito Peruano: del Caudillaje Anárquico al Militarismo Reformista.* Lima: Mejiá Baca.

Vogel, Ezra
1965 "From Friendship to Comradeship: The Change in Personal Relationships in China," *China Quarterly,* No. 6 (April-June), 64-75.
1969 *Canton Under Communism: Programs and Politics in a Provincial Capital, 1949-1968.* Cambridge, Mass.: Harvard University Press.

Wachtel, Howard M.
1973 *Workers Management and Workers Wages in Yugoslavia: The Theory and Practice of Participatory Socialism.* Ithaca, N.Y.: Cornell University Press.

Watson, Andrew F.
1973 "A Revolution To Touch Men's Souls: The Family, Interpersonal Relations and Daily Life," pp. 291-330, in Stuart R. Schram (ed.), *Authority, Participation and Cultural Change in China.* London: Cambridge University Press.

Webb, Richard
1974a "Trends in Real Income in Peru, 1950-1966." Research Paper in Economic Development, Woodrow Wilson School, Princeton University.
1974b "Government Policy and the Distribution of Income in Peru, 1963-1973." Research Paper in Economic Development, Woodrow Wilson School, Princeton University.
1975 "Government Policy and the Distribution of Income in Peru, 1963-1973," pp. 79-127 in Lowenthal (1975).

Weiner, Myron
   1967   *Party Building in a New Nation*. Chicago: University of Chicago
          Press.
Whitehorn, Alan
   1974   "Workers' Self-Management: Socialist Myth or Prognostication."
          Paper presented at the Annual Meeting of the American Political
          Science Association, Chicago, August 29-September 2.
Whiting, Van R., Jr.
   1973   "Agrarian Reform and the Transition to Socialism in Chile." Un-
          published B.A. thesis, Yale University.
   1975   "Capitalism, Agrarian Reform, and Cooperative Organizations in
          Rural Mexico." Unpublished paper, Department of Government,
          Harvard University.
   1977   "The Collective Ejido and the State in Mexico." Paper presented
          at the Latin American Studies Association Meeting, Houston,
          November 2-5.
Whyte, Martin King
   1974   *Small Groups and Political Rituals in China*. Berkeley: University of
          California Press.
Whyte, William F.
   1974   In "Panel Discussion," in Leila A. Bradfield (ed.), *Chile and Peru:
          Two Paths to Social Justice*. Kalamazoo, Mich.: Western Michigan
          University, Institute of International and Area Studies.
Whyte, William F., and Giorgio Alberti
   1976   *Power, Politics and Progress: Social Change in Rural Peru*. New York:
          Elsevier.
Wiarda, Howard J.
   1973   "Toward a Framework for the Study of Political Change in the
          Iberic-Latin Tradition: The Corporative Model," *World Politics*,
          25 (January), 206-235.
Wilkie, James W.
   1974   *Measuring Land Reform*. Los Angeles: U.C.L.A. Latin America
          Center.
Wilkie, Raymond
   1971   *San Miguel: A Mexican Collective Ejido*. Stanford, Calif.: Stanford
          University Press.
Williams, Lawrence K.
   1969   "Algunos Correlatos Sicosociales de los Sistemas de Dominación,"
          pp. 80-94, in José Matos Mar and William F. Whyte (eds.),
          *Dominación y Cambios en el Perú Rural*. Lima: Instituto de Estudios
          Peruanos.
Wilson, Duncan
   1978   "Self-Management in Yugoslavia," *International Affairs*, 54 (April),
          253-263.

Wilson, James Q.
  1973  *Political Organizations.* New York: Basic Books.
Winn, Peter, and Cristobal Kay
  1974  "Agrarian Reform and Rural Revolution in Allende's Chile," *Journal of Latin American Studies, 6* No. 1, 135-139.
Wolf, Eric R.
  1966  *Peasants.* Englewood Cliffs, N.J.: Prentice-Hall.
  1969  *Peasant Wars of the Twentieth Century.* New York: Harper.
World Bank
  1978  *Land Reform in Latin America: Bolivia, Chile, Mexico, Peru, and Venezuela.* World Bank Staff Working Paper No. 275. April.
Woy-Hazleton, Sandra
  1978a "SINAMOS: Infrastructure for Participation," in John Booth and Mitchell Seligson (eds.), *Political Participation in Latin America.* New York: Holmes and Meier.
  1978b "Political Participation in Peru: A Military Model for Mobilization." Unpublished Ph.D. dissertation, University of Virginia.
  1979  "Political Participation in a Non-Electoral System." Paper presented at the International Studies Association meeting, March.
Yglesias, José
  1968  *In the Fist of the Revolution.* New York: Pantheon.
Zammit, J. Ann, ed.
  1973  *The Chilean Road to Socialism.* Austin: University of Texas Press.
Zimbalist, Andrew
  1975a "The Development of Workers' Participation in Socialist Cuba." Paper prepared for the Second Annual Conference on Workers' Management, Cornell University, June 6-8.
  1975b "The Limits of Work Humanization," *The Review of Radical Political Economics, 7* (Summer), 50-60.
Zimbardo, Philip, and Ebbe B. Ebbesen
  1970  *Influencing Attitudes and Changing Behavior.* Reading, Mass.: Addison-Wesley.
Zukin, Sharon
  1975  *Beyond Marx and Tito: Theory and Practice in Yugoslav Socialism.* New York: Cambridge University Press.

# Index

Library of Congress Cataloging in Publication Data

McClintock, Cynthia.
　Peasant cooperatives and political change in Peru

　Bibliography: p.
　Includes index.
　1. Agriculture, Cooperative—Peru.　2. Peru—
Rural conditions.　3. Employees' representation in
management—Peru.　4. Peru—Politics and government—
1968–　　I. Title.
HD1491.P4M33　　334'.683'0985　　80–8563
ISBN 0–691–07627–8
ISBN 0–691–02202–X (pbk.)